CONFLICTING WORLDS
New Dimensions of the American Civil War
T. Michael Parrish, Editor

Loyalty and Loss

ALABAMA'S UNIONISTS in the CIVIL WAR and RECONSTRUCTION

Margaret M. Storey

LOUISIANA STATE UNIVERSITY PRESS
BATON ROUGE

Published by Louisiana State University Press
Copyright © 2004 by Louisiana State University Press
All rights reserved
Manufactured in the United States of America

Louisiana Paperback Edition, 2004

Designer: Laura Roubique Gleason
Typeface: Whitman
Typesetter: Coghill Composition Co., Inc.

Library of Congress Cataloging-in-Publication Data

Storey, Margaret M., 1969–
    Loyalty and loss : Alabama's Unionists in the Civil
War and Reconstruction / Margaret M. Storey.
        p.   cm. — (Conflicting worlds)
Includes bibliographical references (p.) and index.
    1. Unionists (United States Civil War)—Alabama.
2. Alabama—History—Civil War, 1861–1865.
3. Reconstruction—Alabama.   I. Title.   II. Series:
Conflicting worlds.
    E551.S76   2004
    973.7'17'09761—dc22   2003021389

ISBN 978-0-8071-3022-3 (pbk.)

For Jonathan

Contents

Illustrations and Tables

TABLES

Acknowledgments

I have incurred a great many debts in the writing of this book, begun ten years ago as a dissertation at Emory University. At that time, I benefited from generous grant support from Emory and the Andrew W. Mellon Foundation's Southern Studies Dissertation Fellowship. Since then, I have been the fortunate recipient of two summer research faculty fellowships and a paid leave fellowship from DePaul University's College of Liberal Arts and Sciences, a University Research Council grant from DePaul University, as well as a Gilder Lehrman Fellowship in American History for research at the Pierpont Morgan Library. Such support has been much appreciated.

Numerous archivists and librarians likewise assisted me, including the staffs at the George Woodruff Library at Emory University Library; the National Archives in Washington, D.C., and Eastpoint, Georgia; the Southern Historical Collection at the University of North Carolina; the Birmingham Public Library in Birmingham, Alabama; the Pierpont Morgan Library in New York City; the Special Collections of the Perkins Library at Duke University; the Special Collections of the Indiana Historical Society; the John C. Richardson Library at DePaul University; the Newberry Library in Chicago; and the State Historical Society of Iowa in Des Moines. Most notable for their remarkable dedication, however, have been the members of the reference staff at the Alabama Department of Archives and History in Montgomery, Alabama, particularly Rickie Brunner, John Hardin, Debbie Pendleton, and Ken Tilley. In their kindness to me at the archives and helpful responses to telephone calls and requests for long-distance assistance, these specialists have greatly enhanced the quality of this project and made my efforts all the more pleasurable. Thank you.

No scholarly project comes to fruition without intellectual support and camaraderie. I am particularly grateful to my mentors in history. James B. Stewart of Macalester College in St. Paul first encouraged me to study the South. His classes on slavery and the Civil War, and his suggestion that I attend an undergraduate research program at Chicago's Newberry Library, inspired me to pursue a Ph.D. My graduate adviser at Emory, James L. Roark, was unfailingly willing to answer my questions, to challenge my assumptions, and to dispense cups of coffee along with guidance and encouragement. It was he who first suggested that I "take a look at" the Southern Claims Commission records, and I am deeply grateful for his interest in and critical reading of my dissertation. Other teachers at Emory also greatly influenced and helped me, including Patrick Allitt, Dan T. Carter, Elizabeth Fox-Genovese, Eugene Genovese, Kristin Mann, and Randall Packard. I am equally thankful for the friends I made at Emory, folks who were fantastic scholarly colleagues, not to mention great companions for food excursions across Georgia: Daniel Aldridge III, Kristian Blaich, Mary Cain, Sarah Gardner, Winston Grady-Willis, John Hynes, Christine Lambert, Julie Livingston, Steve Oatis, Amy Scott Oatis, Nicolas Proctor, Larissa Smith, Christine Stolba, Belle Tuten, and James Tuten. Since graduate school, I have had the good fortune to gain excellent colleagues at DePaul University, friends whose commitment to teaching and scholarship have been singularly important as I have revised this manuscript over the past five years. My students, especially those in "historical methods" classes, have prompted me to reflect anew on how we do history. I owe much, as well, to the dedicated staff of DePaul's History Department, whose patient assistance and goodwill have been remarkable. Finally, many thanks are owed to Molly O'Halloran, whose remarkable skill and design sense are evidenced in the maps that enhance this book.

A number of scholars have kindly read all or parts of this work at various points, providing many useful insights and suggestions, some of which have kept me from making embarrassing mistakes. These include the anonymous reviewer for Louisiana State University Press, the anonymous reviewers for the *Journal of Southern History*, John Boles, Victoria Bynum, Martin Crawford, Daniel Crofts, Michael Fitzgerald, Robin Grey, Douglas Howland, Bethany Johnson, Julie Livingston, Claudio Saunt, and Randall Shifflett. Equally important have been the interest, insights, and encouragement of my editors at LSU, Michael Parrish and Sylvia Frank Rodrigue. Also significant to my work have been the numerous descendants of loyalists (and other genealogical researchers) who have so kindly shared their family histories with me: Larry Brown, Paula Clack, James Gilbert, Dan Haggard, Stacey Hamby, Thomas E. Jacks, Gerald Jefferson, Greg Johnson, Reita Kelley, Robert L. Palmer, W. S.

Raines, Howell Raines, Wally Rickard, Dan Sniffen, Dottie Theisen, Glenda Todd, and Larry Whitehead. I am grateful for their enthusiasm and commitment to preserving the history of the South's Union people.

I appreciate, as well, permission to republish material originally appearing as an article in the *Journal of Southern History* entitled "Civil War Unionists and the Political Culture of Loyalty in Alabama, 1860–1861," Vol. 69, no. 1 (February 2003): 71–106.

My family has given me great support, as well, never wondering aloud what they must have been thinking: Why is it taking so long? Their humor, grace, and lively interest in everything have been guiding principles for me. Finally, I want to thank my husband, Jonathan Heller, for the inestimable contribution he has made to this work: he has read every word of it more often than he likely cares to remember. Nonetheless, he has always, amazingly, responded with thoughtful criticism, historical expertise, incisive suggestions, and enthusiastic encouragement. His love of history and ideas are the delight of my life.

Abbreviations

ADAH   Alabama Department of Archives and History, Montgomery

AGP   Alabama Governors' Papers, archived by governor's name and term, in Alabama Department of Archives and History, Montgomery

AU   Auburn University, Auburn, Ala.

BPL   Department of Archives and Manuscripts, Birmingham Public Library, Birmingham, Ala.

DU   Duke University Rare Book, Manuscript, & Special Collections Library, Durham, N.C.

EU   Woodruff Library, Emory University, Atlanta

FB-AL   Bureau of Refugees, Freedmen, Abandoned Lands, Alabama District, Record Group 105, National Archives, Washington, D.C.

GLCML The Gilder Lehrman Collection on deposit at the Pierpont Morgan Library, New York

IHS   Indiana Historical Society, Indianapolis

NAB   National Archives Building, Washington, D.C.

NAMS National Archives Microform Series

OR   *The War of the Rebellion: A Compilation of the Official Records of the Union and Confederate Armies.* 128 vols. Washington, D.C.: Government Printing Office, 1880–1901

SCC   Settled Case Files for Claims Approved by the Southern Claims Commission, 1871–1880, Record Group 217, National Archives Building, Washington, D.C.

SHC   Southern Historical Collection, University of North Carolina, Chapel Hill

SHSI   State Historical Society of Iowa, Des Moines

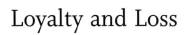

Loyalty and Loss

Introduction

My old father smelt gunpowder in 1776 through that war; and when we were talking about fighting here, I begged our men let us keep the flag of our fathers and set our foot upon the staff, and if we have to fight, fight for our rights in the Constitution and under our old flag; never give up the flag of our fathers, and never give up the Union, die by it.

—Archibald Steele, Madison County, Alabama, 1872

From the 1870s through the 1930s, the Palmer family of northwestern Alabama named its children after Civil War heroes. Like many Southern families, they did so to memorialize the family's sacrifice and loss during the war—but here the similarities ended. Instead of the perennial favorites of Jackson, Lee, and Forrest, Palmer children had names like Alexander *Sherman* and *General Grant,* monikers as close to fighting words as one could choose in postwar Alabama. Later generations bore the names of Republican presidents: *Harrison* Rowe, *Herbert Hoover,* Clover *McKinley.* One man gave his six children, all born in the early years of the twentieth century, names beginning with the letter "R," for "Republican."[1] The Palmers were not alone in their determination to preserve a counternarrative of the war in which unionists and their heroes took center stage. As late as 1968, the descendants of another set of Alabama unionists actively maintained a similar tradition. In that year, a young Colbert County man named Wally Rickard told his grandfather that he might vote for Alabama's ex-governor George C. Wallace in the upcoming presidential election. Although Wallace made his bid on the American Independent Party ticket, everyone in Alabama knew him as a

---

For epigraph, see *Testimony Taken by the Joint Select Committee to Inquire into the Condition of Affairs in the Late Insurrectionary States,* vol. 9, *Alabama* (Washington, D.C.: Government Printing Office, 1872), 944.

1. Robert L. Palmer, letters to author, March 9, 2002, and March 17, 2002. One of the Palmers, Joseph, was a secret service scout for the Union army, and others of the family were partisan fighters for the Federal side. See two entries for Joseph Palmer in "List of Monies Expended for Secret Service, &c. [1863–1864]," Secret Service Files, Grenville M. Dodge Papers (hereinafter Dodge Papers), SHSI.

Democrat. Wally's grandfather certainly viewed matters in this light, and he brusquely responded to his grandson's proposition with "a very strong reprimand and lecture on family traditions of being Republicans for over a 100 yrs." That tradition extended back to William Rikard, a wartime unionist who first set his family on the Republican path during Reconstruction. His son, James Madison Rikard, became Republican commissioner of Colbert County in 1876. From that time on, Alabama Rikards (and Rickards) had consistently voted Republican in keeping with their ancestor's wartime loyalty to the Union. Brought up short, Wally— doubtlessly like many of his kin before him—retreated. "[I]n fear of becoming exiled from the family," he explained, "I *didn't* support George."[2]

This book explores the history of Alabama's Civil War unionists, the men and women whose lives formed the taproot of the Palmer and Rikard traditions.[3] It argues that loyalists' wartime and Reconstruction experiences offer an exceptional opportunity to address a range of issues critical to the study of the South and the Civil War. Such themes include the nature of nineteenth-century Southern loyalty and its relationship to the South's political culture and slave society; the ways the Confederacy viewed and contended with unionists as resisters and traitors; slaves' exploitation of unionists' collaboration with the occupying Union army; the role played by loyalists and slaves in the Federal counterinsurgency strategy; and how the war transformed unionism from a conservative political position into a far more radical ideology that, by Reconstruction, identified unwavering wartime loyalty to the Union and a willingness to punish treason as the key components of postwar political legitimacy.

The study is fortunate to be published at a time when Civil War historiography has begun to take a lively and revealing interest in Southern unionism. New community and local studies of dissenting groups in the Confederacy, in particular, have made great contributions to our understanding of Civil War loyalty by taking into account a range of factors at

2. Wally Rickard, letter to author, November 17, 1997. Colbert County was formed out of the northern half of Franklin County in February 1867.

3. Please note that I will use the terms "unionism/unionist" and "loyalism/loyalist" interchangeably throughout this study. Unlike most studies of Civil War loyalists in the South, this study does not capitalize the words "unionist" and "unionism" simply because I see these words as describing a stance or position (like "secessionist" or "loyalist"), rather than a national identity. Whenever "Union" explicitly refers to the national entity—i.e., pro-Union, Union men, or Union army—the word, like "Confederate," is capitalized.

work in the wartime South.[4] Hoping to understand better "who remained loyal to the Union during the war," these local histories have sought to explain the "Civil War's underlying character, dimensions, and impact" in individual counties or towns, particularly in the upper South and Appalachia. Historians have delved more deeply than ever into the complexities of political allegiances within the states of the Confederacy and, as historian Daniel Sutherland has put it, striven to uncover "the gritty experience of real people."[5]

The trend is part of a larger effort among historians to assert the social, strategic, and military significance of the Southern home front itself. Unlike older works that limited their study of the home front to the civic and "high" political arenas in which internal divisions within the Confederacy played out far away from the battlefield, newer scholarship has explored the interactions of civilians, slaves, and soldiers as an integral part of the war itself. This development integrates fields that have been held apart for too long in Civil War history: the social and cultural from the military and political; the female from the male; the slave from the free. As scholars engaged in these new approaches have argued, understanding of the war itself is greatly enhanced by paying close attention to the ways that civilians and slaves experienced and shaped military action, and the ways that soldiers understood their duty not only to the army, but to society.[6] These dynamics varied markedly over the geo-

4. This new direction is embodied by John C. Inscoe and Robert C. Kenzer, eds., *Enemies of the Country: New Perspectives on Unionists in the Civil War South* (Athens: University of Georgia Press, 2001); Thomas Dyer, *Secret Yankees: The Union Circle in Confederate Atlanta* (Baltimore: Johns Hopkins University Press, 1999); Daniel E. Sutherland, ed., *Guerrillas, Unionists, and Violence on the Confederate Home Front* (Fayetteville: University of Arkansas Press, 1999); Paul S. Horton, "Submitting to the 'Shadow of Slavery': The Secession Crisis and Civil War in Alabama's Lawrence County," *Civil War History* 44, no. 2 (June 1998), 111–36; and Kenneth W. Noe and Shannon H. Wilson, eds., *The Civil War in Appalachia: Collected Essays* (Knoxville: University of Tennessee Press, 1997).

5. Inscoe and Kenzer, eds., *Enemies of the Country*, 3; Martin Crawford, "The Dynamics of Mountain Unionism: Federal Volunteers of Ashe County, North Carolina," in Noe and Wilson, eds., *The Civil War in Appalachia*, 56; Sutherland, *Guerrillas, Unionists, and Violence*, 8.

6. For examples of such work, see Kenneth W. Noe, "Who Were the Bushwhackers? Age, Class, Kin, and Western Virginia's Confederate Guerrillas, 1861–1862," *Civil War History* 49, no. 1 (2003): 5–26; Martin Crawford, *Ashe County's Civil War: Community and Society in the Appalachian South* (Charlottesville: University Press of Virginia, 2001); Victoria E. Bynum, *The Free State of Jones: Mississippi's Longest Civil War* (Chapel Hill: University of

graphic space that was "the South." Whether in the border states, the occupied South, or contested areas of guerrilla conflict, though, the war confronted soldier, civilian, and slave alike with the worst in human suffering and depravity while simultaneously offering up striking instances of honor, courage, and dignity. In the midst of such bewildering experiences, the war's participants struggled to understand the meaning of what was happening to them, their neighbors, and their families.

The present study places unconditional unionists at the center of Alabama's home front maelstrom. For such men and women—firmly loyal to the Union from 1860 through the end of the war—the home front was unmistakably *the* place of conflict. In contrast to the soldiers from Indiana and Illinois who spent so much time in Alabama during the Civil War, unionists' struggles did not occur at a place distant from family and friends, home and farm. From the most significant battles to the briefest skirmishes of partisan guerrillas, fighting in the Civil War occurred amongst civilians and slaves, over rooftops and in kitchen gardens, at gristmills and county courthouses. Many Southerners, black and white, experienced the war in intimate terms and thus reacted to that conflict out of deeply personal interest. Unionists, in particular, were convinced that they would be exiled from the South if the Confederacy won its independence, and so battled not simply to keep the South in the Union, but to keep themselves and their loved ones *in the South*, to remain in the region of their birth. These men and women became and remained unionists not simply out of opposition to something (the Confederacy), but also out of a deep desire to cleave to something, to consolidate and preserve what they valued in their families, neighborhoods, section, and nation.

Key to this study is a focus on unionists' political culture and the way it shaped and fueled their resistance both to the Confederacy during the

---

North Carolina Press, 2001); William W. Freehling, *The South vs. the South: How Anti-Confederate Southerners Shaped the Course of the Civil War* (New York: Oxford University Press, 2001); Daniel E. Sutherland and Anne J. Bailey, eds., *Civil War Arkansas: Beyond Battles and Leaders* (Fayetteville: University of Arkansas Press, 2000); David Williams, *Rich Man's War: Class, Caste, and Confederate Defeat in the Lower Chattahoochee Valley* (Athens: University of Georgia Press, 1998); Noel C. Fisher, *War at Every Door: Partisan Politics and Guerrilla Violence in East Tennessee, 1860–1869* (Chapel Hill: University of North Carolina Press, 1997); Steven V. Ash, *When the Yankees Came: Conflict and Chaos in the Occupied South, 1861–1865* (Chapel Hill: University of North Carolina Press, 1995); and Mark Grimsley, *The Hard Hand of War: Union Military Policy toward Southern Civilians, 1861–1865* (Cambridge, U.K.: Cambridge University Press, 1995).

war and to Democratic control of their state during Reconstruction. The "political," in this sense, represents more than formal, public actions like voting, party affiliation, or legislative action, though such factors are crucial to understanding loyalist history. Like the work of many women's historians, this analysis assumes that the political also embraces relationships and decisions that might be deemed "personal" or "private," but that nonetheless fostered, defined, and gave meaning or active expression to individuals' political ideas.[7] In the case of Alabama unionists, kinship ties, neighborhood business and friendship relations, master-slave relations, as well as the codes of behavior and expectations inherent in an honor-based society, played critical roles in individuals' articulation of their political loyalty to the Union.

Such a broadened definition of the political is especially important when trying to understand loyalty and resistance, for such ideas, while assuredly political, are by their very nature social concepts.[8] In wartime, loyalty is a lived reality with extensive and often violent consequences. For Alabama's unionists—a tiny minority marooned in enemy territory, loathed as traitors best expelled or killed—this was especially true. When these men and women gave their allegiance to the Union in 1860–61, they frequently did so as a matter of obligation. To honor and protect, and not betray, a host of social ties was critical to their understanding of themselves and their role in their communities. At the same time, they relied on that same set of ties to maintain their resistance once the war began. Unionists' political culture and their resistance to the Confederacy were deeply intertwined; the relationship between the two transformed a political identity into a durable code of resistance that individuals were willing to defend with their lives. For loyalists, the po-

7. Laura Edwards, *Scarlett Doesn't Live Here Anymore: Southern Women in the Civil War Era* (Urbana: University of Illinois Press, 2000), 2–4; Drew Gilpin Faust, *Mothers of Invention: Women of the Slaveholding South in the American Civil War* (Chapel Hill: University of North Carolina Press, 1996), xiii; Stephanie McCurry, *Masters of Small Worlds: Yeoman Households, Gender Relations, and the Political Culture of the Antebellum South Carolina Low Country* (New York: Oxford University Press, 1995), 61, 235–7; Linda Kerber, "Separate Spheres, Female Worlds, Women's Place: The Rhetoric of Women's History," *Journal of American History* 75, no. 1 (June 1988), 18, 38–9; and Joan Wallach Scott, *Gender and the Politics of History*, rev. ed. (New York: Columbia University Press, 1999), 24–6.

8. Josiah Royce, *The Philosophy of Loyalty* (1908; reprint, New York: Hafner, 1971), 20, 55; Morton Grodzins, *The Loyal and the Disloyal: Social Boundaries of Patriotism and Treason* (Cleveland: World, 1966), 40–1, 45–7.

litical was anchored in, and resistance was expressed through, the social relations that composed daily life.

Though some historians have agreed that similar patterns shaped Southern rights ideology and fostered Confederate nationalism, scholars have not fully recognized the importance of such sociocultural factors to the growth and development of unionist resistance in the Deep South.[9] To do so is to recognize that though Southerners' loyalty to the Union represented a rejection of the Confederate state, it did not necessarily represent a rejection of Southern culture or values. Unionists, like Confederates, bound the abstraction of political loyalty to widely shared Southern values of personal duty and familial honor. They negotiated the same range of social relations and were steeped in the same cultural and political traditions as were Confederates. They were, as one appalled Alabama Confederate noted, "Southern born."[10] Unionists simply resolved the demands and implications of these social relations differently than did secessionists. Rather than suggesting an imperative for divorce, loyalists believed that duty to kin, friends, and community demanded that they cling more tightly to the Union. As this book will demonstrate, unionism prompted considerable social dislocation for its adherents, but it was also the shelter under which many intimate social ties were crowded together in mutual aid and comfort.[11]

Alabama is a particularly illuminating site in which to explore the complexities of Southern unionism because the state had a recognized unionist population—most but not all of whom lived in its northern counties—and, at the same time, was deeply invested in the Confederate movement and in slavery.[12] Alabama's circumstance in this regard stands

9. See, for example, McCurry, *Masters of Small Worlds*, 259–61, 277–8 and chap. 8, passim; Drew Gilpin Faust, *The Creation of Confederate Nationalism: Ideology and Identity in the Civil War South* (Baton Rouge: Louisiana State University Press, 1988), passim.

10. Mrs. M. E. Thompson to Elias Thompson, November 21, 1861, Benson-Thompson Family Papers, 1803–1936, DU.

11. Although David Potter's *The South and the Sectional Conflict* (Baton Rouge: Louisiana State University Press, 1968) addresses the history and nature of Southern nationalism, I have found his explication of the relationship of local loyalties to national loyalty helpful in this context; see especially the discussion on 47–9. Also helpful was Grodzins, *Loyal and the Disloyal*, 40–7, whom Potter himself cites.

12. Unionists clustered in North Alabama, but they could be found scattered throughout the state, particularly in the southeastern Wiregrass region. William W. Rogers, Jr., in *Confederate Home Front: Montgomery during the Civil War* (Tuscaloosa: University of Alabama

in contrast to the more familiar story of Southern loyalism: a tale of men and women living in the upper South, distant literally and ideologically from slavery and slaveholders and, therefore, from secession. (Whether this story itself obscures the complexities of Union loyalty in the upper South is another question.) Most historians have seen this upper South archetype mirrored in North Alabama, and have thus tended to emphasize the region's poverty and mountainous geography while arguing that its citizens became unionists because they were economically and politically alienated from wealthy slaveholding secessionists.[13]

Closer investigation, however, reveals a more complicated demographic picture, a reality that challenges the usefulness of a class-based, or narrowly antislaveholder/antislavery, explanation of unionism. The designation "North Alabama" should not be equated with an undifferentiated mass of poor people farming poor soil. Census data clearly demonstrate that wealth and slaveholding varied widely across the northern counties of the state, and their distribution was shaped by the geographi-

---

Press, 1999), devotes chap. 7, "Dissenting Voices," to unionists, mostly Northern-born, living in Montgomery, Alabama's capital city, located in the Black Belt.

13. For example, William Stanley Hoole in *Alabama Tories: The First Alabama Cavalry, U.S.A, 1862–1865* (Tuscaloosa, Ala.: Confederate, 1960), 5, argued that loyalists were generally poor and supported the Union out of a simple hatred of "the affluent slave-holder and his 'nigger' alike." Similar themes mark Malcolm C. McMillan, *The Disintegration of a Confederate State: Three Governors and Alabama's Wartime Home Front, 1861–1865* (Macon, Ga.: Mercer University Press, 1986), 2. The earliest treatments of unionism in the South put forward similar impressions regarding Alabama loyalists; see Bessie Martin, *Desertion of Alabama Troops from the Confederate Army: A Study in Sectionalism* (New York: Columbia University Press, 1932), 40–61, 99–120; Albert Burton Moore, *Conscription and Conflict in the Confederacy* (New York: Macmillan, 1924), 151–4; Ella Lonn, *Desertion during the Civil War* (New York: American Historical Association, 1928), 3–4, 31, 100, 200–1; Hugh C. Bailey, "Disloyalty in Early Confederate Alabama," *Journal of Southern History* 23 (November 1957): 522, and by the same author, "Disaffection in the Alabama Hill Country, 1861," *Civil War History* 4 (June 1958): 183–93; Durwood Long, "Unanimity and Disloyalty in Secessionist Alabama," *Civil War History* 11 (September 1965): 268–70; Georgia Lee Tatum, *Disloyalty in the Confederacy* (1934; reprint, Lincoln: University of Nebraska Press, 2000), xxiv; Elbert L. Watson, "The Story of the Nickajack," *Alabama Review* 20 (January 1967): 17–26; Donald B. Dodd, "Unionism in Northwest Alabama through 1865" (M.A. thesis, Auburn University, 1966) and by the same author, "Unionism in Confederate Alabama" (Ph.D. diss., University of Georgia, 1969), which, despite the title, focuses only on the northwestern hill counties, and, again by the same author, "The Free State of Winston," *Alabama Heritage* 28 (spring 1993): 8–19. See also Donald B. Dodd and Wynelle S. Dodd, *Winston: An Antebellum and Civil War History of a Hill County of North Alabama,* vol. 4, *Annals of Northwest Alabama,* comp. Carl Elliot (Jasper, Ala.: Oxmoor, 1972).

cal character of two distinct subregions: the Hill Country and the Tennessee Valley.[14] (See map 1.) The Hill Country did contain mostly small, subsistence farms, located on poor soil, which relied very little on slave labor; slave populations in the subregion ranged from 3.4 percent in Winston County to 16.4 percent in Cherokee County. This is the part of Alabama that seems best to fit a model that links unionism with alienation from the South's slave society; people living here *were* often detached from the mainstream of Deep South commerce and slaveholding. Nonetheless, it should be noted that between 1850 and 1860, even these poorer counties had become increasingly involved in producing cotton, although their contributions to the state's overall cotton production remained very low. The Tennessee Valley counties, by contrast, had long invested heavily in slavery and cotton production; moreover, the subregion exhibited a diversified economy, including lively commercial, manufacturing, and mercantile interests as well as yeoman subsistence farming in the more rolling areas. Slave populations here ranged from 18.6 percent of the total population in Jackson County to 55.1 percent in Madison County. These valley counties had long maintained close eco-

14. Counties of the Tennessee Valley subregion include Franklin, Jackson, Lauderdale, Lawrence, Limestone, Madison, and Morgan. Counties of the Hill Country include Blount, Cherokee, DeKalb, Fayette, Marion, Marshall, St. Clair, Walker, and Winston. When reading the footnote citations for SCC claims, be aware that Alabama created a number of new counties in the decade following the end of the Civil War. Consequently, it is not unusual to find a discrepancy between the county name listed in a footnote and the county name given in the text as the claimant's wartime home. For instance, though a person may have lived in Franklin County during the war, by the time he or she filed a claim, that person's county could have changed to Colbert County. Moreover, at times the SCC misfiled the claim. This was frequently the case if an individual traveled outside his or her home county to give testimony—claim materials were sometimes filed under the county of testimony, not the county of residence. When trying to find a claim in the National Archives, it is best to provide the information given in the footnote citation, as this represents the official filing scheme. Because the maps in this study do not include post-1865 county names, the list at the end of appendix 1, "A Note on the Sources," offers a list of new counties (1865–1874) and their predecessors.

Note that the determination of which counties exactly constitute the particular subregions of Alabama varies among historians. To create map 1, I have taken inspiration from the approaches of Horace Mann Bond, *Negro Education in Alabama: A Study in Cotton and Steel* (Washington, D.C.: Associated Publishers, 1939), 2–3, 7; Peter Kolchin, *First Freedom: The Responses of Alabama's Blacks to Emancipation and Reconstruction*, Contributions in American History, no. 20 (Westport, Conn.: Greenwood Press, 1972), 13; and Samuel L. Webb, *Two-Party Politics in the One-Party South: Alabama's Hill Country, 1874–1920* (Tuscaloosa: University of Alabama Press, 1997), xii.

nomic and political ties to Middle Tennessee, and may well have shared more in common with their neighbors to the north than with the hill counties south of the Tennessee River.[15]

In light of the dramatic demographic differences among subregions, it seems a mistake when trying to understand what factors influenced the development and expression of unionism to ignore these distinctions, treating the slaveholding parts of the region as the exception, while generalizing the Hill Country's demography to North Alabama as a whole. Historian J. Mills Thornton long ago cautioned against this when explaining the ways that Alabamians responded to secession. "The pattern is abundantly clear: south Alabama was for immediate secession and north Alabama was not," he noted. "However straightforward this statement may be, though, it is subject to misinterpretation. First of all, the geographical division is between north Alabama and south Alabama. It is not between plantation counties and small farm counties; if it were, the Tennessee Valley and the Black Belt on the one hand would be grouped against the hill counties and the Wiregrass in the southeast on the other."[16]

The significance of Thornton's caveat is even more convincing upon examination of the economic status of unionists who made successful claims to the Southern Claims Commission (SCC). A postwar agency created in 1871 to hear the claims of loyalists and freedpeople for property lost to the Union army during the war, the SCC preserved in transcription the oral testimony of thousands of loyal black and white Southerners. Men and women, planters and yeomen, artisans and mechanics, freedpeople and former free blacks—all gave testimony to the

---

15. J. Mills Thornton III, *Politics and Power in a Slave Society: Alabama, 1800–1860* (Baton Rouge: Louisiana State University Press, 1978), 285–6, 279–80. Thornton documents a greater than 300 percent increase in cotton production in the poorest Hill Country counties, Winston and Walker, during this period. For a full account of slave populations by county and subregion, see appendix 3, table A.1. The 1860 census also reveals a significant difference in the annual value of manufactured products coming out of the Tennessee Valley and the Hill Country. Franklin, Lauderdale, Limestone, and Madison Counties alone produced nearly four times the value in manufactured goods in 1860 ($1,608,763) as did the Hill Country (not including Winston County, whose data was missing from the census). Indeed, Madison County's annual manufactured production (valued at $725,488) ranked second to that of Mobile County, by far the leading manufacturing county in the state (with annual production valued at $1,500,916). Aggregate 1860 census data for Alabama counties from "United States Historical Census Browser."

16. Ibid., 343.

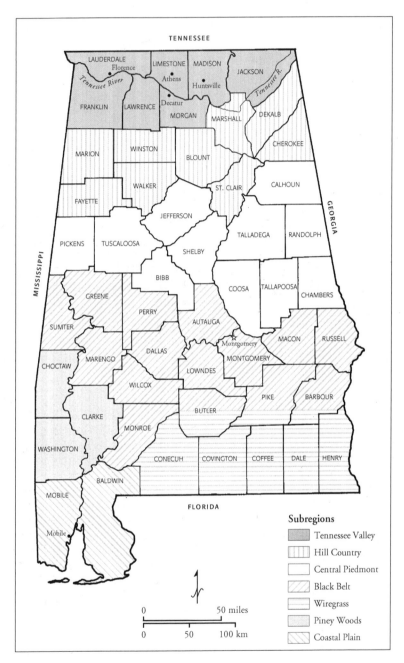

Map 1: Alabama Counties and Subregions, 1860.

SCC. Each case file contains the claimant's (and his or her witnesses') sworn statements about loyalty and the property in question. This testimony reveals the names of friends, political enemies, and slaves, as well as the kinship or community ties among various individuals. Supporting documents such as deeds, discharge papers, wartime affidavits regarding loyalty, or receipts from Union officers were also included. In their own words, individuals revealed their loyalist sentiments during the war, the actions they took to support the Union, and the violent consequences they incurred as a result.[17]

Among all the rich evidence the claims contribute to our understanding of Alabama unionists' experiences is some fairly basic, but heretofore elusive, information: names. With names, unionists take on fixed identities that make it possible to trace them through the 1860 United States census. This, in turn, offers an unparalleled opportunity to understand the particulars of age, wealth, slaveholding, and neighborhood that until now have remained rather murky. For instance, although some white SCC claimants in both the Tennessee Valley and the Hill Country were poor farmers, they also were representative of men and women of mod-

17. This study relies heavily on the testimony of 405 loyal Alabamians, most of whose identities I have been able to trace in the United States census. As with county names, confusion might arise from the dates I have provided for SCC testimony and those one might find in published indexes of the claims. As a rule, I have provided a date that corresponds with the date of the claimant's and his or her witnesses' initial depositions in the case, hoping thereby to help readers understand exactly when the individuals spoke the words transcribed therein. Most indexes, by contrast, provide the date on which the claim was closed, or paid out, by the Congress, usually many years after the original testimony was given. See appendix 1, "A Note on the Sources," for a detailed description of the papers of the SCC, the agency's history and methods, as well as my methodological approach to these materials. In statistical analysis, the total number of claimants will sometimes be smaller than the total number of claims reviewed because not all claimants could be traced through the census, and thus could not be included in databases about wealth or slaveholding, for example. For historical treatments of the Southern Claims Commission, see Frank W. Klingberg, *The Southern Claims Commission,* University of California Publications in History, vol. 50 (Berkeley: University of California Press, 1955), vii–viii; and by the same author, "The Southern Claims Commission: A Postwar Agency in Operation," *Mississippi Valley Historical Review* 32, no. 2 (September 1954): 195–214; Sarah Larson, "Records of the Southern Claims Commission," *Prologue* 12 (winter 1980): 207–8. For other studies that make use of, or comment on, the claims, see Michael K. Honey, "The War within the Confederacy: White Unionists of North Carolina," *Prologue* 18 (summer 1986): 75–93; Daniel W. Crofts, *Reluctant Confederates: Upper South Unionists in the Secession Crisis* (Chapel Hill: University of North Carolina Press, 1989), 348; and Dyer, *Secret Yankees.*

erate to considerable wealth, including a marked number of slaveholders. And, not surprisingly, the wealth of unionists varied according to the subregion in which they lived.[18] (See tables 1 and 2.) Tennessee Valley claimants, though poorer than Hill Country unionists in the tenth (least wealthy) decile, were nonetheless wealthier overall than their Hill Country counterparts. This distinction was largely a consequence of dramatically different rates of slaveholding between the subregions: whereas slaveholders represented just under 5 percent of Hill Country claimants, they made up 30.4 percent of valley claimants.[19] It is important to note that the Valley's slaveholding unionists differed considerably from the grand landowners of Alabama's Black Belt: over half of those for whom exact slaveholding statistics can be confirmed owned four or fewer slaves and were much closer economically to nonslaveholding yeoman farmers than to the planter class owners of twenty or more slaves.[20] (See table 3.) Census data also reveal that although the majority of unionists who lived in North Alabama were farmers, greater numbers of unionist artisans, artisan-farmers, merchants, and professionals lived in the valley than in the Hill Country.[21]

These figures do not offer a tidy causal explanation of unionism's strength in North Alabama. Indeed, if anything, the numbers emphasize the inadequacies of a single socioeconomic model in explaining unionism, for they clearly show that this population contained considerable demographic variation. That diversity does, however, offer an excellent starting point from which to approach the questions of loyalty and resistance within this population. Rather than striving to isolate a single cause for unionism, this book focuses on the multiple factors shaping the formation and expression of Union loyalty on the Deep South home front. In so doing, it illustrates what many would consider a commonplace, but what historians should nonetheless avoid taking for granted:

18. For distribution of wealth among all allowed SCC claimants in the state, see appendix 3, table A.2.

19. SCC; U.S. Census Bureau, *Eighth Census of the United States: Alabama, Free Population Schedule*, NAMS M-653 (hereinafter, 1860 U.S. Census, Alabama, Free Pop.). For percentages of slaveholders by county and subregion, see appendix 3, tables A.3 and A.4.

20. Exact slaveholding numbers could only be confirmed in the 1860 census for a total of three Hill Country claimants and a total of thirty-two Tennessee Valley individuals. The distribution of slaves among these three Hill Country claimants was as follows: one owned one slave; one owned twelve slaves; and the last owned fourteen slaves.

21. SCC; 1860 U.S. Census, Alabama, Free Pop. For occupational data among white claimants, see appendix 3, tables A.5 and A.6.

TABLE 1: *Distribution of Wealth among Allowed SCC Claimants, White (Hill Country Subregion, Alabama, 1860)*

Decile	Total Value of Wealth	% Share of Wealth	Mean Wealth	% Slaveholders
Top decile	$159,939	58.44	$15,379	38.5
Second	34,647	12.66	3,331	9.6
Third	21,876	7.99	2,103	0.0
Fourth	17,186	6.28	1,653	0.0
Fifth	12,904	4.72	1,241	0.0
Sixth	9,334	3.41	898	0.0
Seventh	7,798	2.85	760	0.0
Eighth	5,918	2.16	569	0.0
Ninth	3,571	1.30	343	0.0
Tenth	485	.18	47	0.0
Totals	$273,658	100.00	2,631	4.8

Sources: SCC; 1860 U.S. Census, Alabama, Free Pop. and Slave Pop., NAMS M-653.

Note: The total number of unionists in this table is 104; it includes only those white claimants living in the Hill Country whose real and personal property was recorded in the 1860 census; all men and women eighteen and younger still living in their parents' households were excluded. However, sons over eighteen living in their father's or mother's household were included, regardless of whether or not they independently owned property.

that people of varying background, economic status, and race may choose to support the same cause for markedly different reasons. Indeed, love of the Union may be the only "interest" such individuals shared. By the same token, people in similar socioeconomic situations can come to quite different political understandings despite the apparent commonality of their "interests." Loyalty in wartime, moreover, can motivate people to take more rigid stands than party politics does in peacetime. In war, the stakes are simply higher, and people consequently mute social or cultural distinctions between one another in order to highlight a common cause, the success or survival of which demands united action. The wartime alliances of unionist masters and slaves discussed in this book, for instance, is a prime example of such a circumstance.

Understanding the contrast between wartime loyalty and the workings of peacetime political "interest" is equally important when trying to understand unionists and their postwar relationship with the Republican Party. During the war, Alabama loyalists helped occupying Federal forces

TABLE 2: *Distribution of Wealth among Allowed SCC Claimants, White (Tennessee Valley Subregion, Alabama, 1860)*

Decile	Total Value of Wealth	% Share of Wealth	Mean Wealth	% Slaveholders
Top decile	$695,045	66.31	$55,604	100.0
Second	145,085	13.84	11,607	76.0
Third	87,332	8.33	6,987	44.0
Fourth	50,084	4.78	4,007	44.0
Fifth	28,205	2.69	2,256	32.0
Sixth	18,044	1.72	1,444	8.0
Seventh	11,860	1.13	949	0.0
Eighth	7,850	.75	628	0.0
Ninth	4,307	.41	345	0.0
Tenth	368	.04	29	0.0
Totals	$1,048,180	100.00	8,385	30.4

Sources: SCC; 1860 U.S. Census, Alabama, Free Pop. and Slave Pop., NAMS M-653.

Note: The total number of unionists in this table is 125; it includes only those white claimants living in the Tennessee Valley counties whose real and personal property was recorded in the 1860 census; all men and women eighteen and younger still living in their parents' households were excluded. However, sons over eighteen living in their father's or mother's household were included, regardless of whether or not they independently owned property.

TABLE 3: *Distribution of Slaves among Allowed SCC Claimants, Slaveholding (Tennessee Valley Subregion, Alabama, 1860)*

Number of Slaves Owned	Number of SCC Slaveholders	As % of Total Number of Slaveholders in Subregion
1–4	17	53.1
5–10	4	12.5
11–20	6	18.8
21+	5	15.6
Totals	32	100.0

Sources: SCC; 1860 U.S. Census, Alabama, Free Pop. and Slave Pop., NAMS M-653.

Note: This table includes only those slaveholders whose exact slaveholding could be confirmed through the 1860 census.

destroy their mutual enemy: the rebel army. Frequently, the Union allowed and even encouraged them to indulge a rigid notion of right and wrong in order to prosecute this guerrilla warfare. At the time, Federals' overwhelming mandate for victory, like unionists' all-consuming desire for vengeance, justified acting with little concern for shades of meaning or the niceties of a courtroom. The political battle of the postwar era, however, was quite a different animal, largely because the Federal government no longer sought to crush its enemies as it had during the war. Instead, most Northerners in Congress wanted speedy reconciliation with the South and a relatively painless return to peace and prosperity.[22] The Republican Party was fundamentally unwilling, during both Presidential and Congressional Reconstruction, to sacrifice Northern votes for the sake of severely punishing former Confederates or for the sake of establishing a long-standing military occupation of the South to defend unionists from their wartime enemies.[23] Unionists, by contrast, wanted postwar Federal policy to serve as a reckoning for traitors, and their ideas in this regard could not be easily made to conform to a politics of reconciliation. Indeed, the idea that there could be a return to the prewar "give-and-take of pragmatic politics" was simply inconceivable.[24] Deep and abiding distrust of any leaders associated with the Confederate state, combined with an ever-present awareness of their minority status and fear of violent abuse, made it impossible for wartime loyalists to support the dominant Northern desire for a speedy and gentle reunion with the South.

A final word about the size of this population is necessary. It is quite difficult to know the exact number of loyalists living in Alabama in 1860–61, when individuals made the decision to unconditionally support the Union. Postwar estimates given by wartime unionists to the Joint Committee on Reconstruction in 1866 suggest that the state at that time could have offered anywhere from ten to fourteen thousand "Union votes" out of a statewide white voting strength of about eighty thousand—or about 15 percent.[25] Most of these votes, it was explained, would

22. Michael Perman, *Reunion without Compromise: The South and Reconstruction, 1865–1868* (New York: Cambridge University Press, 1973), 5–10.

23. Richard H. Abbott, *The Republican Party and the South, 1855–1877: The First Southern Strategy* (Chapel Hill: University of North Carolina Press, 1986), x–xi, 49–52, 187–91.

24. Perman, *Reunion without Compromise*, 10.

25. *Report of the Joint Committee on Reconstruction*, 39th Cong., 1st Sess. (Washington, D.C.: Government Printing Office, 1866), 9, 14.

come from North Alabama. There are considerable difficulties with accepting this figure as a reliable indicator of the number of unconditional unionists (i.e., loyal from secession through Appomattox). By the end of the war, disaffection from the Confederacy had sharply increased the numbers of individuals willing to identify themselves as "Union men," especially in the northern counties where the war caused great devastation. Moreover, the Alabamians giving the estimates to Congress tended to present the unionist population in two ways: as a besieged group in need of military protection, or as a healthy voting bloc with great potential for aiding the Republican cause in the South. A tendency to exaggerate numbers was certainly in the interest of anyone painting either of these portraits. Finally, because this 1866 estimate is based upon voter strength, it ignores women unionists. Though invisible in a count of electors, women were critical to the formation and defense of unionism within their families and circles of friends; they also played important roles in the Union army's counterinsurgency efforts during the war. To equate voter strength with the strength of unionist sentiment simply elides female participation in this aspect of loyalist political culture. What is clear despite the above concerns is what anecdotal evidence has long suggested and the SCC claims confirm: with rare exception (notably Winston and Walker Counties) unconditional unionists did not represent majorities in their counties before, during, or after the war.

With these caveats in mind, it seems safe to say that the number of unconditional unionists in 1861 never outstripped 15 percent of the total adult white population, and was likely closer to 10 percent. Such estimates are, however, only informed guesswork, and the statistics used in this study do not come close to incorporating this number of people. Instead, they are based on data collected from just over four hundred allowed SCC claims, as well as any corresponding data available through the Eighth U.S. Census of 1860. Although this information provides us with a better sense of loyalists' demographic "profile" and illuminates certain descriptive factors about unionists in Alabama, these statistics do not provide a census of Alabama's unionist population, and therefore do not represent a reliable estimate for the total numbers of unionists in the state.[26]

In the end, the historical significance of Alabama's loyalists does not really lie in the size of their population. No matter what, it is clear that

26. See appendix 1, "Note on the Sources."

16

unionists in Alabama never had the numbers necessary to marshal the political influence wielded by, for example, William G. "Parson" Brownlow and his followers in East Tennessee. Their significance does, nonetheless, have something to do with the size of their population: Alabama unionists were remarkable because they persisted despite overwhelming odds—despite their very real "smallness." Their early and vigorous opposition to secession and the Confederacy, active alliances with the Federal army as soldiers, spies, and partisan fighters, and postwar association with the Republican Party as the party of loyalty, all shed light on the very nature of resistance itself. They are a reminder that a man's or woman's willingness to sacrifice for a cause does not always hinge on the promise of success, but can, instead, arise defensively in the face of terrible loss. The threat of losing one's nation and home, of betraying one's family and friends, and of abandoning long-treasured ideas about loyalty and honor, can sustain small people in dangerous times. Alabama unionists' notions of how to preserve and protect the future of their homeland were clearly not those of their Confederate neighbors. But their desire to do so was undeniably as strong.

1

"Flag of Our Fathers"

THE POLITICAL CULTURE OF LOYALISM

*I voted for those who said the guns would have to be placed to their breast
and the trigger pulled before they would vote for Alabama to go out of the
Union, but they did not stick to what they said.*

    —Jasper Harper, Marshall County, 1874

*Heavens, I have never been anything else than a union man and expect to
die one. I was born that a way. The wind changes and the moon changes,
but the old man never changes.*

    —Martin Middleton, Monroe County, 1874

In early 1861, a gentleman named Garret Hall arrived unannounced at
the home of unionist Elisha Nelson, bearing the news from Montgomery
that "Alabama had went out of the Union." The revelation was profoundly unwelcome in the neighborhood surrounding Nelson's farm in
coastal Baldwin County. There, in a settlement on a peninsula some
twenty-five miles long and two miles wide, eleven unionist families made
up a "community to ourselves," oystering, fishing, and raising cattle for
a living just south of Mobile Bay. United by their bitter opposition to
secession, Elisha Nelson's neighbors would doubtlessly have concurred
with his terse response to Hall's announcement that Alabama had se-
ceded: "[S]he never went out with my consent."[1]

For epigraphs, see Claim 4190, Jasper Harper, Marshall Co., April 24, 1874; and Claim
2318, Martin Middleton, Monroe Co., December 3, 1874; both in SCC.

1. Claim 3787C, Elisha Nelson, Baldwin Co., March 7, 1878; and Claim 3787A, Samuel
Sebury Strong, Baldwin Co., March 8, 1878: Testimony of Hans Peter Hanson; both in SCC.
When quoting from SCC claims, as well as all other manuscript or published primary material, I have preserved original spellings, only inserting bracketed letters when the word, as
spelled, was very difficult to read or understand. I have silently added punctuation whenever
such additions added clarity to the quotation.

Although most of Alabama's unionists were not as physically segregated from their Confederate neighbors as were these Gulf Coast Union families, during the secession winter all loyalists became equally detached, figuratively speaking, from the mainstream of Alabama citizens. Prior to the 1860 presidential election, loyalists had represented only the most extreme faction of a large body of pro-Union sympathizers, men who opposed secession but who did not necessarily make the preservation of the Union their ultimate priority.[2] Lincoln's election caused many of these moderates to embrace secession as the best, if not only, response to Republican victory. As one shocked citizen observed in the wake of Lincoln's election, men of all parties seemed to catapult themselves into a frenzy of pro-separation speeches and pronouncements. "This people is apparently gone crazy," he remarked to a friend, "Union men, Douglass men, Breckinridge men are alike in their loud denunciation of submission to Lincoln's administration."[3] Everyone, it seemed, had to choose a side—"to be pig or puppy one."[4]

While moderates increasingly came to the conclusion that a pro-Union position was untenable in such a heavily secessionist state, unconditional unionists, for reasons of conviction, pride, community loyalty, and peculiar stubbornness, refused to collapse under the weight of the states' apparent unanimity.[5] Every step unionists took in this regard, however, provoked increasingly hostile opposition from secessionists and diminishing solidarity with moderate pro-Union men who became in-

2. In order to differentiate such moderates from wartime unionists, I have employed the terms "pro-Union," "Union men," "moderates," and "conservatives," to describe pro-Union citizens prior to the presidential election of November 1860. During the secession crisis of 1860–61, I also use the term "cooperationist" (defined in detail later in the text) to refer to this moderate group. I have referred to nascent and active secessionists at different points as "southern rights men," "radicals," "bolters," or "fire-eaters." I have reserved the terms "unionist" and "loyalist" (used interchangeably throughout this study) for individuals who unconditionally maintained their allegiance to the United States after secession.

3. Sereno Watson to Henry Watson, November 17, 1860, Box 6, Folder: Correspondence, 1860, Henry Watson Papers, 1765–1938, DU.

4. Claim 6828, William Mathews, Cherokee Co., May 19, 1874, SCC.

5. Many men who took a pro-Union stance during the secession crisis ultimately "went with the state" once the secession ordinance was adopted. A discussion of the reasons for most Alabamians' decision to support the Confederacy after the election of 1860 lies beyond the scope of this study. Moreover, such a discussion would be redundant in light of the excellent work already done on this subject by historians Thornton, *Politics and Power,* and William L. Barney, *The Secessionist Impulse: Alabama and Mississippi in 1860* (Princeton, N.J.: Princeton University Press, 1974).

creasingly unwilling to resist separation. Throughout the secession winter, unionists thus had to reassess and solidify relationships with others of like mind, slowly circling the wagons against the onslaught from the majority. Both responding to external pressures and cleaving to one another, Alabama's unionists laid the foundations of a community of resisters—isolated, fierce, and profoundly loyal not only to the Union, but to each other: "We knowed one another as a man know his flock."[6]

In the aftermath of Alabama's secession, reluctant secessionist John Moore wrote to friends at home, "The die is cast, the Rubicon is crossed."[7] With these words, Moore highlighted the inevitability, the fatalism, many Alabamians attached to the South's exodus. Unconditional unionists, however, saw nothing inevitable about separation. Refusing to be dragged across the Rubicon, loyalists stubbornly dug in their heels as Alabama crossed over.

Political Ideology

A unionist's identity arose, first and foremost, from a set of political beliefs. Alabama's unionists interpreted secession as irresponsible folly at the least, and a terrible abrogation of one's obligations to family and nation at the worst. In embracing this position, they did not conceive of themselves as radical dissenters (although Confederates viewed them as such). Nor did they take their stance as critical outsiders come lately to the region: Alabama's allowed SCC claimants were overwhelmingly native Southerners (90 percent were born in Southern states, the majority of these in the Deep South) who were tightly bound to the state and region by kinship and community.[8] Instead, they saw themselves as the

6. Claim 2318, Martin Middleton, Monroe Co., December 3, 1874: Testimony of T. E. Feagin, SCC.

7. John E. Moore to Capt. Jack and My Friend Luke, January 14, 1861, John Edmund Moore Papers, 1861, DU.

8. For detailed nativity data, see appendix 3, table A.7. Thomas Dyer's study of the "Union circle" in Atlanta shows that many of the city's unionists were born in the North. The reason that Dyer's study differs with my findings in this regard is likely because he investigated unionists living in an urban setting. I suspect that in more rural areas of Georgia, fewer Northerners populated unionist enclaves. Like Dyer, William Rogers, Jr., found a similar pattern of northern-born unionists living in Montgomery. They, like the Union circle members in Atlanta, were mostly involved in industry, commerce, or urban labor. See Dyer, *Secret Yankees*, 14–5, 24, 36–8, 43, 53, and chap. 7 of William Rogers, Jr.,

defenders of a government that, in their view, had not betrayed its prom-
ises to them. In this regard, most of them shared in common an attitude
or temperament that valued conservatism and was characterized by a
general desire to preserve stability and to pursue strategies for political
accommodation. Indeed, they believed the Union embodied democratic
processes that continued to provide fair and just government, that had
made possible the gains of their parents and themselves, and that promised future security and stability for their children and grandchildren.

Secession, on the other hand, seemed to them to be the antithesis
of these values, an extreme, dangerous, foolish, and illegitimate act that
undermined democratic processes and the intentions of the Founding
Fathers, despite that secessionists claimed to be the real guardians of traditional republicanism against radical new Northern political ideology.[9]
As Creed Taylor, a tanner from Marshall County, explained to the SCC,
"[W]hen smarter persons than I contended with me that we had a right
to secede, I always said we had no right to that privilege—and that the
makers of our constitution never intended to give that [right] to any
state." To farmer James Cloud, secession was simply unjustified by the
situation—nothing, in his view, had been done to warrant breaking
the contract implied in the Constitution. "Mr. Lincoln was elected by the
majority of the people of the Government," Cloud asserted, and therefore had been the legal and constitutional choice. Still others believed
greed and self-interest led secessionists to force an antidemocratic crisis
on the Union. Physician, slaveholder, and former Whig Frederick Anderson, for instance, argued to friends that the "treasonable" act of secession
had been "carried forward by unscrupulous men to promote their own
ambitious schemes for self aggrandisement and not for the good of the
people north or south."[10]

Confederate Home Front: Montgomery during the Civil War (Tuscaloosa: University of Alabama
Press, 1999).

9. For more on the ways secessionists presented themselves as the restorers of the
Revolution's republican order, see George C. Rable, The Confederate Republic: A Revolution
against Politics (Chapel Hill: University of North Carolina Press, 1994), 14; Drew Gilpin
Faust, The Creation of Confederate Nationalism: Ideology and Identity in the Civil War South
(Baton Rouge: Louisiana State University Press, 1988), 30–1.

10. Claim 21220, Creed Lewis Taylor, Marshall Co., February 28, 1874; Claim 5614,
James M. Cloud, Jackson Co., March 26, 1873; Claim 1755, Frederick H. Anderson, Franklin
Co., September 8, 1871: Testimony of Richard S. Watkins; all in SCC.

Perhaps most salient to unionists was the belief that the Confederacy could not replace, much less improve upon, the old Union. As fire-eaters themselves understood all too well, secession was a risky venture.[11] Unionists simply did not want to take that bet. They believed their future happiness, and that of their children, would be seriously jeopardized by separation. Like farmer Miles Craig of Limestone County, they trusted that they "had a better shelter under the old Government than could ever be built for us again." Andrew Hames, a steamboat engineer of Jackson County, likewise treasured "this old government." Change made no sense to him: "I wanted to leave the government just as it was." To farmer John Hutton of Jackson County, the Confederacy was "a desperate government"; to tanner Creed Taylor, secession was "obnoxious" and promised to leave Southerners "in a worse sure fix than Mexico was ever in," meaning that they "would not have any government" at all. Again and again, loyalists expressed a desire to preserve what they had, not to overthrow it for a new venture whose prospects were murky at best. "I loved my government," explained Jasper Harper, "and I was not in favor of no other one."[12]

Worries about future security extended to include concerns over property among those Alabama unionists who owned slaves. As historian Daniel Sutherland has argued in the case of Culpeper County, Virginia, caution among slaveowning unionists was sometimes prompted by fears of losing slaves in any conflict that might result from secession.[13] SCC claimant Thomas Nation certainly counted these anxieties among his reasons for opposing separation. "I had worked a long time and had got a little property," he explained, "and I felt that it would all go up if there was a rebellion." His "little property" included fourteen slaves in 1860. John Morgan Brown, who owned thirty-six slaves and ran a sawmill and plantation just outside Mobile, likewise insisted that the better course of

---

11. David S. Heidler, *Pulling the Temple Down: The Fire-Eaters and the Destruction of the Union* (Mechanicsburg, Pa.: Stackpole Books, 1994), 165–74; 183–8.

12. Claim 18695, Miles S. Craig, Limestone Co., September 2, 1873; Claim 15260/14923, Andrew Hames, Jackson Co., December 13, 1872; Claim 4120, John Hutton, Jackson Co., June 5, 1877: Testimony of Jonathan Beason. SCC, NAB; Claim 21220, Creed Lewis Taylor, Marshall Co., February 28, 1874; Claim 4190, Jasper Harper, Marshall Co., April 24, 1874; all in SCC.

13. Daniel Sutherland, "The Absence of Violence: Confederates and Unionists in Culpeper County, Virginia," in Sutherland, *Guerrillas, Unionists, and Violence*, 79; see also Carl Degler, *The Other South: Southern Dissenters in the Nineteenth Century* (New York: Harper & Row, 1974), 183–4.

action for slaveholders was to "fight for their rights in the union," rather than secede and fight a war which would likely destroy the thing they claimed to want to protect. "I do not mean fighting with arms," Brown explained, "I mean to fight for them in Congress."[14]

Another theme articulated by slaveholders differed in formulation, but not in the conservative impulse it betrayed. These men, all of whom refused to support the Confederacy throughout the war, swore to the SCC that they would have preferred to sacrifice slavery altogether rather than destroy the Union. As planter John G. Winston explained, "The secessionists claimed that the South was compelled to secede to save their negroes. I had twenty, and I told them that I would rather see every one of them go, and not get one cent for them, than see an attempt made to divide the Government." Likewise, when secessionists told Samuel Greenhill, a Franklin County planter, that if the Union side was sustained in Alabama, his slaves would be emancipated, he responded by saying that although "he had worked hard for them," he would nonetheless "rather have them all set free than to have the union dissolved." While their testimony, given after the war to a skeptical Republican commission, was undeniably self-serving, most of these men had long been identified as Whigs or "old-fashioned" conservative Democrats in the late antebellum period.[15] Their postwar claims thus have continuity with an extensive prewar political tradition of endorsing conservative political approaches to solving the sectional conflict over slavery.[16]

Many of the sentiments expressed by unionists were not all that uncommon among moderate Southerners before the outcome of the presidential election of November 1860.[17] Both Constitutional Unionist John Bell and Northern Democrat Stephen Douglas garnered considerable

14. Claim 36834, Thomas Nation, Blount Co., July 17, 1873; Claim 20979, John Morgan Brown Estate et al., Mobile Co., January 30, 1874; both in SCC.

15. Claim 2656, John G. Winston, Marshall Co., February 16, 1874; Claim 10346, Samuel Greenhill, Colbert Co., August 18, 1873: Testimony of George W. Creamer; see also the following: Claim 20979, John Morgan Brown Estate, et al., Mobile Co., January 30, 1874: Testimony of John C. Berry; Claim 2656, John G. Winston, Marshall Co., February 16, 1874; Claim 12231, Thomas E. Potts, Bibb Co., December 7, 1872; Claim 36834, Thomas Nation, Blount Co., July 17, 1873; all in SCC.

16. Clarence Phillips Denman, The Secession Movement in Alabama (Montgomery: Alabama State Department of Archives and History, 1933), 61–4, 94; Barney, Secessionist Impulse, 279–81; Degler, The Other South, 182–4.

17. Barney, Secessionist Impulse, 54–60; Daniel W. Crofts has ably outlined these moderate positions as they took shape in the upper South in Reluctant Confederates, 106–25.

support among pro-Union moderates in the wake of the split in the Democratic Party at its presidential nominating convention in the spring of 1860, and the nomination of John C. Breckinridge as the candidate by the Southern rights wing of the Democratic Party.[18] In an attempt to stay above the sectional fray, Bell and the Constitutional Unionists endorsed vague tenets like strict adherence to the Constitution, enforcement of the laws (i.e., the Fugitive Slave Law), and protection of the Union. Former Whigs, many of them slaveholders who still hoped to avoid secession, gave their support to Bell because of the very blandness and malleability of his platform. Some Democrats, on the other hand, flocked to support Bell's candidacy out of frustrations with the factionalism in evidence at the Charleston nominating convention. As Wetumpka lawyer (and later unionist exile) Robert S. Tharin remembered, "I was disposed then to condemn the persistency of the Douglas wing in keeping their nominee before the convention, when they must have seen the danger of disruption which such a course involved. . . . This I did without any sacrifice of my *national* democracy."[19] Finally, Alabamians, like John Cavin and Benjamin Wilson of Cherokee County, embraced Bell over both Douglas and Southern rights candidate John C. Breckinridge because they emphatically believed that while Bell was not a disunionist, he bore no taint of antislavery either. As Wilson explained, "I was as far from an abolitionist as any man. . . . We voted for [Bell] as a union man, and because he had been represented to us as a union man."[20] Stephen Douglas's well-known doctrine of popular sovereignty had perhaps made the "little giant" suspect to proslavery unionists like Wilson; opposition to secession among such men, however, kept them from endorsing Breckinridge, whom they viewed as the candidate most sympathetic to separation.[21]

18. Thornton, *Politics and Power*, 402–5; Barney, *Secessionist Impulse*, 95–8. For details of the nominating convention, see *Proceedings of the Conventions at Charleston and Baltimore. Published by Order of the National Democratic Convention, Maryland Institute, Baltimore and under the Supervision of the National Democratic Executive Committee* (Washington, D.C.: n. p., 1860).

19. Robert Seymour Tharin, *Arbitrary Arrests in the South; Or, Scenes from the Experience of an Alabama Unionist, by R. S. Tharin, A.M., A Native of Charleston, S. C.; For Thirty Years a Resident of the Cotton States, and Commonly Known in the West as "The Alabama Refugee"* (New York: John Bradburn, 1863), 61.

20. Claim 13839, John Cavin, Cherokee Co., January 8, 1873: Testimony of Benjamin J. Wilson, SCC. At the point in the SCC interview at which Wilson announced that he was "as far from an abolitionist as any man," Cavin chimed in, "I am too."

21. Barney, *Secessionist Impulse*, 102; Thornton, *Politics and Power*, 409.

Illinois Senator Stephen Douglas nonetheless maintained support among some pro-Union Alabamians, although his following was smaller than Bell's.[22] John G. Winston of Marshall County, for instance, explained to the SCC that he had believed that "if Douglas could be elected the thing [secession] could be stopped." Alfred Wall simply "considered him a union man" for the same reasons that Bell supporters like Benjamin Wilson may have chosen to reject Douglas: his commitment to national solutions to the vexing problems surrounding the question of slavery in the territories. Other unionists, however, took a deeply pessimistic view of the entire situation and saw nothing to support in any of the candidates. Like pro-Union physician Rhesa McPherson, they had lost hope in the political process altogether. "I didn't care to vote for Bell or any of the rest," he explained. "I knew it wouldn't amount to anything—that the intention in running three candidates was to ensure the election of Lincoln and pave the way for secession."[23]

For Alabamians, much rode upon the election of 1860. Should Lincoln be elected (as Rhesa McPherson believed he would), the fire-eaters would have the excuse they had so long required to initiate moves toward secession.[24] The election of a "Black Republican," according to the secessionists, was a threat not to be borne. Pressures from fire-eaters in this regard had long been exacerbated in Alabama by the standing call for a state secession convention in the event of Lincoln's election. Passed nine months before the presidential election, the resolution hung like a specter over the presidential campaign.[25] Tensions were further heightened by the vitriol hurled at pro-Union men by various state political organs. One Alabama newspaper editor, for instance, hoped that those who had opposed the disintegration of the Democratic Party at Charleston in the spring of 1860 would be "branded with the mark of Cain, that they might be forever known and despised and excoriated by every true

22. Barney, *Secessionist Impulse*, 102.

23. Claim 2656, John G. Winston, Marshall Co., February 16, 1874: Testimony of William Bryant; Claim 7982, Alfred Wall, Madison Co., August 9, 1873; both in SCC. William B. Irwin of Lawrence echoes Wall's sentiments almost verbatim; see Claim 2664, Charles W. Pitt, Lawrence Co., August 30, 1871: Testimony of William B. Irwin; both in SCC. Claim 12231, Thomas E. Potts, Bibb Co., March 5, 1875: Testimony of Rhesa McPherson, SCC.

24. Thornton, *Politics and Power*, 402.

25. Lewy Dorman, *Party Politics in Alabama from 1850 through 1860* (1935; reprint, Tuscaloosa: University of Alabama Press, 1995), 164; William W. Rogers et al., eds., *Alabama: The History of a Deep South State* (Tuscaloosa: University of Alabama Press, 1994), 181; Thornton, *Politics and Power*, 405–6.

son of the South." Other commentators actually threatened reprisals against pro-Union men. "What execration will be too deep and damning, what vengeance too severe for the traitors . . . ?" questioned a piece entitled "The Southern Treason and Its Possible Consequences."[26] Introducing a dramatic flourish to a similarly damning piece, editor Max Greene published the Charleston Convention edition of the *Huntsville Democrat* with black edges (like those commonly rimming death announcements) in "mourning over the traitorous audacity" of Alabamians who remained loyal to the national Democratic Party after the secessionist "bolters" walked out of the convention.[27]

Sometimes, suspicions about political loyalties merged with Alabamians' ever-present anxiety about potential slave insurrections and the abolitionist interlopers who might foment them. Historian William Barney has characterized the reports of abolitionist plots as "incessant" and "ubiquitous" in Alabama during the summer of 1860. In such instances, community vigilantism often emerged to punish individuals suspected of subversive behavior, further heightening local tensions and fears among those sympathetic to the Union cause.[28] In Union Town, Perry County, for instance, citizens punished James G. Bagley, a native of the North, for having allegedly made remarks like, "If the Union is dissolved and a civil war ensues, I will be damned if I do not go North, shoulder my musket and fight against the South." On the night of October 1, 1860, Bagley was met on the public road by "individuals in disguise" who whipped him for his indiscretion. At a subsequent public meeting, citizens attending wrote and approved resolutions thanking the "unknown persons who assumed the responsibility of inflicting . . . this well merited punishment." In Line Creek, a neighborhood near Montgomery, a white laborer named Sowell was also accused of abolitionism, particularly inciting slaves to commit the rash of arsons that had swept the area in the previous weeks. According to his neighbors, he had informed slaves that if Lincoln was elected, they would all be freed and that he would help them take over Montgomery. The townspeople made Sowell lie across a bench, where they whipped him severely, and then gave him enough money to pay his traveling expenses out of the state. The *Montgomery Advertiser* warned its readers to keep a lookout for Sowell and his ilk.

26. *Montgomery Weekly Advertiser*, May 16 and June 20, 1860.

27. *Huntsville Democrat*, reprinted ibid., May 16, 1860.

28. Barney, *Secessionist Impulse*, 163–80.

"He is an old man, about fifty, and being, as we are informed, a Southerner, and hence a traitor to his section, he is likely to be troublesome to other communities."[29]

During the election itself, political disagreements between moderates and Southern rights supporters led to intimidation and outright conflict. John B. Feemster, a pro-Union tanner, blacksmith, and farmer in Marshall County, quickly got into trouble at the polls. Casting his vote for Constitutional Union Party candidate John Bell, he warned the pollsters not to "steal" his ticket out of the ballot box and nearly got whipped by "some of the Judges and Clerks" for his remark. John Carrithers, a blacksmith in Cherokee, Franklin County, voted for Douglas despite the pressures not to: "I was abused a good deal for that," he remembered. In one oyster-fishing community on Bon Secour Bay in South Alabama, antiunionist officials prevented the polls from opening at all in 1860. "We had no election down here," explained oyster fisherman Abisha Styron. "They would not allow us to vote [b]ecause we were a Union settlement. They knew it and would not open any polls."[30] And, as was the case across the Deep South, had a man been willing to take the risk of voting the Republican ticket—"It wouldn't have been exactly safe for any person to have voted for Lincoln"—they were saved the trouble.[31] Only the upper South states of Maryland, Delaware, Virginia, Kentucky, and Missouri actually allowed Lincoln's name to appear on the ballot.[32] As Murphy Bruce, a Methodist minister from Limestone County, pointed out, "I should of voted for Abraham Lincoln, but there was no electoral ticket for him at our box [in] 1860." Farmer James Blackwell of Walker County also would have chosen Lincoln, but his family, afraid that he would be hurt by political opponents, convinced Blackwell not to go to the polls at all. He did, however, subsequently name his child Abraham Lincoln.

29. *Montgomery Weekly Advertiser,* October 17 and November 7, 1860.

30. Claim 21232, John B. Feemster, Marshall Co., April 7, 1874; Claim 8251, John Carrithers, Colbert Co., September 1, 1874; Claim 3789A, Abisha Styron, Baldwin Co., March 3, 1879; all in SCC.

31. Claim 12230, Lee McGuire, Bibb Co., October 10, 1872, in Barred and Disallowed Case Files of the Southern Claims Commission, 1871–1880 (NAMS-M1407, Fiche 0546), Records of the U.S. House of Representatives, 1789–1990, Record Group 233, NAB; hereinafter SCC Disallowed Claims.

32. Ollinger Crenshaw, *The Slave States in the Presidential Election of 1860,* Johns Hopkins University Studies in Historical and Political Science, series 58, no. 3 (Baltimore: Johns Hopkins University Press, 1945), 197; Emerson D. Fite, *The Presidential Campaign of 1860* (New York: Macmillan, 1911), 233.

(Confederate authorities sent Blackwell a note ordering him to change the child's name within twenty days or be run out of the county.) In a similar gesture of defiance, Walker Countians Cherry Rice and her husband named their daughter, born in 1860, Mollie Ann Lincoln Rice.[33]

The result of the presidential election confirmed the strength of the Southern rights party in Alabama: Breckinridge won 54 percent of the vote; John Bell came in second with 31 percent of the vote; and Douglas brought up the rear with just over 15 percent of the votes polled.[34] While not necessarily indicative of widespread support for *immediate* secession, Breckinridge's success in Alabama indicated a broad-ranging willingness to consider secession as a means to preserve slavery.[35] And, as historian Mills Thornton has pointed out, turnout at Alabama's elections seems to correlate with the weight or importance that citizens ascribed to the issues under consideration. In the 1860 election, fully 80 percent of Alabama's eligible voters participated, the second highest turnout in the state's electoral history to that point. Citizens clearly attached great significance to the vote not simply because it would result in the election of a president but because the question of secession hung like a specter over the entire proceeding.[36]

For unionists, Breckinridge's victory in the state was less important than Lincoln's election to the presidency. That event more than any other precipitated a marked desertion of the middle ground in Alabama politics, much as it did across the South.[37] Significant numbers of moderates became convinced that Lincoln's election was a direct threat to slavery's protection and, by extension, to the future security of their property and personal liberty. Secessionists began exhorting their cause with increased fervor in Alabama's pro-secession press and in public debates.[38] Indeed, by mid-November, fire-eaters' rhetoric was so elevated that one observer noted, "It seems to be their endeavor here as elsewhere to

33. Claim 12483, Murphy Bruce, Limestone Co., February 21, 1873; Claim 5787, James M. Blackwell, Walker Co., December 21, 1871; Claim 12992, Cherry E. Rice, Walker Co., December 13, 1873; all in SCC.

34. Thornton, *Politics and Power*, 404, 409; Clanton W. Williams, ed., "Notes and Documents: Presidential Election Returns and Related Data for Ante-Bellum Alabama," *Alabama Review* 2 (January 1949): 72.

35. Barney, *Secessionist Impulse*, 313.

36. Thornton, *Politics and Power*, 408, 402.

37. Crofts, *Reluctant Confederates*, 90–103, passim.

38. Barney, *Secessionist Impulse*, 267; Dorman, *Party Politics in Alabama*, 164.

browbeat & bully into silence those whom they cannot persuade to go with them & so to make it appear that there is but one opinion throughout the South."[39] As increasing numbers of moderates deserted unionism, accusations of treason seemed more portentous. The *Montgomery Advertiser* warned ominously, "We have no doubt that if there be any enemies of our section amongst us, they are in trouble at the unanimity for secession in this community. We advise all such to seek other quarter. . . . Our citizens cannot be too vigilant."[40]

Local communities often took their cue from such injunctions, making sure that those who advocated unionism felt the heat. In southeast Alabama, for instance, sixty-four-year-old Middleton Martin came "pretty near getting into two or three cutting scrapes" as he fiercely canvassed for the Union cause in Old Texas Beat. "I said to the men 'Don't for God's sake vote that secession ticket.'" When Dick Hathorne, a secessionist neighbor of Martin, told him that the community was planning to run him out of town, Martin reacted threateningly. "I told him he must get away from there, that I had got too mad to talk. Say I, 'Do you see this knife? If you don't get away from here right away I'll cut your guts out!'" James Cloud, a crippled farmer from Jackson County, heard similar threats "when the clash came up." As a consequence of Cloud's open advocacy of the Union at a public sale, secessionists in his neighborhood told him that "the hemp had grown and the ropes had been made for me."[41] When a Hale County citizen used his local newspaper to call a Union meeting in Greensboro, the town's secessionists "stopped the paper," rushed around town tearing down handbills posted to announce the meeting, and said that they would establish a new paper in town that would stand only for secession.[42] John Isom of Limestone County remembered meeting mounting opposition and disapprobation from his secessionist neighbors, but he persisted nonetheless. "I talked boldly and fearlessly and exerted all my influence at all elections for the benefit of the union cause," he explained to the SCC. "[I] forced myself in every meeting of the kind to vote it [secession] down."[43]

---

39. Sereno Watson to Henry Watson, November 17, 1860, Henry Watson Papers, 1765–1938, DU.

40. *Montgomery Weekly Advertiser*, November 21, 1860.

41. Claim 2318, Middleton Martin, Monroe Co., December 3, 1874; Claim 5614, James M. Cloud, Jackson Co., March 26, 1873; both in SCC.

42. Sereno Watson to Henry Watson, November 17, 1860, Henry Watson Papers, 1765–1938, DU.

43. Claim 7104, John C. Isom, Limestone Co., February 3, 1872, SCC.

During the intense and confrontation-laden canvass for delegates to the secession convention in December 1860, three general positions took shape: unconditional unionism, immediate secessionism, and cooperationism. Unconditional unionism held that under no circumstances should Alabama secede from the Union. Immediate secessionists were the old "straight-out" or fire-eaters' faction, whose most visible Alabama spokesman was William L. Yancey; they advocated immediate and unconditional secession. "Cooperationists" bridged these extremes. They represented a still significant, but nonetheless diminished, body of moderates who, like unionists, believed that secession was the least justified response to Lincoln's election. Unlike unionists, however, cooperationists were ultimately willing to acquiesce to separation, but only if the majority of the people ratified the measure and Alabama acted in cooperation with other slaveholding states.[44] As a Mississippian defined the term in 1860, "a cooperationist [was] one who was in favor of united Southern action for the purpose of demanding further guarantees from the North, or, failing in that, the formation of a Southern Confederacy."[45] Of the three positions, only the latter two garnered the support of enough citizens to actually form the foundation of a "party" for whom people could vote. Despite major differences with the cooperationists, therefore, unconditional unionists were so thoroughly a minority during the election for delegates to the secession convention that there was not an unconditional unionist banner under which a delegate could run. Some ran instead as cooperationists, aware that unconditional unionist voters' sole chance for effective action was to throw their support to the "cooperationist" camp; by doing so, they associated themselves with the only viable antisecession vehicle in the field.[46]

The election for delegates was held on December 24, 1860, only four days after South Carolina became the first state to secede from the Union. In Alabama, straight-out secessionist candidates won twenty-nine counties by a majority of almost eighteen thousand votes; all but one of these counties lay in the south-central plantation-rich Black Belt. Cooperationist delegates won twenty-three counties by a much closer margin—ninety-six hundred votes; all but one of the cooperationist counties were in the northern half of the state. (See map 2.) Of the one hundred

44. Barney, *Secessionist Impulse*, 198–9; Denman, *Secession Movement in Alabama*, 94.
45. Quoted in Barney, *Secessionist Impulse*, 199.
46. Denman, *Secession Movement in Alabama*, 94; Dorman, *Party Politics in Alabama*, 167.

delegates elected, fifty-three were secessionists unified in their desire to split from the Union. Against them stood forty-seven cooperationists who represented a variety of ideas about how, when, and under what circumstances to cooperate with secession. Probably less than one-third of these cooperationists were elected as unconditional unionists.[47]

The newly elected delegates gathered in Montgomery on January 7, 1861, to begin their debates. Within three days, a special committee of thirteen had completed a report on the question of Alabama's relations with the United States. William Yancey, the chair of the committee, pre-sented the majority report to the convention. In it, the fire-eaters advo-cated Alabama's immediate secession and called for a meeting to be held with the other seceding states in Montgomery on February 4.[48] The six delegates composing the committee's minority included two men who can be identified as unconditional unionists, William O. Winston of De-Kalb County and Robert S. Watkins of Franklin County. The minority report advocated a more deliberate course and called for a convention to be held at Nashville on February 23, in which the slaveholding states would discuss the "wrongs of which we have cause to complain." More-over, it outlined a "basis for a settlement" of the sectional crisis which required that the North pledge to faithfully execute the Fugitive Slave Law and repeal of all state laws designed to interfere with it; to guaran-tee that slavery would not be abolished in the District of Columbia, "or in any other place over which Congress has exclusive jurisdiction"; to assure that interstate slave trading should be protected from interfer-ence; to protect slavery in the Territories and the right of slaveholders to transport slave property throughout the free states; and to exclude "the foregoing clauses" from repeal by constitutional amendment. The official *Journal of the Convention* makes no mention of any unconditional union-ist protest during the debates, nor does it record what course was envi-sioned by the cooperationists should their demands not be met by the Congress and the president. One issue of prime concern to unionists, however, was addressed by the minority report: it demanded that any secession ordinance passed by the convention be referred back to the people for a vote before taking effect. The minority report was defeated

---

47. Thornton, *Politics and Power*, 422, 427. I do not include as unconditional unionists those who refused to sign the secession ordinance but who, after the war began, supported the Confederacy.

48. Barney, *Secessionist Impulse*, 302.

53 to 45.[49] On January 11, 1861, Alabama's secession ordinance passed by a vote of 61 to 39.[50]

Although opposition was fairly substantial up to the point of secession, most cooperationists ultimately went with the state. Upon passage of the ordinance, four opposing delegates quickly reversed themselves and signed with the majority: James S. Clarke and David P. Lewis of Lawrence County; William S. Earnest of Jefferson County; and John W. Inzer of St. Clair County. Moreover, thirty-three delegates who had voted against the ordinance immediately signed the "Address to the People of Alabama," a document which embodied the heart of cooperationist thinking. In it, the signers committed themselves to "a faithful and zealous support of the State, in all the consequences that may result from the Ordinance of Secession," to the principle of popular referendum as "the foundation of the whole theory of popular government," and to the policy of consulting other Southern states as "consonant with prudence and a wise discretion." This document clearly did not endorse the views of unconditional unionists; it did, however, allow signers to place the ultimate decision about their future action in the hands of the people. "[I]f it should hereafter appear that the public interest or expediency requires the affixing [of the authors'] signatures," the document averred, "they will unhesitatingly and cheerfully do so, their object being in the present statement solely *to defend and maintain the principles and line of policy, the advocacy and support of which was entrusted to them by their constituents,* and which they believed to be of vital importance to the future peace and welfare of the State."[51] Ten of the men who signed this "Address" found that their constituents wanted them to sign the ordinance, and they did so. Even delegates who joined in the "Address" but did not subsequently sign the Ordinance of Secession ultimately took active political or military roles in the Confederacy or state: M. J. Bulger of Tallapoosa County became a brigadier general in the Confederate army; Sidney C. Posey of Lauderdale County was a state legislator from 1861 to 1863; William R. Smith of Tuscaloosa County was a Confederate legislator from 1861 to 1865; and John A. Steele of Franklin County became an

49. William R. Smith, *The History and Debates of the Convention of the People of Alabama, January, 1861* (Atlanta: Rice, 1861), 78–9; Barney, *Secessionist Impulse,* 302.

50. Smith, *History and Debates,* 79–80.

51. Italics added. William H. Brantley, "Alabama Secedes," *Alabama Review* 7, no. 3 (July 1954): 184 n. 37; "To the People of Alabama . . . " [opposing secession without plebiscite], GLC 5987.13, GLCML.

Map 2: Election for Delegates to Alabama's Secession Convention, 1860–61,
by County.

officer in Nathan Bedford Forrest's cavalry. In the end, only three of those signing the "Address"—Henry C. Sanford of Cherokee County, Elliot P. Jones of Fayette County, and Robert Guttery of Walker County—never signed the ordinance and can be confirmed as having maintained consistent unionism throughout the war. Finally, just two unconditional unionists—R. S. Watkins of Franklin County and Christopher C. Sheets of Winston County—signed neither the "Address" nor the Ordinance of Secession.[52]

The majority of Alabamians greeted the state's newfound independence with pride and enthusiasm. Towns and counties came out in ecstatic support for William Yancey and his straight-outs. Politicians held rallies to congratulate themselves, young men formed greenhorn military companies in anticipation of trouble, ladies joined flag-sewing circles to express their devotion to the new nation. Quickly, at courthouses across the state, citizens began removing United States banners and replacing them with homemade Confederate flags. Unconditional unionists, by contrast, greeted the news of secession with despair and anger. Many were furious at "their members for doing which they were directed not to do" by signing the Ordinance of Secession.[53] Others would continue for years to argue that secession was a usurpation of the people's will because the secession convention failed to put the secession ordinance up for popular referendum. One ruefully remembered, "In Alabama we had no chance to vote to reject the ordinance of secession." In Athens, Limestone County, unionist citizens simply did it on their own. They "held a meeting" where many voted to retract the ordinance.[54]

52. Sheets was subsequently elected by his heavily loyalist county to serve as their representative in the 1861–62 state legislature, but his fellow legislators expelled him "on a charge of disloyalty" to the Confederacy. See Claim 14, Robert Heflin, Randolph Co., April 18, 1871: Testimony of Christopher C. Sheets, SCC. For discussion of the delegates and their actions at the convention and during the war, see Brantley, "Alabama Secedes"; Denman, *Secession Movement in Alabama*; and Thomas McAdory Owen and Marie Bankhead Owen, *History of Alabama and Dictionary of Alabama Biography*, 4 vols. (Chicago: S. J. Clarke, 1921).

53. Benjamin A. Smoot to Gov. A. B. Moore, January 24, 1861, AGP: A. B. Moore, 1857–61.

54. Claim 12986, John N. Nesmith, Blount Co., October 31, 1873; Claim 20403, Brooks D. McKinney, Limestone Co., August 5, 1873; both in SCC. It should be noted that when the legislature passed the act to hold a convention on secession, there was no promise of a popular referendum to follow; if any usurpation occurred, this was the moment at which it happened. Most Alabama citizens believed that because they were able to vote for delegates to the secession convention, they had been represented democratically. Unconditional

Unionists' decision to maintain their loyalty to the Union despite Lincoln's election and Alabama's secession made their loyalism "unconditional." Unlike reluctant secessionists who ultimately went with the state, unconditional unionists refused to accept the legitimacy of separation under any circumstances. Herein lies the great irony of unionists' experience: the impulse that drove them to first identify with the Union cause was a conservative one rooted in an unwavering desire for stability and security. The consequences of that identification, however, ultimately undermined the security they sought to preserve and relegated them to the fringes of their communities. Their unionism became a brand—it was as telling about an individual as who his parents were or what church she attended. Not a radical group to begin with, unionists nonetheless seemed radical to their opponents. They were thus made extreme–or "true blue" unionists—by the shifting sentiments of the majority around them.[55]

After 1861, the purpose driving local hostility against unwavering unionists underwent a transformation as well. The opposition that unionists faced after secession was no longer simply geared toward getting them to change their political position. Instead, post-secession intimidation and harassment were designed to humiliate and ostracize dissenters.[56] When "strong-headed secesh" taunted loyalist neighbors with epithets like "damned union son of a bitch," "damned submissionist," and "Lincolnite," they acted in keeping with long-standing Southern traditions for intimidating the wayward. When loyalists refused to fold in the face of community demands for conformity, they solidified their status as pariahs. Jesse Thomas of Lauderdale County, for instance, remembered that his friend John Perryman became so renowned for his determined support of the Union that his "name was a hiss and byword for every rebel in his neighborhood." The public reputation of Susan Thrasher, a single woman planter of Lauderdale County, was also well known by "disloyal persons" in Florence, which resulted in her being

---

unionists lost because their numbers were so small, not because the fire-eaters undermined a promised referendum; nonetheless, unionists believed for many years that had such a popular vote been held, secession would have been defeated in Alabama.

55. Degler, *The Other South,* 120.

56. For community discipline and social control, see Bertram Wyatt-Brown, *Southern Honor: Ethics and Behavior in the Old South* (New York: Oxford University Press, 1982), 435–8 and part 3, passim; Edward Ayers, *Vengeance and Justice: Crime and Punishment in the Nineteenth-Century American South* (New York: Oxford University Press, 1984), 143.

"frequently scoffed at and ridiculed by the female citizens." William Wroten, an oysterman of Baldwin County, testified about the tense public confrontation he had while watching as Mobile citizens removed the United States flag from its prominent place at the central market in January 1861. "I came very near getting into a difficulty . . . when they hoisted the first Confederate flag," he remembered. "The halliards parted and the flag came down. I made the remark that the Confederacy would fall as the flag did. Col. Craig of a Confederate regiment was standing near and took me by the shoulder and told me I would be hung first thing I knew." Likewise, when small slaveholder John Hafley of Limestone County was asked to help raise the Confederate flag at Athens, he refused. "I told them if they never got up a flag until I helped them it would never be raised." Hafley's continued adherence to the Union cause had its price. As his friend John Hayes explained to the SCC, "He was put down as a Yankee during the war by everybody in his neighborhood."[57]

In their willingness to withstand the withering insults and violent threats of the secessionist majority, unconditional unionists took a divergent path from those moderates with whom they had once shared political ideas in common. Their response was rooted, first, in the depth of their affection for the old government; but second in their identification of political loyalty with the cause of personal and familial honor. Southern society and political culture had long operated on the principles of honor and duty; character and dignity were frequently associated with the willingness of a man to stand by his principles, his reputation, and his duty to the larger good.[58] Unionists never accepted that the Confederacy would or could provide for the larger good. The illegitimacy of secession seemed patently obvious to them. To betray one's duty to the United States by endorsing the Confederacy would be to betray one's citizen-

57. Claim 16404, John S. Hayes, Limestone Co., July 19, 1875: Testimony of John H. Gray; Claim 21530, William C. Price, Jackson Co., December 30, 1873: Testimony of W. H. James; Claim 8478, Larkin M. Cox, Cherokee Co., December 19, 1874; Claim 7543, John Perryman, Lauderdale Co., July 9, 1873: Testimony of Jesse Thomas; Claim 3981, Susan Y. Thrasher, Lauderdale Co., August 8, 1871: Testimony of Neander H. Rice; Claim 3789F, William Henry Wroten, Baldwin Co., March 8, 1878; Claim 19873, John W. Hafley, Limestone Co., September 29, 1873 (Hafley owned four slaves); Claim 19873, John W. Hafley, Limestone Co., September 29, 1873: Testimony of John W. Hayes; all in SCC.

58. Wyatt-Brown, Southern Honor, 110; Bertram Wyatt-Brown, The Shaping of Southern Culture: Honor, Grace, and War, 1760s–1890s (Chapel Hill: University of North Carolina Press, 2001), xii, 194–5; McCurry, Masters of Small Worlds, 258–61.

ship, and worse, to give in to cowardice and opportunism. In the end, it would be dishonorable and, for male unionists, unmanly. Consequently, unionists responded to secessionist attacks much as they would have to an offense to personal or familial reputation: they swore to defend it as a matter of personal honor and thereby deepened their commitment to the cause. And the more boldly Union people refused to give way to secessionist threats and violence, the more fully they appeared to be bound by principle, and thus, to be "true" to the cause. So when John DeBoice heard his friend John Hutton declare that he was "dyed two days and a half under the skin" with the Union, DeBoice knew what Hutton meant. The Union was indelibly a part of his identity, impervious to secessionists' attempts to hide or erase it. Moreover, that determination to defend the Union was not simply a matter of politics, but a question of defending his personal honor.[59]

Social and Cultural Contours of Unionism

Despite the anxieties of their Confederate neighbors, Alabama's unconditional unionists were few in number. In their greatest concentrations, most were still able to dominate little more than their rural country neighborhoods or settlements. Such firm status as minorities in society meant that long before the secession of the upper South states and onset of the war, unionists in Alabama had to develop strategies of resistance just to protect themselves from secessionist abuse and intimidation. To do so, they, like groups of resisters everywhere, relied on support systems of like-minded people. The process of building such supportive networks took place in two interconnected, but nonetheless distinct, arenas of daily life: the family and the neighborhood. Setting aside a discussion of the neighborhood for the moment, we will turn first to the question of kinship. Like evangelical Christians who depended on the church and its congregation of disciples to steady them and refresh their faith, unionists turned to trustworthy kin to help them maintain their commitment to the Union in the midst of intense opposition. Of course, complex and deep kinship ties and obligations did not distinguish unionists from their Confederate counterparts; the foundation for most Ala-

59. Claim 4120, John Hutton, Jackson Co., June 5, 1877: Testimony of John DeBoice, SCC.

bamians' loyalties, social and political, was the family.[60] Unionists were in no way distinctive in their reliance on kin in time of trouble. It is nonetheless important to recognize how they coped with the difficulties they faced and how those methods of coping helped them forge an exceptionally resilient sense of identity and purpose. The war required all men and women to make decisions about how fundamental personal loyalties could be accommodated in the face of the society's insistent demands for political constancy. But unionists at cross-purposes to the goals of the Confederacy found kin to be the primary buffer between their principles and the corrosive effect of intimidation by a hostile majority. For a tiny minority isolated among Confederate neighbors, kin relations bore particularly heavy burdens during the secession crisis and the Civil War.[61]

The hierarchical structure of Southern families made it unlikely that loyalty could be understood as anything but a family affair. As Alabama's SCC claims show, middle-aged men were heavily represented among unconditional unionists—of the 221 male claimants for whom age in 1860

60. Historians of the Appalachian regions of the South, especially, argue for the centrality of kinship and neighborhood to upland political ideology, and particularly unionism. See Patricia Duane Beaver, *Rural Community in the Appalachian South* (Lexington: University Press of Kentucky, 1978), 2, 56–7; Ralph Mann, "Family Group, Family Migration, and the Civil War in the Sandy Basin of Virginia," *Appalachian Journal* 19 (summer 1992): 374–92; Joshua McKaughan, "'Few Were the Hearts . . . That Did Not Swell with Devotion': Community and Confederate Service in Rowan County, North Carolina, 1861–1862," *North Carolina Historical Review* 73 (April 1996): 156–61; David H. McGee, "'Home and Friends': Kinship, Community, and Elite Women in Caldwell County, North Carolina, during the Civil War," *North Carolina Historical Review* 74 (October 1997): 365; and Martin Crawford, "The Dynamics of Mountain Unionism: Federal Volunteers of Ashe County, North Carolina," in Noe and Wilson, eds., *Civil War in Appalachia,* 57. For similar themes treated in a non-Appalachian context, see Jean Friedman, *The Enclosed Garden: Women and Community in the Evangelical South, 1830–1900* (Chapel Hill: University of North Carolina Press, 1985), x–xi, 3–4, and passim; McCurry, *Masters of Small Worlds;* Elizabeth Fox-Genovese, *Within the Plantation Household: Black and White Women of the Old South* (Chapel Hill: University of North Carolina Press, 1988), 82–99; Orville Vernon Burton, *In My Father's House Are Many Mansions: Family and Community in Edgefield, South Carolina,* Fred W. Morrison Series in Southern Studies (Chapel Hill: University of North Carolina Press, 1985), 117; and Darrett B. Rutman, "The Social Web: A Prospectus for the Study of the Early American Community," in William L. O'Neill, ed., *Insights and Parallels: Problems and Issues of American Social History* (Minneapolis: Burgess, 1973), 57–188.

61. Jörg Nagler, "Loyalty and Dissent: The Home Front in the American Civil War," in Stig Forster and Jörg Nagler, eds., *On the Road to Total War: The American Civil War and the German Wars of Unification, 1861–1871* (Cambridge, U.K.: Cambridge University Press, 1997), 331.

can be confirmed, the median age was 45.[62] These middle-aged men took it as a matter of duty that they should reproduce their own political loyalty among their sons, grandsons, and nephews. As fathers, grandfathers, and uncles, they frequently demanded that the actions of younger male relatives reflect, and sometimes directly extend, their own loyalty to the Union.[63] Farmer Solomon Lentz, for instance, explained to the SCC that he had sent his son Abraham to the front as a United States soldier, where he "served three years fighting for *my* principles" (italics mine). Samuel Studdard likewise viewed his sons' and son-in-law's service as not only *their* duty, but *his*, to the United States. Having sent young men from his family to the Federal army, he "would have furnished ten thousand in the aid of the glorious cause" if he had been able. Likewise, Daniel Smith enthusiastically sent three sons to the Union army, furnishing them with the necessary money and outfits to do so. All three died for the cause he championed.[64] In this way, loyalism became a matter of intergenerational responsibility, not simply an individualistic concern.

Men who believed that fidelity to the Union was an imperative of family duty did more than order their sons or nephews to fight; they tied their personal sense of honor to a long national history of patriotism. Just as being a good son meant honoring one's father, honoring one's ancestors meant honoring the Union. In this light, it becomes clear how even duty to long-dead relations could exert powerful influences over unionists during the secession crisis and early days of war. Jacob Albright, a yeoman farmer of Franklin County in his sixties, based his refusal to support the Confederacy on his father's service in the Revolu-

---

62. For age data, see appendix 3, table A.8. Age statistics are subject to some inherent bias in the claims, simply because younger people were less likely to own substantial property; thus, they may have been less likely to file claims. Indeed, the prevalence of younger sons as witnesses for their fathers suggests that conscript-aged men may not be fully accounted for in an age analysis of claimants. The best approach—but one beyond the scope of this study—would be to confirm the ages of all SCC witnesses who claimed loyalty, as well as the ages of other individuals named by claimants as fellow loyalists. This age data reinforces an increasingly common historical argument that middle age correlated strongly with Southern conservatism regarding secession in 1860. For discussion of age and conservatism, see Barney, *Secessionist Impulse,* 282, and Sutherland, "Absence of Violence," in Sutherland, ed., *Guerrillas, Unionists, and Violence,* 79.

63. Burton, *In My Father's House,* 96; McCurry, *Masters of Small Worlds,* 56–8.

64. Claim 5202, Solomon Lentz, Limestone Co., June 13, 1876; Claim 6415, Samuel Studdard, Fayette Co., February 23, 1872; Claim 17152, Daniel Smith, Fayette Co., September 23, 1875; all in SCC.

tionary War. As he explained to the SCC, "I told [the local pro-Confederate vigilance committee] that my father fought for the Union and I could not go against it and the request of my father and that sooner than turn over [to the Confederacy] I would die right there." Aaron Bodiford, a yeoman farmer in his early thirties in 1860, likewise remembered, "My father said he had fought in the War of 1812, and his father in the Revolutionary War fighting for the constitution, and he didn't want his boys to fight against it." Edward Frost, a farmer in Walker County, also drew courage and confidence from his ancestors' loyalty. "The names of my parents were enrolled where the rebels dared [not] to show their faces which is at Washington City, D.C. My Grandfather was in the war of 1776 under Gen. George Washington and my Father was in the War of 1812 under command of Gen. Jackson." Frost held the "emblem" of his father's service "sacred" throughout the war, as a talisman of his family's loyalty.[65] The notion of loyalty as a sacred duty passed from parent to child was echoed by Archibald Steele, an established farmer and father of grown children himself at the time of the war's outbreak. Testifying to a postwar committee investigating Klan violence in Alabama, he explained his loyalty to the United States in this way: "I was raised in South Carolina by my old father, and taught first, to reverence my God; second, the Bible; third, the Constitution; and fourth, the Union—to regard all these things as sacred."[66] In this way, loyalists anchored their political ideology to long-held traditions about familial patriotism. Again, this process was not a peculiarly unionist one. The distinction here is a matter of emphasis. Secessionists were inspired by, and claimed as precedent for their actions, the radical zeal of American revolutionaries.[67] Unionists, by contrast, highlighted the sacrosanct quality of the nation those revolutionaries had created.

Not only men, but also white women, in their roles as mothers, wives, and sisters, protected family integrity and honor in standing by the Union. And although William Danly, a farmer from Lauderdale County, dismissively remarked, "You can't tell much about a woman, only from her talk," unionist women and their "talk" could have pro-

---

65. Claim 4805, Jacob Albright, Colbert Co., July 12, 1872; Claim 17530, Alexander Bodiford Estate, Crenshaw Co., April 20, 1875: Testimony of Aaron G. Bodiford; Claim 6636, Edward Frost, Walker Co., February 9, 1872; all in SCC.

66. Testimony of Archibald Steele, *Testimony Taken by the Joint Select Committee*, 9:944; also see Claim 2652, Archibald J. Steele, Madison Co., August 1, 1872, SCC.

67. See Faust, *Creation of Confederate Nationalism*, 14.

found impact on family loyalty.[68] Middle-aged women who held positions of influence—as wives and mothers—over voting- and fighting-aged men had considerable latitude to persuade and harangue those who would listen.[69] Caroline Hayden shocked her young male relative by "abusing secession, regretting that the thing happened, and abusing Jeff Davis and Bob Lee" in a "pretty rough" way. And Caroline Atkisson of Franklin County "kept fast days in her zeal for the union and its cause." Her friends and family certainly took notice of her example; one less-than-sympathetic sister, in fact, thought her "demented on the subject." Rebecca Angle was "hard" "with tongue" on the Confederates in her neighborhood. Eliza Barnard of Cherokee County early in the conflict knew where her loyalties lay and encouraged her husband to follow suit, telling him that she "wanted him to stand for the union." And although Catharine Bowen admitted to the SCC that she had wished that she could "keep her husband at home," she nonetheless encouraged him to "go and join the Union army." Such pressure from women could work upon men's sense of duty and honor in impressive ways. As Louisa Sparks's brother remembered, "I often heard [Louisa] declare that she had rather go into the Union army and die in its cause, than to stay in the Confederacy—this was done in the presence of her husband, and contributed much to make him go into that army."[70]

It was vital that women's energies and sympathies be fully committed to the Union cause, for they embodied a most important link in unionists' familial networks. Through marriage, men who were not blood relations established kinship ties and the mutual obligations such bonds implied. As James Davis explained, he came to associate with fellow unionist Mary Leath as a result of their families' intermarrying. "[O]ne of her sons having married my daughter and he being a strong union man I often heard from her [about the Union cause]." Similarly, John Conner

68. Claim 1197, Bethany Gray, Lauderdale Co., September 29, 1873: Testimony of William Danly, SCC.

69. Like their male counterparts, female claimants tended to be middle-aged in 1860. See appendix 3, table A.8.

70. Claim 17603, Caroline M. Hayden, Dallas Co., March 3, 1874: Testimony of Frank Tipton; Claim 12374, Caroline H. Atkisson, Franklin Co., August 22, 1873: Testimony of Sarah Atkisson; Claim 14450, Rebecca (Webb) Angle, Cherokee Co., August 3, 1874: Testimony of George W. Wester; Claim 18891, Eliza Barnard, Cherokee Co., November 8, 1878; Claim 3352, Catharine Bowen, Walker Co., January 13, 1873: Testimony of Cumberland Conaway; Claim 20139, Louisa Sparks, Colbert Co., November 17, 1875: Testimony of Washington Goin; all in SCC.

remarked of his neighbor, Louisa Echols, "It was natural for her to be [a unionist woman]—her stepfather and all of her relations on her mother's side was strong Union people and friends to the Union cause and all of her husband's family were strong Union people and opposed to the Confederacy and the rebellion."[71] Through Echols, her in-laws and blood relations were united; these ties had to be either confirmed or denied in the context of war. Once joined by marriage, and then again united by faith in the Union, the bonds of kin were deepened and strengthened.

This is not to say that networks of loyalty within families were perfect. For unionists, the onset of the war solidified certain familial relationships and tested, strained, and severed others. Unionists first experienced the real meaning of being a loyalist not on the battlefield but in their homes, where questions of family honor and political values came together to shape responses to the crisis. Conflicting loyalties could destroy the connections that had united families before the war; they also made manifest the ways that loyalty—and a desire to preserve what the Union had bequeathed to its citizens—could shape the way unionists saw the world. Elizay Bell of Winston County, for instance, was quick to realize the implications of her conflict with her brother, Henry, a Confederate sympathizer living in Mississippi. In a letter begging him to change his mind, Elizay made her views plain. "I wrote to you to pick out me a sooter before I got there," she reminded him, "but if thare is none but disunion men thare for god sake let them alone for I would disdain to keep company with a disunionist for if he will cecede from the goverment that has allways sustaned his Rights he would cecede from his famaly."[72] For Elizay, secession violated a near-sacred trust and had profound implications for the morality of young men and their willingness to perform duties to wife and children. Preserving the integrity of the polity was tantamount to honoring the integrity of marriage and family. Elizay Bell was not mistaken in her interpretation. As she predicted, her brother's willingness to "cecede from the goverment" had made it possible for him to "cecede from his famaly." Sometime in 1861, having decided that his true home lay with the new nation and his Confederate

---

71. Claim 6688, Mary Leath, Cherokee Co., June 30, 1875: Testimony of James Davis; Claim 8388, Louisa Echols (*née* Shoemaker), Jefferson Co., June 14, 1877: Testimony of John A. Conner; both in SCC.

72. Elizay Bell to Henry Bell, April 21, 1861, AGP: A. B. Moore, 1857–61.

friends in Mississippi, he submitted the letters of his unionist family members to the Alabama governor's office as proof of their treason.[73]

Family relationships thus formed the field upon which unionists built, and frequently contested, their loyalty to the Union. Neighborhoods represented another, equally important, arena in which Alabamians tested one another's fidelity to the Union.[74] The importance of local community life to unionists is self-evident in their testimony before the Southern Claims Commission, for they almost invariably located their identified circle of loyalist friends within their "neighborhood."[75] The word itself could refer to a fixed area of land, most usually within twelve or fifteen miles of a post office, or to the physical proximity of households within a settlement area. But the term was more flexible—representing what historian Patricia Beaver has called "an ideological entity." It encompassed not only physical space, but also the body of civic and personal contacts and shared histories that were a part of daily life.[76]

In North Alabama, the "size" of neighborhoods, both geographical and metaphorical, varied according to subregion, occupational status, wealth, and race. As a consequence of the subregion's rugged terrain and poor roads, individuals living in Hill Country neighborhoods were often

73. Bailey, "Disloyalty in Early Confederate Alabama," 528. Bailey states that Henry took the letters to the postmaster of Choctaw County, Mississippi. He also states that the only Bells named to the governor as traitors were John, James, and Robert (the last of whose letters I have not found), omitting Elizay Bell.

74. My understanding of rural neighborhoods in Southern society has been greatly informed by Robert C. Kenzer's *Kinship and Neighborhood in a Southern Community: Orange County, North Carolina, 1849–1881* (Knoxville: University of Tennessee Press, 1987); Frank L. Owsley, *Plain Folk of the Old South* (Baton Rouge: Louisiana State University Press, 1949); Daniel W. Crofts, *Old Southampton: Politics and Society in a Virginia County, 1834–1869* (Charlottesville, Va.: University of Virginia Press, 1992); and Beaver, *Rural Community in the Appalachian South*.

75. To some degree, the standard battery of SCC questions (preserved in preprinted questionnaires; see appendix 2) encouraged what was a preexisting tendency to place unionism within the neighborhood. For instance, the SCC asked, "Who were the leading and best-known Unionists of your *vicinity* during the war? Are any of them called to testify to your loyalty; and if not, why not?" (italics mine). The commissioners were interested in obtaining names of people with whom they could check stories.

76. Friedman, *The Enclosed Garden*, 3; Beaver, *Rural Community in the Appalachian South*, 56–7, 140–1; Stephen V. Ash, *Middle Tennessee Society Transformed, 1860–1870: War and Peace in the Upper South* (Baton Rouge: Louisiana State University Press, 1988), 21–2.

only marginally engaged in state political life and Alabama's staple crop and slave economy. Consequently, inhabitants of these areas were less likely to have frequent contacts with individuals outside the immediate proximity of the homeplace, especially people who were not farmers. Their neighborhoods could be quite small and insular; community ties were often coterminous with kinship ties. For example, unionist Clarissa Crane lived "on the top of Lookout Mountain" in DeKalb County. When the SCC asked her what neighbors would testify to her loyalty, she named two related families, both by the name of McNew. "The mountain was very thinly settled," she explained. "Those were the only families that lived near me."[77]

By contrast, in areas of heavier commercial traffic, a neighborhood could extend quite dramatically beyond the confines of home. In the Tennessee Valley, cotton planters and nonslaveholding yeomen, white and black artisans, skilled slaves and town dwellers, all cultivated a broader set of political, economic, and social connections that extended further afield in their counties, stretching the physical, social, and demographic scope of their neighborhoods.[78] Historians' tendency to homogenize North Alabama has generally submerged these important distinctions between the subregions, which in turn has failed to show us the diversity of social and economic exchanges in which Valley men and women were engaged, including their involvement with slavery and its social imperatives. The great majority of slaveholding North Alabamians, as well as black Alabamians whose resistance to the Confederacy is documented by the SCC, lived in the Tennessee Valley, not in the Hill Country. For these individuals, the neighborhood frequently split into two additional "sub-neighborhoods," the white and the black, adding yet another dimension to the physical space of neighborhood relations.

77. Claim 8189, Clarissa Crane, DeKalb Co., December 13, 1878, SCC.

78. Yeomen in slaveholding counties clearly hired slave labor and interacted with slave artisans who hired themselves out for independent trading and contracting. A number of planters who testified to the SCC hired their slaves out or allowed their slaves to hire themselves, which suggests a nonslaveholding population who paid for this labor; moreover, a number of former slaves who testified to the SCC also refer to being leased or hired out. For nonslaveholders and the slave economy, see Kenneth Noe, "'A Source of Great Economy'? The Railroad and Slavery's Expansion in Southwest Virginia, 1850–1860" and Wilma A. Dunaway, "Put in Master's Pocket: Cotton Expansion and Interstate Slave Trading in the Mountain South," both in John C. Inscoe, ed., *Appalachians and Race: The Mountain South from Slavery to Segregation* (Lexington: University Press of Kentucky, 2001), 99–100, 105–10; and 117–9, respectively.

Unionist associations were influenced by a range of friendly, cooperative, and hierarchical neighborhood relations. Because the neighborhood, as a public space, became the proving ground for loyalists, close
investigation of unionists' neighborhood life can reveal how their political culture developed and operated. Three general "levels" of association
became fertile ground for unionists seeking to make alliances. At the
level of friendship, unionists' connections operated much as kinship relationships did by drawing upon long-time affection, familiarity and trust,
and a mutual history of interdependence for their strength. Moreover,
such relationships were generally private, both as a consequence of their
personal character but also because unionists preferred to keep their exchanges secret from the larger secessionist community. Associations of
Union people in semiprivate settings, like businesses or stores, offered
ways for unionists who were less personally familiar with one another to
make sympathetic connections. Finally, public displays of unionism by
particularly "strong and noisy" loyalists created opportunities for friends
and strangers alike to learn who would be willing to risk themselves for
the sake of the Union and, implicitly, for the sake of fellow unionists.
Such individuals became known "by everybody and by all parties" as
"bold and outspoken" people—their stoutness was impressive to those
less resolute in the face of public threats, intimidation, and shame.[79] In
these individuals, networks of loyalists found their leaders.

The significance of neighborhood friendships in fostering and sustaining unionism is nowhere more apparent than in SCC witness testimony. When making a claim, unionists were required to bring witnesses
to testify to their loyal words and deeds. These witnesses were most commonly other unionists, sometimes kin relations, but usually close neighborhood allies. The SCC was interested in gauging the worth of witness
testimony and, as a result, asked witnesses to state how long they had
known the claimant, whether their relationship was "intimate," whether
or not they were related to the claimant, and where they had lived in
relationship to the claimant during the war. In the answers to these ques-

---

79. Claim 14480, Jeremiah R. Jack, Cherokee Co., November 17, 1874: Testimony of
Levi Tramel; Claim 6091, James Ellis, Walker Co., December 28, 1871: Testimony of A. J.
Sides; both in SCC. The phrase "bold and outspoken" appeared with marked frequency as
the descriptor of choice of witnesses for such leading unionists; see, for example, Claim
6888, John H. Austin, Morgan Co., November 18, 1871: Testimony of Lewis Hobart; Claim
6701, Ebenezer Leath, Cherokee Co., July 2, 1875: Testimony of Joseph Baker; Claim 6514,
Samuel Studdard, Fayette Co., February 23, 1872: Testimony of J. V. Tirey; all in SCC.

tions, friends explained their loyalty to the Union in both personal and political terms. Take the example of Mial Abernathy, a schoolteacher, farmer, and miller of Limestone County who had been a fierce and outspoken unionist and a Union army soldier. His case before the SCC drew on the testimony of John Baker and James Tucker, both of whom were Union men themselves. Baker, a farmer, was Abernathy's senior, a friend to Abernathy's father, and had known Mial "ever since he was a little boy." Tucker, also a farmer, was Abernathy's contemporary: "We were schoolboys together," he explained, "[and] have been intimate ever since." These men all lived within ten to fourteen miles of Athens; the younger men had been "born within sight of" the places where they lived in 1860. Long-term friendships between them and their families influenced, and were strengthened by, mutual support of the Union. Similarly, Gallant Kelley came to know the sentiments of his neighbor Alexander Bodiford over the course of two decades of shared work and camaraderie. "We neighbored together, hunted, fished, and rolled logs together a good deal . . . were at meeting . . . and at each others' houses a good deal." Their physical proximity and shared habits existed alongside their mutually held political values; when secession came up, it was only natural that they discuss that as well. "I frequently heard of him speak of his father as in the revolutionary war, to fight for this constitution the rebels were trying to break up," Kelley recalled. "[And] that he himself was in the war of 1812, [and had] utter abhorrence for secession." Likewise, Emmanuel Isom, a carpenter whose family was well known for unionism, explained that he had known his friend John D. Thomas for many years before the war. Thomas was, according to Isom, "as much opposed to secession and the rebellion as any man I knew." The men "were neighbors and of the same sentiments and generally went to elections together," and became confidants about the Union during the secession crisis. Because of their close friendship, Thomas was drawn into the Isom family circle as a fellow loyalist: "He is a very reserved man," explained Isom, "and there were but few of us with whom he talked about the war. Our conversations were generally private or only in the presence of my family."[80]

80. Claim 4806, Mial S. Abernathy, Limestone Co., July 23, 1875: Testimony of John C. Baker and Testimony of James M. Tucker; Claim 17530, Alexander Bodiford Estate, Crenshaw Co., April 20, 1875: Testimony of Gallant Kelley; Claim 4852, John D. Thomas, Limestone Co., August 4, 1873: Testimony of Emmanuel Isom; all in SCC. Kin were almost always called upon to give testimony about the property taken, but this was a separate interrogation from the loyalty testimony.

Semiprivate gatherings at the homes or businesses of known Union men likewise encouraged unionism to flourish among men of similar bent. Such sites became refuges for individuals searching for news, congenial conversation, and support. William Walker, a farmer and clerk in a store in Chickasaw, Franklin County, lived within two miles of blacksmith John Carrithers and "met with him frequently at his shop" where the "general scope" of their conversations was pro-Union. James Sykes of Morgan County was himself the owner of a mill in 1860–61; there he met weekly with George Thrasher, who came to do his milling with Sykes. "I was a union man," explained Sykes, "and when I met him we talked right smart." Although Sykes and Thrasher had only been business acquaintances before the war, their conversations at the mill at the outbreak of the conflict cemented their relations into friendship. J. S. Smith of Cherokee County had a dry goods store from which he "kept the Post Office," and where he met frequently with James Crain and other unionists after business hours to talk about the war. And Jacob Whitehead, a well-known unionist farmer of Lauderdale County, held a "meeting of the neighbors" at his house during harvest after the war began in earnest. As they shucked corn together, the men "openly expressed" their unionist sentiments to one another. Public conversations among neighbors and business associates were critical to learning how a man stood on the issues of the day. As tanner Robert Chandler explained, he knew that his friend, cabinetmaker Milton Irvin, "was no secessionist" by "[b]eing with his neighbors and hearing them talk."[81]

Unionism was also fostered through the leadership of men with prewar standing in their communities, men who frequently felt it their duty to publicly advocate for the Union cause. Such men had influence in their communities because they had engaged in public service in the past, or because their neighbors thought them wise and sensible people.[82] Pleasant Taylor, a popular small slaveholder in the Tennessee Val-

81. Claim 8251, John Carrithers, Colbert Co., September 1, 1874: Testimony of William A. Walker; Claim 18264, George Thrasher, Morgan Co., June 3, 1876: Testimony of James M. Sykes; Claim 7381, James Crain, Cherokee Co., February 18, 1878: Testimony of J. S. Smith and Testimony of J. R. Dorsey; Claim 4858, Jacob Whitehead, Lauderdale Co., May 7, 1875: Testimony of William A. Harrey; Claim 20847, Milton V. Irvin, Limestone Co., April 16, 1876: Testimony of Robert Chandler; all in SCC.

82. Crawford, "Dynamics of Mountain Unionism," 64. Such patterns were, of course, part of Confederate political influence as well. See Ralph Mann, "Ezekiel Counts's Sand Lick Company: Civil War and Localism in the Mountain South," in Noe and Wilson, eds., Civil War in Appalachia, 83.

ley, actively used his influence over those living near him to advance the Union cause during the December 1860 election for delegates to the state secession convention. "I advised my neighbors to vote against secession and I so voted," Taylor remembered. "The vote at the precinct at which I voted I think, was 300 for the union and 9 for secession, I voting with the majority." Similarly, James R. Dorsey, a unionist farmer known for his political savvy in Cherokee County, advised James Crain "on election occasions." As Dorsey explained, "He had made me his confidante and always came to me for advice and counsel. Wanted to know all about each candidate and their standing politically and all the different bearings connected with each election." In all cases, Dorsey claimed, Crain "invariably voted against secession and everything tending in that way." In similar fashion, slaveholder Archibald Steele of Madison County frequently advised his neighbor, farmer George W. Campbell, about "the union cause" during the canvass on secession in late 1860. As Campbell noted, Steele's reputation made him a trustworthy confidant. "He was a man smart enough to give one information," explained Campbell. "I had confidence in what he said."[83]

Sometimes influence was markedly hierarchical in nature, rooted in the influence of wealthy, propertied men over employees or neighbors of considerably smaller fortune. Edward Hooper, for instance, "carried on the boot and shoe making business" on the Franklin County plantation of Frederick H. Anderson. In 1860, Hooper's total property was valued at seven hundred dollars; with this he supported seven dependents. By contrast, Anderson was quite wealthy, owning twenty-seven thousand dollars in property, including twenty-one slaves, for whom Hooper was doubtlessly producing shoes. Their proximity to one another was not one born of equal social and economic status, but it nonetheless produced a high level of familiarity between the men. As Anderson explained, "I met him . . . almost daily while he kept his shop at my house."[84] During these

---

83. Claim 2670, Pleasant Taylor, February 25, 1873, Franklin Co.; and also Claim 5637, William Rikard, February 26, 1873, Franklin Co.; Claim 7381, James Crain, Cherokee Co., February 18, 1878: Testimony of J. R. Dorsey; Claim 2652, Archibald J. Steele, Madison Co., August 1, 1872: Testimony of George W. Campbell; all in SCC. According to the 1860 U.S. Census, Steele owned $55,000 in property, including twenty-three slaves.

84. Claim 8722, Edward W. Hooper, Franklin Co., November 26, 1874: Testimony of Frederick H. Anderson; Claim 1765, Frederick H. Anderson, Franklin Co., September 8, 1871; both in SCC. See also 1860 U.S. Census, Alabama, Free and Slave Pop., NAMS M-653. Although the men allied themselves to one another during the war, their unionism did not

conversations, the men came to know and trust one another's unionism. Similarly, James Bell of Madison County ran the mill on John Ogden's plantation. His house was "about half a mile in sight" of the big house and the men met very frequently, "some times every day," at Bell's mill, where they would talk about the war. As Ogden explained, "I was one of the true blue original union men and [Bell] recognized me [as such]" and, as a consequence, came to Ogden, his employer and social better, "for advice what to do" at the elections in 1860–61. Apparently, Bell took Ogden's advice: "He voted with me against secession candidates in all elections." And William B. Irwin, a physician, planter, and owner of fifty-one slaves, cultivated a similar relationship with John C. Blalock, a miller of modest means living near Irwin's plantation. Blalock, who lived within easy distance of Irwin's home, described Irwin as "a wealthy man" with whom he had from the first been on "terms of friendship and intimacy." The war, however, deepened that relationship considerably. "[W]e became sort of confidantes; we took a great deal of pains to consult, advise, and post each other, and would meet in all sort of circumstances and in diverse places day and night."[85]

Private communications between like-minded neighbors, either in the course of business or at social gatherings, were very important to establishing networks of support among unionists. But public displays of loyalty to the Union in the presence of hostile secessionists also played a vital role in establishing who would not shirk or renounce their beliefs in the face of social proscription or threats. To risk one's social reputation, business relations, and personal safety was to prove one's mettle and trustworthiness. William Brooks, a sawmill owner and planter of Russell County in the Central Piedmont, solidified his reputation as a unionist by abandoning his church "because the minister preached secession sentiments from the pulpit." And George Watkins of Limestone County— who described his occupation to the SCC as "sorter of a farmer, blacksmith, and wagon maker"— had a reputation of being "notoriously

---

erase the social distinctions between them. While Hooper called Anderson to testify on his behalf before the SCC, Anderson did not call Hooper, preferring instead to rely on the testimony of his friends and equals, two leading lawyers of his community.

85. Ogden claimed to own $11,000 in property, much of which was slave property, in 1860. His exact slaveholding is not recorded in the 1860 census, however. James Bell is also missing from the census. Claim 7962, James T. Bell, Madison Co., June 13, 1874: Testimony of John Ogden; Claim 1369, William B. Irwin, Lawrence Co., April 13, 1872: Testimony of John C. Blalock; all in SCC.

loyal, one of the true blue, [with] no flickering in him," largely because he was an "independent sort of fellow and a fighting kind of man." When his tendency to "fight if he is crowded" got him "into licks" with a local secessionist at a country store, his friends and enemies were standing by, taking notice.[86]

Public displays of loyalty were not limited to male interactions at the blacksmith shop, on the election ground, or during the political canvass. Although women's views were often publicly and politically subordinated to those of their families, especially those of the male head of the household, women could still make good on private "talk" by backing it up with public action. Rebecca Webb, for instance, refused to put her household's funds in support of an independent South. When "some of the women of the neighborhood" began a campaign for financial subscriptions to buy a Confederate flag for the community, "she would not have a thing to do with it." In those cases in which women lived independently of men (especially husbands), they took full responsibility for defending their family's public honor as loyalists. Spinster Margaret Mapp and her female kin, for example, learned that "the secesh all got up and left" when Union men had gotten up to speak at a recent public meeting about secession in the winter of 1860–61. In response, the ladies in question planned a counterdemonstration. As a male neighbor recollected, "[W]hen the parties came to speak at Blue Pond where the Mapp girls lived [and] when the secesh got up to speak, Miss Margaret Mapp, her mother and sisters . . . got up and left" in protest. As a family, the Mapp women identified themselves as unionists as clearly as they would have if they had been able to vote. Once the war began, some unionist women grew even bolder in their denunciation of the Confederate effort. Planter Martha Hobgood "spoke in favor of the Union amongst neighbors whenever the question arose." She explained to the SCC that she "[o]ften told Confederate soldiers they were engaged in the wrong cause." Elizabeth Kelly, the spinster daughter of a devoted unionist farmer, also made it her business to challenge local men signing up as soldiers. "The first volunteers that ever turned out here for the rebs, I just told them what I thought—they was doin' the worst work they ever

86. Claim 4807, William Brooks, Lee Co., March 26, 1873: Testimony of James Johnson; Claim 6858, George W. Watkins, Limestone Co., July 24, 1875: Testimony of Isaac Gatlin and Testimony of John M. Clark; all in SCC. The SCC interviewer who questioned Watkins noted in the transcript of the testimony that Watkins had, at the appropriate moment, proudly pulled up his pants leg to display the scars he still bore from that knife fight.

done." These moments of public identification and conflict were the keys to solidarity among loyalists, both male and female, in the early part of the war, for it was through risking personal security that unionists demonstrated their trustworthiness to one another. Within a short time, as T. E. Feagin of Monroe County remarked, Union people "knowed one another as a man know his flock."[87]

The neighborhood was the site of vital network-building among white unionists, but it also included wide-ranging interracial interactions between unionist whites and African Americans. Indeed, the great significance of small slaveholding among unionists in Tennessee Valley neighborhoods is that the "union people" with whom slaveholders, and some nonslaveholders, associated also included slaves. This factor is frequently overlooked by historians of Alabama who, by broadly applying the demography of the Hill Country to all of North Alabama, tend to represent unionists as white antislavery poor people. The omission distorts considerably our understanding of how loyalism survived, for it ignores an important set of social relations that ultimately gave unionism succor and vitality. Moreover, it "whitens" unionism in a way that simply fails to reflect historical reality. SCC testimony clearly demonstrates what historians of black activism during the Civil War have long argued: that free and enslaved blacks paid close attention to the schisms in the dominant white community, and that slaves who lived in proximity to white unionists saw loyalists as potential allies, witting or otherwise, in slaves' own campaigns for freedom.[88] While little common cause united

87. Claim 14450, Rebecca (née Webb) Angle, Cherokee Co., August 3, 1874: Testimony of George W. Wester; Claim 14482, Margaret Mapp, Cherokee Co., November 2, 1877: Testimony of Abraham Starling; Claim 2650, Martha A. Hobgood, Colbert Co., November 21, 1872; Claim 18264, George Thrasher, Morgan Co., June 3, 1876: Testimony of Elizabeth Kelly; Claim 2318, Martin Middleton, Monroe Co., December 3, 1874: Testimony of T. E. Feagin; all in SCC.

88. See Leon F. Litwack, *Been in the Storm So Long: The Aftermath of Slavery* (New York: Knopf, 1979); Barbara J. Fields, *Slavery and Freedom on the Middle Ground: Maryland during the Nineteenth Century* (New Haven: Yale University Press, 1985); Clarence L. Mohr, "Before Sherman: Georgia Blacks and the Union War Effort, 1861–1864," *Journal of Southern History* 45, no. 3 (1979): 331–52, and by the same author, *On the Threshold of Freedom: Masters and Slaves in Civil War Georgia* (Athens: University of Georgia Press, 1986); Ira Berlin, Barbara J. Fields, Thavolia Glymph, Joseph P. Reidy, and Leslie S. Rowland, eds., *Freedom: A Documentary History of Emancipation, 1861–1867* (Cambridge, U.K.: Cambridge University Press, 1992); Ira Berlin, Barbara J. Fields, Steven F. Miller, Joseph P. Reidy, and Leslie S. Rowland, *Slaves No More: Three Essays on Emancipation and the Civil War* (Cambridge, U.K.: Cambridge University Press, 1992), and also by the same authors, *Free at Last: A Documentary History of*

white and black unionists during the secession period, the war thrust them into overlapping patterns of subversion and pro-Union activity, which included collaboration between unionist masters and their slaves.

Such collaboration was particularly attractive once white unionists found themselves forced to go "underground" after the war began, what unionists referred to as the "shut mouth time."[89] The increasingly closed nature of unionist communications encouraged surreptitious conversations between slaveholding unionists and their slaves, men and women who were both subject to their master's orders and deemed likely, by whites, to be sympathetic to the cause of the Union. Moreover, the inherently private character of such conversations made them safer for African Americans, who had to keep their views about the war hidden, mostly out of fear of the violent repercussions that could follow any evidence of slave insurrection. As white loyalist Joseph Doyle explained to the SCC, "Colored men did not speak to white men, as to their loyalty, unless they knew well to whom they were speaking. They were afraid, and it was dangerous for them to do so."[90] The whites whom blacks were most likely to "know well" were their owners or the members of their owners' families. Thus, the impulse to cooperate—if not to trust—traveled both directions.

Loyalist slaveholders often spoke more frankly to their slaves than they would have dared do in the presence of most whites. Early in the conflict, for instance, a young loyalist physician named William Irwin told his slaves that he was a unionist and that they would likely be freed as a consequence of the war. As one of the doctor's slaves, Nelson Irwin, remembered, "He took us in his room and shut the door, and told us that he expected we would be free, but for us to make ourselves comfortable at home and he would let us know when the time came." Richard Mosely, a slave and later Union soldier from a neighboring plantation,

---

Slavery, Freedom, and the Civil War (New York: New Press, 1992); Freehling, *The South vs. the South*. I discuss the collaborative efforts of unionist masters and slaves in further detail in chaps. 3 and 4.

89. Many claimants and witnesses noted the advent of this "shut mouth time," but for examples of others who use that particular phrase, see Claim 15549, John M. Gasque, DeKalb Co., December 21, 1875: Testimony of Martha Gasque; Claim 36834, Thomas Nation, Blount Co., July 17, 1873; and Claim 12483, Murphy Bruce, Limestone Co., February 21, 1873; all in SCC.

90. Claim 14648, Sandy Bynum, Madison Co., May 2, 1874: Testimony of Joseph P. Doyle, SCC.

testified to the SCC that Irwin was one of only two men in the neighborhood who were known by the slaves to be Union men. "[W]e could get very little help from any other men except them." Likewise, Anthony Steele knew well the sentiments of his master, Archibald Steele of Madison County, in part because Steele had asserted to Anthony that "the old flag was the only flag that ought to be." But Steele's reputation was further solidified, at least in the minds of his slaves, by the fact that the master's "rebel neighbors said that he was a damned old union man."[91]

Together, white loyalists and the African Americans with whom they associated formed a sort of shadow community for the purposes of sharing information and aiding the cause they supported. Such networks were peculiar to loyalism within a slave society, for they relied upon the boundaries of race and class—and slaves' mechanisms for coping with those boundaries—for their success. Indeed, the very nature of slavery made it possible for white unionists to maintain secret communications with black resisters and to benefit from their established habits of subverting the larger white community. Slaves had long cultivated secret underground networks through which they hid runaways and obtained information about kin and friends abroad. Now white unionists found themselves taking advantage of—indeed, trusting their own safety to— systems of communication and movement that had heretofore been used against them by their own slaves.[92]

Even when slaves and white unionists did not belong to the same "family," they took notice of one another's interests and loyalties. Thomas Williams, an enslaved farm laborer of Franklin County, shared in the unionist confidences of Meredith Thompson, a nonslaveholding white farmer and trader whom Williams had known for twenty-six years. Likewise, former slave George Miller explained that he and other slaves had long watched the actions of a Madison County unionist named

91. Claim 1369, William B. Irwin, Lawrence Co., April 13, 1872: Testimony of Nelson Irwin and Testimony of Richard Mosely; Claim 2652, Archibald J. Steele, Madison Co., August 1, 1872: Testimony of Anthony Steele; all in SCC. At least six of the slaveholding individuals here addressed discussed collaborations with their slaves in their claims to the SCC; more than that doubtlessly put their power as masters of slaves to the service of the Union cause.

92. See, among others, John W. Blassingame, *The Slave Community: Plantation Life in the Antebellum South*, rev. ed. (New York: Oxford University Press, 1979); Eugene D. Genovese, *Roll, Jordan, Roll: The World the Slaves Made* (New York: Random House, 1972); Herbert G. Gutman, *The Black Family in Slavery and Freedom, 1750–1925* (New York: Pantheon, 1976); and Benjamin Quarles, *The Negro in the Civil War* (Boston: Little, Brown, 1953), xi.

Thomas McFarland. "I knew he was a union man because I heard him say he was for the Union before the war commenced. . . . The rebels thought he was a union man and that's the reason they was against him. I gathered that from what I heard them say . . . I have heard rebels in the neighborhood say that he ought to be hung because he was a union man. Some said he ought to be burnt up." Another former slave, Andrew Rogers "lived a neighbor by" McFarland and explained that "us colored people" based their assessment of the man first on his attitude toward slavery. "Well, we thought he was one of the upright and just's men in the country. We thought so because he had a heap of property and could own slaves and he would not do it." Well informed as to McFarland's views on slaveholding, and emboldened by the disfavor shown him by local rebels, slaves in the neighborhood began to approach him for information. "He talked with me in the presence of . . . colored men," Rogers explained, "fifteen or twenty at a time. It would be when we could catch him out from his house, when nobody would be present." Likewise, in Tuscaloosa, enslaved carpenter Dudley Smith made arrangements with a few other "colored men" in town to have "a club or society which was for the purpose of communicating with the loyal whites and learning how the war was progressing." These African Americans secretly "met at night with these whites who would talk with us and tell us about the war."[93]

These meetings proved vital to the slaves' understanding of the war's significance to their lives. But such meetings also reveal a great deal about the lives of white unionists. When individuals like McFarland and the Tuscaloosa white unionists chose to trust slaves by bringing them into intimacies about delicate, indeed insurrectionary, matters, they did so largely because their associations with the white community had become so circumscribed. They now belonged, at least in the eyes of Confederates, in categories of Southern society long inhabited by slaves—the dishonorable, the statusless, the potentially criminal. To be approached by anyone who claimed to be a friend, even if those friends arrived in the form of slaves, prompted behavior from white unionists that probably would never have been considered or countenanced before secession.

93. Claim 13286, Meredith Thompson, Colbert Co., August 23, 1873: Testimony of Thomas Williams; Claim 10249, Thomas McFarland, Madison Co., April 16, 1872: Testimony of George Miller and Testimony of Andrew Rogers; Claim 18746, Henry Hall, Dallas Co., June 12, 1874: Testimony of Dudley Smith; all in SCC.

* * *

If it is true that loyalty is a product of the expectations and values of individuals in relation to their families and communities, it is equally true that the means and methods to maintain and defend that loyalty arise from the same set of social relations. The experiences of Alabama's unionists during the election season of 1860 and into the secession winter demonstrate the critical role played by such supportive networks in the early days of loyalist resistance. After secession, as the Confederate community turned away from efforts to intimidate men into "voting right" and moved toward controlling dangerous domestic enemies, these connections began to bear an even greater burden as dissenters endeavored to stand by the Union, their consciences, and their personal relationships.

The political culture that gave rise to unionism in the Confederacy was a Southern political culture—it was premised on hierarchical and reciprocal kinship and neighborhood relationships, and it was often refracted through the prism of slavery and the values and challenges of a slave society. For white unionists in Alabama, to remain faithful to the Union meant relying upon and risking virtually all their closest ties, while building new ones to meet new exigencies. In so doing, they hazarded, as historian Carl Degler has argued, "familiar surroundings, esteem of friends, long associations, and, not infrequently, love of family itself."[94] But at the same time, they deepened the obligations embedded in personal loyalties by linking them so clearly to the defense of Union and the sacred duty it represented. Consequently, although strong feelings of patriotism and a desire to preserve the old government lay at the root of unionists' stubborn commitment to the Union cause, the "traditions and sentiments" of their families and neighborhoods tied the abstraction of loyalty to personal honor, duty, and identity.[95] Like Avilla Hendrix of Cherokee County, many unionists ultimately saw loyalty as a fundamental, indissoluble aspect of themselves. "I am a union woman," Hendrix once proudly declared, boldly stretching out her arm for a neighbor to inspect. "And have not a drop of secession blood in me."[96]

94. Degler, *The Other South*, 121.
95. Nagler, "Loyalty and Dissent," 303.
96. Claim 6820, Avilla Hendrix, Cherokee Co., March 3, 1871: Testimony of Joseph Matthews, SCC.

2

"To Evade the Conscript"

RESISTING THE CONFEDERATE DRAFT

Disgracefull as it might be to the fair name of Alabama, and painful as [it] would be . . . to have to proceed against any disaffected and disloyal citizens within the limits of the State, you may rest assured, that the most prompt & effective measures shall be adopted for the apprehension of every man—wherever located—who engages in any open act of Rebellion against the authorities of Alabama, or of the Confederate States.

—John Gill Shorter, governor of Alabama, December 1861

I never fired a gun or done any other duty to aid the rebellion . . . my occupation was to evade the conscript, which I did very well.

—David Studdard, Fayette County, 1872

As Alabama boys rushed into volunteer companies to fight for the South's independence, unionists hunkered down. They had plenty to fear, for during the months leading up to the war, pro-secession men had made their attitudes toward loyalists clear. Alabama's government, however, like those of many states in the Confederacy, had not yet prepared itself to meet the challenge of internal dissenters, and it had no clearly articulated policy for responding to continued resistance among its citizens. Indeed, state officials usually outlined remedies on an ad hoc basis, as citizens informed them of problems with local "tories." This did not mean that Alabama's officials failed to take action against dissenters, quite the contrary. But it did mean the consequences for dissent varied considerably from place to place within the state. Nonetheless, whether subjected to arrest and put into jail with no trial, or simply dragged before a local vigilance committee to be publicly chastised, unionists across

For. epigraphs, see Gov. John Gill Shorter to Messrs. H. A. Gamble, J. W. Hampton, L. T. Gilbert, D. L. Stovall, & Jonathan M. Wallace, December 23, 1861, AGP: John Gill Shorter, 1861–63; and Claim 9461, David Studdard, Fayette Co., February 10, 1872, SCC.

the state were quickly inculcated with the same lesson: submit to the reality of things and be silent—or be punished.[1]

The state's attitude toward unionists only intensified and hardened after April 1862, when the Confederate Congress passed the Act to Provide for the Public Defense, the fledgling nation's first draft. As one loyalist put it, "Things got . . . hot about the time the conscript law passed."[2] Conscription transfigured the implications of unionists' dissent and raised the stakes for resistance because it flattened out the distinctions that Alabama's governors and the Confederacy had made between "treason" (disloyal acts) and "sedition" (disloyal speech). Both offenses had been punished, but not usually in the same manner or to the same degree. Conscription—by making criminals of those who refused the Confederacy not only their hearts and minds, but ultimately their bodies—redefined a subsection of the unionist population as treasonous, and therefore legally subject to arrest and imprisonment without trial. Moreover, because conscription was a national matter, efforts to suppress resistance were no longer simply a question of state and local governance, but a problem to be solved in part by military authorities.[3] Consequently, all unionists now became subject to harassment and arrest by both state officials and Confederate conscript cavalries. After 1862, it thus became a regular occurrence, in the words of one Walker County man, "for union men to be arrested, put in the county jail, others sent to military

1. Mark Neely, *Southern Rights: Political Prisoners and the Myth of Confederate Constitutionalism* (Charlottesville: University Press of Virginia, 1999), 88–9; William M. Robinson, Jr., *Justice in Grey: A History of the Judicial System of the Confederate States of America* (Cambridge, Mass.: Harvard University Press, 1941), 383–6, 389–90, 393–5, 452; Curtis Arthur Amlund, *Federalism in the Southern Confederacy* (Washington, D.C.: Public Affairs Press, 1966), 106–7. On the Confederacy and the writ of habeas corpus and other questions of civil liberties, see Frank L. Owsley, *States Rights in the Confederacy* (Chicago: University of Chicago Press, 1925); J. G. DeRoulhac Hamilton, "The State Constitutions and the Confederate Constitution," *Journal of Southern History* 4 (November 1938): 425–48; Memory F. Mitchell, *Legal Aspects of Conscription and Exemption in North Carolina* (Chapel Hill: University of North Carolina Press, 1965); Emory Thomas, *The Confederacy as a Revolutionary Experience* (1971; reprint, Columbia: University of South Carolina Press, 1991); John B. Robbins, "The Confederacy and the Writ of *Habeas Corpus*," *Georgia Historical Quarterly* 55 (summer 1971): 83–101; Robert Neil Mathis, "Freedom of the Press in the Confederacy: A Reality," *Historian* 37 (August 1975): 633–48; George C. Rable, *The Confederate Republic: A Revolution against Politics* (Chapel Hill: University of North Carolina Press, 1994).

2. Claim 6813, Aquilla Ferguson, Cherokee Co., May 14, 1874: Testimony of John Terry, SCC.

3. Robinson, *Justice in Grey,* 385.

prisons, some hung and others shot, families of some . . . abused, their property taken, others . . . forced to go within the union lines for safety."[4]

Despite intensifying Confederate recriminations, conscripted unionists were determined not to serve. Charles Brewer of Jackson County swore that "as long as there was a hole in the mountain to hide in," he would resist the Confederate draft. Thomas Gordon of Macon County contended that he would rather "go to Hell" than to fight for the South.[5] Men like these devised schemes ranging from wrangling legal exemptions established by the conscript law to "lying out" from Confederate conscript officers in hills, caves, woods, and swamps for days and months at a time. For success, such arrangements demanded more than individual enterprise, however. Instead, draft resistance was often a family and community effort, one doomed to failure without the cooperation of women, older men, and even slaves. Lie-outs relied upon these supporters to provide vital assistance, including food, clothing, and news of rebel movements. This fact was not lost on Confederate authorities, of course. Local officials and conscript officers strategically targeted such support networks with threats, intimidation, and violence. The conscription law thus transformed the significance of dissent for the collaborators of lie-outs, too.

Although the state's demand for soldiers markedly raised the stakes for unionists determined to resist the Confederacy, the draft and its enforcement also fostered conditions that strengthened and made more intimate union people's bonds. Willingness to suffer at the hands of state and military authorities—without shrinking, shirking, or betraying fellow believers—ultimately compounded the esteem of unionists in the eyes of friends and kin, for it proved a man's or woman's trustworthiness and dependability. As one Franklin County unionist remarked about a friend and neighbor he called "a red hot Union man": "If he had been tinctured with rebel principles I would certainly [have] known it."[6]

---

4. Claim 3128, Robert Guttery, Sr., Walker Co., January 17, 1872, SCC.

5. Claim 6807, Charles B. Brewer, Jackson Co., December 29, 1874: Testimony of William Allen; Claim 19439, Thomas F. Gordon, Lee Co., February 25, 1878: Testimony of A. S. Grigg; both in SCC.

6. Claim 10893, Pleasant Thorn, Colbert Co., September 11, 1877: Testimony of Samuel Pounders, SCC.

Treason and Sedition

The actions taken by Alabama's governors in response to unionist resistance illustrate the importance of historian Mark Neely's recent interpretation of the Confederacy's attitude toward civil liberties. Neely demonstrates convincingly that much evidence from across the South does not fully support the long-standing scholarly contention that the Confederate state exhibited notable restraint in its handling of political prisoners. Rooted in the distinction drawn by various Southern officials between disloyal speech (sedition) and disloyal action (treason), the old argument suggested that Confederate officials advocated the tolerance of the first, and strict punishment of the second. Neely notes, however, that by late 1861, Confederate officials no longer tolerated sedition in practice, though they maintained the fiction of doing so in their rhetoric and in many public policy pronouncements. The key to understanding this seeming contradiction, according to Neely, is to recognize that the absence of a law to *try* those accused of sedition did not prevent the Confederacy, or state and local officials, from *arresting* those accused of sedition, despite that the writ of habeas corpus remained in place.[7]

Alabama's history certainly confirms much of Neely's argument. The state's first two wartime governors—A. B. Moore (1857–1861) and John Gill Shorter (1861–1863)—promulgated most of their remedies for dissent in response to complaints from Confederate citizens about loyalist resistance. The state equivocated little with unionists who actually threatened open rebellion. Such instances of armed resistance were especially common in the northern counties in 1861. In Fayette County, for instance, loyalists began meeting together in July, "huzaing for Lincoln," and forming "Companys to protect themselves."[8] In Randolph County, a small band of unionists spent the early summer months hoarding ammunition, presumably for defense against local Confederate authorities or to deploy as Union soldiers.[9] In the little settlement of Lentzville, Limestone County, the male members of some twelve union families formed "an independent Union home guard" and regularly held "Union meetings" to hear speeches advocating continued resistance to

7. Neely, *Southern Rights,* 1–2; 87–98.
8. J. H. Vail to A. B. Moore, July 8, 1861, AGP: A. B. Moore, 1857–61.
9. James M. Adams to A. B. Moore, June 19, 1861, AGP: A. B. Moore, 1857–61.

the Confederacy.[10] Walker County loyalists, led in part by secession convention delegate and slaveholder Robert Guttery, formed "Union-Com-
panies" that "hoisted the flagg" and vowed to fight for Lincoln should he
come "down South."[11] Similarly, on July 16, 1861, W. H. Musgrove, captain of the Blount County militia, reported to Governor A. B. Moore that
"a very considerable number of the inhabitants of the counties of Winston, Marion, Fayette, and some of Walker and Morgan, are . . . actually
raising and equiping themselves to . . . sustain the old Government of
the United States." Musgrove felt confident the unionists could convene
at least nine hundred men, armed with 250 pounds of powder accumulated over recent months. Faced with a well-organized band, Musgrove
begged for Moore's advice, wondering what action should be taken and
by whom. If "not prevented soon," Musgrove warned ominously, the
problem would "amount to a considerable insurrection in these parts."[12]
By December, Winston County unionists had indeed effected such an
"insurrection" in their neighborhoods by infiltrating the state militia responsible for home defense. Their intention: to "prevent the organization and defeat the end aimed at."[13]

Alabama's first wartime governor, A. B. Moore, initially applied per-
suasive tactics to nip such resistance in the bud, for he was convinced
that anti-Confederate sentiment arose from "ignorance and not understanding fully and clearly the true principles of our Government." He
even commissioned respected Confederate citizens to re-educate the
wayward, but they had little success. At the same time, however, Moore
and his successor John Gill Shorter, endorsed from the beginning the use
of regular legal mechanisms and official authority—sheriffs, posses, state
militias, and the courts—to arrest and suppress open resisters.[14] As
Shorter explained to a correspondent in December 1861:

10. Claim 5202, Solomon Lentz, Limestone Co., June 13, 1876: Testimony of Green W.
Grisham, SCC.

11. F. R. Baker to Gov. A. B. Moore, June 28, 1861, AGP: A. B. Moore, 1857–61; Claim
3128, Robert Guttery, Sr., Walker Co., January 17, 1872, SCC.

12. W. H. Musgrove to Gov. A. B. Moore, July 16, 1861, AGP: A. B. Moore, 1857–61.

13. M. R. Kinsey to Gov. John Gill Shorter, December 6, 1861, and Gov. John Gill
Shorter to M. R. Kinsey, December 24, 1861, both in AGP: John Gill Shorter, 1861–63; L. W.
Jenkins to Gov. A. B. Moore, December 8, 1861, AGP: A. B. Moore, 1857–61.

14. A. B. Moore to Josephus W. Hampton, July 12, 1861, AGP: A. B. Moore, 1857–61;
Gov. John Gill Shorter to Brig. Gen. L. W. Jenkins, December 19, 1861; Gov. John Gill
Shorter to the Sheriff of Walker Co., December 23, 1861; Gov. John Gill Shorter to H. A.
Gamble et al., December 23, 1861; Gov. John Gill Shorter to Col. M. R. Kinsey, December
24, 1861; all in AGP: John Gill Shorter, 1861–63.

All the power of the State shall be promptly used, if need be, at any time, to maintain the allegiance due to its authority; and if individuals are found within our jurisdiction who are charged, upon affidavit and probable cause, with acts of Hostility to this State or to the Confederacy—all the Executive Officers of the State will be expected—on notice, to proceed with their arrest with the utmost diligence & promptitude; and, if necessary, to call in a posse Comitatus, either civil or military, to aid in the execution of the Laws.[15]

According to Shorter, the sheriff could arrest individuals who behaved in a manner that seemed to indicate conspiracy to take action against the state as well as action itself, because "under our Statutes, all Citizens are empowered to arrest persons guilty of Treason—or other felonious crime." At all times, as Shorter explained to the sheriff of Walker County, "[T]here is a manifest difference between the peaceful assemblage of loyal citizens, for the purpose of reforming and sustaining their Government, to which they owe their allegiance, and Collections, or Combinations of disloyal men—whose purpose may be to overturn their State organisations, by giving countenance and aid to the public Enemies of the State of Alabama, and of the Confederate States." Anyone engaged in the latter class of behavior was to be apprehended and jailed immediately. In the case of the unionists infiltrating Winston County's militia, for instance, the governor did not hesitate to advocate quick and decisive action. He instructed local officials to immediately arrest "all disloyal persons," to rescind the commissions offered to the elected officers, and to readminister both the elections and the oath. When the "Right of free discussion and of the citizens—peaceably, to be assembled together for their Common good" was transformed into a means to foster active resistance against the government, Shorter declared himself willing to "use the military power of the State until the last Traitor is hunted down and brought to merited punishment."[16]

In theory, prosecuting sedition was a trickier matter, simply because it involved punishing people for behavior that, during peacetime, would

15. Gov. John Gill Shorter to Brig. Gen. L. W. Jenkins, December 19, 1861, AGP: John Gill Shorter, 1861–63.

16. Ibid.; Gov. John Gill Shorter to the Sheriff of Walker Co., December 23, 1861; Gov. John Gill Shorter to Col. M. R. Kinsey, December 24, 1861; Gov. John Gill Shorter to H. A. Gamble, et al., December 23, 1861; all in AGP: John Gill Shorter, 1861–63.

have been protected under law even if it was obnoxious to the larger community. The state of Alabama nonetheless advocated that sedition, like treason, be punished, and the governors recommended a range of official and extralegal responses. Governor Moore early categorized as seditious "any citizen declaring himself in favor of the Lincoln Government, hoisting the United States flag, or declaring a readiness to fight on that side, or any other act of the like character." Though less dangerous than actual armed rebellion, Moore understood that seditious behavior nonetheless implicitly held a threat for the state. If not curtailed, he believed it could form a nucleus for full-fledged disaffection, undermining home front morale. Thus, Moore believed that those guilty of sedition should be subjected to "severe punishment," explaining to at least one local official that "should . . . men persevere in their course of hostility against the Government of the state, . . . [t]hey can be apprehended, brought before a magistrate, and on due proof of their sedition . . . committed to jail."[17]

Under Governor Shorter's subsequent administration, the state put forward yet more recommendations to Confederate citizens contending with disloyal speech. In minor cases, Shorter emphasized the power of ostracism to quell unionists' remonstrations: "a man may talk & bluster [but] he can, perhaps, do little or no harm—beyond exciting the just contempt of all good men." In other circumstances, the Shorter administration advocated that offenses be adjudicated by extralegal tribunals composed of members of the community. A. B. Moore, now Shorter's aide-de-camp, explained this to a constituent complaining about a fellow citizen who had publicly expressed support for Lincoln: "I am not aware of any Statute passed by Congress, for the punishment of sedition, and am therefore of the opinion, that the language referred to, does not constitute any legal offense." Sedition, in this case at least, could not be brought to trial in a regularly convened court in Alabama. Moore quickly added, however, that the man in question was doubtless "a bad man, and guilty of a moral offense of a high character" and deserved to be disciplined. The burden of correction, he suggested, lay with local officials and the community at large: "One of the objects of the Vigilance committees—as I understand them—is to reach such cases, as are not provided for by Law."[18]

17. Gov. A. B. Moore to Josephus W. Hampton, July 12, 1861, AGP: A. B. Moore, 1857–61.

18. Gov. John Gill Shorter to Brig. Gen. L. W. Jenkins, December 19, 1861; A. B. Moore to Col. Lewis E. Cato, June 14, 1862; both in AGP: John Gill Shorter, 1861–63.

Antebellum Southern society had long utilized such extralegal courts and tribunals to adjudicate matters of community safety, particularly anything pertaining to slave insurrections.[19] During the secession crisis, Alabama had seen a marked increase in its numbers of operative vigilance committees, many of which bullied pro-Union men.[20] Once the war began, these locally constituted groups persisted, now composed of men too old for soldiering. They played a major role in silencing opposition among citizens. Formed to defend against individuals who threatened the "good & safety of the Community," the committees were seen as the first line of defense against domestic and alien (i.e., Northern- or foreign-born) enemies.[21] Their means of enforcement was the "home guard," a mounted civilian posse (similar to an antebellum slave patrol) that arrested suspected dissenters and brought them before the committee for trial.[22] John Hardy, a prominent and politically active resident of Selma, reported that the "aspects and purposes" of Dallas County's vigilance committee "were to ferret out and arrest and try all persons suspected of being friendly to the United States." The group was "self constituted" and not formed "in accordance with any law."[23]

As was the case in Dallas County, most vigilance committees were bound by no particular statute; consequently, any punishment of guilty

19. Barney, *Secessionist Impulse*, 177. For more on vigilance committees, see Charles S. Sydnor, "The Southerner and the Laws," *Journal of Southern History* 6 (February 1940): 3–23; Clement Eaton, "Mob Violence in the Old South," *Mississippi Valley Historical Review* 29 (December 1942): 351–70; James Smallwood, "Disaffection in Confederate Texas: The Great Hanging at Gainesville," *Civil War History* 22 (1976): 349–60; Chris Morris, "An Event in Community Organization: The Mississippi Slave Insurrection Scare of 1835," *Journal of Social History* 22 (1988): 93–112; and Winthrop Jordan, *Tumult and Silence at Second Creek: An Inquiry into a Civil War Slave Conspiracy*, rev. ed. (Baton Rouge: Louisiana State University Press, 1995).

20. Barney, *Secessionist Impulse*, 211, and see chap. 1.

21. For classification of Northerners as alien enemies, see Neely, *Southern Rights*, 145–9.

22. For examples of such interrogations, see Claim 36834, Thomas Nation, Blount Co., July 17, 1873; Claim 13839, John Cavin, Cherokee Co., January 8, 1873; Claim 7212, James M. Downey, Cherokee Co., June 8, 1872; Claim 6815, Matthias Firestone, Cherokee Co., May 12, 1874; Claim 6837, John Smith, Cherokee Co., May 13, 1874; Claim 783, Jacob Albright, Cleburne Co., October 5, 1875; Claim 781, William H. Albright, Cleburne Co., October 4, 1875; Claim 14453, P. T. F. Black, DeKalb Co., March 2, 1878; Claim 8720, John A. Conner, Jefferson Co., May 12, 1873; Claim 1750, John Shugart, Jefferson Co., September 4, 1873; Claim 4825, Thomas Lefan, Lauderdale Co., July 22, 1875; Claim 5455, Andrew J. Morris, Lawrence Co., September 15, 1873; all in SCC.

23. Claim 16730, John C. Waite, Dallas Co., December 2, 1873: Testimony of John Hardy, SCC.

individuals was left up to the "sound discretion" of the members of the committee itself.[24] Moreover, such local vigilance committees frequently cooperated with what historian Mark Neely has called the Confederate government's "shadow system of courts," through which Confederate political prisoners were arrested, interrogated, and held without trial, even when the writ of habeas corpus was still in effect. These political prisoners were frequently sent to jail by "[a]uthorities as different as mayors and major generals," as well as "self-styled committees of public safety."[25]

Alabama's vigilance committees thus assumed the power to implement a wide range of punishments for unionists, from humiliation and intimidation to incarceration, exile, and even death. No one brought before such a committee failed to understand this: History had shown that, given cause, Southern committees of public safety had been willing to mete out extreme punishments.[26] However, at least before the passage of the Conscription Act in 1862 (and the bodily coercion it would demand), it appears that most vigilance committees refrained from inflicting capital punishment, limiting their pressure on unionists to temporary arrest, threats of bodily harm, and charivari. Franklin County's vigilance committee, for example, acted in typical fashion when it sent a home guard composed of nine citizens to arrest an old man named Jacob Albright at his farm. As a witness recalled, Albright "was charged with being a Tory—a union man—and with interfering with volunteering in the Confederate Service." (By his own admission, Albright had actively discouraged young men in his neighborhood from enlisting.) Albright appeared as ordered before the vigilance committee, which detained him for two hours, demanded why he wouldn't "turn over to the Confederacy," and insisted that he recant his unionism. After the interview, the committee "hung their heads" at Albright's recalcitrance, but released him unharmed.[27]

Incidents similarly intimidating but nonetheless restrained occurred across the state in 1861 and early 1862. A twenty-two member vigilance committee in Winston County, for instance, demanded in December 1861 that every man in the county take the Confederate oath of alle-

---

24. A. B. Moore to Col. Lewis E. Cato, June 14, 1862, AGP: John Gill Shorter, 1861–63.

25. Neely, *Southern Rights*, 81, 88.

26. Barney, *Secessionist Impulse*, 174–5; Eaton, "Mob Violence," 367.

27. Claim 4805, Jacob Albright, Franklin Co., July 12, 1872: Testimony of Robert A. Goodloe; Claim 4805, Jacob Albright, Franklin Co., July 12, 1872; both in SCC.

giance. "All those who refuse to do so [will] be dealt with as Aliens," it announced.[28] Though the committee promised to exile such "Aliens," no evidence suggests that the committee carried out its threats. Sometimes, vigilance committees sent threatening notices to men who continued to express their unionist views. Thomas F. Gordon, a lawyer of Macon County, received a message from "a prominent citizen," a member of the local vigilance committee; the note threatened Gordon with arrest and trial before the committee, to be followed by hanging or imprisonment if he "did not desist in expressing union sentiments." Nonetheless, Gordon was never incarcerated.[29] Other unionists did not get off so lightly. A Walker County vigilance committee arrested a citizen in July 1861 for "uttering black republican sentiments," but (luckily for the unionist) did not feel authorized "from the proof . . . to hang him." Instead, "he was ridden on a rail by some young men, and was ordered to leave the state in Two days."[30] Hartwell Huskey of Franklin County was repeatedly threatened both by the county vigilance committee and the town of Chickasaw's committee. On May 14, 1861, Huskey was "taken by the vigilance committee and tried at Cherokee, Alabama," where he "had pistols drawed" on him and was "threatened to be hung with a grapevine."[31]

Through such means, vigilance committees achieved their primary goal: silencing unionists. Many loyalists responded to intimidation and public chastisement by ceasing public discussion of their views and retreating into their circles of fellow-believers. William Irwin of Lawrence County, for example, remembered that "as long as we were suffered to talk against [the Confederacy] I opposed it openly and boldly; but times got so warm . . . that we were not suffered to talk, and we had to lie very still." Threatened "time and again," Irwin—like many other unionists in the state—felt that for self-preservation he had to "keep mighty quiet."[32] And until April 1862, the state of Alabama and the Confederacy tolerated this state of affairs. As long as unionists stopped public demonstrations

28. A. Kaiser to Gov. John Gill Shorter, [December 1861], AGP: John Gill Shorter, 1861–63.

29. Claim 19439, Thomas F. Gordon, Lee Co., February 25, 1878: Testimony of A. S. Grigg, SCC.

30. L. W. Hampton to Gov. A. B. Moore, July 8, 1861, AGP: A. B. Moore, 1857–61.

31. Claim 6501, Hartwell Huskey, Franklin Co., July 1, 1877, SCC.

32. Claim 1369, William B. Irwin, Lawrence Co., April 13, 1872, SCC. For a similar formulation, see Claim 6790, William Baker, Cherokee Co., April 30, 1872, SCC.

against the Confederacy, and submitted to intimidation or arrest by vigilance committees, little else in the way of official sanction seemed necessary. The advent of conscription, however, changed this dynamic. The draft required not only men's silence but also their bodies; when unionists refused to ante up their pound of flesh, their punishment bore all the force Alabama and the Confederate army could muster.

Conscription: Enforcement and Resistance

Politicians in Richmond arrived reluctantly at the decision to compel the Confederacy's male citizens to do military service in the spring of 1862. Only a deepening certainty that their nation could no longer rely on volunteers to provide the manpower necessary to defeat the ever-expanding Union army spurred them to institute conscription. The threat of continual military pressure in Virginia and disastrous reversals at Nashville, New Orleans, and Memphis lent urgency to their deliberations. Even after the Confederate Congress admitted the military necessity of a draft, few politicians (or citizens, for that matter) could disregard the disturbing implications of the conscript law. Many worried about the power such a law vested in the centralized government.[33] For others, the stigma of conscription was the mark of cringing cowardice and emasculation, a far cry from the heroic stuff from which epic struggles were supposed to arise. Alabama Governor J. Gill Shorter himself doubted the character of men who would allow themselves to be conscripted in what seemed a humiliating failure of duty and manly honor. Disheartened at the passage of the draft, he confessed to a friend, "If we are to depend upon [conscription] to maintain the liberty of the South, I should almost despair of our ultimate triumph."[34] Conscription suggested that the South's people lacked the revolutionary fervor necessary for victory.

The draft nationalized the requirement of enlisting men into the army, but the Confederacy's tactics for enforcing conscription remained, like its approach to dissent, highly localized. Depending on the circumstances, responsibility for conscription fell to a variety of officials all at once. Soon after the passage of the draft law, for example, Alabama's Governor Shorter endorsed a plan to send state cavalry forces to the aid

33. Moore, *Conscription and Conflict*, 12; 16–26.
34. Gov. John Gill Shorter to Randolph, May 30 and June 24, 1862, quoted in McMillan, *Disintegration of a Confederate State*, 41.

of local authorities in areas especially troubled by draft resistance. Deeming it important "that those who think they can oppose effectual resistance to the law, should understand, clearly and distinctly, that it will be enforced," Shorter relied on a combination of "civil authorities"—including local sheriffs, vigilance committees, and home guards—to assist Richmond's Bureau of Conscription enrolling officers as they used mounted posses to arrest draft evaders and shepherd them either to one of Alabama's two military training centers (called camps of instruction) or to jail.[35]

Shorter had intended to enhance the Confederacy's effort to enlist the men necessary to prosecute the war and thereby support the national interest. However, his methods ultimately further destabilized the home front. As part of the governor's enforcement guidelines, Alabama agreed to pay bounties to anyone apprehending deserters (including any conscript evading the draft): thirty dollars for each deserter delivered to an army officer, and fifteen dollars for each deserter put in a local jail.[36] From December 1861, however, the government had been offering potential conscripts only a little more, fifty dollars (plus a sixty-day furlough), as a one-time bounty for volunteering.[37] Governor Shorter heartily endorsed monetary incentives for enhancing voluntary enlistment, and once curtly remarked to a correspondent, "If they volunteer, they get $50 bounty for their families, but if they are drafted, they will receive not a dollar for bounty."[38] What he failed to understand was the extent to which the bounty system undermined volunteer enlistment—if a man could continuously make money as a "home guard member" by hauling in deserters in his neighborhood, why would he choose to enlist in the Confederate army for a one-time payment of fifty dollars and a chance to die far from home? For unionists, moreover, local incentives for civilians to take part in conscription enforcement had another, even more significant consequence: it gave local enemies more than an ideological reason to turn them in. Conscription thus intensified localized conflicts between unionists and their rebel neighbors.

35. Gov. John Gill Shorter to Hon. G. W. Randolph, Secretary of War, September 10, 1862, AGP: John Gill Shorter, 1861–63; Moore, *Conscription and Conflict*, 114–7; McMillan, *Disintegration*, 40–1.

36. Gov. John Gill Shorter Proclamation, July 5, 1862, AGP: John Gill Shorter, 1861–63.

37. Moore, *Conscription and Conflict*, 7.

38. Gov. John Gill Shorter to J. A. Hill, February 7, 1862, AGP: John Gill Shorter, 1861–63.

Such a system, which appeared to undermine the conscription effort as much as bolster it, annoyed military leaders who saw it as weak, inefficient, and vulnerable to abuses. One vocal opponent of the Bureau of Conscription was Lieutenant General Leonidas Polk, who proposed instead a national military organization called the Department of Reserves. Under this institution, a general officer would oversee the enforcement and maintenance of conscription for all the states, including the punishment of deserters. As historian Kenneth Radley has argued, such an individual would have acted "as the chief of military police for the nation."[39] Not surprisingly, the Confederate government balked at creating such a centralized power. Polk's bureau was never established, but in early 1863, Confederate adjutant and inspector general Samuel Cooper issued a circular designed to help remedy the failings of the civil conscription machinery. Cooper instructed military commanders to begin recruiting men directly, rather than waiting for officers of Richmond's Bureau of Conscription to arrest and deliver new recruits to the army. General Braxton Bragg, whose recent losses at Perryville and Murfreesboro had made him especially sensitive to the growing problem of desertion in his ranks, embraced Cooper's plan with enthusiasm, ordering General Gideon Pillow to take full advantage of Cooper's circular to bolster the Army of Tennessee.[40] Pillow reported to the War Department that he believed eight to ten thousand "deserters and tory conscripts" could be found in North Alabama alone, and immediately dispatched conscript officers and supporting cavalry forces to the region.[41] There they behaved, according to one critical War Department official, much like a "press gang, sweeping through the country with little deference either to law or the regulations designed to temper its unavoidable rigor, without detracting from its legal force."[42]

Pillow knew that Alabama had established various incentives to encourage local authorities to catch draft dodgers, and that the state had employed "independent cavalry" to enforce the law. He quickly acted to fold these local groups into new Confederate conscription units, for he

39. Kenneth Radley, *Rebel Watchdog: The Confederate States Army Provost Guard* (Baton Rouge: Louisiana State University Press, 1989), 9.

40. Douglas Clare Purcell, "Military Conscription in Alabama during the Civil War," *Alabama Review* 34, no. 2 (1981): 94–5.

41. Quoted in Bessie Martin, *Desertion of Alabama Troops from the Confederate Army: A Study in Sectionalism* (New York: Columbia University Press, 1932), 31, 99.

42. Quoted in Purcell, "Military Conscription in Alabama," 104.

needed men who knew the terrain and the methods used by the draft evaders. But just as Shorter's incentive system had undermined volunteering, Pillow's conscript cavalries attracted men attempting "to circumvent the very thing that they were trying to enforce—conscription." The cynicism of this effort was not lost on the unionists struggling to avoid the draft. As John Smith of Cherokee County remarked about one of Pillow's locally drawn conscript cavalry, "[T]heir business was to gather up conscripts and deserters from the Confederate army, but their main business was to keep from going to the front themselves and to do as little as possible and stay about home."[43]

Because most posses employed in Southern society were formed to hunt down runaway slaves, it was probably inevitable that conscript cavalries would pursue lie-outs using strategies long employed by slave patrols. This was most apparent in the use of slave dogs to catch shirkers, a technique that led one group of unionists living in Fayette County to begin deriding the conscript posse as the "Rebel and Dog Cavalry." It was an effective approach, for escaping a pack of hounds—especially well-trained animals run by men experienced at hunting runaway slaves—was no mean feat. Tom Coker and Isham Bodiford of Lowndes County, for example, were chased by some fifty dogs one night toward the end of 1862. They covered "twenty-eight miles before day" to avoid being captured, even though "it was an awful cold rainy night." Likewise, during the spring of 1864, Jesse Cranford and a friend, both unionists of Cherokee County, were also hunted with dogs. "A party of Rebel scouts or Cavalry got after us with a pack of negro hounds and gave us a long chase." The men ran for hours before escaping their pursuers.[44] In the prewar South, white men, unless heinous criminals, were never subjected to the humiliation and terror of being hunted with dogs. When white conscripts received such treatment during the war, there was no question in their minds, the minds of secessionist neighbors, or even in the minds of neighborhood slaves, that "tories" were outcasts in Southern society.

While the localized nature of the draft was in many ways a terrible burden for unionists, fighting this battle on familiar ground allowed

43. Ibid., 104, 103; Claim 6837, John Smith, Cherokee Co., May 13, 1874, SCC.

44. Claim 17152, Daniel Smith, Fayette Co., September 23, 1875; and Claim 17152, Daniel Smith, Fayette Co., September 23, 1875: Testimony of William D. Crow; Claim 17530, Alexander Bodiford Estate, Crenshaw Co., April 20, 1875: Testimony of Isham Bodiford; Claim 5399, Jesse F. Cranford, Cherokee Co., September 7, 1875; all in SCC.

union men to call upon local networks and connections within their neighborhoods and families. With the help of supporters, they generally embraced two broad strategies to "evade the conscript": taking advantage of legal exemptions and "lying out," or hiding, from the conscript cavalry.[45] At the top of a long list of legitimate draft exemptions employed by unionists were those resulting from age restrictions on conscription. (In April 1862, white males aged eighteen to thirty-five had to enlist for at least three years; by September 1863, the Congress had raised the age limit to include everyone from eighteen to forty-five.)[46] Physical handicaps also warranted exemptions.[47] By far the largest class of legitimate exemptions, however, arose from occupation or class. Ministers, certain schoolteachers and college officials, railroad workers, among many others, were exempted from service under the earliest version of the conscription law. By October 1862, the list had expanded to encompass factory owners, all manner of artisans and skilled tradespeople, saltmakers, masters and overseers (one white man for every twenty slaves owned or overseen), state and local elected officials, teachers, and newspaper editors and staff, and more.[48]

Loyalists lucky enough to belong to one of these exempted occupations quickly took advantage of it. Having a legal exemption, however, did not guarantee relief from harassment. Unionists were by this time well known and loathed by their Confederate neighbors. It was clear that the exemption taken by a unionist protected a man who was disloyal to the Confederacy. Besides offending the sensibilities of rebel families who had dutifully sent their men to the front, the continued presence of exempted unionists on the home front threatened morale. Pressure against them, therefore, could remain intense. Green Haley, an especially outspoken unionist of Marion County, was "continually interfered with" by home guards and conscript officers throughout the war, even though he was over the conscript age. And William Irwin, a large slaveholder and physician of Lawrence County, "was conscripted . . . as many as three times and was carried up for trial" by home guard cavalry to the local conscript officer despite having two exemptions—one as a slaveholder

45. Claim 9461, David Studdard, Fayette Co., February 10, 1872, SCC.

46. Moore, *Conscription and Conflict,* 114–5; McMillan, *Disintegration,* 40–1.

47. Claim 3362, Thomas Sawyer, Blount Co., December 19, 1873; Claim 4855, George W. West, Limestone Co., September 12, 1871: Testimony of James Danforth and Testimony of Joel West; all in SCC.

48. Moore, *Conscription and Conflict,* 53, 54, 62–8, 118–9, 129–30.

and one as a doctor. "They would issue an order at headquarters," he explained, "and send a posse of men after me to carry me to their bureau." Once there, Irwin had to bring out his "credential as a practicing physician" to prove the legality of his exemption.[49]

For every unionist who had legitimate grounds for exemption, there were others who wrangled, obfuscated, lied, cheated, and bribed to get into an exempted status. One Walker County farmer simply let his prematurely white hair mislead his neighbors: "[E]verybody thought I was above 50 years of age; consequently I was not interrupted by any person trying to force me into the service on that account." Meredith Miller had begun an independent business at an unusually young age and by the time of the war "showed age a good deal." His community erroneously thought he was older than he was. "I said nothing and my mother said nothing about my age & my father was dead, and there was nothing said about it." At times, more active manipulation of the facts was required, however. Melvin Carr, for instance, changed the record of his birth in the family Bible, to make him too "young" to be conscripted.[50]

Disability, like age, could also be faked. Men, unionists and otherwise, who had friends or kin in the medical profession were able to obtain false certificates attesting to a debilitating handicap. Ebenezer Leath, only twenty years old when the war began, found himself under "heavy pressure" to join a local Confederate company. After the authorities threatened to force Leath to go no matter what, he "underwent an examination" by a unionist uncle, a physician who concocted a fake medical discharge for his nephew. When some months later the enrolling officer of Cherokee County, Rice Prichett, arrested Leath despite his medical discharge and sent him to a Talladega conscript camp, his uncle again convinced the medical board to release him. "[T]hey never got me in," Leath remembered.[51] John Holcomb, a unionist living in Cherokee County, applied an even more ingenious method to avoid capture. His wife rubbed him "with a weed known as dog fennel—which caused him

49. Claim 2177, Green M. Haley, Marion Co., March 28, 1872; Claim 1369, William B. Irwin, Lawrence Co., April 13, 1872; both in SCC.

50. Claim 3129, John Guttery, Walker Co., February 15, 1878; Claim 10249, Thomas McFarland, Madison Co., April 16, 1872: Testimony of Meredith Miller; Claim 7204, Melvin B. Carr, Cherokee Co., May 21, 1874: Testimony of Elijah C. Carr; all in SCC.

51. Moore, Conscription and Conflict, 93; Claim 6701, Ebenezer Leath, Cherokee Co., July 2, 1875, SCC.

to break out like he had the small pox—so the scouts were afraid to go to his house." When the local enrolling officer demanded that Holcomb be examined by an expert, he turned for confirmation to a man known to have had smallpox, Alexander Ellenburg. Presumably unbeknownst to the authorities, Ellenburg was also a unionist and sympathetic to Holcomb. As he recalled, "I saw it was not small pox but I told [Holcomb] I would report that it was not sufficiently developed to tell for certain it was small pox." After thus creating a window of time for escape, Ellenburg secretly gave Holcomb directions to "Buck's Pocket, a most secluded hiding place in the Sand Mountains where the rebels could not find him." Covered with dog fennel sores, Holcomb fled and did not return home for three years.[52]

While many gained exemption legally through their profession, others sought relief by taking up new jobs. The scramble for exempted employment stunned observers. As one Covington County resident acidly remarked, "Since the advertisements have gone out for the conscripts to meet, every one that has been able has procured little mail routes and others have made up little schools, and many of them can not write their own names."[53] Unionists often conspired to elect their friends to local office, though this was only possible in beats where loyalists could marshal a voting majority. Farmer Larkin Cox ran for the office of constable for the sole purpose of avoiding the draft. "[M]y union friends all voted for me with that end in view," he explained. "It was the last resort I could see to avoid the rebel service or be forced to run to the union lines and leave five small children to the tender mercies of the fanatical rebels to be starved, for my wife had died just before." Unionist farmers also took on a wide range of new artisanal occupations to avoid the draft; others went to work as laborers for artisans who ran sizable businesses. Farmer and minister Levin Clifton of Cherokee County, for example, approached his friend Francis Howell, an exempted wagon maker, for a protective job in the summer of 1862. Howell remembered, Clifton "came to me and told me that he wanted to work for me as a mechanic . . . he threw himself upon my mercy saying I could pay him or not or just what I chose to give him that I could help him out of the rebel

52. Claim 7213, Alexander E. Ellenburg, Cherokee Co., May 28, 1874, SCC.
53. W. J. Prater to Gov. John Gill Shorter, August 24, 1862, AGP: John Gill Shorter, 1861–63.

army." Howell hired Clifton and the two worked together throughout the war.[54]

Most wage labor jobs were innocuous vis-à-vis the war effort, but some—including those in iron factories, saltpeter mines, or for the railroad—directly aided the Confederate cause. Loyalists were aware of the implications when they took employment in war industries, but most believed they had few alternatives. This was especially true in counties lacking strong unionist networks. For instance, John Waite, a native of Rhode Island who lived in the Black Belt county of Dallas, had worked on the railroad before the war. A Northerner by birth and "bitterly opposed to secession," Waite had virtually no unionist friends in his neighborhood. Although he had not wanted the "union broke up," he continued to work on the railroad after the war began, knowing that the Confederacy depended heavily upon the railroad in its war effort. "I was a poor man, unable to leave the Confederacy. I had a family, wife and children, dependent upon my exertions for support, and I was forced to work at something to support myself and them." His job on the railroad provided income and an exemption from service after 1862. Waite believed that he was not "giving aid or comfort to the rebellion," but simply protecting his family from starvation. Likewise, in Marshall County, farmer James Henry Morris was "compelled to work in the [saltpeter] cave to avoid being conscripted, as the country was full of armed rebel soldiers, conscripting and catching and tying men and hunting them down with dogs and carrying them off to the army." Although his labor doubtless aided the Confederate war effort, Morris felt he had no choice. "I knew I could not avoid conscription in any other manner."[55]

Moreover, many unionists were able to obtain work in exempted war industries because the men running the industries wanted to help conscripted loyalists in addition to profiteering from the conflict. The Cornwall Ironworks in Cherokee County, for example, was owned by a man by the name of Nobles who "aided union men every way he could," espe-

54. Claim 11122, Thomas W. Gaylord, Bibb Co., October 4, 1872: Testimony of William R. Gaylord; Claim 8478, Larkin M. Cox, Cherokee Co., December 19, 1874; Claim 4858, Jacob Whitehead, Lauderdale Co., May 7, 1875; Claim 6785, (Rev.) Levin A. Clifton, Cherokee Co., November 18, 1874: Testimony of Francis A. Howell; all in SCC.

55. Claim 16730, John C. Waite, Dallas Co., December 2, 1873; Claim 18293, James Henry Morris, Marshall Co., July 18, 1876; both in SCC.

cially "through his employment" of loyalists.[56] And in Randolph County, a unionist tanner named S. A. Striplin, who had "knot bin concidered tru to his country in the vicinity round about whare he live," had managed to procure a government contract to make shoes. Once he had the contract, he immediately hired a number of his friends to help him, and thereby exempted them all from conscription. Striplin's machinations outraged his strongly Confederate neighbors, some of whom remarked that if Striplin "lived in som [other] country and acted as it was said he did thare he wold be hung."[57]

Lie-Outs and Their Collaborators

Many union men were able to avoid service through exemption, but most avoided the Confederate army "by good running." For them, "lying out," or hiding, in the wooded, swampy, or mountainous areas near their farms and neighborhoods became a condition of daily life. As John M. Clark explained, "We had to bush it many and many a time lying around our plantations day and night." While men occasionally undertook this effort alone, they more commonly hid out in the company of at least one or two, and often more, unionist friends or relations. Moreover, lie-out camps frequently came to be safe places for all loyalists to congregate, whether drafted or not. As George Cook of Fayette County explained, it was common for "all of us union men" to "meet together of nights in woods" and converse about the "war and its progress."[58] But even with good friends for company, life in the "bushes" was a liminal existence. Men who resorted to it became outlaws in every sense of the word. Constantly in danger of violence or capture, they established a furtive, den-of-thieves culture among themselves, in which repeated evidence of loyalty to one's group became increasingly important. Moreover, their conceptions of loyalism both expanded and narrowed when a man went on the run. In one sense, they began to identify acts of loyalty in a much wider range of transactions than they had prior to becoming outlaws: a

56. Claim 8650, William H. Hawkins, Cherokee Co., June 30, 1875, SCC.

57. John Ware to Gov. John Gill Shorter, September 11, 1862, AGP: John Gill Shorter, 1861–63.

58. Claim 6807, Charles B. Brewer, Jackson Co., December 29, 1874; Claim 6858, George W. Watkins, Limestone Co., July 24, 1875: Testimony of John M. Clark; Claim 21671, George W. Cook, Fayette Co., May 28, 1877; all in SCC.

shared confidence, a loaf of bread, a bit of news, or a piece of warm clothing demonstrated unionism. But in another, their loyalty to the Union narrowed to become coterminous with their commitment to one another: one's friends and family, one's fellow lie-outs, came to embody the Union. To betray a fellow unionist was to betray the cause itself.

In order to endure, lie-outs constantly strove to strengthen their own and others' resolve. Tales of resistance against Confederate authorities were thus especially popular, for in their telling, such stories offered news and inspiration and, most importantly, reminded men what they were fighting for.[59] While gathered together in their camps and hiding places, union men exchanged information, heard stories from men who had escaped capture, and received reports from spies who had been sent out by groups of lie-outs to gather information about Confederate activities. John Kennamer remembered learning about his friend Jasper Harper's capture in this way: "[H]e was arrested by the rebels (so I heard) and taken off to the mountain and kept for two or three days. They took his boots off and cursed and abused him and threatened to kill him. That was the news which come to our camp." And James Tucker of Limestone explained in regard to his friend Mial Abernathy, "I heard of Roddy's men going to his house and abusing his wife and taking everything they had and capturing claimant and taking him out and threatening to shoot him." Tucker was "in the bushes" when the events happened, but believed firmly that the tales were true. Likewise, Jacob McGee learned that Jacob Stutts "had been threatened by rebel soldiers and at one time some soldiers cocked a pistol in his face threatening to shoot him for his Union principles," not by witnessing the abuse, but by hearing about it from Stutt's son, Dock, "who was present at the time."[60] Such stories were vital for unionists who needed to know how a fellow lie-out behaved under pressure in order to assess his trustworthiness and dependability. When victims of violence or witnesses to outrages returned to their group in the woods, their tribulations became part of a communally owned, oft-repeated litany of Confederate wrongs. Their heroes were the

59. For a similar pattern among female refugees, see Phillip Shaw Paludan, *Victims: A True Story of the Civil War* (Knoxville: University of Tennessee Press, 1981), 23.

60. Claim 4190, Jasper Harper, Marshall Co., April 24, 1874: Testimony of John B. Kennamer; Claim 4806, Mial S. Abernathy, Limestone Co., July 23, 1875: Testimony of James M. Tucker; Claim 1200, Jacob Stutts, Lauderdale Co., September 5, 1873: Testimony of Jacob McGee; all in SCC.

men who did not break under the pressure by revealing their friends and hiding places or by volunteering in the Confederate army.[61]

For instance, farmer Green Stovall's actions in 1862 left no doubt about his loyalty in the minds of his union friends. When arrested as a conscript, Stovall was not forcibly taken to a camp of instruction. Rather, the officers instead tried to threaten and browbeat Stovall into *volunteering* in the army. Stovall's friend and fellow unionist prisoner, James Studdard, witnessed the treatment Stovall received at the hand of his captors. "[T]hey, the rebels, would try to get him to volunteer and he would tell them he would suffer death before he would fight against the United States and he did suffer almost death but he was true to his word, he never did volunteer." Even though his jailers threatened to shoot him if he would not submit, Stovall stood his ground. "He would tell them that they would have to shoot for he would not [enlist]." Stovall's arrest was as much an exercise in will-breaking and humiliation as it was in military enlistment. The distinction between volunteering and being conscripted was significant: to be conscripted implied a reluctance to serve and could represent a man's continued resistance against the state. By contrast, if the conscript officers could force a unionist to volunteer, they would break him, forcing him to dishonor himself by betraying his friends and cause. By keeping his word in front of his fellow prisoners, Stovall both thwarted his enemies and impressed his comrades with the depth of his commitment, proving himself a true union man. After more than two months of imprisonment, Stovall escaped and made his way back to North Alabama with great difficulty. "I travailed [from Selma] through the woods all the way home and remained in the woods near home until the close of the war."[62]

Some unionists took less confrontational routes in the face of vio-

---

61. See, for instance, Claim 9376, Edwin Templeton Ellis, Lauderdale Co., February 13, 1878: Testimony of Jonathan D. Lautroop; Claim 11640, Green P. Stovall, Fayette Co., February 9, 1872: Testimony of James Studdard; Claim 3362, Thomas Sawyer, Blount Co., December 19, 1873: Testimony of Jesse G. Jones; all in SCC. For heroes, see Claim 8397, John A. McClintock, Jefferson Co., September 29, 1873: Testimony of Phillip T. Griffin; Claim 10017, William Fowler, Fayette Co., February 24, 1873: Testimony of H. L. Bolton; Claim 9461, David Studdard, Fayette Co., February 10, 1872: Testimony of J. F. Files; Claim 3537, William R. Brown, Jackson Co., June 12, 1874: Testimony of Bayless E. Ladd; Claim 4369, James M. Wallace, Lawrence Co., October 2, 1877: Testimony of Elijah S. Masterson; all in SCC.

62. Claim 11640, Green P. Stovall, Fayette Co., February 2, 1872: Testimony of James Studdard; Claim 11640, Green P. Stovall, Fayette Co., February 9, 1872; both in SCC. The distance between Selma and the county seat of Fayette is approximately one hundred miles.

lence, believing that if they did nothing *voluntarily* to aid the Confederate army or government, they would have, in all good conscience, maintained their fidelity to the Union. In particular, any sentiment stated or oath of loyalty to the Confederacy taken while under duress was not binding and did not constitute a betrayal as long as it served as a strategy to obtain freedom from arrest or harassment.[63] As attorney Robert Heflin of Randolph County explained, "In January 1863, I was required to take an oath, or affirmation, on being released [from prison]. . . . I regarded it as taken under duress in every sense of the term, and the whole thing passed from my mind with the occasion." Likewise, Robert Tharp also took an oath to gain release from arrest, "it not being known I was a conscript." The oath meant nothing to him, except as a way to gain his freedom. "I always regarded these oaths as of no effect because taken under duress and under threats of great personal harm." James Henderson, a twenty-eight-year-old farmer from Cherokee County, also took "an oath on being released" from a four-month stay in a Montgomery prison. "I don't know what it was and did not care, as all I wanted was to get out," he explained to the SCC. "I was near dead at the time, never saw the sun from the time I was incarcerated until liberated."[64] In the end, deeds, not oaths, mattered most among unionists trying to decide who was trustworthy and who was not.

Similar sensibilities prevailed even among unionists whom the Confederate authorities ultimately captured and forced into the army. All were determined that, even if they had been made to take an oath and shoulder a gun, they would desert as soon as possible and never actually fight. David Studdard, for instance, was "forced into the rebel camp by conscription," but once freed of handcuffs looked for a way to desert. His friend J. F. Files, an Alabama Union army scout, felt assured that Studdard "never fired a gun . . . during the war." James M. Smith of Limestone County also viewed his forcible enlistment as meaningless. "I do not consider that when I was conscripted and put in the army giving [the Confederate States] aid and comfort, for I entered it against my will

63. As scholars have long noted, the very nature of oaths in an honor-based society demanded that they be voluntarily undertaken to be binding. See, for instance, Julian Pitt-Rivers, "Honour and Social Status," in *Honour and Shame: The Values of Mediterranean Society*, ed. J. G. Peristiany (Chicago: University of Chicago Press, 1966), 34–5.

64. Claim 14, Robert Heflin, Randolph Co., April 18, 1871; Claim 19003, Robert Tharp, Jr., Franklin Co., September 6, 1873; Claim 6686, James M. Henderson, Cherokee Co., April 23, 1872; all in SCC.

and got out the first chance I had." Likewise, Joanna Sutterlin's husband—"a union man of the unyielding sort"—was arrested and put on a train bound for a conscript camp in Rome, Georgia. He soon escaped, jumping from the train and running all the way back home. And when two young conscriptable men, Frank and Jasper Ridge of Jackson County, decided to go with a local company of cavalry, they did so to protect their father, who had been threatened with hanging as a consequence of his sons' resistance. When the boys set out on the road to Bridgeport, where they would report to the conscript officer, they were accompanied by their father, William, and older brother, George. "[W]e all talked along the road how they would escape from the Rebels to the Federal army," George explained. "Frank told Father not to be uneasy—not to go out after them, for if he [i.e., Frank] did not get through to the Federal army, he would come back home and take to the Mountain." True to their word, when after fifteen days they had failed to cross the lines, Frank and Jasper deserted, came home, and fled to the mountains.[65]

Although situated beyond the edges of settled life, lie-out communities remained firmly tethered to their homes. Indeed, draft evaders owed their security to the extensive networks of friends and family who continued to live in the world beyond the woods. Of utmost importance were a steady supply of food, information about safe places to hide, and warm clothing and blankets. Such necessities were increasingly difficult for lie-outs to obtain unassisted. When a man had been living in the woods for days or weeks at a time, he changed physically. Men made ragged by lying out could not simply wander into town to ask for food or for guidance to a new hiding place. They had to depend on those who, on sight, would not betray them. As Jefferson Cook explained, "Those of us who were keeping out were very careful who we let see us. . . . Some people would have shot us or had the dogs after us in a few hours."[66]

Conscripts were frequently assisted by their fathers or other older men who were able to remain at home safely. Jesse Thomas, for instance, regularly fed his son and his friends as they hid out in the woods. As one of the lie-outs remembered, "He carried victuals to us, and protected us,

65. Claim 9461, David Studdard, Fayette Co., February 10, 1872: Testimony of J. F. Files; Claim 17226, James M. Smith, Limestone Co., June 15, 1874; Claim 6670, Joanna Sutterlin, Cherokee Co., July 3, 1875: Testimony of Elijah McNew; Claim 20467, William Ridge Estate, Jackson Co., November 10, 1875: Testimony by George W. Ridge; all in SCC.

66. Claim 17714, Randall Taylor Estate, Crenshaw Co., October 11, 1875: Testimony of Jefferson Cook, SCC.

and gave us word whenever there were rebels about, or we were in danger." Such assistance was especially important when a conscript did not have kin of his own to whom he could turn. William McNew credited his ability to successfully "keep out of the way of the rebels" to John Bowman, who offered to care for McNew like one of his own. Lying out around Bowman's "house and place with his sons," McNew received both sustenance and information on the whereabouts of conscript cavalry. The only consideration that might stand in the way of aid between the generations was the survival of the provisioner's immediate family. For instance, while Isham Bodiford and his wife "cooked and toted" food for "some of the boys to lie out on" in his neighborhood, they stopped when Bodiford no longer "had the rations to spare and was running the risk of leaving my wife destitute."[67]

As a general rule, women ventured into the lie-out world with far less regularity than did men and usually only if male relatives were unavailable. Nonetheless, mothers, sisters, wives, and female neighbors assisted lie-outs in important ways. Women cooked and prepared the "victuals" that their husbands and fathers carried into the woods, when they did not carry the provisions to the men themselves. Melissa Turbyfill and her daughters, for instance, kept vigilant watch for her husband and the nearly twenty union men who "lay out with him and were in the Mountains" nearby. The women "fed and washed for them" and always gave them "timely warning of the approach of the rebels." Likewise, Winnie Helms was always "ready and willing" to feed any draft evader in need. Phila Brooks of Lee County also provided lie-outs with "clothing and provisions," and Margaret Shoe, a widow from Cherokee County, "smuggled provisions" to her brother and brother-in-law, who were "often hunted and watched so closely that neither of them could slip in home to get anything to eat for fear of being caught." This she did for six months until the Confederate conscript cavalry "ran both of them off from the country with hounds."[68]

67. Claim 16196, Jesse Thomas, Lauderdale Co., July 23, 1875: Testimony of Jacob A. Paulk; Claim 8188, John Bowman, Cherokee Co., July 23, 1875: Testimony of William McNew; Claim 17530, Alexander Bodiford Estate, Crenshaw Co., April 20, 1875: Testimony of Isham Bodiford; all in SCC.

68. Claim 19870, Wilson Turbyfill, Madison Co., June 3, 1875: Testimony of Melissa Turbyfill; Claim 14479, Winnie Helms, Cherokee Co., August 12, 1874; Claim 4807, William Brooks, Lee Co., March 26, 1873: Testimony of Phila Brooks; Claim 5399, Jesse F. Cranford, Cherokee Co., September 7, 1875: Testimony of Margaret Shoe; all in SCC.

Slaves also became abettors of lie-outs, a situation that involved varying levels of risk for both parties. Because slaves were frequently viewed
by white Southerners as the extension of their masters' wills, it is possible that, if caught helping a master or his son lie out, a slave would face
no serious repercussions. Authorities might simply assume that the slave
had only been acting on orders. Nevertheless, owners who brought their
slaves into such arrangements had no assurances of the slave's safety,
and the slave likely had little leeway to protest being implicated in such
dangerous activities. At the same time, ordering a slave to help a lie-out
meant revealing the details of illegal acts and hiding places to someone
with considerable interest in betraying his or her oppressor. In being
trusted with information that could result in the lie-out's capture, then,
bondspeople also gained a measure of power over the draft evader.

These tensions, however, did not prevent such arrangements from
working successfully. For example, Riley Tirey, one of the twelve slaves
owned by Robert Guttery of Walker County, "carried blankets to [Gut-
tery] and waited on him to help him keep out of the way of the Rebel
cavalry." Likewise, when unionist Stephen Haynes began keeping "his
son hid out to prevent his being conscripted," Benjamin Haynes often
carried provisions to the son "in the mountain nearby." And J. J. Giers,
a prominent white unionist of Hill Country Morgan County, found support in Henry Slaughter, a neighborhood slave who was hiring his own
time as a wagonmaker and farmer. "He expressed sympathy for me, [I]
having been driven out from my family by the rebels," Giers explained
to the SCC. "He gave me information about the location of the rebel
troops and advised me to look out for myself." And while Albert Morris,
a slave of Jackson County, did not assist a lie-out with supplies or information, he did make a deal to do so. When hired out by his master to
another farmer, Morris was put in charge of cultivating a leased farm.
There he met unionist Allen Isbell, who lived next door. "[T]here was
only a turning row between my crop and [Isbell's]," Morris remembered.
"[W]e could stand in each other's doors and talk." The men developed a
good neighborly relationship, "swapping work" and feeding the livestock
when one or the other was away from home. As a consequence of this
intimacy, the men made an arrangement to protect Isbell from conscription and, presumably, Morris from impressment as a slave laborer. "If
the rebels got too hot for him and he had to lay out, I was to feed him,"
Morris explained, "and the same if I had to lay out . . . he was to feed

me. We were to feed each other until the moss grew on our backs if necessary before going into the rebel army."[69]

Whether free or slave, aiders and abettors of lie-outs carried a burden of immense weight: the trust of those they protected. Many could have, at any point, turned in the lie-out and thereby got themselves a bounty or simply some favor from Confederate authorities. In carrying out this duty faithfully, the aiders gained considerable standing in the eyes of the lie-outs. Jeptha Ware, for example, esteemed his friend David Abernathy because, although "he had every opportunity to do so," Abernathy had never "betrayed" Ware. By coming to his hiding place in the woods on a regular basis, bringing him information and encouraging Ware to "remain in the woods," Abernathy had convinced Ware of his trustworthiness. John Elliot, in like fashion, "was not afraid to see" his friend Thomas Sawyer when he approached Elliot's lie-out camp in the woods. "I had not fears that he would betray me." Once such trustworthiness had been clearly established, unionists repeatedly turned to their support network for help. Andrew Linn repeatedly entrusted his life to Elizabeth Hardin, whose house he early identified as a place of refuge. "[S]he all the time give me the information about the cavalry and fed me and gave me provisions to take with me in the woods." Most important, Linn remembered, "I was not afraid of being betrayed by her."[70]

Confederates quickly realized how heavily lie-outs depended upon networks of supporters for food, information, and protection. Locating and tracking conscript-avoiders took days or weeks of effort, and officers were often foiled by an active network of civilians who helped unionists escape. As three members of a Coosa County home guard reminded Governor Shorter in the fall of 1863, "If we go into these mountain districts

69. Claim 3128, Robert Guttery, Sr., Walker Co., January 17,1872: Testimony of Riley Tirey; Claim 4357, John Ogden and Stephen Haynes, Madison Co., September 11, 1871: Testimony of Benjamin Haynes; Claim 319, Henry S. Slaughter, Morgan Co., September 23, 1873: Testimony of John J. Giers; Claim 6028, Allen Isbell, Jackson Co., March 8, 1876: Testimony of Albert Morris; all in SCC. Henry Slaughter was a "good farmer" who had established substantial financial resources through his self-hire and consequently owned "horses, mules, wagons & other property." Giers reported that he would have been willing to take Slaughter's "bond for a thousand dollars, but not for two thousand, though he might have been good for that." For more on self-hire by slaves, see chap. 3.

70. Claim 7829, David W. Abernathy, Jefferson Co., August 1, 1873: Testimony of Jeptha M. Ware; Claim 3362, Thomas Sawyer, Blount Co., December 19, 1873: Testimony of John Elliot; Claim 12976, Elizabeth Hardin, Jefferson Co., August 29, 1873: Testimony of Andrew J. Linn; all in SCC.

to arrest deserters we will be obliged to exercise some control over the citizens, for many of them are infected with a feeling of disloyalty and consequently would aid the deserters in evading of us."[71] Moreover, many believed that such civilians and their successful resistance had a corrosive effect on Confederate morale. James Hogan, for instance, was threatened by Confederates in 1863 when one Sid Walker, "a Captain in the rebel army, said that I ought to be hung, for I was a dangerous man to their cause, that I was educated and had an influence in my neighborhood, and that I must be got rid of in some way."[72]

Consequently, collaborative loyalist networks became one of the Confederate conscript cavalry's favorite targets. The goals were simple: to humiliate, intimidate, and punish the supporters of lie-outs until the networks broke and the lie-out came in of his own accord, or until the unionist's family fled the South, thereby rendering further resistance on the home front impossible. Confederates employed a range of strategies to exert this pressure. Punitive robbery and foraging helped to diminish the resources of lie-outs' supporters and force them to capitulate or flee. For instance, after learning that the Reverend Levin Clifton frequently "counseled" men to "keep out of the military service," six hundred Confederate cavalrymen rode into the preacher's yard, waving pistols and cursing him as a "D——d Lincolnite." Clifton explained, "They wasted and destroyed about one hundred and fifty bushels of corn and about eight thousand binds of fodder. It rained all night and these soldiers pulled down and scattered all this fodder so it was rained on all night and ruined." Simultaneously, a number of soldiers "crowded into" Clifton's house, where they stayed all night, cursing and "vilifying" him. He was later reminded—through the rumor mill—that he should have been grateful for such treatment: "I heard often that the rebels had said that if I had received justice I would have been hung."[73]

"Burning out" a family, which usually meant destroying outbuildings but could include setting fire to a house, was another oft-employed tactic to cow loyalists' supporters. Jesse Tiara, for instance, had joined a group of lie-outs in Marion County, men who not only avoided the draft, but who sought "to protect union men in that section of the country from being forced into the rebel army" through open resistance to the con-

71. O. P. Dark, G. M. Gamble, and T. G. Slaughter to Gov. John Gill Shorter, October 31, 1863; and Adj. and Insp. Gen. S. Cooper to Gov. John Gill Shorter, December 24, 1862; both in AGP: John Gill Shorter, 1861–63.

72. Claim 2346, James Hogan, Walker Co., December 4, 1871, SCC.

73. Claim 6785, (Rev.) Levin A. Clifton, Cherokee Co., November 18, 1874, SCC.

script officers. His activism cost him dearly, for Confederates burned down his house, his outbuildings, twenty-one bales of cotton, thirty bushels of oats, fifteen hundred bundles of fodder, a wagon, and a set of blacksmithing tools. As the coup de grace, they "cut the ears off" two of Tiara's horses. The slave of Jesse's father, Riley, was astounded that Tiara had survived: "I do think the good Lord took care of him, and kept the rebels from killing him."[74]

Confederate cavalry also used the threat of arson, as well as the act itself, to force women to reveal the hiding places of spouses or sons. A rebel officer confronted Elizabeth Linn, for instance, and demanded that she reveal the hiding place of her husband, Andrew. Believing that if Andrew had been found, he would "have been killed by [the rebels] as quick as they would have killed a snake," Elizabeth refused. The officer then told her that he would burn down the house with Elizabeth and her six children inside if she would not tell them where to find Andrew. She again refused. Instead of burning the house, the soldiers broke in and stole the Linns' store of bedclothes—valuable household items. That the cavalry robbed Elizabeth rather than burning her up as they threatened to do suggests that there were, at least in certain times and places, limits to what men were willing to do, even in war. Nonetheless, Elizabeth Linn and her husband understood that had the men wanted to, they could have done terrible damage; moreover, one instance of restraint did not ensure future "kindnesses." The threat of burning along with the robbery inflicted limited damage and served to remind the Linns of their vulnerability to Confederate power. Less fortunate were the Watkinses of Limestone County. The conscript cavalry abandoned restraint over George Watkins, probably because he had repeatedly escaped arrest. They went to Watkins's home, confronted his wife, Martha, and demanded—at pain of burning her house down—to know her husband's whereabouts. Watkins himself was hidden close nearby and overheard the leader of the "squad" telling Martha that he would shoot George on sight. That threat, not surprisingly, failed to convince Martha to budge. She remained silent about her husband and watched as the conscript cavalry set the house on fire.[75]

74. Claim 7552, Jesse V. Tiara, Fayette Co., December 10, 1871; Claim 7552, Jesse V. Tiara, Fayette Co., December 10, 1871: Testimony of Riley Tiara; both in SCC.

75. Claim 9454, Andrew J. Linn, Jefferson Co., August 30, 1873: Testimony of Joseph Hand (see also Linn's testimony on his own behalf); Claim 6858, George W. Watkins, Limestone Co., July 24, 1875; both in SCC. According to historian Michael Fellman's interpretation of similar events in guerrilla-plagued Missouri, however, the theft of the bedding might

The posturing and intimidation that frequently marked these encounters could quickly spill over into bodily abuse of the families of draft evaders. Thomas Molloy, for example, recalled that while he was fleeing from the conscript officers, "[M]y Wife was knocked down with a Gun by the Cavilery because she refusd to tell them where I was." Molloy went on to explain that his daughters were also abused, but this time were nearly raped as well. "[M]y Daughter was scandlausly insulted, my D[a]ughtering law they drew a knife on her and tride to intimidate her that they might gratify there evil passions with her."[76] Alfred Southern of Marion County learned with horror that his "little son & daughter" had been kidnapped by the conscript cavalry, who then threatened the children with hanging if they refused to reveal their father's hiding place. And George Ridge of Jackson County, exempted as a railroad worker, was accosted by a conscript officer furious that Ridge and his father, William, had been aiding and abetting George's three younger brothers. "He told me if Father did not bring in them boys out of the mountain . . . that he, Lieutenant Horn, would take the damned old Yankee out and hang him," Ridge remembered. Not content to leave it at that, Horn cursed Ridge, saying, "And you, damn you, ought to be hung now, you are carrying nurse to your Brothers in the Mountain." Ridge then rose up and challenged Horn's honor: "I answered him in the presence of the hands, and told him, 'You, God damn you, cannot hang me, and if you will turn out man to man, you can't hang me atall yourself.' I also told him to take off them shoulder straps and I would whip him. He then went off." But Horn, doubtlessly enraged over Ridge's impudence, did not "go off" for good—within a few months, one of the Ridge boys and William Ridge, the father, had been killed by Jackson County conscript cavalry.[77]

*   *   *

also represent a violation of Elizabeth Linn's person in lieu of raping or otherwise physically abusing her. Considering that wartime black markets thrived throughout North Alabama, however, the linen could also represent handy trade goods for future exigencies. Michael Fellman, *Inside War: The Guerrilla Conflict in Missouri during the Civil War* (New York: Oxford University Press, 1989), 207–8.

76. Thomas Molloy to Hon. Arty C. Cadley, May 28, 1867, AGP: Wager Swayne, 1867–68; for instructive examples of Confederate and guerrilla soldiers refraining from raping women in Missouri, see Fellman, *Inside War*, 206–8.

77. Claim 4848, Alfred B. Southern, Marion Co., March 23, 1875; Claim 20467, William Ridge Estate, Jackson Co., November 11, 1875: Testimony of George W. Ridge; both in SCC.

For Confederates and unionists, conscription markedly intensified the conflict over loyalty on the home front. Rebel families who had sent sons and husbands to the front were outraged when good Confederates risked life and limb while "tories" got away with shirking. Government and military officials heartily concurred in the citizenry's denouncement of unionist draft evaders, and put intense and frequently violent pressure on lie-outs and their networks of support to force compliance with the law. Most Confederates were thoroughly satisfied with the government's willingness to pursue these "traitors" with a vengeance. "I hail the conscript raids about here with delight," one such citizen announced. "There are some in these piney woods & hills that are as wiley as a fox."[78]

The other side of this equation, however, was that Confederate efforts to humiliate, abuse, and arrest lie-outs only bred deeper resentments and hatreds in the hearts of union people. Prior to the war, reverence for the Union had been one of a range of shared values among white Southerners; now, however, adherence to that value had not only forced loyalists into a defensive and radical position, it had opened the door for a level of social correction never before experienced by men and women such as themselves. Slaves and suspected abolitionists, horse thieves and bandits, gamblers and arsonists—these were the sorts of people traditionally set up for community sanction. Now, however, time-honored traditions of humiliation, intimidation, and terror were brought to bear upon unionists who, by maintaining their stubborn loyalty to the Union and by violating the law of conscription, threatened to destabilize Confederate morale and purpose.

Thus, even as such measures became increasingly important tools for Confederate social and political control, they provided continually renewed justification for unionist resistance. Harsh treatment by neighbors and the Confederate army simply confirmed for most unionists that "the *Devil* was the father of the Confederacy."[79] The more corrupt the Confederacy appeared to be, the more righteous seemed resistance to it. The ceaseless menace of conscription thus changed unionists—it transformed a resistant stance, attitude, and temperament into active, dangerous, and sometimes deadly rebellion. The consequences of this shift

78. Robert Anderson McClellan to Father, August 15, 1863, Robert Anderson McClellan Papers, DU.

79. Claim 6091, James Ellis, Walker Co., December 28, 1871: Testimony of A. J. Sides, SCC.

extended well into the war and beyond. The skills and thirst for vengeance lying out bred became a prized commodity among union commanders who invaded Alabama and enlisted these men into the Federal ranks as soldiers, scouts, and spies. Moreover, unionists' experiences during the ordeal of wartime conscription filled them with moral outrage not simply at the wrong done the Union, but the wrongs done to themselves and their families. This outraged sense of justice—or what historian Phillip Paludan has called "justice in personal terms"—became the heart of unionists' wartime, and eventually postwar, identity and purpose.[80]

80. Paludan, *Victims*, 23.

"Union Southern Men Welcoming Our Gun-Boats in Alabama," *Harper's Weekly Magazine*, March 1, 1862.

Courtesy The Newberry Library, Chicago.

"Searching for Rebels in a Cave in Alabama," *Harper's Weekly Magazine*, August 16, 1862.

Courtesy The Newberry Library, Chicago.

"Huntsville, Alabama, From General Logan's Headquarters," *Harper's Weekly Magazine,* March 19, 1864.

"Charge of the First Alabama and Fifth Kentucky, Under Colonel Spencer, at White Pond—Sketched by Theodore K. Davis," *Harper's Weekly Magazine,* February 5, 1865.

"The Escaped Slave—From
Photography by T. B. Beard [?],"
Harper's Weekly Magazine, July 2,
1864, and "The Escaped Slave in the
Union Army."

Courtesy The Newberry Library,
Chicago.

Brigadier General George E. Spencer, Commander, First Alabama Cavalry; and U.S. Senator from Alabama, 1868 to 1879.

Photograph ca. 1868 by Mathew Brady. Photography of Civil War–Era Personalities and Scenes, 1921–1940, Record Group 111, Records of the Chief Signal Officer, 1860–1982, NAB.

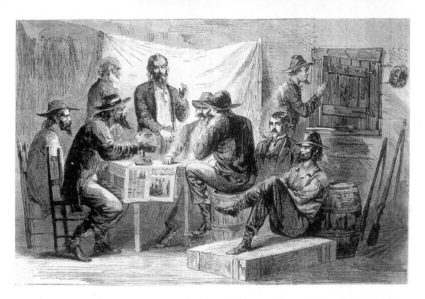

"Secret Meeting of Southern Unionists—Sketched by our Special Artist, A. R. Waud," *Harper's Weekly Magazine*, August 4, 1866.

Courtesy The Newberry Library, Chicago.

"Alabamians Receiving Rations," *Harper's Weekly Magazine*, August 11, 1866.

Courtesy The Newberry Library, Chicago.

"Scene Upon the Assembling of the Southern Loyalists' Convention at the 'National Hall' in Philadelphia, September 3, 1866," *Harper's Weekly Magazine*, September 22, 1866.

Courtesy The Newberry Library, Chicago.

Dr. Thomas Haughey, Surgeon, Third Tennessee Infantry, U.S.A., 1862 to 1865; and U.S. Representative from Alabama, 1868 to 1869.

Photograph ca. 1868 by Mathew Brady. Photographs of Civil War–Era Personalities and Scenes, 1921–1940, Record Group 111, Records of the Chief Signal Officer, 1860–1982, NAB.

Grave marker of Shedrick Golden, Bragg Family Cemetery, Hurricane Valley (near New Market), Alabama.

Photograph: Gene Frost, October 1966. Permission to reproduce courtesy David Frost.

3

"The Loyal Alabamians Are Invaluable"

UNIONISTS, SLAVES, AND FEDERAL OCCUPATION

[W]hen we re[a]ch the brow of the hill there stood a fare speciman of N. Alabama. [T]here was from 75 to 100 of men women and children, and such shouting at the sight of troops and the old flag [I have] not herd but few times.

—Corporal John C. Wysong, Company H, Thirtieth Indiana
Infantry Volunteers, 1863

I didn't go into the [Confederate] army until I was forced to go. They catched me with dogs, and I hadn't been with them long until I snapped off their clothes for better ones; I crossed over the lines.

—Henry Long, Crenshaw County, 1875

When Colonel Abel D. Streight invaded North Alabama in 1862, he and his Fifty-first Indiana Infantry Volunteers were overwhelmed by the numbers of unionists they encountered. "Suffice it to say," Streight remarked in a letter to his superiors, "that I have never witnessed such an outpouring of devoted and determined patriotism among any other people; and I am now of the opinion, that, if there could be a sufficient force in that portion of the country to protect these people, there could be at least two full regiments raised of as good and true men as ever defended the American flag."[1] Navy lieutenant S. L. Phelps was likewise staggered by the reception his gunboat troops received as they reconnoitered south on the Tennessee River. Over the course of this expedition, which

---

For epigraphs, see August 21, 1863, John C. Wysong Diary, F80, Indiana Historical Society, Indianapolis, Indiana; and Claim 17530, Alexander Bodiford Estate, Crenshaw Co., April 20, 1875: Testimony of Henry Long, SCC.

1. Report of Col. Abel D. Streight, July 16, 1862, *The War of the Rebellion: A Compilation of the Official Records of the Union and Confederate Armies,* ed. U.S. War Department (Washington, D.C.: Government Printing Office, 1880–1901), Ser. I, vol. 16, pt. 1, 789 (hereinafter *OR*).

stretched from Tennessee through Mississippi and finally into Alabama, Phelps and his men were "astonished . . . not a little" by the unionism evident among the people they encountered. "We have met with the most gratifying proofs of loyalty everywhere across Tennessee and in the portions of Mississippi and Alabama where we visited," Phelps noted. "Men, women and children, several times gathered in crowds of hundreds, shouted their welcome, and hailed their national flag with an enthusiasm there was no mistaking." Phelps and his men looked out in amazement at the crowds, where "tears flowed freely down the cheeks of men as well as of women" at the approach of the Union boats. The Northern commander understood how dangerous it was for Southern people to express their love of the Union publicly. "Those people braved everything to go to the river-bank, where a sight of their flag might once more be enjoyed."[2]

The invasion of Alabama in 1862 offered loyalists their first sustained contact with friendly forces since secession. Those living in towns where the army headquartered, like Huntsville and Athens, or whose farms surrounded those towns, eagerly traveled to the provost marshal or commanding officer to take oaths of allegiance, thereby reaffirming their United States citizenship.[3] Others enlisted in the Union army, a step that allowed men who had previously lain hidden in the woods—dependent on women, children, old men, and slaves—to face their enemies well armed and clad in Union blue. In return, the Union army granted these men and their families extensive assistance in the form of food rations, military protection, and transportation away from dangerous neighborhoods. Many would have agreed with Alfred Southern, who remarked that Federal soldiers "afforded me . . . all the genuine protection I had during the Rebellion, to keep from being robbed, murdered, or killed for my principles."[4]

The Union occupation of North Alabama also offered slaves their first chance to escape to the protection of Northern lines. Until the war came to them, slaves had little opportunity to take action. As one slave of Jackson County explained, until the invasion "De war am on, but us don't see none of it."[5] Once the Federal army arrived in Alabama, slaves could

2. Report of Lt. Comdr. S. L. Phelps, February 10, 1862, OR, Ser. I, vol. 7, 155–6.

3. Ash, When the Yankees Came, 108, and chap. 4, passim.

4. Claim 4848, Alfred B. Southern, Marion Co., March 23, 1875, SCC.

5. Narrative of Thomas Cole in The American Slave: A Composite Autobiography, Ser. 1, vol. 4 of Texas Narratives, pt. 1, ed. George P. Rawick (Westport, Conn.: Greenwood Press, 1972), 228, 230–1.

not only see the war, but also use the disruption it created to free themselves and to aid the Union cause. In this way, they served their own
interests while directly challenging the Confederacy by robbing their
state of precious labor and undermining slavery.

For both white unionists and slaves, Union occupation brought difficulties as well as benefits, however. Proximity to Federal soldiers frequently prompted severe Confederate recriminations against loyalists
still behind rebel lines, simply because unionists, their families, and
friends represented weak links in the state's defenses. African Americans, too, were viewed with suspicion; moreover, even those blacks who
successfully crossed the lines into "friendly" territory continued to struggle, for they frequently met a far less enthusiastic welcome than that
given to white unionists. Throughout 1862, the Union army rebuffed
black activists who volunteered as soldiers, instead relegating them to
manual labor (frequently impressed) and occasional guard duty. Even
after the military fully lifted the ban on black soldiering in 1863, the relationship between Alabama's free and freed blacks and the Union army
remained distrustful and uncertain; throughout the Federal occupation,
black enlistment in Federal forces remained a contested right, not a
given.

As was the case throughout the South, difficulties such as these were
exacerbated by the ravenous character of Union forces who repeatedly
foraged from the farms surrounding their encampments and lines of
march. North Alabama was traversed by multiple army divisions. Consequently, tens of thousands of soldiers might move through a given county
at any one time, and even "small" garrisoning forces, which usually numbered fewer men, represented hundreds of new mouths to feed. Even if
well supplied by a nearby railroad, occupation troops regularly foraged
the countryside for extra sources of nourishment, especially fresh meat,
fruit, and vegetables. The larger the number of Northern soldiers, the
more voracious the occupation seemed to civilians, Confederate, unionist, and enslaved alike. The presence of so many hungry men, even those
long looked for, could simply be overwhelming, as it was to J. B. Hyatt
of Franklin County, who said that when the Union troops moved in, it
seemed that the "whole face of the earth was covered with soldiers."[6]
Confronted by this onslaught, loyal men and women struggled to do

6. Claim 8251, John Carrithers, Colbert Co., September 1, 1874: Testimony of J. B.
Hyatt, SCC.

their duty while still protecting themselves and their families from destitution. For white unionists, the loss of stockpiled food could be truly
devastating. Seen as deserving targets by pro-Confederate society and
military authorities, many had been repeatedly singled out for punitive
Confederate foraging and had little left to give when Union troops arrived. Because loyal people had only themselves and fellow unionists
upon which to depend, Federal foraging sometimes caused them to abandon home and hearth for refugee camps inside Union lines. For prop-
erty-owning slaves, army confiscation threatened the only measure of
independence most had; without it, many felt totally vulnerable to the
uncertainties of war and what might follow.

For both black and white loyalists in Alabama, then, the Union occupation coupled protection with a new kind of instability. As historian
Stephen Ash has argued, "Wherever the Northerners invaded they imposed a new pattern on the South's social and economic landscape."[7]
Moreover, the Northern invasion marked the beginning of a difficult and
contentious triangulation of three separate interests; the alliances among
white unionists, the Union army, and African Americans would remain
crucial throughout the war and into Reconstruction. From the beginning, this alliance was both exceptionally fruitful and fraught with mis-
understandings and ongoing conflicts. Nevertheless, in the midst of the
confusion lay great opportunities for both white unionists and black activists to take part in the war in a tangible, concrete fashion.

Boundaries of Union Occupation

From the very early days of the conflict, Federal and Confederate strategists alike had recognized the value of Alabama's stretch of the Tennessee River and the state's railroads.[8] (See map 3.) The river represented a
way into the Deep South, for it linked western Kentucky to northern
Mississippi, northern Alabama, and eastern Tennessee. During rainy

7. Ash, *When the Yankees Came*, 76.

8. Stephen D. Engle, *Struggle for the Heartland: The Campaigns from Fort Henry to Corinth*
(Lincoln: University of Nebraska Press, 2001), 32; George Edgar Turner, *Victory Rode the
Rails: The Strategic Place of the Railroads in the Civil War* (New York: Bobbs-Merrill, 1953),
120–1. Also see Maj. Gen. Don Carlos Buell to Maj. Gen. O. M. Mitchel, June 12, 1862, *OR*,
Ser. I, vol. 16, pt. 2, 17; Gen. in Chief Henry W. Halleck to Maj. Gen. Stephen A. Hurlbut,
October 4, 1863, *OR*, Ser. I, vol. 30, pt. 4, 73; Maj. Gen. William T. Sherman to Lt. Gen.
Ulysses S. Grant, April 24, 1864, *OR*, Ser. I, vol. 32, pt. 3, 466.

winter months when overland travel was difficult, if not impossible, domination of such a throughway was strategically advantageous. Moreover, occupation of port towns along the Tennessee, such as Tuscumbia and Florence, meant control and diminution of some of Alabama's more significant cotton trading centers.[9] North Alabama's railroads—the Memphis & Charleston and the Nashville & Decatur (sometimes called the Tennessee and Alabama Central)—were equally attractive to Federal commanders, although considerably more difficult to maintain and protect. The first connected the eastern South to the vital western trading centers of Memphis and New Orleans via Chattanooga, Tennessee, and Corinth, Mississippi.[10] The Nashville & Decatur Railroad linked Middle Tennessee and the Tennessee River. Moreover, because the Decatur Junction lay on the Memphis & Charleston, the Nashville & Decatur offered a secondary way to travel from Nashville to Corinth or to Chattanooga.

All these factors placed Alabama at the crossroads for important Federal campaigns into the Deep South. On the state's western border sat Corinth, which early in the war took on considerable significance to General U. S. Grant as he planned to plunge southward from Tennessee. In Grant's eyes, the north Mississippi town represented "the great strategic position at the West between the Tennessee & Mississippi Rivers and between Nashville and Vicksburg."[11] Chattanooga, situated just northeast of Alabama, was long viewed as singularly important for any Federal occupation of eastern Tennessee, a goal close to President Lincoln's heart. Its capture was the goal of Major General William S. Rosecrans's Chickamauga campaign through northern Alabama and western Georgia in the autumn of 1863. Finally, during the Atlanta campaign in 1864, Alabama's Tennessee Valley formed Major General William T. Sherman's "base of operations."[12] Control of North Alabama's railroads allowed the Union army to transport and supply some twenty thousand troops moving west from Mississippi, Memphis, and Alabama toward Chattanooga in the winter and spring of 1863–64.[13]

9. Engle, *Struggle for the Heartland*, 9, 86.

10. Turner, *Victory Rode the Rails*, 120.

11. Quote ibid., 123.

12. Maj. Gen. William T. Sherman to Maj. Gen. Nathaniel P. Banks, January 16, 1864, *OR*, Ser. I, vol. 32, pt. 2, 115.

13. Maj. Gen. William T. Sherman to Maj. Gen. John A. Logan, December 21, 1863, *OR*, Ser. I, vol. 31, pt. 3, 459; and Maj. William T. Sherman to Maj. Gen. James B. McPherson, April 29, 1864, *OR*, Ser. I, vol. 32, pt. 3, 534.

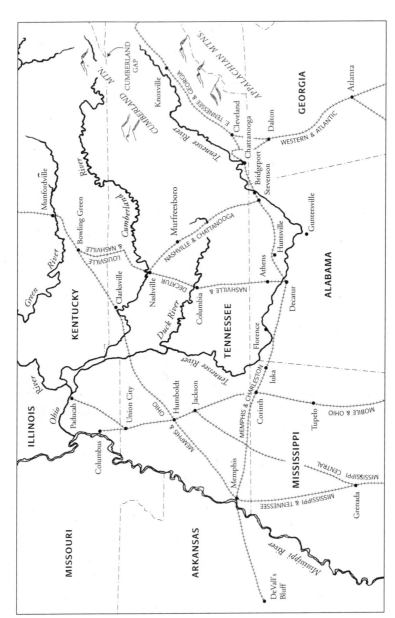

Map 3. Rivers, Ports, and Railroads of the Confederate Heartland.

Though the Federals conducted significant campaigns in and around North Alabama, the Union army's zone of occupation remained quite small throughout the war, comprising at most the four Valley counties lying north and west of the Tennessee River—Lauderdale, Limestone, Madison, and most of Jackson. These counties first came under sustained Union control in the spring of 1862, as the Union army pressed its advantage south after the fall of Forts Henry and Donelson in February.[14] Following this early invasion, Federal occupation was interrupted on two occasions. In late August 1862, Federal troops under the command of Major General Don Carlos Buell withdrew from northern Alabama to cut off Confederate General Braxton Bragg's counteroffensive into Middle Tennessee and Kentucky.[15] Federal forces regained control of Alabama north of the Tennessee River in the summer of 1863, after which much of the region served as a staging ground for Major General William S. Rosecrans's Chickamauga campaign (August–September 1863) and later for Major General William T. Sherman's Atlanta campaign (May–September 1864).[16] Union forces briefly withdrew from northern Alabama again in September 1864, this time to defend Middle Tennessee

14. Brig. Gen. O. M. Mitchel to Hon. E. M. Stanton, April 17, 1862; Brig. Gen. O. M. Mitchel to Hon. Edwin M. Stanton, May 1, 1862, OR, Ser. I, vol. 10, pt. 2, 111, 156.

15. Malcolm C. McMillan, The Alabama Confederate Reader (Tuscaloosa: University of Alabama Press, 1963), 139; William Letford and Allen W. Jones, Location and Classification and Dates of Military Events in Alabama, 1861–1865 (University: Alabama Civil War Commission, 1961), 197; Maj. Gen. Don Carlos Buell to Maj. Gen. Ulysses S. Grant, August 25, 1862; Maj. Gen. Don Carlos Buell to Maj. Gen. Lovell H. Rousseau, for Gov. Andrew Johnson, August 30, 1862, OR, Ser. I, vol. 16, pt. 2, 417, 451.

16. McMillan, Alabama Confederate Reader, 139. On Rosecrans's campaign, see Maj. Gen. William S. Rosecrans to Maj. Gen. Henry W. Halleck, August 6, 1863, OR, Ser. I, vol. 23, pt. 2, 594; Maj. Gen. William S. Rosecrans to Adj. Gen. U.S. Army, August 15, 1863; Maj. Gen. William S. Rosecrans to Maj. Gen. Ambrose E. Burnside, August 19, 1863; Maj. Gen. William S. Rosecrans to Col. John C. Kelton, August 21, 1863, 11:15 A.M., OR, Ser. I, vol. 30, pt. 3, 32–3, 80–1, 98–9; Joseph Jones to Nancy Jones, August 31, 1863, Joseph Jones Letters, GLC 2739, GLCML. For Sherman's preparations for the Atlanta campaign, see Maj. Gen. William T. Sherman to Maj. Gen. Jonathan A. Logan, December 21, 1863, OR, Ser. I, vol. 31, pt. 3, 459; Maj. Gen. William T. Sherman to Maj. Gen. Nathaniel P. Banks, January 16, 1864, OR, Ser. I, vol. 32, pt. 2, 113–5; Maj. Gen. William T. Sherman to Maj. Gen. Stephen A. Hurlbut, March 14, 1864; Maj. Gen. William T. Sherman to Maj. Gen. James B. McPherson, April 24, 1864; Maj. Gen. James B. McPherson to Maj. Gen. Jonathan A. Logan, April 28, 1864; Brig. Gen. Grenville M. Dodge to Brig. Gen. T. W. Sweeny, April 28, 1864, 6 P.M.; Maj. Gen. William T. Sherman to Maj. Gen. James B. McPherson, April 29, 1864; all in OR, Ser. I, vol. 32, pt. 3, 70–1, 479, 524, 525, 534.

against Confederate General John B. Hood's counteroffensive following Sherman's defeat of Atlanta. Federal forces returned once and for all after Hood's defeat at Nashville and subsequent withdrawal south of the Tennessee River in late December 1864. From this point until the end of the war, the Union army remained in control of the counties north and west of the Tennessee.[17]

In southern Alabama, the situation was quite different. Union forces did not actually occupy this part of the state until the final days of war. Nonetheless, Federal forces in control of West Florida began to press Alabama's southeastern border at about the same time Union troops occupied northern Alabama in 1862. Consequently, border counties of Alabama's Wiregrass and Coastal Plain subregions experienced sporadic military action throughout the remainder of the war. Here, the Union army's objectives developed as part of a larger plan to starve the Confederacy into submission through the Federal naval blockade of the Gulf of Mexico.[18] In particular, Union infantry and cavalry stationed in West Florida attempted to undermine, thwart, and destroy Alabama's ability to produce one essential substance: salt.[19] Necessary for the preservation, and thus the storage and transportation, of meat, salt had become increasingly rare in many parts of the South by 1862, largely as a result of the naval blockade. Before the war, almost all of the South's domestic salt was produced in Virginia, Kentucky, Florida, and Texas. But this domestic production represented less than half of the total consumed in the Southern states. The balance of the region's salt supply, 3.3 million bushels, was imported through New Orleans.[20] After the Union blockade cut off regular shipments of the vital preservative, various Southern states began to mine salt independently. Alabama, for example, relied on the relatively meager yields from salt works in Clarke and Washington Counties, just north of Mobile, and the determined efforts of individual

17. McMillan, *Alabama Confederate Reader*, 139–40.

18. For the Union blockade of the Gulf Coast, see Bern Anderson, *By Sea and by River: The Naval History of the Civil War* (New York: Knopf, 1962); James M. Merrill, *The Rebel Shore: The Story of Union Sea Power in the Civil War* (Boston: Little, Brown, 1957).

19. Ella Lonn, *Salt as a Factor in the Confederacy* (New York: Walter Neale, 1933), 13–5, 31–2, 221–30. Lonn's study is the classic treatment of this subject. George E. Buker, *Blockaders, Refugees, and Contrabands: Civil War on Florida's Gulf Coast, 1861–1865* (Tuscaloosa: University of Alabama Press, 1993) updates this issue in the context of Alabama's struggle; see especially 46–7.

20. Buker, *Blockaders, Refugees, and Contrabands*, 47; for a detailed treatment of the salt war on the Gulf Coast, see chap. 5.

citizens to supplement salt supplies.[21] As one Confederate citizen of Eufaula remembered, no measure was considered too great to get salt. "In some cases the salty soil under old smokehouses was dug up and placed in hoppers," she recalled. "Water was then poured upon the soil, the brine which percolated through the hopper was boiled down to the proper point, poured into vessels, and set in the sun, which by evaporation completed the rude process."[22] Under these circumstances, the mineral became so rare that Governor Shorter believed Alabama to be in real danger of salt famine. Should soldiers' families begin to starve for want of salt, the governor (like other officials throughout the Confederacy) feared that large-scale desertion of Alabama troops would result. Union forces occupying Pensacola, Florida, well understood the importance of the salt works in southern Alabama to maintaining the civilian and military population. Desirous of undermining Confederate abilities to supply the new nation's wants, Federal raiders conducted frequent invasions to disrupt production, terrorizing those making salt and stealing what reserves had been established.[23]

Union occupation thus fostered a range of transformation on the Southern home front. In North Alabama, garrisoned towns like Huntsville, Athens, Stevenson, Decatur, and Bridgeport were very well defended, for they were situated at critical railroad junctures and river ports. Here, as historian Stephen Ash has explained, "citizens lived constantly in the presence, and under the thumb, of the Northern army." Directly outside the garrisoned towns, in an area Ash has termed "no-man's-land," matters were less clear-cut. Here, Union troops stood picket and regularly foraged for stock and provisions, but they did not exercise control sufficient to prevent incursions by rebel cavalry. In North Alabama, the Tennessee River itself was a no-man's-land, representing both barrier and conduit for whichever side could control a par-

21. Sherry Harris, ed., *1862 Alabama Salt List* (Granada Hills, Calif: Harris Press, 1993). See also Gov. J. Gill Shorter to Prof. J. Darby, May 15, 1862; Alfred Turner to Gov. J. Gill Shorter, August 27, 1862; both in AGP: John Gill Shorter, 1861–63; and Gov. John Gill Shorter to Secretary of War G. W. Randolph, September 22, 1862, and to Messrs L. F. Johnson and Co., September 22, 1862, Governors' Unprocessed Administrative Records (Shorter, 1861–63), ADAH.

22. Parthenia Hague, "A Blockaded Family . . . in South Alabama during the Civil War, 1888," quoted in McMillan, *Alabama Confederate Reader*, 371.

23. Gov. John Gill Shorter to Messrs. L. F. Johnson and Co., September 22, 1862, and to Secretary of War G. W. Randolph, September 22, 1862, Governors' Unprocessed Administrative Records (Shorter, 1861–63), ADAH.

ticular port or fording place. Beyond this point, most of Alabama represented what Ash calls "the Confederate frontier," or what is commonly understood as "behind the lines." Here, with the exception of sporadic Federal forays, Alabama remained firmly in Confederate control.[24]

These divisions help to illustrate the consequences of Union occupation for the Southern landscape. However, conditions in Alabama were far more changeable than a map of occupation zones might seem to suggest. As Ash himself notes, any given area might be transformed rapidly by events, for "in the ebb and flow of military campaigns some captured districts were at one time or another temporarily relinquished by the Union army, and what was a garrisoned town or no-man's-land one day might be Confederate frontier."[25] In North Alabama, the fluidity and unpredictability of Federal occupation was compounded by continual patrolling of the Tennessee River by cavalry from both armies. Immediately following the Union invasion of 1862, Alabama dispatched newly created partisan cavalry units to the northern counties. Ordered by Governor Shorter to "hang upon the Enemy's border, and secure the homes and property of our people against depredation," partisan rangers were a highly mobile and volatile presence who frequently raided no-man's-land.[26] Likewise, Federal troops regularly challenged Confederate defenses along the river and, despite the risks of running into "armed men" sent "to dispute the right to reconnoiter," sporadically visited or temporarily occupied towns south of the river, like Chickasaw or Tuscumbia in Franklin County, and Moulton in Lawrence County.[27] Throughout occupied Alabama, the status of neighborhoods or roads could change so rapidly as to make most civilians quite unsure from moment to moment which army commander, or group of guerrilla cavalry, controlled what. Instability was thus a constant feature of life in and adjacent to the occupied zone.

Crossing the Lines

One boon of the occupation of North Alabama and West Florida was that it made unionists mobile again. Drafted loyalists had been confined to

24. Ash, *When the Yankees Came*, 77.

25. Ibid.

26. John Gill Shorter Proclamation, April 24, 1862, AGP: John Gill Shorter, 1861–63.

27. Daniel Lovejoy, *Adventures of a Varied Career* (Chicago: n.p., 1894), 138. Lovejoy was a member of the Thirteenth Wisconsin Volunteer Infantry.

hiding places, moving only on the best assurance of safety and to find another secure refuge. Their families, as well, had found themselves increasingly circumscribed by the hostility of neighbors and conscript cavalry. The Federal presence held out the promise of escape to these individuals. For men, the chance to enroll in, or get a job with, the Union army lay in the safety of a Federal camp or garrisoned town.[28] For their families, the camps held the promise of protection from the abuse of conscript cavalry, along with food and shelter.

Escaping one's neighborhood, however, required careful planning and calculation, and was not equally practicable for all unionists. Men who lived within or near Union garrisoned towns of North Alabama, such as Huntsville or Florence, found volunteering relatively easy. However, unionists who had to get to the lines from the Confederate frontier, as well as those living in no-man's-land, had to navigate a perilous stretch between home and the perimeter of Union camps or garrisoned towns.[29] Few young men, especially those without horses, relished the odds of striking out without assistance into land heavily patrolled by Confederate partisan rangers and regular cavalry.

As had been the case for unionists since the beginning of the war, success depended heavily upon collaborators. Resistance networks now became sources for the supplies, information, and contacts necessary for escape. Assistance could be as simple as monetary support. For instance, Hartwell Huskey, exempted as a schoolteacher, subsidized the trips of his drafted brother and eight other men. "I was poor but I spent over five hundred dollars in that way," he explained. John Perryman of Lauderdale County sent his son, Alexander, to the army with thirty dollars in his pocket, as well as a horse bridle and saddle. So outfitted, Alexander volunteered with the Sixth Tennessee Cavalry, U.S.A. Likewise, Matthias Firestone loaned silver to his half-brother and two other unionists to help them "reach the Federal lines." Sometimes, rather than loaning cash, Union people purchased property from men seeking to join the army. Alexander and James Greenway scrounged together enough specie to leave by selling their stock to fellow unionist Levin Clifton.[30]

28. Fisher, *War at Every Door*, 68.

29. Richard Nelson Current, *Lincoln's Loyalists: Union Soldiers from the Confederacy* (New York: Oxford University Press, 1992), 105, 107.

30. Claim 6501, Hartwell Huskey, Franklin Co., July 1, 1877; Claim 7543, John Perryman, Lauderdale Co., July 9, 1873; Claim 6815, Matthias Firestone, Cherokee Co., May 12, 1874; Claim 6785 (Rev.) Levin A. Clifton, Cherokee Co., November 18, 1874; all in SCC.

Money was key, but often more important was company. Setting off with a group felt safer than venturing forth alone. When Henry Rikard left his home in Franklin County, for instance, he did so with several cousins. After traveling thirty-five miles west to Iuka, Mississippi, the young men all volunteered together in Company F of the Sixty-fourth Illinois Volunteer Infantry. Similarly, twenty-eight Cherokee County loyalists "made an arrangement" to meet one night and set off together to the Federal lines at Rome, Georgia.[31] Another large group of unionists— "four companies" of them, according to a Union army informant— simply gathered together in the woods on the top of barren Sand Mountain in Jackson County in August 1863, "waiting the crossing" of the Army of the Cumberland "to join it." Rather than risk fighting Confederate cavalry guarding the Tennessee River, these men camped out to wait for the army to come to them. Others were confident or desperate enough to push through the lines despite the considerable danger. In October 1863, Major General Stephen A. Hurlbut, commanding headquarters at Memphis, enlisted some "120 recruits" from North Alabama, men who had "fought their way in handsomely." They arrived bearing an impressive offering of loyalty, too: ten rebel prisoners.[32]

Although some unionists banded together in sizable groups, circumstances dictated that others set off in two's and three's. Perhaps loyalist men could find no more than a companion to accompany them; others may have eschewed a crowd because they feared unwanted attention from citizens. At times, the small number of comrades was simply a consequence of the spontaneity of the escape. For example, after Silas Morphew made up his mind "to leave the Confederacy and go north," one of his friends, who was already harboring a relative on his way to the Union lines, told Morphew to come to his house, have supper with his kinsman, after which the two could leave together. With a friend acting as watchman, the two refugees left that night.[33]

Men traveling considerable distances relied even more heavily on sympathetic friends and networks of collaborators for help. For example,

31. Claim 5416, Henry F. Rikard, Franklin Co., October 18, 1875; Claim 6815, Matthias Firestone, Cherokee Co., May 12, 1874; both in SCC.

32. Col. E. M. McCook to Maj. James A. Garfield, Chief of Staff, August 26, 1863, *OR*, Ser. I, vol. 30, pt. 3, 179; and Maj. Gen. Stephen A. Hurlbut to Brig. Gen. John A. Rawlins, October 2, 1863, *OR*, Ser. I, vol. 30, pt. 4, 29.

33. Claim 21108, William W. Beard, Walker Co., October 28, 1873: Testimony of Silas Morphew, SCC.

John Bowman, who farmed forty acres of land alongside the "forks of Little River" in Cherokee County, kept a canoe ready at all times so that he "might set union men across that was going to the union lines." Unionists in Bowman's neighborhood quickly learned that he had set up a refugee ferry into Union territory. "[M]y union friends knew it and many came and were set over." Bowman sent not only neighbors and friends across the river, but also five sons, two of whom served in the Sixth Tennessee Mounted Infantry, U.S.A. On occasion, unionists were helped to the lines by slaves. Elijah Carr, for instance, ordered his slave Willis Carr to take Elijah's three sons across the Coosa River to Union encampments just inside the Georgia border, some fifteen miles east. Willis remembered, "We lay over along the river till evening when we found a canoe lodged against a tree top on the opposite side of the river." One of the boys swam across the river to get the boat, bring it back, and then take the others to the other side as Willis stood by and watched. "When I saw them safely over the river," he explained, "I made my way back home to master's in the night and reported to my master the successful trip of his sons."[34]

Unionist runaways also depended upon strangers who had established themselves as willing to assist refugees. Long-distance kin and business relationships frequently formed the basis of these elongated networks, which could stretch considerable distances. One such network, anchored in Chattanooga, Tennessee, likely aided numerous refugees from northeast Alabama. It extended north of Chattanooga through the Sequatchie Valley, and continued until ending at Possum Creek, Kentucky, traversing in total nearly three hundred miles.[35] As one soldier of the Fifty-first Indiana observed, these networks operated very much like "a sort of 'underground railroad' system by which the former runaway slaves made their escape from their brutal masters."[36] Unionists moved covertly from one safehouse (an identified unionist household or slave quarter) to another until they made it to the safety of a Union encampment or garrisoned town. The members of one escape network in Cleburne County

34. Claim 8188, John Bowman, Cherokee Co., July 3, 1875; Claim 7204, Melvin B. Carr, Cherokee Co. May 21, 1874: Testimony of Willis Carr; both in SCC.

35. John S. Daniel, Jr., "Special Warfare in Middle Tennessee and Surrounding Areas, 1861–1862," (M.A. thesis, University of Tennessee, 1971), 206.

36. William M. Hartpence, *History of the Fifty-First Indiana Veteran Volunteer Infantry: A Narrative of Its Organization, Marches, Battles and Other Experiences in Camp and Prison, from 1861 to 1866, with Revised Roster* (Cincinnati: Robert Clarke, 1894), 58–9.

maintained utter secrecy to protect one another and the network itself. "[I]t was the practice not to give names when calling for information . . . to screen the party upon whom [travelers] called." Because these men lived near the Georgia border, they provided important assistance not just to unionists, but to Northern prisoners escaping from Andersonville Prison as well. Directed to the next safe haven by the last, Southern unionists and Federal prisoners picked their way through the countryside to Union lines.[37]

Relying on long-distance connections, Ezekiel Bird of Monroe County in southern Alabama sent a number of unionists to join the "First Floridy" Federal regiment by way of his brother-in-law's home in Holmes County, Florida. "I got Tom McMillan and Dick McMillan of the neighborhood of Burnt Corn in this county to go, [as well as] Benjamin Martin, Jasper and Oliver Braxton, my brothers-in-law." With directions from Bird, the men located safe places to stay on their trek; when they arrived in Holmes County, they simply explained from whom they had been sent and why. Armed with a similar set of instructions, a small group of unionists in northwest Alabama arrived unannounced at the door of steamboat engineer and miller William Nance of Franklin County, asking for assistance crossing the lines. The wandering band of unionists had been sent to Nance by a man named James Potts, a member of Nance's network of trustworthy Union friends, whose farm lay some miles south of Nance's home. Nance hid the refugees for one day, and then took them across the Tennessee River to a Federal gunboat stationed at nearby Eastport, Mississippi, then occupied by Union forces. He did so at considerable risk to himself, for wartime rural communities were quick to note unfamiliar faces in their midst. In the climate of the home front, unfamiliarity bred fear and hostility. "I knew it was very hazardous to help them away," Nance acknowledged. "If they had been caught about me I would have had to suffer for it. These men were perfect strangers, and would have been picked up. I put myself out of the way to help them, because I sympathized with them."[38]

Women played significant roles in these networks, largely because they were numerous on the home front, but also because they had

37. Claim 783, Jacob Albright, Cleburne Co., October 5, 1875: Testimony of James M. Thrasher, SCC.

38. Claim 6756, Ezekiel Bird, Monroe Co., December 11, 1874; Claim 8262, William S. Nance, Franklin Co., September 3, 1874; both in SCC.

broader leeway for unrestricted travel. Unless known for sheltering wanted men, women were usually less likely to be stopped and arrested by conscript officers.[39] This was especially true of women who had no husbands hiding from the conscript cavalry. Margaret Shoe, for example, believed that her status as "a widow with some small children" meant that Confederates "did not care much" about her, which made it easier for her to aid and abet her draft-dodging brother and brother-in-law.[40] A soldier of the Fifty-first Indiana was astounded to see coming into his camp near Decatur one morning "a company of about twenty men . . . preceded by a woman."[41] The woman was "old Mrs. Campbell," who had crossed Confederate lines to find her husband and son, who had fled from the conscript cavalry to the mountains.[42] Fifty-five years old, and mounted on "a poor old horse," she had made a seventy-mile round trip in thirty hours to bring them safely to the Federal camps, all the while "hunting for other friends, and cooking their breakfast." The group was "received with cheers of delight" and Mrs. Campbell's story left "few dry eyes in that camp."[43]

Similarly Rachel Cole, a divorced woman farmer in DeKalb County, established herself as a trustworthy member of a long-distance network in northeastern Alabama. When a man named William Key, whom Cole had known for many years, came to her house for protection and aid crossing the lines, she and Key sought help from other unionists in the area. "Key and myself thought James R. Dorsey, that we knew to be a union man, could help us get his family through and I went and got Dorsey to come to my house to meet Key and we in connexion with Mr. Dorsey devised means to get Key's family and himself to the Union lines." Dorsey had established a fairly elaborate system by which he concealed unionists south of the Tennessee River until they could cross the lines. After Cole allied with Dorsey, she became a full-fledged member of his network. As Dorsey recalled, "I . . . made an arrangement with her that when I sent a union man to her who was trying to get through the rebel lines and he gave her a certain sign she should give him proper directions, or conceal him till he could go on." Cole faced considerable

39. Fisher, War at Every Door, 72.

40. Claim 5399, Jesse F. Cranford, Cherokee Co., September 7, 1875: Testimony of Margaret Shoe, SCC.

41. Hartpence, History of the Fifty-First Indiana, 60.

42. Report of Col. Abel D. Streight, July 16, 1862, OR, Ser. I, vol. 16, pt. 1, 789.

43. Hartpence, History of the Fifty-First Indiana, 60.

verbal abuse and threats, but was never arrested or physically abused. Prevailing gender conventions toward single or widowed women likely gave Cole greater latitude than that enjoyed by men, or even that enjoyed by women whose husbands were lie-outs or in the Federal army. Although she was not "molested," her partner in crime, Dorsey, ended up having to flee Cherokee County altogether because his activities had made him the target of violence.[44]

Crossing the lines was just the first step to greater security for Union men. Once in Federal territory, those of fighting age usually enlisted with any of a number of regiments, depending on where they crossed. Over the course of the war, more than 2,500 whites and at least 4,969 blacks successfully volunteered their services in the Union army. In its white enlistments, Alabama fell far behind the volunteer levels in the upper South, where more unionists lived and Union army presence was more extensive. Historian Richard Current has estimated that Tennessee sent approximately 42,000 white men to the Federal ranks; Virginia and West Virginia about 30,000; Arkansas somewhere around 10,000; North Carolina about 5,000. But after Louisiana and its approximately 6,500 recruits, Alabama appears to have outstripped volunteering elsewhere in the Deep South. While Texas sent at least 2,220 white men, Current has estimated that combined white enlistments from Florida, Mississippi, and Georgia probably equaled less than 2,500 recruits.[45]

The regiment a unionist joined depended largely upon luck and timing. A white man escaping northern Alabama between 1862 and 1865 could have encountered soldiers hailing from Indiana, Illinois, Michigan, Wisconsin, Ohio, and Pennsylvania, and belonging to the Army of the Cumberland, the Army of the Ohio, and the Army of the Tennessee. During the early months of the 1862 occupation, the Federal army put unionist volunteers into whatever regiments were available, believing it too "difficult for them to organize companies and regiments of their own" because they fell so far out of the normal recruiting and organizational structure of the army. As Colonel James B. Fry explained to Colonel

44. Claim 18376, Rachel R. Cole, DeKalb Co., December 15, 1876; and Claim 18376, Rachel R. Cole, DeKalb Co., December 15, 1876: Testimony of James R. Dorsey; both in SCC.

45. Current, *Lincoln's Loyalists*, 106, 215–7; Ira Berlin, Joseph P. Reidy, and Leslie S. Rowland, eds., *Freedom's Soldiers: The Black Military Experience in the Civil War* (New York: Cambridge University Press, 1998), 17. The experience of African American soldiers will be treated in detail later in this chapter.

A. D. Streight, such men faced the problem of having "no Governor to aid them, no clothing, arms or equipments . . . and no officers to assist them." Moreover, Fry noted, by joining the regiments at hand, the recruits would begin to receive pay immediately.[46] For this reason, many of the regiments participating in the initial occupation of Alabama mustered at least a few (and in the case of the Fifty-first Indiana, some 400) unionists into their ranks.

By late 1862, however, the Union army had managed to systematize the enlistment of loyal Alabamians by creating regiments composed mostly of Southern soldiers.[47] Perhaps the most well known of these was the First Alabama Cavalry, U.S.A.[48] Brigadier General Grenville M. Dodge began recruiting the First Alabama from his garrison at Corinth, Mississippi, in late 1862; his first efforts garnered over one thousand Southern enlistees, most from Alabama.[49] By design, the regiment performed the bulk of its duty in northern Alabama, western Tennessee, and northeastern Mississippi, though it later marched with Sherman to Savannah in 1864.[50] Over the course of the war, the First Alabama experienced numerous organizational shifts, but it always maintained its identity as a regiment of loyal Southern men.

Another important loyalist regiment was the First Tennessee & Alabama Independent Vidette Cavalry, organized at Stevenson and Bridgeport, Jackson County, Alabama, in late August 1863; it later augmented its ranks at Tracey City and Nashville, Tennessee.[51] The regiment formed around a nucleus of self-constituted unionist partisans under the command of a Jackson County man named Ephraim Latham, who came

46. Col. James B. Fry to Col. A. D. Streight, July 10, 1862, *OR*, Ser. I, vol. 16, pt. 2, 118. Also see the Secretary of War's authorization to recruit loyal Alabamians in Edwin M. Stanton to Maj. Gen. Don Carlos Buell, July 21, 1862, *OR*, Ser. I, vol. 16, pt. 2, 193.

47. Current, *Lincoln's Loyalists*, 217.

48. The classic regimental history of the First Alabama is Hoole, *Alabama Tories*.

49. Current, *Lincoln's Loyalists*, 105.

50. Hoole, *Alabama Tories*, 23–5.

51. Marcus J. Wright, *Tennessee in the War* (Williamsbridge, N.Y.: A. Lee, 1908), 164–5; Johnny L. T. N. Potter, *First Tennessee and Alabama Independent Vidette Cavalry, 1863–1864: Roster, Companies "A," "B," "C," "D," "E," "F," "G," "H"* (Chattanooga: Mountain Press, 1995); First Tennessee Independent Vidette Cavalry, Civil War Soldiers and Sailors Database: http://www.civilwar.nps.gov/cwss/template.cfm?unitcode = UTN0001RC03&unitna me; eq1st%20Regiment%2C%20Tennessee%20Independent%20Vidette%20Cavalry; last accessed April 25, 2002. Official Union army records refer to this regiment simply as the First Tennessee Independent Vidette Cavalry.

across the Federal lines at the Tennessee River town of Larkinsville. Colonel Edward M. McCook, commanding the Second Brigade of the Army of the Cumberland's Cavalry Corps, reported from Larkinsville on August 26, 1863, that "Seventy-six partisans of Mr. Latham's company [are] waiting here to be mustered in."[52] Ephraim Latham himself later testified to the SCC that he began service as captain of Company A in the Vidette Cavalry on August 28, 1863.[53] By early September, the cavalry had reported to the commanding officer at Stevenson, who was directed "to furnish the company with arms" and horses; the men were then posted "in the vicinity of Larkinsville and along the line of the Stevenson and Huntsville railroad."[54]

These Southern cavalry regiments had two main objectives, both of which allowed them to remain near home while they fought. First, loyal Southern regiments supported the counterguerrilla operations of the Union army, scouting enemy movements and skirmishing with regular Confederate cavalry and irregular rebel guerrillas (subjects examined in greater detail in chapter 4). Second, unionist regiments used their familiarity with the social and physical geography of the home front to locate, rescue, and recruit beleaguered unionists still behind Confederate lines. Because the soldiers who made up regiments like the First Alabama were intimate with area unionists, they were perfectly suited for surreptitious recruiting missions. Many who joined the First Alabama did so via connections between already enlisted Alabamians and their kin and friends still on the home front. Burrell Earnest of Walker County organized "several squads of union men" from northwest Alabama and piloted them to First Alabama soldier "J. F. Files and other scouts who were recruiting for the Union Army from this part of the country." Files, a Walker County farmer who left home in September 1863, had traveled at least sixty miles to cross the lines at Glendale, Mississippi. By December 13, 1863, he had returned home to recruit fifty new soldiers for the First

52. Col. E. M. McCook to Maj. William H. Sinclair, August 26, 1863, *OR*, Ser. I, vol. 30, pt. 3, 179.

53. Claim 2657, Perry L. Harrison, Madison Co., October 3, 1871: Testimony of Ephraim Latham, SCC. Latham's testimony about his enlistment and rank is confirmed by his service record at the National Archives, available online at the Civil War Soldiers and Sailors Database: http://www.civilwar.nps.gov/cwss/PersonzDetail.cfm?PERNBR=1262536; last accessed April 25, 2002.

54. Brig. Gen. James A. Garfield, Chief of Staff, to Brig. Gen. King, September 4, 1863, 1:15 P.M., *OR*, Ser. I, vol. 30, pt. 3, 343.

Alabama. Files undertook similar missions on at least two subsequent occasions, always relying on the help of men like Burrell Earnest to alert potential recruits and arrange rendezvous places.[55]

Alabamians in the southern half of the state followed a similar pattern of enlistment. Fleeing south toward Federally occupied Forts Pickens or Barancas, these men most often joined the First Florida Cavalry, U.S.A. Composed largely of loyal Floridians, the regiment also recruited Alabama enlistments. Eighteen-year-old Alabama recruit Wade Richardson remarked that the rank and file of the regiment "were a motley crew of as dare-devil fellows as can be collected at any seaport town, I guess. Among them were Spaniards, French creoles, half-breed Indians, Germans, a few Poles and a host of crackers and gophers—the western Floridians were derisively called gophers." These Southerners did not always find Union commanders enthusiastic to accept them. Richardson was especially struck by the slowness with which he and other Southerners were inducted. "Nearly the whole summer was spent in drill as infantry with arms borrowed for the occasion. . . . We often surmised that the reason we were not armed was that our officers were suspicious of our loyalty." Richardson concluded that his superior officers eventually gained full confidence in the Alabamians' patriotism and abilities, but the men had to earn that trust.[56]

Once allowed to fight, Richardson's "motley crew" engaged in warfare primarily along the Alabama-Florida border, a mission for which most were especially eager and qualified to undertake. "From our ranks volunteers would step forth at any moment to conduct an expedition, however perilous, through any of the border country. Every road, I had almost said every cowtrail of southern Alabama and Florida, was known to some of our men."[57] Like the First Alabama Cavalry, these unionist enlistees scouted Confederate territory, piloted Northern commanders through the region, and encouraged frightened unionist lie-outs to flee. According to Richardson, by January 1864, "there were several hundred men in hiding in southern Alabama and Florida, and squads of our recruits were passed through the lines to assist these men to our camp."

55. Claim 6092, Burrell Earnest, Walker Co., February 6, 1873; Claim 11631, Jeremiah F. Files, Fayette Co., January 30, 1873; both in SCC.

56. Wade H. Richardson, *How I Reached the Union Lines,* 2d ed. (Milwaukee: Meyer-Rotier Print Co., 1905), 25, 26.

57. Quote ibid., 25–6; Current, *Lincoln's Loyalists,* 107–9; see Buker, *Blockaders, Refugees, and Contrabands* for more on the Second Florida Cavalry, U.S.A.

Within two months, Union recruiters had ferried enough men into Federal camps in Florida to form five companies, most of whom were mustered into the army.[58]

In the wake of such enlistments by Union men, their wives, like all Southern women whose husbands left home, frequently struggled to manage home front affairs. Nonslaveholding women faced difficulty planting and tending crops, taking care of livestock, and watching over family affairs previously the purview of men. Elizabeth Cranford of Cherokee County, for instance, resorted to her own labor and that of her children (all between the ages of four and fourteen in 1864, the oldest boy being only eight) to raise and harvest a corn crop "of some eighteen or twenty acres" after her husband left. She did so with horses borrowed from friends because Confederate soldiers had taken her mare shortly after her husband left. Catharine Bowen of Walker County began "working on the farm to make a support for her family" when her husband fled to the woods to lie out; once "she gave him up to go to the Union Army," she continued to do so, apparently with only her young children's help.[59]

Confederate women faced similar circumstances, to be sure. However, unionist women's difficulties were exacerbated by their isolation from the broader community. Confederate neighbors and the state deliberately made it difficult for these women to survive unassisted. Unlike wives of rebel soldiers, for instance, the wives of Federal enlistees were not eligible to receive state-allotted rations.[60] In the absence of government assistance, though, local charity readily available to Confederate spouses (including the wives of conscripted men) rarely found its way to the doors of "tory" women. Many could only rely on the help of the small number of unionists in their neighborhood. William B. Irwin, a wealthy physician and planter of Lawrence County, took his paternalistic duty to such women seriously, at one point bringing wagons to his "crib" and loading them with corn for "the families of men who had left home and

58. Richardson, *How I Reached the Union Lines*, 24–5.

59. Claim 5399, Jesse F. Cranford, Cherokee Co., September 7, 1875: Testimony of Elizabeth Cranford; Claim 3352, Catharine Bowen, Walker Co., January 13, 1873: Testimony of Cumberland Conaway, and Testimony of George W. Phillips; all in SCC.

60. "An act [of the Alabama State Legislature] to provide a fund for the aid of indigent families of Volunteers absent in the Army," November 11, 1861, and "An act [of the Alabama State Legislature] to provide for the support of Indigent Families of soldiers in the Army of the Confederate States," November 12, 1862, Folder 18, Clyde E. Wilson, Summary of Carlotta P. Mitchell WPA Study #1584, Civil War and Reconstruction Files, SG 17131, ADAH.

gone through the lines, leaving their families in a destitute condition." As his friend John Blalock explained, "[H]e was sending them this corn without measure, money or price." The total amount came to some thirty wagonloads. Less wealthy individuals were likewise known to share "their last morsel" with "union soldiers and their wives and children." Thomas Sawyer of Blount County, a farmer and miller exempted from Confederate service as a "crippled man," repeatedly fed the "wives and children of men who was in the Union Army," despite being arrested and threatened with hanging. After each confrontation, he promised to stop supporting the soldiers' families, but immediately went back to his mission. "I fed them all the time as I had done before."[61]

Even when unionist women could get corn, they still faced the substantial obstacle of how to mill it, because many of them were refused by neighborhood millers. Exempted unionist millers could be found, but they were often few and far between. Louisa Sparks, for instance, knew of no friendly millers in her community, so turned to a stranger, loyalist Calvin Dillard. She came to him one day in 1863, asking for help making her cornmeal. "As a means of obtaining the service," Dillard remembered, "she told me her husband had gone as a soldier into the union army—that she was destitute of provisions, and was dependent upon union people for supplies." In similar fashion, Union women of Walker County learned they had an ally in William Keeton, who was the only local miller who "would venture" to grind meal "for the wives of men who were gone to the Union army," despite nearly having his mill burned by local Confederates as a consequence. To help Keeton maintain as low a profile as possible, the women began carrying their corn to him "in sacks with rebel brands on them to keep him . . . from being hung."[62]

Unionist women's struggles extended beyond experiencing instances of community ostracism. Because Alabama's Union soldiers, especially those in the First Alabama, maintained communication with unionist civilians, Confederate authorities were highly suspicious of soldiers' kin and friends, especially their wives, for the intelligence they might transmit to enlisted men acting as scouts and spies for the Union army. Fre-

61. Claim 1369, William B. Irwin, Lawrence Co., April 13, 1872: Testimony of John C. Blalock; Claim 6514, Samuel Studdard, Fayette Co., February 23, 1872: Testimony of J.V. Tirey; Claim 3362, Thomas Sawyer, Blount Co., December 19, 1873; all in SCC.

62. Claim 20139, Louisa E. Sparks, Franklin Co., November 17, 1875; Claim 2066, William Keeton, Walker Co., December 29, 1871; Claim 2066, William Keeton, Walker Co., December 29, 1871: Testimony of Phillip P. Pike; all in SCC.

quently, these officials found it pointless, if not counterproductive, to make distinctions between actual agents of the Union army and their networks of supporters on the home front. Confederate officials thus employed severe measures to cut Federal connections to the home front by forcing the kin of unionists to leave Confederate territory altogether, usually by carrying out a campaign of punitive foraging and theft, along with verbal and physical violence. Unionist women experienced some of the most devastating effects of such efforts. When George Ridge of Jackson County escaped to the Federal lines, for instance, his wife was immediately visited by furious local soldiers who threw her spinning "wheel, dresser, dishes all in the yard as far as they could throw them," and yelled at her "that her god dam'd Yankee husband had escaped from their prison and had gone to the Yanks." Another farm wife, left at home in Cherokee County with small children after her husband fled to the Union army (chased the whole way by a pack of slave hounds), turned to an elderly couple for support, but they could offer little but sympathy. As their friend remembered, "The rebel scouts and bushwhackers plundered . . . [their] five or six little children of all they had—even taking their clothes and what cloth she had made—because her husband had gone to the Yankees. This poor family was shamefully treated."[63]

Pressures like these frequently had their desired effect, forcing women and children to flee to the lines for safety. Indeed, only severe threats compelled John Nesmith to stop harboring his daughter and grandchildren, left in his care when his son-in-law enlisted. Confederate cavalry arrived at Nesmith's house and ordered him to remove his daughter, "Mrs. Benjamin," from the family home by the following morning or have his place torched. Faced with the total destruction of his home, Nesmith acquiesced. "I carried [my daughter] across the lines and left her and her children within the Federal lines." Likewise, the wife and children of First Alabama Cavalry scout Jeremiah Files made "their way as best they could to the union lines" after Confederates took "all they had to subsist on." That the family "was totally broken up by the rebels" was really no surprise—Files later claimed to have "influenced about five hundred men to go into the [Union] army."[64]

63. Claim 20468, George W. Ridge, Jackson Co., November 22, 1875; Claim 8779, Mariah L. Howard, Cherokee Co., December 18, 1874; both in SCC.

64. Claim 12986, John N. Nesmith, Blount Co., October 31, 1873; Claim 11631, Jeremiah F. Files, Fayette Co., January 30, 1873; both in SCC.

Like their men, women refugees looked to networks of friends, slaves, and the Federal army itself, to make their escape. Thomas Carroll of Winston County, for instance, took through the lines at Decatur "about 60 women and children" who had been "broken up by the Rebbs." Similarly, when a number of Union soldiers' families grew desperate to escape the persecutions of Confederate cavalry in Franklin County, William "Buck" Rikard (who had two sons in the Union army) and his brother-in-law, Pleasant Taylor, conveyed four harassed families of Union army volunteers thirty-five miles west to Iuka, where they crossed the lines. The wife of an Alabama surgeon who had joined the Union ranks relied on a neighborhood slave, Woodson Armistead, to help her join her husband because "she could not get any white man to convey her." Finally, Elizabeth Wright was continually harried by rebel soldiers after her husband joined the Federals at Bridgeport, Jackson County. "[They] would come to my house and would take anything I had and rob me, taking my bed clothing and children's clothing." After repeated instances of robbery and death threats from Confederate soldiers and citizens—including a tenant farmer living on Wright's 960-acre plantation—she fled with her children to the Tennessee River, where they were rescued by Union soldiers.[65]

The numbers of fleeing refugees at times staggered the army. A private belonging to the Sixth Wisconsin Artillery Battery noted in the fall of 1863 that some thirteen hundred white refugees had gathered around the headquarters of the First Alabama at Glendale, Mississippi, on Alabama's northwestern border. "Anticipating the presence of an army, they are leaving bag and baggage, trusting to the tender mercies of Uncle Sam."[66] These people posed wide-ranging problems for the Federal army, for the presence of large numbers of men, women, and children in military camps exacerbated demands on scarce resources, limited the mobility of soldiers, and reinforced men's desire to stay close to camp. And though male refugees represented prospective soldiers or laborers, elderly, female, and child refugees seemed like dead weight. William Holbrook of Vermont, for example, called the white refugees gathering at Pensacola, Florida, "an ignorant, lazy and worthless lot" who "formed

65. Claim 2180, Thomas Carroll, Winston Co., June 29, 1876; Claim 2670, Pleasant Taylor, Franklin Co., February 25, 1873; Claim 3957, Woodson Armistead, Lauderdale Co., August 10, 1871; Claim 7555, Elizabeth A. Wright, Marshall Co., February 19, 1874; all in SCC.
66. Jenkin Lloyd Jones, *An Artilleryman's Diary* (n.p.: Wisconsin History Commission, 1914), 106.

quite a large camp," and noted that "it became something of a problem to decide what to do with them."[67] A soldier of the Eleventh Indiana Cavalry stationed at Larkinsville, Alabama, described the women in his camp as living in "little shanties about like chicken coops" and drawing "ther rations from the government" just like soldiers.[68] By January 1864, the numbers of white refugees at Camp Davies in Corinth had become a matter of great concern to commanding officer Brigadier General Jonathan D. Stevenson. "I have at least 600 wives and children of Federal soldiers that require to be cared for," he complained when ordered to move his troops north and abandon the post. In the end, he simply moved the white families, along with an equally large number of freedpeople—"an immense train of refugees"—to Memphis, to be cared for by Federal authorities.[69]

The army quickly developed policies governing the duties and behavior of male refugees. Only by working or shouldering a gun could a unionist adequately demonstrate his loyalty and thereby guarantee himself Union army protection.[70] Because the army needed any labor it could get, it sometimes preferred to use a unionist for his skills rather than as a private. Most unionists were more than happy to exchange labor for safety. Numbers of "good Union men" worked to "keep the cars in motion" for General O. M. Mitchel in the spring of 1862.[71] Likewise, carpenter and lumber supplier Levi Snow helped occupying forces at Bridgeport repair Jackson County's railroad. His lumber and skills were handy for constructing soldiers' winter quarters, too. After Memory C. Reynolds fled from his home in Cherokee County to Rome, Georgia, the quartermaster assigned him to work at the hospital. Oysterman Elisha Nelson was hired by the army within three days of his arrival at Fort Morgan, just off the Alabama Gulf Coast. There he remained for nine months,

67. William C. Holbrook, *A Narrative of the Services of the Officers and Enlisted Men of the 7th Regiment of Vermont Volunteers (Veterans) from 1862 to 1866* (New York: American Bank Note Co., 1883), 137.

68. Joseph Airhart to Stephen Emmert, June 30, 1864, Stephen Emmert Letters, F80, IHS.

69. Brig. Gen. Jonathan D. Stevenson to Maj. Gen. Hurlbut, January 12, 1864, 9:10 P.M., and January 23, 1864, *OR*, Ser. I, vol. 32, pt. 2, 76, 191.

70. Grimsley, *Hard Hand*, 113.

71. Brig. Gen. O. M. Mitchel to Hon. Edwin M. Stanton, May 6, 1862, *OR*, Ser. I, vol. 10, pt. 2, 174.

"part of the time building at the barracks at Fort Morgan and part of the time oystering and fishing for the soldiers."[72]

Federal encampments represented only a temporary haven for men and women who ended up moving to the North. As historian Stephen Ash has demonstrated, the Federal army willingly put men to work, but in certain cases did not have enough work to go around. In such circumstances, Northern missionary societies and the Federal army transported refugees to towns and cities where jobs were more plentiful. Thomas Spencer, a farmer from Franklin County, moved in 1863 to Brooklyn, Illinois, where he ran steamboats and maintained a wood yard, from which government steamboats purchased fuel. Hartwell Huskey, also of Franklin County, was likewise able to move to the rural county of Spencer in southern Indiana, where he farmed for a living until the war was over, at which point he returned to Alabama. Pleasant Woodall of Marshall County fled the rebel conscript cavalry in December 1863 and moved to Illinois, where he farmed and "worked some as a hireling." Planter Henry R. Beaver refugeed with his two sons, both of conscriptable age, to Rockport, Indiana, in February 1862. One of the sons joined a Kentucky mounted infantry regiment and another joined up with the Rockport home guard.[73] For refugees like these, the only promise of returning home again lay with Union victory.

Escaping Slavery

White unionists were, of course, not the only people "liberated" by the arrival of Federal forces on Alabama's home front. For slaves, "crossing the lines" meant leaving slavery as well as the Confederacy behind; it meant the opportunity to establish a means of self-defense against bondage. Some joined the army; others labored for a wage or traded in goods and services in Federal camps. In various ways, such men and women prepared for future independence. Ultimately, black Alabamians used

72. Claim 11505, Levi Snow, Jackson Co., March 1, 1878; Claim 8090, Memory C. Reynolds, Cherokee Co., November 23, 1874; 3787C, Elisha Nelson, Baldwin Co., March 7, 1878; all in SCC.

73. Claim 17359, Thomas Spencer, Colbert Co., February 22, 1878; Claim 6501, Hartwell Huskey, Colbert Co., July 1, 1877; Claim 5841, Presley Woodall Estate, Jackson Co., October 14, 1874: Testimony of Pleasant S. Woodall; Claim 21109, Mary Beaver, Jackson Co., August 21, 1873; all in SCC.

the Union army's proximity to reshape what the war itself meant and what kind of Union would be established at the end of it. The pressures they put upon Union commanders through their flight from slavery, combined with the Union army's move toward military tactics designed to destroy the Confederacy's ability to sustain itself, brought Northern forces into collaboration with slaves' own designs for freedom.[74]

Historian Mark Grimsley has persuasively argued that emancipation was the "touchstone of hard war," and signaled a critical shift in the Union's conciliatory policies toward Southern slaveholders. From the beginning, however, the Union policy of respecting slaveowners' rights to their slave property faced difficult challenges, not the least of which came from slaves themselves.[75] As Grimsley has argued, the "army might not be interested in the slave, but the slave was fervently interested in the army." Commanders in the South, faced with thousands of runaways, grew increasingly restive over the government's demand that bondspeople fleeing to their lines be returned to disloyal owners. Benjamin Butler's May 1861 decision to confiscate rebel slave property as "contraband" was hugely important in this regard, for it seemed to many commanders and politicians to embody compelling logic: Why protect any resources— even slaves—used by the enemy to wage war? This pragmatic response to a growing problem was quickly transmuted into official policy through the passage of the First Confiscation Act in August 1861, which allowed for Federal appropriation of any slave found working in the service of the Confederacy—laboring to build breastworks or digging trenches, for example.[76]

In 1862, Congress moved closer to emancipation by passing the Militia Act, which authorized the recruitment and employment of blacks "for any military or naval service for which they may be found competent." The act led to some minor military organizing of slaves in the South, but most white commanders remained decidedly opposed to arming free or enslaved African Americans—they doubted black men's abilities and

---

74. Studies emphasizing slave agency in provoking changes in military and governmental policy toward emancipation include Litwack, *Been in the Storm So Long*; Fields, *Slavery and Freedom*; Ira Berlin et al., *Freedom*; for the confiscation of slave property by the Union army, see Grimsley, *Hard Hand*, 121–41.

75. Grimsley, *Hard Hand*, 123–4; Ash, *When the Yankees Came*, 150–4.

76. Grimsley, *Hard Hand*, 123.

courage and argued that they were not "competent" to serve as soldiers.[77] African Americans in Federally occupied North Alabama, like their counterparts elsewhere, however, pressed for the right to fight. In June 1862, some fifty Huntsville black men (whether free or slave remains unclear) organized their own military unit, armed themselves with Enfield rifles, and began to drill in public. They were quickly arrested by the Union provost marshal, much to the relief of local Confederate citizens.[78] Not until the Emancipation Proclamation took effect in January 1863 did the army begin to recruit both free and enslaved black men in a dedicated way.[79]

Regardless of the Union's ambivalence toward slaves and slavery, black men and women in Alabama certainly believed that they could only guarantee their freedom by escaping to the safety of a Union or contraband encampment within a garrisoned area. As historian Clarence Mohr noted in his study of black refugees escaping Confederate Georgia, "logistical factors," not Union policy, "were of central importance in determining the rate of black escapes." As in Georgia, liberty in Alabama depended largely on slaves' "physical opportunity to obtain it" by crossing the lines.[80] In North Alabama, the Tennessee Valley counties controlled by the army had significant slave populations. (See appendix 3, table A.1.) Freedom for these men and women came with the occupation and the chaos it created, as Benjamin Haynes of Madison County explained. "I come to be free after General Mitchell came in this country

77. Quoted ibid., 134, 135; Litwack, *Been in the Storm So Long*, 66–7, 98; Louis S. Gerteis, *From Contraband to Freedman: Federal Policy toward Southern Blacks, 1861–1865*, Contributions in American History, no. 29 (Westport, Conn.: Greenwood Press, 1973), 17–8.

78. June 10, 1862, Mary Jane Cook Chadick Diary, 1862–1865, DU.

79. Grimsley, *Hard Hand*, 134, 138. Many historians have addressed the history of black soldiers and their relations with the Federal army; the list is too long to name all but a few particularly noteworthy ones here: Benjamin Quarles, *The Negro in the Civil War* (Boston: Little, Brown, 1953); Dudley T. Cornish, *The Sable Arm: Negro Troops in the Union Army, 1861–1865* (1953; reprint, New York: Norton, 1966); Gerteis, *From Contraband to Freedman*; Mohr, *On the Threshold of Freedom*; Joseph T. Glatthaar, *Forged in Battle: The Civil War Alliance of Black Soldiers and White Officers* (New York: Free Press, 1990); Howard C. Westwood, *Black Troops, White Commanders, and Freedmen during the Civil War* (Carbondale: Southern Illinois University Press, 1992); James G. Hollandsworth, Jr., *The Louisiana Native Guards: The Black Military Experience during the Civil War* (Baton Rouge: Louisiana State University Press, 1995).

80. Mohr, *On the Threshold of Freedom*, 70–2.

with the Northern army." Or, in the words of Nancy Jones, "I got free after both set of soldiers had been in our country, but it was the Yankee soldiers who told us we was free."[81]

Slaves living in the Confederate frontier faced a very different set of challenges. Confederate cavalry stood between them and Union-occupied territory. As Moses Hampton, a free black preacher from Cherokee County, remembered, there "were small parties of rebel guerrilla bands hovering around the Union Army that were always ready to shoot a colored man that went about the Union Army." Despite the dangers, enslaved people, especially men, took the sizable risk of absconding from plantations and farms behind rebel lines. As Louisa Pinson of Cherokee County explained to the SCC, "Whenever any of the colored males could get a chance they would go through the lines to the union army."[82]

Whatever their means of escape, the sanctuary of Union-controlled areas offered African Americans a number of opportunities to support the North's war effort. Many men immediately attempted to join the army before 1863, but were refused. Once the Emancipation Proclamation opened the door to enlistment, these men insisted on being allowed to fight.[83] Eugene Marshall, a Union soldier stationed near Huntsville in late fall 1863, noted in his diary that when two black men arrived in his camp one night, they were first asked "if they wished to work." Their short answer was "that they did not come to work but to fight & wanted to enlist." Marshall's comrades sent the volunteers to a recruiting station, along with two hundred other men who came in to sign up over the course of the subsequent week.[84]

An influx of black soldiers into the Federal ranks was seen throughout the occupied South in the wake of emancipation. Recent estimates suggest that 179,000 black men served in the Union army and about 18,000 African Americans (including a very small number of women), served in the navy. The vast majority of these black enlistees came from slave states. Alabama contributed to this number some 4,969 African American soldiers, or 6 percent of the state's black male population aged

81. Claim 18674, Benjamin Haynes, Madison Co., May 14, 1875; Claim 2753, Nancy Jones, Madison Co., February 18, 1876; both in SCC.

82. Claim 14476, (Rev.) Moses Hampton, Cherokee Co., March 6, 1874; Claim 14487, Louisa Pinson, Cherokee Co., November 7, 1877: Testimony of Ellen Hampton; both in SCC.

83. Grimsley, *Hard Hand*, 138–9; Litwack, *Been in the Storm So Long*, 97.

84. November 11, 1863, Eugene Marshall Diary; and Eugene Marshall to Sister Olive, November 15, 1863, Correspondence, 1860–1863; both in Eugene Marshall Papers, DU.

eighteen to forty-five, and furnished at least five separate regiments of African American soldiers.[85] The earliest to be organized was the Third Regiment Alabama Volunteers, A.D. (African Descent), later redesignated the 111th U.S. Colored Infantry; it originated on January 13, 1863, and received volunteers until April 5, 1863. Soldiers mustered for three-year tours at various towns in southern Tennessee and at Sulpher Branch Trestle, Alabama. In May and June 1863, the First Regiment Alabama Volunteers, A.D. (Fifty-fifth U.S. Colored Troops) and the First Alabama Siege Artillery, A.D. (Sixth U.S. Colored Heavy Artillery) began mustering soldiers at Corinth, Mississippi, which also served as the First Alabama Cavalry's primary enlistment spot.[86] In November 1863, the Second Regiment Alabama Volunteers, A.D. (110th U.S. Colored Infantry), was organized next, also at Pulaski, Tennessee. And lastly, in the spring and summer of 1864, the Fourth Regiment Alabama Volunteers, A.D. (106th U.S. Colored Infantry) organized at Decatur, Alabama; it later merged with the Fortieth U.S. Colored Infantry.[87] Because they were primarily employed as garrison forces for towns or important bridges and fords along the Tennessee River, such African American soldiers were visible across the North Alabama home front.

Recruiters of African American soldiers stationed in Union garrisoned towns also made forays into no-man's-land, and even behind the lines, using "both persuasion and strong-arm methods" to canvass for enlistees.[88] In November 1863, for instance, Union soldier Eugene Marshall

85. Berlin et al., *Freedom's Soldiers,* 20–1; 17. Alabama's black Federal personnel was significantly smaller than that of Mississippi, which had 17,869, or Louisiana, which had 24,052; among Southern states, only Texas and Florida are credited with fewer black soldiers than Alabama. The disparity is largely explained by the proximity of Union troops to black Southerners—very little of Alabama's territory was occupied by Federal soldiers; moreover, the land lying between the occupied Tennessee valley and the Black Belt had very few slaves. To escape from the Black Belt in a northerly direction would have required traveling through a mountainous region heavily guarded by Confederates.

86. The First Alabama Siege Artillery, A.D., also enlisted men at Lagrange, Lafayette, and Memphis, Tennessee. Members of this regiment were among those stationed at Fort Pillow when Nathan Bedford Forrest's men captured and massacred hundreds of black soldiers garrisoning the fort in April 1864.

87. Frederick H. Dyer, *A Compendium of the War of the Rebellion,* 3 vols. (1908; reprint, New York: Thomas Yoseloff, 1959), 1:113; Charles Hubert, *History of the Fiftieth Illinois Volunteer Infantry in the War of the Rebellion* (Kansas: Western Veteran, 1894), 198.

88. Litwack, *Been in the Storm So Long,* 74; quote in John Hope Franklin, ed., *The Diary of James T. Ayers, Civil War Recruiter,* Occasional Publication (Springfield: Illinois State Historical Society, 1947), 5.

noted such a party leaving Madison Station in search of black recruits. The expedition was a success: one hundred black men enlisted. "They appear proud to be soldiers," Marshall commented.[89] Brigadier General Grenville Dodge authorized a recruiter to enlist slaves from the country-side around Athens, Alabama, in December 1863. "As soon as he gets a company," Dodge ordered, "send him up [to Pulaski] with them."[90] Throughout 1863, most such recruitment was done by white officers; however, some armies, most notably Benjamin Butler's Army of the James in Virginia, employed black troops as recruiters in Confederate territory.[91]

The matrix of factors involved in the recruitment of slaves by enlisted black soldiers can be understood more clearly by examining the experience of Richard Mosely. Before he joined the army, Mosely had been the slave of one of the two unionist planters in Lawrence County, situated south of the Tennessee River in Confederate territory. Shortly after the nearby town of Decatur was occupied in 1863, Mosely left his family and friends to journey the eleven miles east to the Union encampment. Despite the dangers, Mosely made it safely across the lines, where he enlisted in the army and was quickly assigned to return to Confederate territory to recruit other enslaved blacks from his neighborhood. For each new enlistee, Mosely was promised one dollar in payment.[92]

Even as he received his assignment, Mosely knew exactly where he would go to do his recruiting. Before leaving home, he had learned that his master's close Union friend, a young doctor named William Irwin, had early intimated to his slaves that they would be freed as a consequence of the war.[93] One of the doctor's slaves, Nelson Irwin, remembered his master's words when the war broke out. "He took us in his room and shut the door, and told us that he expected we would be free, but for us to make ourselves comfortable at home and he would let us

89. November 22, 1863, Eugene Marshall Diary, Eugene Marshall Papers, DU.

90. Brig. Gen. Grenville M. Dodge to Lt. Col. J. J. Phillips, December 2, 1863, *OR*, Ser. I, vol. 31, pt. 3, 309.

91. Edward G. Longacre, "Black Troops in the Army of the James, 1863–1865," *Military Affairs* 45, no. 1 (1981): 2; Litwack, *Been in the Storm So Long*, 73; Mohr, *On the Threshold of Freedom*, 75–6, 85.

92. Claim 1369, William B. Irwin, Lawrence Co., April 13, 1872: Testimony of Richard H. Mosely, SCC.

93. Ibid. The doctor owned fifty-one slaves and two plantations, comprising a total of twenty-six hundred acres.

know when the time came." Because he had friends and acquaintances on the Irwin plantation, Richard Mosely knew of the planter's plan. But as Mosely discovered when he returned to his old neighborhood three days after having joined the army, most of Irwin's slaves had not waited for their master's command. Upon the incursion of the Union army into the area, these men and women had decided for themselves that the time to flee had arrived. Abandoning Irwin's plantation to hide in the woods, they lay in wait for their opportunity. With Irwin's full knowledge and permission, Mosely stayed overnight and the next day sought out the refugees in the woods. He remembered, "[T]here were nine of them and we took twelve mules and a horse and started off for Decatur."[94]

Not all African American men who crossed the lines enlisted in the army, however. Before the Emancipation Proclamation allowed them into the Federal ranks, many African American men were instead put to work as laborers for the army.[95] Moreover, even after emancipation, some, like white unionists chose to labor rather than fight for the Union cause. Robert Brandon of Madison County, for instance, worked for a government-run machine shop, where he built forges, erected furnaces, and did general repair work as required. Likewise, Albert McDavid, a free black man living in Huntsville when Brigadier General O. M. Mitchel occupied the city, worked for the army as a paid blacksmith during the first five months of the army's 1862 occupation. Slave Spencer Harris also made money "cutting wood for the Government" when the army occupied his county of Limestone.[96]

Though the stated policy of the Federal army was to compensate any and all for such work, regardless of race, some slaves were clearly exploited as unpaid, impressed laborers.[97] Jackson Daniel, for instance, was never paid for the three weeks of labor he did for the army just after it occupied Huntsville. Daniel had been extremely enthusiastic to help and

94. Claim 1369, William B. Irwin, Lawrence Co., April 13, 1872: Testimony of Nelson Irwin, and Testimony of Richard H. Mosely; both in SCC.

95. James M. McPherson, *The Negro's Civil War: How American Negroes Felt and Acted during the War for the Union* (New York: Pantheon, 1965), 144. Almost two hundred thousand black men and women from across the nation are estimated to have worked for the army in such nonmilitary capacities.

96. Claim 18663, Robert Brandon, Madison Co., February 16, 1878; Claim 9929, Albert McDavid, Madison Co., September 25, 1871; Claim 19483, Spencer Harris, Limestone Co., March 30, 1876; all in SCC.

97. Gerteis, *From Contraband to Freedman,* 19.

claimed to have been "the first darkee who went with [the Federals] from Daniel Plantation." Daniel "went and borrowed [a] team in my own name, from one of the neighbors" and, taking the horses with him to the army's encampments, signed on to do hauling work. Despite his effort and labor, the army "never paid me a particle of nothing for my work for them." Similarly, when William Richardson worked himself to the bone shoeing horses for Union cavalry regiments in Limestone County, he never received any pay for labor or materials. "I just shod for all of Hatch's command and for all of Rousseau's command. I shod for them from morning to night, day in and day out, all the time, on Sundays and nights for weeks at a time. I furnished my own shoes and nails and never refused them."[98]

Some slaves eliminated the risk of nonpayment, preferring instead to trade with the army on their own terms and for cash on the barrel. Men and women with previous experience and established capital were the most likely to thrive as traders or hired workers in occupied zones. Prior to the war, such individuals had been allowed by their masters to hire their own time in order to pursue independent money-making enterprises.[99] Some kept the full proceeds from these efforts; most, however, paid their masters a certain percentage of the profits for the "privilege."[100] As Edmond Moss of Shelby County explained to the SCC, "[F]or

98. Claim 14957, Jackson Daniel, Madison Co., May 25, 1874; Claim 20134, William Richardson, Limestone Co., April 1, 1873; both in SCC.

99. See appendix 3, table A.9, for occupational data on enslaved and free black claimants. For studies of property ownership among slaves and free blacks based on testimony in allowed SCC claims, see Dylan Penningroth, "Slavery, Freedom, and Social Claims to Property among African Americans in Liberty Co., Georgia, 1850–1880," *Journal of American History* 84, no. 2 (September 1997): 405–35; and Loren Schweninger, *Black Property Owners in the South, 1790–1915* (Urbana: University of Illinois Press, 1990).

100. Although these insights into slaves' market involvement are tantalizing, it should be remembered that the SCC claims are biased toward those who, at the time of emancipation or before, had the skills to engage in substantial moneymaking enterprises. While field slaves had stores of foodstuffs as a matter of course—extra corn or bacon, preserved game, or small livestock like chickens—it was rarer for them to possess more valuable property coveted by the Union army, such as horses, cattle, mules, wagons, or blacksmithing tools. Slave artisans, by contrast, enjoyed greater mobility that allowed for access to the marketplace, and they often owned a wider array of property. For evidence of this pattern elsewhere in the South, see Roderick A. McDonald, "Independent Economic Production by Slaves on Antebellum Louisiana Sugar Plantations," in Ira Berlin and Philip D. Morgan, eds., *The Slaves' Economy: Independent Production by Slaves in the Americas,* special issue of *Slavery and Abolition* 12 (May 1991): 199; Schlotterbeck, "The Internal Economy of Slavery in Rural Pied-

a good many years I hired my time and had my master's tan yard under control . . . all I made over my time was mine to keep." With his profits, Moss "bought a town lot in Montevallo for $125.00 when cheap," and when the railroad began building track through Montevallo, sold the lot for $975. Likewise, carpenter Henry Slaughter of Morgan County "hired my time from my master for four years before I was set free. I was a carpenter and paid three hundred dollars a year for my time." William Richardson, a blacksmith of Limestone County, set up a similar system with his owner. "I worked at the blacksmith trade and I hired myself of my master. I paid him four hundred a year." Moreover, Richardson also hired the time of his brother, George, "who was learning to be a black-smith," as well as the labor of one of his nephews; he paid his master two hundred dollars per year for the boys' time. Robert Brandon, an en-slaved brick mason of Madison County, likewise turned over one hun-dred and twenty dollars to his master every year for the right to work for himself. "[W]hatever [Brandon] made was his undisputed property, free and uncontrolled, by his master," explained Brandon's neighbor and judge of probate, James H. Scruggs. Scruggs was in a unique position to know. At the outbreak of the war, Brandon had accumulated so much cash that the judge was able to borrow some twelve hundred dollars from him.[101]

Slaves who had never "worked for themselves" before the war none-theless found that the Union occupation created that opportunity by changing the dynamics of master-slave relationships. As historian Stephen Ash has argued, in "districts that lay close to the Federal lines and where Confederate authority was unusually weak" slaveholders had no choice but to "relax discipline rather than tighten it." Henry Hall's owner, for example, only allowed him to work independently after the occupation of North Alabama. From 1862 to 1864, Hall paid his owner between

---

mont Virginia," in Berlin and Morgan, *Slaves' Economy,* 174–5; Larry E. Hudson, Jr., "'All That Cash': Work and Status in the Slave Quarters," in Larry E. Hudson, Jr., ed., *Working toward Freedom: Slave Society and Domestic Economy in the American South* (Rochester, N.Y.: University of Rochester Press, 1994), 77; and Mary Beth Corrigan, "'It's a Family Affair': Buying Freedom in the District of Columbia, 1850–1860," in Hudson, *Working toward Free-dom,* 171–2.

101. Claim 21676, Edmond Moss, Shelby Co., October 25, 1873; Claim 319, Henry S. Slaughter, Morgan Co., September 23, 1873; Claim 20134, William Richardson, Limestone Co., April 1, 1873; Claim 18663, Robert Brandon, Madison Co., February 16, 1878: Testimony of James H. Scruggs; all in SCC.

twenty-five and fifty dollars each month for the "privilege" of pursuing his own business. "I painted, and afterwards peddled and traded and ran a hack in the summer," Hall explained. In other cases, the Federal presence undermined the master-slave relationship, or perhaps slaveholders' finances, to such a degree that masters relinquished control over their slaves altogether. As slave Alfred Scruggs explained, "I was turned loose by my old master to make a living for myself," once the army invaded. In similar fashion, Benjamin Haynes's owners seemed to have lost faith in mastery after the first Union invasion in 1862, whereupon they gave him some land, saying they wanted "nothing more to do with me, and for me to go to work for myself."[102]

For bondspeople, the entrepreneurial pursuit of capital represented one of the few open routes to economic security and limited independence. Thus, when the Union army occupied North Alabama, slaves who had the means to trade eagerly turned to Northern soldiers as a new and excellent market to be exploited. Many arrived at army encampments bearing homemade goods such as "sweet milk and corn bread," with which soldiers supplemented their sometimes monotonous and unsavory rations. "We have plenty to eat," Private John Barnard of the Seventy-second Indiana Infantry reassured his family in December 1863. "[The] Negroes is constantly coming in with pies cakes &c to trade for Sugar [and] Coffe." Indiana artilleryman William A. Swayze rose in his Huntsville camp at "day light and stop the negrows as they pass and get milk." Another soldier reported regularly paying not insignificant amounts of money to civilians (whether black or white he does not explain) for fresh items like these: "25 cts for a good pie" and "10 cts for some cakes." Such sales provided an industrious trader with specie or greenbacks at a time of considerable economic instability and terrible inflation in Confederate currency. Others obtained cash by working as servants or cooks for individual soldiers. One infantryman paid "Negro Bill" two dollars to cook for him in the summer of 1863. John Barnard joined with six Huntsville messmates to pay for the services of "a Negro waiter," who "gets our wo[o]d car[ri]es our watter & tends to our Horses &c." Such an experience was not only costly (requiring the pay of seven of them to afford it), but something of an exotic adventure for these white boys from the

102. Ash, *When the Yankees Came*, 164; see Claim 18746, Henry Hall, Dallas Co., June 12, 1874; Claim 2391, Alfred Scruggs, Madison Co., July 31, 1872, SCC; Claim 18674, Benjamin Haynes, Madison Co., May 14, 1875; all in SCC

Midwest. "See," he pointed out to his wife, "we are putting on Southern Style."[103]

The potential for African American entrepreneurs to make substantial sums of money trading with army men could be very high. One Athens woman, Emily Frazier, took full advantage of her opportunities. Well known among friends and acquaintances as "a very smart woman and a great trader," who before the war had "got high enough to hire her own time and to take in work," Frazier was the slave of a lawyer named William Richardson. For five or six years prior to secession, however, she had worked almost exclusively for Danger Rhodes, "a colored man who belonged to a man in Tennessee," and who ran a brick-making and contracting business in Athens. She cooked for Rhodes's laborers, took in washing from young men in Athens, and sewed as well. With the money she earned, Frazier purchased a hog for one dollar and a mule for forty dollars. Once she had the mule, she turned around and hired it to Danger Rhodes to "haul water and tramp mortar," and thus immediately began to make money on her investment. As a neighbor remarked admiringly, "She was a remarkable woman for industry and economy." Moreover, Frazier undertook these activities openly. "My master knew all about my trading," Frazier explained, and was in general "very kind to all his servants." Richardson's reputation for "liberality" with his slaves was indeed familiar to both blacks and whites in Athens. The Reverend James C. Elliot, a white man living across the street from Frazier, remarked, "Her owner Mr. Richardson did allow her to trade and own property in her own name. It was the understanding in the community that anyone trading with her received a good title to any property received from her."[104]

When Union troops arrived in Athens in 1862, Frazier had thus already built up a significant amount of property and a reputation for being a hardheaded businesswoman. Shortly after General O. M. Mitchel occu-

103. Robert H. Crowder to his wife, January 29, 1863, Robert H. Crowder Papers, M208; John M. Barnard to Margaret Barnard, December 6, 1863, John M. Barnard Letters, F80; William A. Swayze to Mother, May 12, 1862, William A. Swayze Civil War Letters and Papers, SC 1915; June 26 and June 14, 1862, George W. Baum Civil War Diaries, M674; July 26, 1863, Mahlon Floyd Account Book, Helen Floyd Carlin Papers, M39; John M. Barnard to Margaret Barnard, December 2, 1863, John M. Barnard Letters, F80; all in IHS.

104. Claim 19479, Emily Frazier, Limestone Co., April 22, 1875: Testimony of Martha Scott, Testimony of James C. Elliot, and Testimony of George Richardson; Claim 19479, Emily Frazier, Limestone Co., April 22, 1875; all in SCC.

pied the town, Frazier began trading with the soldiers. "I made . . . money off the Yankee soldiers by cooking for them, and I went out in the country and bought whiskey from the poor whites and brought it home and sold it to the soldiers. I kept that up until the soldiers cut up so bad that the officers found it out and forbid me selling it." Threatened with arrest by the Union provost marshal, Frazier gave up her liquor business and, after purchasing a cow from soldiers for five dollars, turned instead to selling the wholesome alternative of milk. She also put her wagon and team to use "hauling water and wood . . . [and] cotton" during the war. Frazier made a significant amount of money in this way; by 1875, she had parlayed her prewar and wartime earnings into a sizable estate, including two cows, two horses, a pair of oxen, a number of hogs, and a house and lot in Florence.[105]

Nancy Jones, an enslaved woman of Madison County, also built up a successful wartime trade. Both Nancy and her husband, Marshall Jones, belonged to "an old bachelor" named Alexander Jones, who had a plantation some four miles west of Huntsville. "He let any of us black ones have any stock we·could buy," Nancy explained. By the time the war began, the Joneses owned both hogs and cattle, which Nancy used after 1862 to foster a milk and butter trade with occupying Union soldiers. In addition, she "baked them bread," did their washing, and "knit and sewed" for money. Likewise, Nelson and Matilda Mason earned money "by cooking for the soldiers, and washing for the soldiers and selling cakes and pies in the army." The couple used the cash they earned from trading with the soldiers to purchase a horse, which proved very useful to them when they rented forty acres for farming corn in 1864. Trade with the army and later investments ultimately secured the Nelsons real independence: by 1867, they had purchased their own farm. Through furnishing soldiers with goods and services, the Nelsons and others like them took advantage of wartime chaos to accumulate wealth, and in the process, took their first steps toward securing freedom.[106]

---

105. Claim 19479, Emily Frazier, Limestone Co., April 22, 1875, and Claim 19479, Emily Frazier, Limestone Co., April 22, 1875: Testimony of Julia Richardson, Marginal notes of B. J. Spaulding, claimant's attorney; both in SCC. Apparently not everyone approved of Frazier's entrepreneurial spirit. During the Federal occupation, Frazier bought a horse from "a citizen by the name of Johnson," paying the man sixty dollars for the animal. Frazier noted this in her testimony: "my father whipped me for buying him. I never will forget that."

106. Claim 2753, Nancy Jones, Madison Co., February 18, 1876; Claim 19492, Matilda Mason, Limestone Co., September 1, 1873; both in SCC.

Foraging and Destruction

North Alabama was occupied just as the Union army began to implement the tactics of punitive destruction that historian Mark Grimsley has termed a "rigorous application of the pragmatic policy."[107] Under this approach, Union commanders occupying Southern territory tolerated little in the way of guerrilla attacks on their garrisons, or on surrounding railroads and infrastructure, but retaliated against such activities with a firm hand. Alabama's landscape showed signs of this as early as 1862, when one soldier of the First Minnesota Light Artillery passed through Decatur, situated just south of the Tennessee River in Morgan County. "[S]ince the war broke out the boys on both sides have distroyed the houses and tore down all the fences and laid things to waste in genrel . . . the river at this place is about half mile wide there was once a rail road bridge a cross the river but the rebles has burned it down so our boys could not get a cross the river."[108] A soldier of the Ninth Illinois Volunteer Infantry met with a similar scene upon arriving in the town of New Albany, Alabama: "Finding the town nearly deserted by citizens, and used as a general Headquarters for guerrillas, and a supplying point for them, it was entirely destroyed, after any stores of value that could be carried away were taken."[109] Decatur, the only town south of the Tennessee River to come under Federal control for any extended period, was evacuated of most of its citizens in March 1864. Brigadier General Dodge's Special Orders No. 72 explained that the army needed "the use of every building in Decatur," and that the only people allowed to remain in the town were "Gov't employees and families of persons in our army." Everyone else had to choose to move at least one mile "north or south as they choose," taking with them "all their movable effects."[110]

Thus, while the Union army's occupation of Alabama and Florida offered both black and white unionists protection and greater personal

107. Grimsley, *Hard Hand*, 143.

108. D. H. Duryea to My Dear Wife, May 27, 1862, D. H. Duryea Letters, 1864–1865, SHC; also see McMillan, *Alabama Confederate Reader*, 139–40.

109. Chaplain Marion Morrison, *A History of the Ninth Regiment Illinois Volunteer Infantry* (Monmartin, Ill.: John S. Clark, 1907), 56.

110. Quote from March 19, 1864, Daily Ledger of Gen. Grenville M. Dodge, Secret Service Files, Grenville M. Dodge Papers (hereinafter Dodge Papers), SHSI; also see Special Orders, No. 72, March 19, 1864, enclosure with Brig. Gen. Grenville M. Dodge to Brig. Gen. Jonathan D. Stevenson, March 19, 1864, *OR*, Ser. I, vol. 32, pt. 3, 94–5.

freedom, it also brought danger and devastation.[111] Of the many unpleasant consequences of having soldiers in one's neighborhood, the one most frequently experienced, and usually most distressing, was foraging—the taking of food and supplies from the countryside for the use of army personnel and their animals. From the first months of Union occupation, the rich farms of North Alabama represented longed-for supplies to commanders overseeing the logistics of moving large armies in hostile territory. Officers' relief at finding foodstuffs along the line of march or in the vicinity of a garrisoned town is palpable in their military communications. Brigadier General William S. Rosecrans, for example, reported with evident pleasure his findings upon reconnoitering North Alabama between Corinth, Mississippi, and Tuscumbia, in late summer 1862. "The Tennessee Valley," he wrote, "for 70 miles long and from 5 to 7 miles wide, is one immense corn field." Brigadier General Grenville Dodge likewise sang the praises of the northwestern Tennessee valley in December 1863. "The country your troops will occupy from Huntsville," he explained to Major General Jonathan A. Logan, "is very rich, full of forage and meat. Thus far I have subsisted my command entirely off of the country except coffee, sugar, and salt, which I have from Nashville."[112] Logan was commander of the Fifteenth Army Corps; his command in January 1864 thus included some 15,500 men stationed in Madison and Jackson Counties.[113]

Federal commanders clearly preferred that unionist civilians be protected from the most harmful effects of foraging—soldiers were to avoid unionists' farms unless absolutely necessary, and when they could not do so, they were to offer payment or receipts for the items taken. Nonetheless, loyalist civilians could not help but feel painful consequences of the army's actions. The mandate governing the foraging operations was fundamentally vague. According to General Order 100, or "Lieber's Code," the "military necessity" of feeding soldiers and their animals, and of winning the war, allowed for "all destruction of property, and obstruction of the ways and channels of traffic, travel, or communication, and of all withholding of subsistence or means of life from the enemy; of the ap-

111. Ash, *When the Yankees Came,* 76.

112. Brig. Gen. William S. Rosecrans to Maj. Gen. Henry W. Halleck, August 11, 1862, 3 P.M., *OR,* Ser. I, vol. 16, pt. 2, 309; Brig. Gen. Grenville M. Dodge to Maj. Gen. Jonathan A. Logan, December 24, 1863, *OR,* Ser. I, vol. 31, pt. 3, 486.

113. Abstract from returns of the Army of the Tennessee, Maj. Gen. William T. Sherman, U.S. Army, commanding, for the month of January 1864, *OR,* Ser. I, vol. 32, pt. 2, 297.

propriation of whatever an enemy's country affords necessary for the subsistence and safety of the Army."[114] The breadth of this definition made it possible for soldiers to justify a wide range of actions against civilians. This was even more true once Union commanders like General William T. Sherman began advocating the army's use of punitive measures "to make citizens earn good treatment."[115] The destruction of local buildings, bridges, crops, and stock, even if directed at active rebel civilians, meant that loyalists' worlds were thrown into upheaval, too.

In the end, the Union army rarely avoided "eating off" any citizen whose farm offered sustenance, rebel and unionist alike, leaving loyalists like Pleasant Taylor with the impression that soldiers "took property indiscriminately from union men, as well as others."[116] This perceived indifference caused a great dilemma for unionists. Unlike their Confederate neighbors, who understood such depredations as the actions of an unjust and wicked enemy, white loyalists struggled between their desire to serve the cause they identified as their own and their fear of losing all ability to feed and shelter themselves and their families. The contest over property and its dispensation deeply complicated the relationship between loyalist civilians and invading troops.

White loyalists' reactions to loss of property at the hands of Union soldiers varied considerably. Some unionist civilians believed that the soldiers had every right to anything they wanted, almost as payment-in-kind for the military service provided by the army. When George Davis of Walker County saw U.S. soldiers coming toward his farm, for example, he felt nothing but relief and gladly gave them what he had. "I had been so basely treated by the rebels that I did not care one farthing for anything [the Union soldiers had] taken. I was so proud to see them come, knowing they would scatter the rebels and drive them out of the country, and leave us at home in peace that I could freely give up everything I possessed." In like fashion, Young Amerson "made no complaint" when the Union soldiers took his property because he was "willing to make any sacrifice to bring the war to a close." And Caroline Atkisson (a fervent Union woman who "kept fast days" for the cause) opened her home to soldiers camped nearby. "[S]he gave them meal and butter and had

114. Grimsley, *Hard Hand*, 145; quote, 150.
115. Gen. William T. Sherman to Gen. Grenville M. Dodge, November 18, 1863, Miscellaneous Correspondence Files, Dodge Papers, SHSI.
116. Claim 2670, Pleasant Taylor, Franklin Co., February 25, 1873, SCC.

washing done for them free of charge." In a broad gesture of welcome, Joshua Mullins, a planter who owned 1,250 acres just south of the Tennessee River, put "everything he had" at the disposal of the Third Michigan Cavalry in 1862. What Mullins had was considerable: in 1860, the fifty-nine-year-old unmarried planter had a personal estate worth fifteen thousand dollars and real estate equaling ten thousand. He cultivated about two hundred and fifty acres using the labor of twelve slaves.[117] Finally, Hiram Gibson, a farmer living near Bridgeport and a unionist "from the first to the last," managed to support the Federal army while exacting revenge on a hated neighbor. Gibson invited soldiers to forage on his land, but not on his crop—instead, Gibson offered up the crop of his tenant, a man named Poe, who was "a scout and guide in the employ of the Confederate States." Ninety-five Federal wagons were sent down to Gibson's farm, where soldiers loaded them with over a thousand bushels of Poe's corn.[118]

Occasionally, unionists' generosity could extend beyond foraging and transform into a hospitable arrangement through which Union soldiers were regularly made welcome in a loyalist home for extended periods of time. James Cargile, for instance, a yeoman farmer of Jackson County, lived two miles away from the garrisoned town of Stevenson. At various times, he relinquished his land to the army for use as the headquarters of Generals Thomas, Rosecrans, and Stanley. And after Stephen Haynes, a farmer living near Huntsville, procured a Union guard for his home, he regularly invited Union officers stationed in town to come to his house "to dine, eat supper, &c." Likewise, planter Martha Hobgood of Franklin County frequently had Federal soldiers to her house for food and other provisions. "I considered it a gratuity, never asked for pay— and when payment was made [by the soldiers], it was voluntarily done." Olivia Ricks, also of Franklin, "cooked for the soldiers" and gave them meals "when they did not have their rations" even though she was a "poor widow." Henry Stutts, Sr., of Lauderdale made his house a reliable place of refuge for soldiers: "This was their stopping feeding place," he

117. Claim 6090, George Davis, Walker Co., February 7, 1873; Claim 7531, Young R. Amerson, Fayette Co., March 16, 1872; Claim 12374, Caroline H. Atkisson, Colbert Co., August 22, 1873: Testimony of Sarah Atkisson; Claim 18929, Joshua Mullins, Franklin Co., September 11, 1873: Testimony of William Taylor; all SCC; also 1860 U.S. Census, Alabama, Free Pop. and Slave Pop.

118. Lt. Col. William G. Le Duc to Maj. Gen. O. O. Howard, October 8, 1863, 3 P.M., OR, Ser. I, vol. 30, pt. 4, 191–2.

explained.[119] Soldiers on scouting expeditions from the Twelfth Indiana Cavalry had a similar "stopping place" near the town of Vienna at the home of the Welches—the family cooked the soldiers' rations and let them sleep on the porch.[120] Similarly, while members of the First Illinois Light Artillery Volunteers were encamped at Larkinsville during the frigid winter of 1864, they regularly took respite with a unionist family by the name of Baker, "which lived up the mountain, and included several young ladies." A few of the artillerymen returned to the Bakers' repeatedly for dinner and conversation, visits they enjoyed so much that they found it difficult to say goodbye when they decamped in April. Evidently, the Bakers felt equal regret, as one soldier recounted: "Mr. Baker came in camp to see us off. He brought a bag full of nice cakes from the young ladies for their friends in the Battery."[121]

Nevertheless, as historian Mark Grimsley has argued, even if handled carefully, foraging was far from a "benign affair" and indeed was "economically devastating" and "psychologically stressful for civilians."[122] Unionists were frequently torn between their desires to help the cause and an understandable impulse, in the face of a ravenous army, toward self-preservation. While most white unionists were happy, even eager, to offer a meal or two to individual soldiers, it was rare that even the most devoted loyalist did not balk at sacrificing the last cow in the barn or ham in the cellar. In particular, unionist men and women living in areas recently occupied by rebel armies were the least likely to have supplies to spare, having been repeatedly "foraged on" by hostile rebel cavalry. Union Colonel Abel D. Streight noted in 1862 the declining economic circumstances of the unionists he met. "[M]any of them are, or rather have been, in good circumstances."[123] As William Rikard recalled, Confederate soldiers had regularly taken his corn, fodder, bacon, flour, and other resources, telling him they did it "because I was a Damned Union

119. Claim 13285, James Cargile, Jackson Co., December 7, 1872: Testimony of William A. Austin; Claim 4357, Ogden and Haynes, Madison Co., September 11, 1871: Testimony of Benjamin Haynes; Claim 2650, Martha A. Hobgood, Colbert Co., November 21, 1872 (and see also *History of the Ninety-Second Illinois Volunteers* [Freeport, Ill.: Journal Steam, 1875], 123); Claim 2666, Olivia Ricks, Colbert Co., June 15, 1871; Claim 1199, Henry Stutt (Stutts), Sr., Lauderdale Co., September 14, 1871; all in SCC.

120. July 24, 1864, Charles A. Harper Diary, Charles A. Harper Papers, F84, IHS.

121. Quote in Charles Kimbell, *History of Battery "A," First Illinois Light Artillery Volunteers* (Chicago: Pushing, 1899), 72.

122. Grimsley, *Hard Hand,* 105.

123. Report of Col. Abel D. Streight, July 16, 1862, *OR,* Ser. I, vol. 16, pt. 1, 789.

Man." Green Haley of Marion County lost at least "thirty head of cattle" to Confederate depredations throughout the war; every year Confederates stole about a hundred bushels of his corn. "[E]verything that they could appropriate was taken," he explained. "They were sent on me by my secession neighbors on [account of] my being a union man."[124] After being stripped to near nothing, unionist civilians were deeply upset when U.S. soldiers, thought of as friends and allies, were just as willing as Confederates to pillage treasured stores.[125]

The relationships between foraging soldiers and the unionists they encountered could be markedly adversarial, for troops were not unwilling to use intimidation and force to get what they wanted. The power evinced by foragers prevented many unionists from protesting when their property was confiscated. Solomon Lentz, a well-known unionist of Limestone County, was reluctant to have the army take his property, but said nothing out of fear. "I dare not say they daresn't take it." Presley Thorn of Franklin County simply became so "flustrated by the officers and soldiers" that he failed to request "a receipt or voucher." All he could think about were the consequences of his loss. "I did not know what to do, provisions being scarce & horses very scarce to commence a crop with . . . it was about planting time and I had a large family to support without anything to commence a crop on."[126]

Even those who protested rarely prevailed. Upon learning that Yankee soldiers were in his neighborhood, Jonathan Barton of Winston County returned home from hiding and arrived to find the soldiers "taking my property," including quantities of cornmeal, syrup, honey, sweet potatoes, peas, hogs, and bacon. "I begged of [the captain] not to take all

---

124. Claim 5637, William "Buck" Rikard, Franklin Co., February 26, 1873; Claim 2177, Green M. Haley, Marion Co., March 28, 1872; both in SCC. For other claims discussing such punitive depredations, see Claim 3787C, Elisha Nelson, Baldwin Co., March 7, 1878; Claim 7230, Thomas N. McCarley, Cherokee Co., July 29, 1874; Claim 6815, Matthias Firestone, Cherokee Co., May 12, 1874; Claim 6837, John Smith, Cherokee Co., May 13, 1874; Claim 20467, William Ridge Estate, Jackson Co., November 10, 1875: Testimony of George W. Ridge; Claim 9454, Andrew J. Linn, Jefferson Co., August 30, 1873; Claim 1369, William B. Irwin, Lawrence Co., April 13, 1872; Claim 19870, Wilson Turbyfill, Madison Co., June 3, 1875; Claim 2757, Benjamin B. Rogers, Madison Co., August 30, 1871; Claim 7555, Elizabeth A. Wright, Marshall Co., February 19, 1874; Claim 3111, Claborne C. Ballinger, Walker Co., May 16, 1877; all in SCC.

125. Grimsley, *Hard Hand*, 105.

126. Claim 5202, Solomon Lentz, Limestone Co., June 13, 1876; Claim 15769, Presley Seaborn Thorn, Colbert Co., September 4, 1877; both in SCC.

I had as I was in an enemy's country, and that I would be obliged to move or starve." Barton explained to the captain of the foraging party that he himself was an honorably discharged First Alabama Cavalry soldier. "On my wife producing [my discharge], he ordered the men remaining to empty what they had in their sacks." The soldiers initially complied, but later that night, after the captain had gone away, they sneaked back and took what had been left. When soldiers confiscated Alfred Wall's horse as he was taking it for shoeing in Huntsville, they had to soundly threaten the man before he would give up his animal. After stopping Wall in the middle of the public road, the soldiers told him "that they wanted that horse." Wall angrily protested the order. "I told them I wasn't the cause of their coming down here and for God's sake to let me have my horse." His pleading was to no avail. "[T]hey rode up and took him by the bridle and said if I didn't get down they would take me too." Wall "lit" off the horse, put his saddle on his back, and walked the six miles home, wondering all the way how in the world he would support his family without that horse.[127]

Though soldiers proffered the officially prescribed vouchers and receipts for the property, many white unionists remained dissatisfied. A voucher meant nothing when the item could not be replaced immediately.[128] Moreover, individuals were often frightened to have a Union receipt in their possession, indicating as it did the owner's cooperation with the Federal army. Ebenezer Leath of Cherokee County refused to keep one on precisely these grounds. "[I]f it was known that I had [taken] a voucher," Leath explained, "it w[ould] endanger my life after their army was gone, from those scouts and plunderers that were robbing and killing union men . . . I knew the desperate character of the rebel scouts and so I got no receipt or voucher."[129]

White unionists were not the only loyal civilians to suffer at the hands of foraging Union troops. Slaves and free blacks who lost property had similar reactions. Some, of course, viewed the loss of goods as negligible in light of the security and opportunities Federal occupation brought them. Alfred Scruggs, for example, was "willing" to let the soldiers take his supply of corn, fodder, meat, and cornmeal. He believed

127. Claim 2167, Jonathan Barton, Winston Co., March 14, 1872; Claim 7982, Alfred Wall, Madison Co., August 9, 1873; both in SCC.

128. Grimsley, *Hard Hand*, 98–9.

129. Claim 6701, Ebenezer Leath, Cherokee Co., July 2, 1875, SCC.

his contribution would "help the United States Government that much for what they done for me." Upon receiving his freedom, John Langford of Madison County used the hundred and fifty dollars he had saved to rent land from his old master, on which he made a crop. He also used the profits of his labors to support the Union cause, welcoming Federal soldiers into his home for meals, "free of charge."[130]

Most slaves and free blacks, however, were more likely to be reluctant to part with their goods. For slaves in particular, obtaining property was an exceptionally difficult and painstaking process, often requiring, as has been discussed, complicated arrangements with masters and regular payments for "hiring one's time." As Nancy Jones explained in regard to her savings, "I tell you we were a long time making that little money." Furthermore, at the time the Union army took people's property, slaves had no firm idea who would win the war; it was not at all clear that their freedom would be preserved or recognized in the future. In their calculations, loss of even small property meant increased vulnerability to whatever white people won the war. Planning for all exigencies, Dudley Smith, a carpenter in Tuscaloosa, hedged his bets. On the advice of a fellow slave, Smith invested some one thousand dollars of Confederate currency in property. If the United States won the war, the currency itself would be worthless. If the Union lost, he would at least have the property.[131]

The interaction between resisting slaves and foraging Union soldiers could thus become heated and violent. Benjamin Turner of Selma "was pleased enough" when Union soldiers occupied his town, that is "until [the Federal army] took everything I had." Turner had hired his time from his master for two hundred and fifty dollars per year and thereby made a good living as the operator of a livery stable business. As he explained, when the Union army took all the property that he had so carefully accumulated, "I got mad." Adding insult to injury was the fact that the soldier confiscated "a very large strong mule named Tom, to which I was much attached." The mule was virtually worthless to the army because he was almost blind. Turner remonstrated with the captain of the foraging team. Already disgruntled at the thought of fighting on behalf

130. Claim 2391, Alfred Scruggs, Madison Co., July 31, 1872; Claim 8917, John Langford, Madison Co., January 7, 1878; both in SCC.

131. Claim 2753, Nancy Jones, Madison Co., February 18, 1876; Claim 18746, Henry Hall, Dallas Co., June 12, 1874: Testimony of Dudley Smith; both in SCC.

of slaves, the Federal soldiers viewed Turner's resistance as an outrage to be met with threats of force. "[A]fter receiving some hard words . . . the officer pointed his pistol at me," Turner remembered. The soldiers got the mule. Similarly, Jackson Daniel, a slave from Madison County, became very afraid for his wife—deemed "a very fractious woman" even by her husband—when she protested loudly over soldiers' confiscation of her cornmeal. "She objected to it," her husband remembered, and the soldiers "talked about slaying of her, see. I just told her to hush and say nothing and it would be best for us."[132]

Some soldiers, especially those from border slaveholding states, appeared to be shocked to find a sizable amount of property in the possession of bondspeople. Take the case of Stephen Coleman, a slave from Lawrence County who had hired his time for seven years prior to the war. A minister and laborer, Coleman had "accumulated by industry and economy a very pretty little property in Horses, cattle and hogs, and had a good deal of good household and kitchen furniture." In May 1863, a group of Federal troopers from Missouri attempted to take Coleman's property, whereupon he resisted, holding on to his horses for dear life. At this point, one of the cavalrymen "presented his Pistol to [Coleman's] head . . . and told him to let go the horses or he would shoot him as he knew that no negro had that much property."[133]

Even those soldiers who regretted having to take slave property tended to be immovable on the subject. Late in the war, Matilda Mason lost her mule and horse, despite her protests. "[O]ne of the soldiers said, 'Go away, Auntie. We are obliged to take the stock. We have orders from Gen. Rousseau to take them.'" In tears, Mason went to the general to plead for the return of her animals. She found General Rousseau reclining before his fire. He repeated his soldiers' admonition to her: "Don't cry, Auntie. I am obliged to have them or I would not take them." Like-

132. Claim 285, Benjamin S. Turner, Dallas Co., April 21, 1871; Claim 14957, Jackson Daniel, Madison Co., May 25, 1874; both in SCC. In fact, Turner had long been financially able to buy his freedom and had offered his master sixteen hundred dollars "cash in gold" for his freedom in 1856. But upon doing so, he found "the laws of Alabama would not permit me to buy my freedom except through a third person who would stand the relation of master to me." This seemed a raw deal. "I preferred to remain with my old master and keep my money," Turner explained. He was right about his mule's uselessness as a work animal, but was chagrined to see the army's solution: "I saw Tom afterwards in the dining room of the Mobile House in Selma, they had him in there for show."

133. Claim 5809, Stephen Coleman, Lauderdale Co., August 24, 1871: Testimony of Cyrus Kirkman, SCC.

wise, slave peddler Henry Hall of Dallas County lost horses to "five or six private soldiers" who came to his house, "sat down in the yard and conversed on indifferent subjects with myself and others for an hour or so." Only at that point did the men get up to do the business they came to accomplish. Upon wandering around the farm, they found the horses. "Two of the soldiers immediately seized [them] and rode them off to the camps." The remaining men apologized to Hall, telling him that they "hated to take my horses as I was a colored man, but were compelled to do so."[134] Whatever economic and civil opportunities the army's presence afforded Alabama bondspeople, its voracious need could just as easily strip them of vital property.

In Alabama, the invasion of Federal troops irrevocably shifted the balance of power among white unionists, black activists, and Confederate society. White and black Alabamians both embraced the Union army as a protector and as a way to gain leverage for self-determination. Their motives, however, remained incongruent. White unionists used the army as a tool to defeat the forces threatening to destroy the old Union, and their families and neighborhoods along with it; slaves and free blacks saw the army as an ally in the fight to end their own enslavement and that of their race. Thus, though all the parties to the pro-Union alliance in Alabama were bound by a shared desire to prosecute the war and overthrow the Confederacy, conflicting interests abounded. Ongoing and sometimes bitter conflicts over how much of their personal property and labor, and therefore security and independence, loyal whites and blacks were willing to sacrifice for the army dramatically illustrates the limitations of cooperation. The roles, responsibilities, and obligations of all three parties to the anti-Confederate effort on the Alabama home front remained unclear and contested. As unionist Presley Thorn put it, "Every thing was in confusion in the country."[135]

134. Claim 19492, Matilda Mason, Limestone Co., September 1, 1873; Claim 18746, Henry Hall, Dallas Co., June 12, 1874; both in SCC.

135. Claim 15769, Presley Seaborn Thorn, Colbert Co., September 4, 1877, SCC.

4

"Wild Justice"

UNIONISTS, SLAVES, AND THE FEDERAL COUNTERINSURGENCY EFFORT IN NORTH ALABAMA

[S]ometimes when I would lay down at night I would never expect to see daylight again.
—Valentine Cagle, Jackson County, 1875

Toward the last it was considered a waste of time to surrender, even if cornered without hope of escape. The recognized practice was to sell out as dearly as possible and keep shooting as long as a trigger could be pulled.
—John Wyeth, former Confederate soldier stationed in North Alabama, 1914

In the summer of 1863, George Ridge, a farmer of Doran's Cove, Jackson County, was living at the Federal headquarters in Nashville, having only recently escaped from a Chattanooga prison where he had been incarcerated as a political prisoner. While there, he reunited with his brother Jasper and "several" cousins and uncles, all of whom had enlisted in the Tenth Tennessee Cavalry, U.S.A., and were stationed at Nashville. From his relations, George Ridge learned terrible news: his father, William ("Old Yankee Bill"), and brother James had been murdered by a "squad" of "Rebbles, Thieves, Robbers & Bushwhackers." Another brother, Frank, had been shot and wounded by the same group of men, some of whom "belonged to different companies," and some of whom "did not belong to none." From the first days of conscription, William Ridge had actively encouraged his four sons to "lie in the mountain until the moss would grow on their backs a foot long" before submitting to the rebel draft. This commitment had proved his ruin. One night in May 1863, a local Confederate had "put on an old pair of shoes, and old Clothes and went

For epigraphs, see Claim 15659, Valentine Cagle, Jackson Co., January 4, 1875, SCC; and John Allen Wyeth, *With Sabre and Scalpel: The Autobiography of a Soldier and Surgeon* (New York: Harper & Brothers, 1914), 317.

to William Ridge's," with the story that he had come to get provisions for William's sons hiding in the mountains. "The old man Ridge gave him a pair of shoes, a pair of britches, and . . . a big sack of bread and meat." Having caught William red-handed in the act of aiding and abetting his deserter sons, the Confederates "had Ridge just where they wanted him," and executed him for treason. Brothers James and Frank were soon thereafter shot while fleeing the same gang.[1]

George Ridge was determined to find a way home to protect his remaining siblings, as well as his wife and children. The way he managed to do it was as a Federal scout and recruiter for the Tenth Tennessee Cavalry, U.S.A. Ridge's experience as a draft dodger, familiarity with area unionists, and intimate knowledge of the Tennessee Valley and surrounding mountains made him an ideal candidate for the Union army's counterinsurgency work. During the Federal reoccupation of northern Alabama in August 1863, he performed service that was doubtless important to the major troop movements of the Chickamauga campaign. As a guide for Major General Philip H. Sheridan, then commanding the Third Division, Twentieth Corps of the Army of the Cumberland, he employed his understanding of "all the fords" across the Tennessee River in northeastern Alabama to help Sheridan and Major General William S. Rosecrans push south and east toward unseating the Confederates at Chattanooga. But contributions of this sort, while points of pride to Ridge, were never uppermost in his mind or heart. Shortly after helping the Army of the Cumberland across the river, Ridge asked to be relieved of duty, telling his commanding officers that he "wanted to come back and look after" his family. Granted leave to return home, he remained loosely assigned to the Federal post at Bridgeport, close to his family's farm in Doran's Cove.[2]

1. Claim 20467, William Ridge Estate, Jackson Co., November 10, 1875: Testimony of George W. Ridge; Claim 20468, George W. Ridge, Jackson Co., November 22, 1875; Claim 20467, William Ridge Estate, Jackson Co., November 10, 1875: Testimony of Henry Dawson; all in SCC.

2. Claim 20467, William Ridge Estate, Jackson Co., November 10, 1875: Testimony of George W. Ridge, SCC. For correspondence relative to Rosecrans's crossing of the Tennessee River, see Maj. Gen. William S. Rosecrans to Maj. Gen. Henry W. Halleck, August 6, 1863, OR, Ser. I, vol. 23, pt. 2, 594; Maj. Gen. William S. Rosecrans to Adj. Gen. U.S. Army, August 15, 1863; Maj. Gen. William S. Rosecrans to Maj. Gen. Ambrose E. Burnside, August 19, 1863; Maj. Gen. William S. Rosecrans to Col. John C. Kelton, August 21, 1863, 11:15 A.M.,

George Ridge's experience with the Union army was one of many instances in which Alabama civilians worked to support and facilitate the Federal counterinsurgency strategy. Indeed, the energies and commitment of white unionists seeking to revenge themselves on rebels, as well as slaves hoping to undermine slavery, were critical to the successful destabilization of the Confederate home front. Alliances with unionists and slaves allowed the Union army to overcome a basic weakness of its position as an occupying force. Unlike their Confederate opponents, Federal commanders were in enemy territory; when they arrived, they did not have established and long-standing relationships with sympathetic civilians and home front officials like conscript cavalry and home guards. Confederate commanders and guerrilla fighters had long rested their offensive upon this "stable infrastructure"; through it, they had obtained vital intelligence and material support for fighting the invading Northern army.[3]

To launch an effective counterinsurgency effort, Union commanders had to tap into the layers of unionist and slave networks already in place on the home front. In a range of capacities, white and black civilians aided Union troop movements, thwarted the Confederacy's guerrilla campaign against Federal occupation, and enabled pro-Union resistance behind Confederate lines. Men who did not enlist as soldiers in regiments like the First Alabama Cavalry nonetheless acted as guides, scouts, and spies skirting around the edges of garrisoned towns and no-man's-land, and probing deep into the Confederate frontier looking for rebels. North Alabama's bondspeople likewise undermined the guerrilla efforts of their masters and other whites in their neighborhoods. The correspondence and reports of Union commanders are littered with references to "negro reports," the regularity and accuracy of which the army came to rely heavily upon.[4] Slaves chipped away at the stability of the Confederacy with studied habits of careful listening, a whisper here and there to

---

OR, Ser. I, vol. 30, pt. 3, 32–3, 80–1, 98–9; Joseph Jones to Nancy Jones, August 31, 1863, Joseph Jones Letters, GLC 2739, GLCML.

3. Daniel, "Special Warfare in Middle Tennessee," 291–2.

4. See for example, Brig. Gen. O. M. Mitchel to Hon. E. M. Stanton, May 4, 1862, OR, Ser. I, vol. 10, pt. 2, 162–3; Brig. Gen. C. L. Matthies to Lt. Col. R. M. Sawyer, May 16, 1864, OR, Ser. I, vol. 38 pt. 4, 215; Brig. Gen. R. S. Granger to Maj. Gen. Thomas, October 9, 1864, OR, Ser. I, vol. 39, pt. 3, 171; Col. William P. Lyon to Lt. Samuel M. Kneeland, December 23, 1864, OR, Ser. I, vol. 45, pt. 2, 326.

passing soldiers, and directions and assistance to generals at garrisons. They helped dismantle the Confederacy's defenses in the heart of slavery's kingdom.[5]

To successfully stamp out enemy guerrillas, however, an army needs guerrillas of its own. Thus, though the intelligence provided by civilians and slaves was critical to the counterinsurgency effort, the Union army also relied on unionist partisans to locate and kill the Confederate partisans threatening Federal control of North Alabama's railroads and the Tennessee River. Federal commanders found such fighters in men who, like George Ridge, had watched their homes and families torn asunder by the Confederacy. Desperate and determined, and given wide latitude by the army to which they were only nominally responsible, these unionist partisans used Federal counterinsurgency efforts as a tool in their own war for vengeance.

Confederate Guerrillas and Their Aims

Confederate control of the Hill Country south of the Tennessee River, when combined with uneven Federal occupation north of the river, fostered excellent conditions for guerrilla warfare. Pinning down who these guerrillas were can be, as it was then, rather difficult. They are perhaps best described through an examination of their tactics and aims. In North Alabama, most guerrilla warfare was prosecuted by small groups of mobile, often mounted Confederate fighters. They sought to sabotage any and all Federal forces and installations in the area; intimidate, arrest, and sometimes murder civilians they believed were unionists or assisting the Union; and, frequently, indulge in considerable thievery and reckless destruction of property in the process. Within this broad description, however, distinctions can be made about how such forces were constituted and organized. Historian Mark Grimsley's typology of Civil War

5. In *South vs. the South*, chaps. 4–8, passim, historian William W. Freehling has recently argued for the influence of anti-Confederate Southerners, including slaves, in weakening the Confederate nation. See as well similar arguments regarding slave agency in the war throughout the South: Fields, *Slavery and Freedom*; Grimsley, *Hard Hand*; Gerteis, *From Contraband to Freedman*; Victor B. Howard, *Black Liberation in Kentucky: Emancipation and Freedom, 1862–1884* (Lexington: University Press of Kentucky, 1983); Hollandsworth, *Louisiana Native Guards*; Ash, *When the Yankees Came*.

guerrillas is helpful when trying to understand who these men were and why they fought the way they did.[6]

Grimsley's first type, "guerrillas only by extension of the word," were regularly organized cavalry units on detached service from the infantry division to which they were assigned.[7] In Alabama, the Confederate Army depended heavily upon such detached cavalry, particularly those commanded by Major General Nathan B. Forrest and Brigadier General Philip D. Roddey, to defend the Tennessee Valley and its railroads. Partisan rangers, a second type of guerrilla fighter, were organized by an act of the Confederate Congress in 1862 to defend their home states and were not assigned to any larger body of Confederate troops.[8] These units remained subject to military authority, usually wore regular uniforms, and counted as regularly enlisted troops.[9] Nevertheless, they had a distinctly independent flavor. Drafted men not interested in fighting far from their home found deserting to join a partisan unit on the home front highly attractive.[10] Moreover, being part of a partisan ranger outfit could be financially rewarding. The Secretary of War promised to pay such fighters, in addition to their regular wages, the "full value" of "any arms and munitions of war captured from the enemy," offering a practical incentive to enlistment, particularly for men facing wartime deprivation.[11]

Uneasiness over the autonomy of partisan rangers quickly surfaced among Confederate officials and leaders, however. Criticism was such that, three months after the act passed, the War Department established measures to "restrain the partisan movement." On July 31, 1862, the Secretary of War issued General Orders No. 53, making partisan rangers liable to conscription and limiting partisan service to those over thirty-five. The enforcement of these restrictions went so poorly, however, that in

6. Daniel Sutherland's recent work on the Confederacy's guerrilla war has also influenced my understanding of this subject. See in particular, Daniel E. Sutherland, "Guerrillas: The Real War in Arkansas," in Bailey and Sutherland, *Civil War Arkansas*, 135–8, 143–5; and Daniel E. Sutherland, "Guerrilla Warfare in the Confederacy," *Journal of Southern History* Volume 68, no. 2 (May 2002): 273. Also see Noe, "Who Were the Bushwhackers?," 7–8; Fisher, *War at Every Door*, 62; and Fellman, *Inside War*, 81.

7. Grimsley, *Hard Hand*, 112; Sutherland, "Guerrillas: The Real War in Arkansas," 136, 142.

8. Thomas Alton Smith, "Mobilization of the Army in Alabama, 1859–1865" (M.A. thesis, Alabama Polytechnic Institute, 1953), 32–6; C. E. Grant, "Partisan Warfare Model," *Military Review* 38 (1958): 44–5; Fellman, *Inside War*, 98.

9. Grimsley, *Hard Hand*, 112; Grant, "Partisan Warfare Model," 44.

10. Sutherland, "Guerrilla Warfare in the Confederacy," 282–3.

11. Quote from Grant, "Partisan Warfare Model," 44; Fellman, *Inside War*, 98–9.

February 1864, the Confederate Congress simply repealed the Partisan Ranger Act, ordering all units to be assimilated into the regular army except those who were operating behind enemy lines. This last caveat, however, meant that partisan rangers remained active until the end of the war.[12]

The two final types of guerrillas straddled the line between regular military and civilians. These outfits—"politicized civilians who fought covertly, masquerading as noncombatants" and "outlaws for whom the war was mainly an excuse to indulge in mayhem"—were the least formal and accountable guerrilla fighters in North Alabama, and they remain the most poorly understood by historians. Self-constituted and subject to little, if any, military oversight, their motivations ranged from deep political conviction to a wanton desire for plunder. Perhaps most important, these categories bled into one another with some frequency—fighting for the Confederate cause and to protect one's home did not preclude slipping into outlawry. Many political guerrillas were by the end of the war hard to distinguish from the bandits who from the first had taken advantage of the chaos of the home front to plunder civilians for personal profit and to steal horses or cotton from the armies for sale on the black market.[13]

Together and independently, detached cavalry, partisan rangers, and other local ad hoc guerrilla forces worked to disrupt the Federal attack on Alabama by wreaking havoc on Union forces. They provoked skirmishes, burned bridges, pulled up railroad track, hijacked and destroyed supply trains, captured mail and dispatches, stole stock and materiel, demolished telegraph communications, and ambushed and assassinated foraging and reconnaissance parties.[14] In the Tennessee Valley, guerrillas concentrated on undermining the communications and transportation

12. Jerry McDowell King, "Shadow Warriors of the Confederacy" (M.A. thesis, University of South Florida, 1990), 28–32.

13. Quote in Grimsley, Hard Hand, 112; Sutherland, "Guerrillas: The Real War in Arkansas," 143–4, 285–6. When testifying before the SCC, unionists frequently referred to such rebel groups as "home guards," "rebel squads," or "bushwhackers." The word "bushwhacker," however, was employed freely by both Confederates and unionists to denigrate any enemy partisan or irregular fighter. Thus, unionist partisans organized as loyalist "home guards" were viewed as "bushwhackers" by Confederate soldiers. The term simply underscored the perceived illegitimacy of the enemy's actions; it cannot be relied upon as a precise descriptor.

14. Grimsley, Hard Hand, 112. See also S. J. Hamilton to his cousin, [1863], Eb Allison Papers, GLC 3523.24; and Edward W. Amsden to Cousin Lill, September 27, 1863, Edward W. Amsden Papers, GLC 2156; both in GLCML.

structure provided by the river itself and the adjacent railroad. Frequent practice at the task made them good at it. "I think I can keep the railroad so crippled that it will be of very little use to the enemy," Confederate Brigadier General P. D. Roddey reported to Major General Joseph Wheeler in October 1863. "[I] have such plans as will cut the track every day."[15]

Although the Union army established a fairly efficient system for repairing damage done by such guerrillas, the railroad remained the repeated site of deadly Confederate attacks throughout the war. Sergeant Eb Allison of the Fifteenth Pennsylvania Cavalry experienced a typical series of "narrow escapes" from guerrillas on a railroad trip from Rossville, Georgia, west through Stevenson, Scottsboro, and then north to Nashville via Huntsville. The train was repeatedly "fired into by guerrillas," men hidden along the track in the "heavy woods, thickets and marshes" lining the railroad and "splendidly adapted for guerrilla operations." The engineer and fireman of the train were killed in the action, and Allison counted himself lucky to be alive. "Between the danger of ordinary railroad accidents, and that of being shot or pitched over an embankment by guerrillas," he confessed to his father, "it is about as much as a man's life is worth to go by rail from [Nashville] to Chattanooga, or vise versa."[16]

The second broad objective of Confederate guerrilla activity included what has been called the enforcement of "the secessionist political order in occupied regions where the Confederate government could exert no direct influence."[17] This purpose extended beyond safeguarding the "political order," to defending the entire Confederate military and social

15. Brig. Gen. O. M. Mitchel to Edwin M. Stanton, May 4, 1862, OR, Ser. I, vol. 10, pt. 2, 161–2; Maj. Gen. Don C. Buell to Brig. Gen. James D. Morgan, July 29, 1862, OR, Ser. I, vol. 16, pt. 2, 225; Col. Louis D. Watkins to Brig. Gen. James A. Garfield, August 27, 1863, 9:45 P.M., OR, Ser. I, vol. 30, pt. 3, 194; Brig. Gen. E. A. Carr to Maj. Gen. Stephen A. Hurlbut, October 3, 1863, OR, Ser. I, vol. 30, pt. 4, 55; Maj. Gen. William T. Sherman to Brig. Gen. J. A. Rawlins, October 14, 1863, OR, Ser. I, vol. 30, pt. 4, 356; Brig. Gen. Philip D. Roddey to Maj. Gen. Joseph Wheeler, October 14, 1863, OR, Ser. I, vol. 30, pt. 4, 748; Brig. Gen. Grenville M. Dodge to Lt. Col. Bowers, February 16, 1864, OR, Ser. I, vol. 32, pt. 2, 404. Quote in Brig. Gen. P. D. Roddey to Maj. Gen. Joseph Wheeler, October 14, 1863, OR, Ser. I, vol. 30, pt. 4, 748.

16. Eb Allison to James Allison, May 20, 1864, Eb Allison Papers, GLC 3523.24, GLCML. For an earlier instance, see Brig. Gen. O. M. Mitchel to Gen. Don C. Buell, June 6, 1862, OR, Ser. I, vol. 10, pt. 2, 265.

17. Grimsley, Hard Hand, 112.

order in areas proximate to Federal occupation.[18] By spring 1864, cavalry commander Brigadier General Philip D. Roddey had made policing North Alabama a primary objective. Ordered to use his Confederate cavalry force "to picket the whole front from the Mississippi State line across the State, and along the Tennessee River," Roddey hunted down and arrested "tories, conscripts, and deserters." Any found "in arms offering resistance" were to be punished "with death upon the spot."[19] Roddey was so relentless in his pursuit that one loyalist sarcastically remarked after the war, "I think General Roddey would be the best witness I could get to prove my loyalty by."[20]

Aid, Comfort, and Intelligence

Union commanders serving in Alabama, like all those stationed along Confederate lines, quickly learned that regular warfare would not suffice to combat guerrilla tactics.[21] By building on the networks originally erected for unionists' and slaves' self-defense, however, the Federals were able to construct a counterguerrilla effort from a dependable force of loyal collaborators. Driven by the twinned desires for Union victory and personal vengeance, many loyal Southerners eagerly took the oppor-

18. Jonathan Sarris, " 'Shot for Being Bushwhackers': Guerrilla War and Extralegal Violence in a North Georgia Community, 1862–1865," in Sutherland, ed., *Guerrillas, Unionists, and Violence*, 38–43.

19. Quote in Lt. Gen. Leonidas Polk to Maj. Gen. French, April 26, 1864, *OR*, Ser. I, vol. 32, pt. 3, 825; also see Lt. Gen. Leonidas Polk to Maj. Gen. Stephen D. Lee, April 26, 1864, and Brig. Gen. Philip D. Roddey to Maj. Gen. Stephen D. Lee, April 26, 1864, in *OR*, Ser. I, vol. 32, pt. 3, 825, 828–30.

20. Claim 8262, William S. Nance, Franklin Co., September 3, 1874, SCC. Though by 1865, Roddey had actively negotiated with Ulysses S. Grant for peace, this should not obscure the fact that he and his men prosecuted the war on the home front with fervor, especially against unionists. As Pleasant Sivley of Lawrence County remembered, his friend William Hightower "on one occasion had his finger on the trigger of his gun to shoot Gen. Roddey, a rebel officer, for the abuse he received at the hands of his men, on account of his unionism"; see Claim 8393, William Hightower, Lawrence Co., September 16, 1873: Testimony of Pleasant Sivley, SCC; for Roddey as a more benign figure than some unionists claimed, see Horton, "Submitting to the 'Shadow of Slavery,'" passim.

21. Fisher, *War at Every Door*, 96; Ash, *When the Yankees Came*, 47–9; Kenneth W. Noe, "Exterminating Savages: The Union Army and Mountain Guerrillas in Southern West Virginia, 1861–1862," in Noe and Wilson, *Civil War in Appalachia*, 105–6; Fellman, *Inside War*, 166.

tunity to assist the war effort in their own backyards and against well-known enemies.

White unionists participated in a wide variety of subversive activities on behalf of Federal forces. The chance to do so could arise at virtually any time. One of the most basic forms of assistance occurred when, after a skirmish, Union soldiers were left for dead in no-man's-land or the Confederate frontier. Quite a number of wounded Northern soldiers owed their very lives to aid offered by loyal white and black Alabamians.[22] White unionist Susan Thrasher of Lauderdale County, for instance, nursed one soldier "for upwards of a month" and "waited upon and showed him every attention . . . and kindly treat[ed] him" until he was recovered sufficiently to return to his command.[23] Corporal J. J. Ferris of Company K, Seventy-third Indiana Volunteers, fell injured in a skirmish with General Nathan B. Forrest's cavalry. Left behind Confederate lines, Ferris was rescued by "Union people of the neighborhood" and a "citizen doctor," who nursed him until he was able to recross to Union territory.[24] A unionist family also cared for John McCarty, a Federal soldier serving under Major General Joseph Hooker, when he was hurt during a skirmish at Shoal Creek on the Tennessee River. At the home of unionist John Burrows, McCarty and another wounded soldier had their bodies and souls "tended" by the womenfolk of the household. "Mrs. Burrows was a very religious woman and in fact the whole family are religious and I am a little the reverse myself," McCarty explained. "Mrs. Burrows used to get down and wash my feet and talk to me of better times when I would get well, and would sing hymns &c —. She and her two daughters took care of us and paid us every attention and made us as comfortable as possible."[25]

Union soldiers especially appreciated the care loyal citizens showed their wounded and dying in light of the dangers they faced in taking such action. After the Forrest–Streight skirmish of 1863, a soldier of the Seventy-third Indiana explained, "The loyal citizens of the vicinity would have gladly assisted in the care of the stricken ones . . . but not even a cup of milk or a piece of bread was allowed to be given them by these

22. Seventy-third Indiana Regimental Assoc., *History of the Seventy-Third Indiana*, 139.

23. Claim 3981, Susan Y. Thrasher, Lauderdale Co., August 9, 1871: Testimony of Neander H. Rice, SCC.

24. Seventy-third Indiana Regimental Assoc., *History of the Seventy-Third Indiana*, 137.

25. Claim 5804, John Burrows, Lauderdale Co., August 20, 1873: Testimony of John McCarty, SCC.

sympathizing friends, and it was only when the vigilance of the guards could be evaded that our wounded could receive the slightest favor from this source."[26] Nevertheless, unionists persisted despite intimidation. For instance, after the fight at Sulpher Branch Trestle in September 1864, John Hayes, a farmer of Limestone County, went purposely to the church where the Northern army had housed sixteen wounded Federals. "I found one young man who had been shot through the lungs," he explained. "[He] said if he had a bed to lay on he thought he would get well." So Hayes put the soldier in his buggy and drove him the two miles to his farm, the man bleeding from his undressed wounds. "He tried to tell me his name but could not speak it plain enough for me to understand it," Hayes remembered. "His greatest desire was to see his mother." Hayes planned to care for the soldier at his home, but local Confederate cavalry began to threaten him so heavily that the surgeon at the church encouraged Hayes to return the boy, "as he considered that I was endangering my life in keeping him." Hayes brought the soldier back, but gave him "a full suit of clothes" and bedding "for him to lay on." Soon thereafter he died. Despite being threatened with hanging, Hayes continued to aid the wounded at the church until Union troops came from Huntsville to take them under the protection of the garrison: "I sent them chickens, soup, biscuits, coffee and ever thing which I thought they would relish, and I carried up as many of my clothes as I could spare, for the wounded, for their clothes were all bloody and nasty."[27]

Similarly, Mariah Howard and her husband rescued a soldier wounded in the same skirmish between the Seventy-third Indiana and Forrest's cavalry. The conflict had occurred three miles south of the Howards' home, and afterward one of "the Union soldiers named White was left badly wounded at an outhouse by the road side. . . . None of the near neighbors would do anything for him." The soldier had been shot through his torso, a wound which almost always proved mortal. Nonetheless, "Mr. Howard went and brought him and we nursed and took the best care of him we could until he died some three or four days afterwards." The Howards buried him and sent his wife an ambrotype they had found among his possessions. Mariah explained that she had tried to get a local doctor to help the dying man, but he had refused, saying that

26. Seventy-third Indiana Regimental Assoc., *History of the Seventy-Third Indiana,* 137.
27. Claim 16404, John S. Hayes, Limestone Co., July 19, 1875, SCC.

"he would rather give him something to put him out of the way" than help him live; indeed, their "rebel neighbors talked very harshly" about the Howards for helping a Yankee soldier. Opprobrium did not dissuade Mariah or her husband from doing the best they could for the soldier. "The wounded man seemed to be a man of intelligence and was the most thankful man for our kindness I ever saw. This was the most trying case I ever had and I did what I thought right, what I felt like doing for the friends of the union right in the face of persecution and opposition."[28]

Slaves assisted in similar ways. John Langford, the uncle of a black Federal soldier, took six sick soldiers of the Fourth Ohio Cavalry into his home outside Huntsville. Edmond Moss and his wife kept a wounded soldier at their home in Shelby County. "He bled through a feather bed and almost spoiled it. He was wounded in the breast and shoulders." Five or six days after they took him in, the soldier died, after which the Mosses made him "burying clothes" out of two "clean sheets." Washington Patterson, the enslaved carpenter of a unionist in Franklin County, was ordered by his master to go with him to retrieve the body of a Federal officer who fell on the plantation grounds during a skirmish. "I [then] took him to the house and made him a decent coffin and buried him in the corner of Master's orchard," Patterson remembered.[29]

Assisting wounded Federals was frequently a matter of coincidence, but unionists and slaves also took active steps to provide intelligence to the Union. In all cases, the moment of initial contact with Union troops was no easy matter for Alabama civilians. It required a cool head and a steady hand. When strangers arrived asking for information, one did not always know who was doing the asking—uniforms were notoriously unreliable as indicators of a man's allegiance. Moreover, if it became known to local Confederates that a unionist or slave had entertained or assisted a Federal soldier or spy, the repercussions could be serious. A male unionist might be killed for it; his family might be run off, or his home burned down. Slaves, if caught, faced all the usual consequences for conspiring against one's master and the slave society, including sale, severe punishment, or death. All loyal people, then, were wary of walking into a rebel trap, and extreme caution marked these exchanges.

28. Claim 8779, Mariah L. Howard, Cherokee Co., December 18, 1874, SCC.

29. Claim 8917, John Langford, Madison Co., January 7, 1878; Claim 21676, Edmond Moss, Shelby Co., October 25, 1873; Claim 4348, John C. Goodloe, Colbert Co., February 1, 1872: Testimony of Washington Patterson; all in SCC.

Take, for instance, the experience of Porter Bibb, a "very strong union man" who was "devoted to the United States government" and was threatened with hanging by Confederates on numerous occasions.[30] Bibb was part of an "intimate" group of "loyal neighbors" in Mooresville, Limestone County, a largely pro-Confederate town. Just before the first occupation of Huntsville in the summer of 1862, he was visited by James Pike, a Texas-born spy for the Fourth Ohio Cavalry. Pike's autobiography relates how he spent most of his dangerous career behind enemy lines, determining the location and strength of Confederate forces, and burning or otherwise destroying bridges, telegraph wires, and other Confederate infrastructure. He was on just such a mission in North Alabama when he arrived at Bibb's home looking for a meal, assured by another unionist in the neighborhood that Bibb was a "good Union man." Bibb, however, was immediately suspicious, despite that Pike wore a Federal uniform. As Pike recalled, "He took me for a rebel in disguise, sent there to try him and ascertain his sentiments. He gave his name as Porter Bibb, and I gave mine as Gabe Fitzhugh. I was trying to sound him and he was trying to sound me." Before Pike parted, the men "spent about two hours in lying to each other, to discover each the other's opinions," but neither felt enough convinced of the other's trustworthiness to abandon the elaborate play-acting.[31]

If trust could be established, the circumstances under which loyalists and slaves gave information to the Union army varied. Most information came from casual informants who shared observations of Confederate activities with Union soldiers as the opportunity arose. For instance, James Haynes of Lauderdale County, who had never spied before and never would again, was given a letter by a Confederate and asked to deliver it to the man's wife. Haynes knew that the letter "conveyed intelligence of rebel movements." Although twinged by guilt over purposely diverting the correspondence, Haynes did so anyway. "I gave the letter

---

30. Claim 19873, John W. Hafley, Limestone Co., September 29, 1873: Testimony of Henry S. Bibb, SCC.

31. James Pike, *The Scout and Ranger: Being the Personal Adventures of Corporal Pike of the Fourth Ohio Cavalry . . . Fully Illustrating the Secret Service* (Cincinnati: J. R. Hawley, 1865), 219. Pike also appears in the regimental history of the Fourth Ohio Cavalry, where he is described helping fellow soldiers cut off behind enemy lines. At one point, Pike gave the name of "Jabe [sic] Fitzhugh," very likely the same alias he used with Porter Bibb; see Lucien Wulsin, ed., *The Story of the Fourth Regiment Ohio Veteran Volunteer Cavalry . . .* (Cincinnati: n.p., 1912), 90–1.

to the Federal Colonel Murphy instead of the woman. Under the circumstances I thought I was excusable." Likewise, Green Haley provided intelligence on only one occasion, when he "carried a dispatch" to Sam Looney, a Union recruiting officer from Winston County, informing him that "the Rebel Cavalry was in the country." John Hayes of Limestone County simply notified Union troops "when I thought there was danger about when they were scattered around" the neighborhood. And when William H. Wroten and S. S. Strong left Confederate territory together from their neighborhood on the southern peninsula of Baldwin County on the Alabama Gulf Coast, they brought valuable information along. After dragging a small boat overland "across the Peninsula from Bon Secour Bay which is the east part of Mobile Bay to the Gulf of Mexico," they launched themselves into the Gulf and sailed toward Union-occupied Fort Barancas, Florida. When the boys arrived, they "reported to Gen. Asboth in command of Barancas," to whom Wroten gave "a lot of Confederate newspapers printed in Mobile which I carried with me and all the information I could about Fort Morgan."[32]

White unionists, of course, were not the only ones to offer information to soldiers on a casual basis. From the first Federal invasion of Alabama, slaves represented a critical source of intelligence to Union forces, who knew that bondspeople were well informed about rebel movements, living as they did in Confederate households. Unlike Confederates, who according to one former slave "never trusted us black folks" for any information, Federal soldiers came to rely very heavily on the intelligence offered by slaves.[33] Such casual informants brought in news gathered on their journey to refugee camps, shared intelligence about troop strength and location with federal soldiers marching through their neighborhoods, and reported news of skirmishes or battles to unionists and Federal spies they encountered in woods, fields, or swamps.[34]

A fairly typical example of this sort of information sharing happened in October 1863, when two Ohio cavalrymen made contact with slaves

32. Claim 14221, James H. Haynes, Lauderdale Co., April 3, 1873; Claim 2177, Green M. Haley, Marion Co., March 28, 1872; Claim 16404, John S. Hayes, Limestone Co., July 19, 1875; Claim 3789F, William Henry Wroten, Baldwin Co., March 8, 1878; all in SCC.

33. Claim 14957, Jackson Daniel, Madison Co., May 25, 1874, SCC.

34. Brig. Gen. E. A. Carr to Maj. Gen. Stephen A. Hurlbut, September 15, 1863, OR, Ser. I, vol. 30, pt. 3, 642; Brig. Gen. C. L. Matthies to Lt. Col. R. M. Sawyer, May 16, 1864, OR, Ser. I, vol. 38, pt. 4, 215; Brig. Gen. R. S. Granger to Maj. Gen. George Thomas, October 9, 1864, OR, Ser. I, vol. 39, pt. 3, 171.

living on a plantation situated on the Tennessee River. Assigned to take a secret message behind enemy lines to General Sherman, who was at that point marching eastward from Memphis through North Alabama, the two Ohioans were ordered to follow their "own judgment as to the best and safest way to get to him." Traveling by canoe as surreptitiously as possible, they became confused about where they were. After landing at the foot of a large cornfield, they made their way to the plantation's slave quarters. There, they asked the "old Deacon" for the location of the closest Confederate camps. In response, he explained that the Yankees had come "very near capturing his young master and his whole company, at Florence" the previous night. Brant then inquired where "his young master was" and the old man replied that "he was with some other officers in the big house, and the big company was camped up the lane, in the woods." After getting directions to Florence, the men left the plantation, taking to their commanders valuable information: the name of a leading Confederate soldier as well as the location of his plantation.[35] A similar incident occurred to W. L. Curry of the First Ohio Cavalry. Having been cut off from his command south of the Tennessee River, Curry was carefully picking his way to safety when he met "a colored man going to mill with a sack of corn on his back." The soldier questioned this man on the whereabouts of Decatur, and learned that he had only ten miles to go to reach it. "He directed me the way I should go and cautioned me to keep away from the public roads, as the country was full of rebel cavalry and I was liable to be picked up at any moment."[36]

Slaves were also uniquely able to identify "true union men" among a host of dissembling white people who would willingly profess loyalty to a Federal soldier, provide false information, and then turn around and report back to local rebels. Bondspeople thus represented valuable intermediaries—through them, Federal soldiers could test their own intelligence without actually risking being deceived or captured. A detachment of the Twelfth Indiana Cavalry operating near Huntsville, for instance, relied on "the guidance of a negro" to find "an old fellow by the name of Murry," who was a "tolerable good union man" from whom the cavalry hoped to get names of local rebels.[37] Soldiers of Company K, Fifth Iowa

35. Wulsin, *Story of the Fourth Regiment Ohio Veteran Volunteer Cavalry,* 91, 97.

36. W. L. Curry, *Four Years in the Saddle: History of the First Regiment Ohio Volunteer Cavalry: War of the Rebellion—1861–1865* (Columbus: Chaplin, 1898), 343.

37. Charles A. Harper to his family, July 27, 1864, Charles A. Harper Papers, F84, IHS.

Cavalry, were saved from making a serious mistake by a network of informed slaves. "At night we stopped at a planter's a little off the road who claimed to be a union man," Corporal Eugene Marshall wrote in his diary, "but his Negroes said that he was a secessionist." They instead directed the soldiers to the planter's brother, whom the slaves knew to be "true to the Union cause."[38] Similarly, slave Willis Carr of Cherokee County was living on the farm of Elijah Carr, himself a unionist, when he was approached by a Union spy in the autumn of 1864. "His name was Joseph Smith," Willis Carr explained to the SCC. "[He] came to me and told me who he was and that he was from Sherman's Army." Smith had been directed to contact Carr's master, but he wanted to confirm the man's unionist sentiments with Carr before going forward. "I told him how things stood and he staid all night at my master's." Having found Willis Carr trustworthy, Smith called on the slave again the next day, asking for guidance to another safe house. Carr pointed out the house of "Mr. William Matthews," a unionist with whom the spy stayed another night and day before he "went on his way."[39] In this way, a chain of espionage and protection extended out of slave quarters into the houses of unionist masters and back again.

A different "type" of unionist informant was the regular spy, an individual whose presence was critical to Union soldiers undertaking reconnaissance operations. Such spies were so important to the secret service of Huntsville, in fact, that one Federal soldier stationed there kept a list of "union men" in the surrounding area "who can be relied on for information"—the list went to twenty-one names, and included two entire families, the Fisks and the Hills, spread over multiple households; farmer Seaborn Jones and factory-owner Thomas McFarland; as well as two women, Sarah Bevil and Jane Ferguson.[40] Unionists acting as regular spies generally identified themselves to Federal forces as loyalists or were vouched for by others, and thereafter maintained regular communication with soldiers in or near their neighborhoods. Loyalist spies living within Union lines were more likely to visit Federal headquarters with informa-

38. March 2, 1862, Eugene Marshall Diary, Eugene Marshall Papers, DU.

39. Claim 6828, William Mathews, Cherokee Co., May 19, 1874: Testimony of Willis Carr, SCC.

40. Secret Service Ledger of E. Bourlier, Edward F. Reid Papers, SC 1068, IHS. McFarland and Jones both made successful claims to the SCC; see Claim 19875, Seaborn Jones, Sr., Estate, Madison Co., January 26, 1874, and Claim 10249, Thomas McFarland, Madison Co., April 16, 1872; both in SCC.

tion than those living south of the Tennessee River. However, Franklin County planter John C. Goodloe, considered by Federal commanders "one of the best posted [men] on the south side of the river," crossed the river a few times in 1864 with news of Confederate activities.[41] Similarly, the repeated delivery of accurate information by another "Union woman" south of the river had gained the "entire confidence" of Colonel Doolittle, commanding officer at Decatur in 1864. In what was likely a typical communication, she sent Doolittle a dispatch conveying news about an imminent cavalry campaign, as well as Southern newspaper reports noting the whereabouts of Forrest's troops.[42] Similarly, Elizabeth Wright, also living south of the Tennessee, repeatedly gave Federal forces "all the information about the rebels that I could learn from any source." Wright had always "felt it was a mighty wrong thing to attempt to break up [the] government" and had sworn that she "would never aid in breaking it up." She believed, instead, that duty to the Union and to her husband, who had crossed the lines to work for the garrison at Bridgeport, required that she aid and abet the Union however she could.[43]

Federal soldiers also cultivated regular spies among the slave population of the Tennessee Valley. Early in Alabama's first Federal occupation, Brigadier General O. M. Mitchel was so impressed with the willingness of slaves to assist him, as well as their exceptional ability to obtain information, that he fashioned a plan to deputize "watchful guards among the slaves on the plantations bordering the river from Bridgeport to Florence." Facing the task of protecting some one hundred and twenty miles of riverfront from guerrilla incursions, Mitchel believed that he would only be able to hold the territory with the help of these slave guards, to whom he promised Federal protection in exchange for information. "With the aid of the negroes in watching the river," he commented, "I feel myself sufficiently strong to defy the enemy." Stanton concurred with Mitchel's view, asserting that the "assistance of slaves is an element

41. Quote in Brig. Gen. G. M. Dodge to Lt. Col. William T. Clark, April 24, 1864, *OR*, Ser. I, vol. 32, pt. 3, 482. See also Col. Richard Rowett to Capt. J. W. Barnes, April 23, 1864, *OR*, Ser. I, vol. 32, pt. 3, 460; and Claim 4348, John C. Goodloe, Colbert Co., February 1, 1872; Claim 4348, John C. Goodloe, Colbert Co., February 1, 1872: Testimony of George E. Spencer, in SCC. Spencer commanded the First Alabama Cavalry and served as Gen. Dodge's adjutant general.

42. Brig. Gen. R. S. Granger to Maj. Gen. Lovell H. Rousseau, October 17, 1864, *OR*, Ser. I, vol. 39, pt. 3, 342.

43. Claim 7555, Elizabeth A. Wright, Marshall Co., February 19, 1874, SCC.

of military strength which, under proper regulations, you are fully justified in employing" and which was a legitimate "means to suppress the rebellion and restore the authority of the Government."[44]

Although Federal soldiers developed independent relationships with slave spies, some of the more remarkable loyalist espionage networks involved collaborations between unionist slaveholders and their slaves. By converting the master-slave relationship into a weapon, unionist masters and slaves together could become highly effective saboteurs. Spinster Caroline Atkisson, for instance, relied heavily on one of her slaves to be her personal spy and messenger, through whom she sent information about Confederate movements to Union soldiers.[45] Another regular informant, to whom Union commanders referred to simply as "old Kelley," sent at least one dispatch to Federal forces "by negroes"—in it he reported the location and strength of rebel cavalry congregating in his neighborhood east of Bridgeport.[46] And Henry Gargis, an avowed unionist and merchant farmer who owned four slaves and an estate worth fourteen thousand dollars in 1860, regularly employed one of his slaves, Sam, "for the purpose of carrying information and provisions to Union prisoners, refugees and Union men as occasion required." As a consequence of his actions, Gargis acquired a good reputation among Union secret service agents, one of whom, William W. Jones, became especially close to the Gargis family and married one of Henry's daughters after the war. Jones, a soldier from Ohio working as a spy in North Alabama, explained to the Southern Claims Commission that he had been "instructed by my superior officer to place implicit confidence in [Gargis] as a union man and to send all Union refugees, and escaped federal prisoners to his . . . house and was assured he would furnish them with food and cause them to be safely guided into the federal lines." Jones, Gargis, and Gargis's slaves collaborated throughout the war with great success, assisting many soldiers and civilians on their escape through the lines.[47]

44. Quoted passages in Brig. Gen. O. M. Mitchel to Secretary Edwin M. Stanton, May 4, 1862, OR, Ser. I, vol. 10, pt. 2, 162; and Secretary Edwin M. Stanton to Brig. Gen. O. M. Mitchel, May 5, 1862, OR, Ser. I, vol. 10, pt. 2, 165.

45. Claim 12374, Caroline H. Atkisson, Colbert Co., August 22, 1873: Testimony of Sarah Hicks, SCC.

46. Brig. Gen. William H. Lytle to Maj. Gen. Philip H. Sheridan, August 15, 1863, 7:30 P.M., OR, Ser. I, vol. 30, pt. 3, 39.

47. Claim 5195, Henry Gargis, Colbert Co., December 16, 1872; and Claim 5195, Henry Gargis, Colbert Co., December 16, 1872: Testimony of William W. Jones, SCC.

The Union army actively encouraged these master-slave informant networks. For instance, Joshua Mullins, the owner of a sizable plantation behind Confederate lines in Franklin County, and William Taylor, one of Mullins's slaves, began to conspire together only after being approached by Federal troops. In August 1862, Lieutenant Colonel Gilbert Moyers of the Third Michigan Cavalry led his soldiers through the town of Russellville and arrived at Mullins's plantation seeking food and forage, large quantities of which the planter willingly furnished him. The exchange marked the beginning of what could have been a deadly project for both Taylor and Mullins. As Taylor remembered it, various soldiers of Moyers's command encouraged him to leave the plantation and go North. Moyers, however, offered the slave another option: if Taylor would stay, he might serve as a spy for the army. Mullins, Taylor, and Moyers all understood that the person of a slave was one of the best disguises possible for a spy, especially behind Confederate lines. Taylor, cloaked by his own enslavement, had access to, as his master put it, "intelligence not otherwise . . . safely attained." The espionage scheme evolved as part of Taylor's work as a traveling preacher for surrounding slave communities. As he recalled later, "I was a minister of the Gospel and in attendance on my congregations, was enabled through my membership to get much information of value." The arrangement was, according to Taylor, a very fruitful one. "I became, I think, quite useful to the union soldiers," he explained. In fact, the setup was so successful that "William W. Jones and others of the United States Secret Service" made the Mullins house "their headquarters," where they lived disguised as civilians and received from Mullins and Taylor all the information they could discover from their various sources.[48]

The collaboration between Mullins and Taylor, however, neither erased nor preempted the difficulties that arose between unionist masters and slaves when the Union army occupied the slaveholding South. The two parties rarely shared the same understanding of their roles in the affair, and their cooperation did not imply a lessening of either man's desire for freedom or mastery. Mullins continued to believe that he had given Taylor permission, as his slave, to act on his behalf for the Union army, regardless of Taylor's obvious opportunity to leave the plantation

48. Claim 18929, Joshua Mullins, Franklin Co., September 11, 1873: Testimony of William Taylor; and Claim 18929, Joshua Mullins, Franklin Co., September 11, 1873; both in SCC.

for the North. Tellingly, Taylor clearly distanced himself from his former master after the war ended. In his postwar testimony as a witness for Mullins's Southern Claims Commission claim, he eschewed his slave name—"Monk"—by which he had been known on the plantation and which his former master continued to call him after the war. Moreover, he had moved away from Mullins's plantation, his home since birth.

Regardless of the ambivalence evident in the postwar relationship between master and slave, both Mullins and Taylor had found their wartime arrangement useful. Taylor pursued his objective of undermining the Confederacy and, he hoped, destroying slavery; Mullins distinguished himself as loyal to the Union army by offering up his slave to be the army's servant, thereby distancing himself from the mass of planters in the South. Slave and master were not the only players carefully crafting this interchange, however. The Union army effectively manipulated its powerful position vis-à-vis these very different types of Southern dissenters. By granting the slave more freedom than his master would, the army gained his trust and loyalty. But, by allowing the espionage to remain rooted in the regular routine of plantation life, the army did not totally disrupt Mullins's mastery of his domain.

Guides and Scouts

The Federal army required more than a stable of stationary informants to satisfy their counterintelligence needs. To even come close to understanding, much less navigating, the unfamiliar terrain and society in which they had to operate, Union officers required guides whose main service was to lead soldiers as they moved through the landscape. White unionists acting in this capacity were sometimes attached to a Federal post or garrison, after having come there as refugees or to do business. George Mann of Madison County, for instance, sometimes visited the garrison at his county's seat, Huntsville, and made himself known as an informed loyal man ready to help the troops. "[W]hen I would be in Huntsville," he explained, "I went out with commands to show the roads to places where they wanted to go." Potential guides living behind the lines were more likely to be contacted at their homes by soldiers who had been given their names and locations ahead of time. Edward Frost, who lived well south of the Tennessee River in Walker County, was, for instance, roused from sleep "at the dead hours of the night" to serve "as a pilot" for scouts and soldiers operating behind the lines. "[I] taken them to where they could get all the information they wanted to secure on their march," he explained. John Hayes, a guide from Limestone County, remembered, "It seemed as if when they wanted a company to [pilot them] to a place they could come to me. Whenever a command would leave here I would remain and when the next one would come in, I would go to them for employment."[49] The army preferred to use established, well-known guides with reputations for reliability and trustworthiness, but when troops moved into new territory, they frequently had to rely on strangers for help. As Chaplain Marion Morrison of the Ninth Illinois explained, his regiment turned to such a man as they marched through North Alabama in October 1863. As the surrounding countryside was "poor, rough, broken country" which wreaked havoc with the regiment's sense of direction, they stopped their march to get information. Luckily, they came across "a good Union man, with a clever family," and asked the "old man to go with us, as a guide."[50]

Some Federal commanders believed that the difficulties in finding a trustworthy white unionist to guide them in unfamiliar territory could be best avoided by depending upon slaves. Bondspeople had long since developed methods of secret travel to facilitate interplantation relationships, religious worship, independent hunting and trading, or escape.[51] They easily adapted such skills to aid Federal soldiers. James Pike, the Texas-born Union spy, received vital assistance from slaves he encountered while struggling to find his way back to his command in northern Alabama in late summer 1862. Having spent the night soaking wet after falling into a swamp, Pike crept up to the edge of a rear field on a plantation, where he could see the slaves "just turning out to work." Pike made his way to the quarters, where he found "a gray-haired veteran" and informed him of his identity, begging for something to eat. The man went into his cabin and returned with "an ash-cake, and a very large, thick slice of ham, and gave it to me, saying, he was glad to be able to do something for 'his people.'" After spending some time eating and speak-

49. Claim 22000, George W. Mann, Madison Co., August 25, 1876; Claim 6636, Edward Frost, Walker Co., February 9, 1872; Claim 16404, John S. Hayes, Limestone Co., July 19, 1875; all in SCC. For other Union scouts, see Claim 1459, Isaac Brunston, Marshall Co., August 23, 1871: Testimony of James R. Johnson; and Claim 889, John Miller Estate, Marshall Co., June 10, 1874; both in SCC.

50. Morrison, *History of the Ninth Regiment Illinois*, 73.

51. Genovese, *Roll, Jordan, Roll*, 654–6; Blassingame, *Slave Community*, 196–202, 254; Jordan, *Tumult and Silence*, 58–9.

ing with the old man, Pike asked if there was someone who could guide him out of the swamp that had caused him so much trouble the night before. A young boy was assigned to lead Pike away from the plantation and toward Huntsville. "My guide seemed to be perfectly at home in the swamp, and piloted the way for three miles over a string of logs, which seemed to be arranged by accident, and not design, so as to form a complete chain across it, so that we were landed on the opposite side without wading a step." Pike, amazed as this secret pathway was revealed to him, was the lucky beneficiary of the slaves' system of surreptitious travel.[52]

Guides, white and black, were important to Federal troops, but scouts were invaluable. Their responsibilities, while sometimes including guide work, were nonetheless more expansive, more dangerous, and less serendipitous than those of guides. Most scouts were regularly and repeatedly employed by the Union army and, like the cavalry forces with whom they frequently cooperated, functioned as the eyes and ears of Federal commanders. On foot or mounted, they undertook reconnaissance and espionage missions to learn about Confederate troop strength and plans; to visit and pick up any information from networks of known unionists and cooperative slaves in no-man's-land or the Confederate frontier; to recruit whites and blacks into the Union army; and sometimes to act undercover for weeks or months at a time as secret service agents.[53] Along with regularly enlisted Union troops from the North, local unionists represented a significant portion of these scouts, bringing to the job long months of experience hiding in the woods and traveling through the river valley and the mountains, experience that proved invaluable to Federal commanders. Very few, if any, scouts seem to have been African American, probably because they were less able to travel and interact freely among Confederates.

Many loyalists were eager to serve in this capacity. Wherever Union

52. James Pike, Scout and Ranger, 225–6.

53. For discussions of scouts and their duties, see Brig. Gen. McCook to Maj. Gen. Don Carlos Buell, August 6, 1862, OR, Ser. I, vol. 16, pt. 2, 267; Maj. Gen. Don Carlos Buell to Commanding Officer at Athens [Ala.], August 10, 1862, OR, Ser. I, vol. 16, pt. 2, 301; Brig. Gen. Grenville M. Dodge to Maj. Gen. Stephen A. Hurlbut, July 17, 1863, OR, Ser. I, vol. 23, pt. 2, 539; Maj. Gen. George H. Thomas to Brig. Gen. James A. Garfield, August 2, 1863, OR, Ser. I, vol. 30, pt. 3, 199; Maj. Gen. Hurlbut to Brig. Gen. John A. Rawlins, October 2, 1863, OR, Ser. I, vol. 30, pt. 4, 29; Brig. Gen. Grenville M. Dodge to Lt. Col. [Jesse] Phillips, February 23, 1864, OR, Ser. I, vol. 32, pt. 2, 453; Brig. Gen. James C. Veatch to Brig. Gen. Grenville M. Dodge, April 16, 1864, 7:50 P.M., OR, Ser. I, vol. 32, pt. 3, 379.

troops arrived on the Alabama home front, groups of local white unionists presented themselves at the camps or garrisoned towns to offer their
services for hire. James Morris of Marshall County was part of such a
company of "scouts and guides" that operated "under the direction of
the different Generals who would be stationed near us."[54] Once a man
demonstrated reliability and trustworthiness, the army might repeatedly
use him in their maneuvers. Colonel William Lyon, stationed at Claysville, Alabama, in June 1864, made a scout out of a "refugee" who had
independently provided Lyon with useful intelligence, and who was
"well vouched for" as a "loyal and reliable man." Thereafter, Lyon sent
the scout back across the lines "to obtain information and keep me
posted of the movements and intentions of the enemy."[55]

Brigadier General Grenville M. Dodge, the organizer of the First Alabama Cavalry, U.S.A., was an assiduous recruiter of scouts and secret
service agents. As commander of the Federal post at Corinth, Mississippi, during much of 1863, as well as Union headquarters at Pulaski,
Tennessee, during the Atlanta mobilization, Dodge developed a "stable"
of loyal whites from northern Mississippi, northern Alabama, and southwestern and middle Tennessee, as well as Northern secret service agents.
Dodge had a simple philosophy about trusting unionists with the sensitive responsibilities of scouting: "I never ask them to take the [loyalty]
oath," he explained to Colonel Henry R. Mizner, "but treat them as they
act. . . . I know no Union man in this country unless he openly declares
and shows by his acts that he is willing and ready to shoulder a musket
in our cause."[56] Unionist scouts proved their loyalty by willingly undertaking the considerable risks of operating undercover.

Commanders other than Dodge also recruited spies to their personal
service. Very early in the war, Brigadier General T. L. Crittenden, stationed at Battle Creek, Alabama, employed a spy to travel east to Chattanooga to learn Confederate troop strength. The spy reported "some
21,000 men between [Chattanooga] and Bridgeport [Alabama], many of
them conscripts undrilled, McCown in command." Other information
included the artillery strength of the forces, as well as information on

54. Claim 18293, James Henry Morris, Marshall Co., July 18, 1876, SCC.

55. Col. William V. Lyon to Capt. and Asst. Adj. Gen. Charles Gardner, July 20, 1864,
Box 1. RG 393, Records of the United States Continental Commands, Records of the Department of Alabama.

56. Brig. Gen. Grenville M. Dodge to Col. Henry R. Mizner, November 27, 1863, OR,
Ser. I, vol. 31, pt. 3, 262.

Confederate supplies in Atlanta. "My agent is a good Union man and well vouched for," Crittenden reported to his headquarters.[57] In July 1862, unionist Meredith Thompson, a farmer from Franklin County, took a trip from his home at Frankfort to Confederate camps at nearby Russellville "at the request of Major General [George] Thomas." His mission was to move "among the Confederates to obtain information" and report back to Thomas. Likewise, Lieutenant Colonel Jesse J. Phillips, commanding the Ninth Illinois Mounted Infantry at the county seat of Athens in 1864, hired unionist Mial Abernathy of Limestone County "as a government scout," in which capacity Abernathy "learned information" and "conducted cavalry through the country."[58] Major General Alexander McCook also employed numerous loyalists to scout out rebel territory. He was cautious, however, and created checks to ensure that his system would not fail on account of misinformation fed to him by what latter-day idiom would term "double-agents." "I have four men in the mountains," McCook reported to Major General Buell's chief of staff in July 1862, "neither of whom knows the others are there."[59]

Unionist guides and scouts were, unlike other informants, frequently compensated, and their dangerous work could be lucrative.[60] William G. Douthit, for instance, received a per diem of $1.50 for acting as a guide for Federal troops stationed in Corinth in mid-December 1863. A. J. Lentz, the son of a unionist patriarch and denizen of infamously loyal "Lentzville" in Limestone County, was paid a hundred dollars in November 1863, for acting as a Federal guide from November 1, 1863, through November 20, 1863. Well-known unionist and scout William B. Looney received fifty dollars from the Union army for traveling from Corinth to his home county of Winston as a spy in April 1863. Particularly dangerous or long assignments garnered even higher payments. J. T. Evans, for example, received five hundred dollars for undertaking a mission in June 1863, at the time when the Union army's Vicksburg campaign was under-

57. Brig. Gen. Thomas L. Crittenden to Col. James B. Fry, July 19, 1862, OR, Ser. I, vol. 16, pt. 2, 183–4.

58. Claim 13286, Meredith Thompson, Colbert Co., August 23, 1873; Claim 4806, Mial S. Abernathy, Limestone Co., July 23, 1875; both in SCC.

59. Brig. Gen. Alexander McD. McCook to Col. James B. Fry, July 19, 1862, OR, Ser. I, vol. 16, pt. 2, 217.

60. Maj. Gen. Don Carlos Buell to Brig. Gen. McCook, August 6, 1862, OR, Ser. I, vol. 16, pt. 2, 267; Maj. Gen. James S. Negley to Lt. Col. George E. Flynt, September 7, 1863, 5 P.M, OR, Ser. I, vol. 30, pt. 3, 409.

way. Evans managed to infiltrate Confederate General John C. Breckinridge's army and travel with it as far behind Confederate lines as Selma,
deep in Alabama's Black Belt. There he learned that Breckinridge was
taking his troops to reinforce General Joseph E. Johnston's forces at Jackson, Mississippi. He returned to Corinth and reported that intelligence
to Dodge.[61] Likewise, Alabamian John Stout, later recalled by one veteran
Federal officer as "General Dodge's favorite spy" for having "performed
some wonderful service during the war," traveled extensively through
the border areas between Alabama and Mississippi in the autumn of
1863. For over a month's worth of scouting he was compensated three
hundred dollars. Finally, women, too, were sometimes paid handsomely
for this risky work. Mary Malone, for instance, received a total of eight
hundred dollars for taking three separate trips in the summer of June
and July 1863 "for secret service," journeying from Corinth to Selma,
Alabama, then on to Meridian and Columbus, Mississippi, and back
again to Corinth.[62]

Loyalists had more than a fiscal incentive to act as informants, scouts,
and spies. Their position as trusted advisers could give them considerable
power over specific enemies, for they knew the names and character of
the rebels in their region and were all too eager to share them with the
Union. Being an informant thus meant not simply serving the larger
cause of the Union. It also meant punishing enemies, or at the very least,
exposing citizens pretending to be loyal. This knowledge could turn the
tables on old enemies, guaranteeing them an uncomfortable and circum-

61. Payment Voucher for W. G. Douthit, January 9, 1863; List of Monies Expended for
Secret Service, &c. [1863–64] and Payment Voucher for A. J. Lentz, November 24, 1863 (also
see Claim 5202, Solomon Lentz, Limestone Co., June 13, 1876, SCC); Payment Voucher for
William B. Looney, April 21, [1863]; Payment Voucher for J. T. Evans, June 31, 1863; all in
Secret Service Files, Dodge Papers, SHSI. I want to thank Paul Horton for first alerting me
to the existence of Dodge's secret service papers. For Breckinridge's movements, see Jefferson Davis to Gen. Joseph E. Johnston, May 30, 1863, and Report of Gen. Joseph E. Johnston,
C.S. Army, of Operations March 12–July 20, 1863, November 11, 1863, OR, Ser. I, vol. 24,
pt. 1, 194, 242.

62. The first quote is from Thomas Fullerton, the attorney of record in numerous Alabama SCC cases and a former adjutant of the Sixty-fourth Illinois Volunteer Infantry. The
Sixty-fourth Illinois recruited numerous Alabama unionists during the war. Fullerton made
this comment about Stout in a marginal note in Claim 21671, George W. Cook, Fayette Co.,
May 28, 1877, SCC; for more evidence of Stout's service, see Payment Vouchers for John
Stout, both dated November 1, 1863, Secret Service Files, Dodge Papers, SHSI; and Claim
4042, Peter Ingle, Marion Co., March 1, 1878, SCC. Second quote in Payment Vouchers for
Mary Malone, June 1, 1863; June 30, 1863; and July 25, 1863; all in Secret Service Files,
Dodge Papers, SHSI.

scribed existence in occupied parts of North Alabama. Army Brigadier General Thomas Crittenden, for instance, was informed by "a good Union man," that a rebel deserter bringing in information to the Union camps at Battle Creek, Alabama, was not to be trusted. "I am told he is a bad boy and a great rebel," Crittenden reported. Unionist information undermined the deserter's chances of gaining more than grudging Federal protection. Major General William Rosecrans ordered that a suspicious ferryman by the name of Love, living in Jasper, Tennessee, on Alabama's border, be arrested on the strength of unionist reports: "[He] better be sent away as a prisoner; or at least be carefully watched," the general's chief of staff ordered. "Union citizens regard him as a dangerous man." Another group of Confederate deserters, four in number, arrived in Claysville, Alabama, after fleeing General Hood's army in Georgia, only to find a former neighbor ensconced in the camp as a Union informant. "William Clapp knows these deserters," Brigadier General R. S. Granger reported to his superiors, "and says they were reliable men before the war." Clapp's tepid endorsement was enough for the Federal authorities to accept as truthful the deserters' intelligence about Hood's troop strength; it is notable, however, that Clapp made a point to vouch only for their prewar character of "reliability." He did not say they were "union men" who had been forced into the Confederate army against their will, nor was he willing to endorse their wartime character.[63] E. Bourlier, a Union spy in Huntsville, likely relied on similar sources of information to identify potentially troublesome rebels who needed "watching," the names of whom he carefully catalogued in a diary. Among those recorded was the name of William Acklin, reported to have said "that families of Unionists should not stay in Huntsville during the occupation by the confeds" and to have "always been very officious against unionists." The keeper of the "Billiard Salloon in the Huntsville Hotel" was recorded as "very insulting and threatening to Unionists"; John and William Tilson had "used the expression that men who expressed Union sentiments be hung and their property confiscated."[64]

---

63. Brig. Gen. Thomas Crittenden to Lt. Col. James B. Fry, July 15, 1862, *OR*, Ser. I, vol. 16, pt. 2, 152; Brig. Gen. James A. Garfield to Maj. Gen. Reynolds, August 26, 1863, 9:30 A.M., *OR*, Ser. I, vol. 30, pt. 3, 173–4; Brig. Gen. Robert S. Granger to Maj. Gen. George Thomas, October 26, 1864, *OR*, Ser. I, vol. 39, pt. 3, 450.

64. E. Bourlier Diary, 1864, 3–4, 5, 11, Edward F. Reid Papers, SC 1068, IHS. The diary was originally believed to be written by Edward F. Reid, a captain in the Thirteenth Indiana Cavalry with whose papers it is currently stored at the Indiana Historical Society. However, internal evidence suggests that the diary was kept by E. Bourlier (his first name remains a

Unionist intelligence was not simply used to keep an eye on potentially troublesome rebels, but frequently led Federal authorities to take
action against rebel citizens. For example, in October 1863, three Union
scouts working for General Dodge traveled to Pikeville, Marion County,
deep behind Confederate lines in the Hill Country, and "arrested the
sheriff of [the] county, took jail keys away from him, and released 75
Union prisoners," all of whom "got safely away."[65] Federal forces took
less aggressive, but equally dramatic action late in 1862 or early 1863,
when a "general rumor" reached the garrison at Bridgeport, Jackson
County, Alabama. The soldiers learned that living in the county was a
man named Augustus Gunter, a "base rebel" renowned among union
men as a "bitter, vindictive and overbearing man" who reveled in "cursing and abusing union soldiers." Gunter had traveled with fellow rebel
sympathizers to Virginia to visit his brother, a Confederate soldier, directly after the Confederate victory at Manassas (Bull Run). According
to unionists, he and his friends went all that way "to view and pillage
over the battleground" and then came back to Alabama "with the fin-
gerbones & rib bones of what they said was Yankee[s] . . . picked up
on the battlefields." These they showed around to any interested people,
bragging that they were "going to make pipe stems & finger rings out of
them." Upon hearing the rumor, Federal soldiers set out and captured
Gunter, "put him between two feather beds, and piled all the blankets
they could get on him." When bystanders asked why they were doing
this, the soldiers "said it was to sweat the rebel out of him."[66]

For the Union army, information like this was the stuff of good counterintelligence: commanders benefited from unionists' intelligence because it allowed Federal forces to know who was who and to protect
themselves from trickery and betrayal (although it must be acknowledged that commanders could be fooled, as well). But something else

mystery) who clearly operated as a spy behind enemy lines in Alabama, as well as a spy in
Huntsville during the occupation of 1864. It is unclear to what regiment he was officially
connected, or under whose command he operated; the diary also suggests that he lived in
Pennsylvania at some time, but had many acquaintances in and around the Huntsville area.
He apparently made the record to give to a potential successor—Reid may have been that
man.

65. Brig. Gen. G. M. Dodge, to Asst. Adj. Gen. Harris, October 19, 1863, OR, Ser. I, vol.
30, pt. 4, 477.

66. Claim 20467, William Ridge Estate, Jackson Co., November 10, 1875: Testimony of
George W. Ridge, SCC.

was going on, too. Incidents like these doubtlessly delighted unionists. The information they provided led not only to the advancement of the Union cause in the South, but to personal vindication and the punishment of their enemies. When Union soldiers decided on the strength of unionist reports to spy on Huntsville's billiard keeper, to imprison a deserter rather than hire him as a spy, or to humiliate a man like Gus Gunter, they became party to a fight that, while in some ways was their own, would have continued with or without their help. Unionists and men like Gus Gunter would have hated one another and done whatever they could to avenge themselves upon the other whether the army got involved or not. When it did intervene, the army itself became a tool in a highly personalized fight.

Unionist Partisan Fighters

The ambiguous nature of the counterinsurgency effort was nowhere more apparent than in the agendas and operations of partisan fighters for the Union. The experience of unionist scout George Ridge, whose story opened this chapter, is particularly revealing. After being relieved of duty following his stint as a guide for Generals Sheridan and Rosecrans in September 1863, Ridge returned to Doran's Cove to search for the bodies of his father and his brother. Despite weeks of searching, however, he never found his father, William, although it was rumored that the guerrillas had disposed of his body in a cave near the town of Stevenson. He did manage to locate the corpse of his brother James "a quarter of a mile from Stevenson on the side of the mountain, crammed down betwixt two big rocks and covered with a chunk and leaves." The body bore all the signs of James's capture. "He had hickory bark tied on his neck, wrists and ankles," George Ridge remembered. "I taken his remains and buried them." What Ridge could not bury were the deep-seated feelings of rage and guilt he felt about these deaths. Prior to the murders and his enlistment in the army, Ridge had worked on the railroad as a way to gain exemption from the draft. There he had an altercation with one of his family's persecutors, Lieutenant Newton Horn, leader of the conscript cavalry. In hindsight, Ridge rued missing what he saw as his final opportunity to save his loved ones. "I have been sorry a thousand times that I did not take my pick and kill [Horn] when he accosted me," he explained to the SCC. Ridge's feelings of guilt, when combined with fury he felt toward the rebels who persecuted his family, was a powerful motivator. After Ridge had laid his dead to rest and moved his remaining family to Nashville for protection, he came back to Jackson County and enlisted as a partisan scout and fighter under Brigadier General Wladimir Krzyzanowski, commanding the garrison force at Bridgeport. For the rest of the war, George Ridge spent his days "in charge of twenty-five and thirty men," roaming "through these mountains after the rebels," seeking his own personal vengeance while he fought the Union's fight.[67]

Ridge's story illuminates an important aspect of North Alabama's, and the South's, guerrilla war. Especially after 1863, distinctions between "formal" and "informal" soldiers grew less and less sharp across the occupied South, largely because, as historian Noel C. Fisher has argued, participants in Civil War guerrilla warfare rarely drew neat lines between "violence motivated by political ends and violence originating in personal grievances."[68] For unionists, this blurring of purpose was far more than a cynical excuse for men to indulge their baser and bloodier instincts. Rather, the distinction between the political and personal was simply impossible, for it required a disaggregation of concerns about family, home, and property from concerns about the war's purpose and conduct.[69] For unionists, the war had long been coterminous with defense of kin and community; when kin and community suffered humiliation and brutality, desires for personal justice only intensified. As one Federal soldier from southern Alabama pointed out, "There was a strong thirst for revenge among men whose housetops had been burned over the heads of their defenceless wives and children." The intensely personal and local nature of the guerrilla war in North Alabama made it, like that in East Tennessee and elsewhere in the South, "inherently ambiguous, both militarily and morally" and "best understood not as a set of clearly defined categories but rather as a spectrum, with much overlapping and much blurring."[70] Ultimately, as historian Daniel Sutherland has argued in the case of Arkansas, Alabama's guerrilla conflict was not

67. Ibid.; Claim 20468, George W. Ridge, Jackson Co., November 22, 1875; both in SCC.

68. Fisher, *War at Every Door*, 62–3.

69. Sutherland, "Guerrillas: The Real War in Arkansas," 136–7.

70. Richardson, *How I Reached the Union Lines*, 24.

"a war within a war," but was "*the* war."[71] It did not simply arrive from outside as a neatly demarcated "stage" or exception to the "real war."[72] Instead, partisan conflict was organic to North Alabama's social and political history; the real intensity of the Federal counterguerrilla effort was generated from the fusion of the larger military strategy to "clear the bushwhackers out" with long-standing local conflicts.[73]

Like their Confederate adversaries, most unionist guerrilla bands in North Alabama seem to have been fairly compact, usually numbering between twenty and a hundred men. They were independently organized but loosely associated and actively supported by occupying Union forces.[74] For example, unionist George Cook joined a "Home Guard" after he was liberated from a Marion County jail by fellow union men. By Cook's own description, his group was highly informal and irregular. "We were not uniformed," he explained. "I armed myself." But it nonetheless operated "under the direction of [Federal] General Mallory," who endorsed as his own the home guard's objective of putting down "bushwhacking and horse stealing."[75] Such groups were not uncommon. In August 1863, "a party of citizens from the mountains" came into Federal camps at Larkinsville, Alabama, in Jackson County, and asked to be "mustered into service for six months as partisans operating in this vicinity, furnishing their own horses and arms." The First Alabama Cavalry, U.S.A., and various Federal scouts allied with and helped to organize groups of unionist partisans. Brigadier General Grenville M. Dodge reported in April 1864, "several companies of at least 100 men, each led by our scouts and members of the First Alabama Cavalry," were having

71. Sutherland, "Guerrillas: The Real War in Arkansas," 133.

72. B. Franklin Cooling, "A People's War: Partisan Conflict in Tennessee and Kentucky," in Sutherland, *Guerrillas, Unionists and Violence,* 113–4; Sutherland, "Guerrillas: The Real War in Arkansas," 133.

73. Brig. Gen. Jefferson C. Davis to Col. G. P. Thruston, September 2, 1863, 12 M., *OR,* Ser. I, vol. 30, pt. 3, 204. Also see Sutherland, "Guerrilla Warfare in the Confederacy," 291.

74. For size of partisan bands, see Brig. Gen. Jefferson C. Davis to Col. G. P. Thruston, September 2, 1863, 12 M., *OR,* Ser. I, vol. 30, pt. 3, 204; Lt. Col. P. E. Burke to Capt. C. H. Dyer, October 13, 1863, *OR,* Ser. I, vol. 30, pt. 4, 332; Brig. Gen. Grenville M. Dodge to Maj. Gen. J. B. McPherson, April 6, 1864, *OR,* Ser. I, vol. 32, pt. 3, 274.

75. Claim 21671, George W. Cook, Fayette Co., May 28, 1877, SCC. Cook was probably referring to Union commander Robert H. Milroy rather than anyone named "Mallory." Milroy commanded the defenses of the Nashville and Chattanooga Railroad from July 1864 to April 1865.

considerable success in foiling the efforts of Confederate cavalry to cross the Tennessee River. "[T]hey hold the mountain district [south of Decatur] in spite of all efforts of the rebels to catch them."[76]

Union guerrillas cooperated and coordinated with Federal soldiers in a variety of ways. E. G. Richards, the chief musician and bandleader in the 102nd Regiment of the Ohio Volunteer Infantry, described in some detail a typical Federal alliance with irregular unionist partisans. During the summer of 1864, the 102nd was assigned to patrol the length of the Tennessee River between the towns of Bellefonte and Dodsonville. The duty was difficult: Confederate guerrillas patrolled the opposite side of the river and had already engaged Federals in a number of firefights, during which two Union soldiers had been killed. In the course of their work, members of the 102nd Ohio were approached by a group of native Alabamians from the Confederate side of the river who had "organized a company and called themselves 'Home Guards.'" As Richards remembered, "I think the Home Guards first broached the subject to our officers to unite our force with theirs, go across the river early some morning and exterminate the bushwhackers." The officers of the 102nd welcomed the plan, for as much as they had wished to "exterminate the bushwhackers" they had no idea whom to target or how to find them. The unionists, on the other hand, had plenty of knowledge but little in the way of firepower. Acting together, the two groups quickly arranged to carry a plan into fruition.[77]

The next day, around three o'clock in the morning, a squad of about one hundred and fifty men from the 102nd gathered and marched the two miles to the river, and in three separate trips crossed the river on a flatboat. The troops marched up the bank into an "immense cornfield," which stood so tall that it was only upon exiting the corn that the men caught sight of the mountain they were to climb. Coming to a grass-covered path at the foot of the mountain, they headed into the hills. As the soldiers neared the point of rendezvous with their unionist partisan allies, their captain gave them instructions on how to recognize their friends, and what to do with their foes. "'Now,' says the Captain, 'remember that the homeguards and the bushwhackers are dressed alike,

76. Lt. Col. Edward M. McCook to Maj. William H. Sinclair, August 17, 1863, 4 P.M., OR, Ser. I, vol. 30, pt. 3, 61–2. Brig. Gen. Grenville M. Dodge to Maj. Gen. J. B. McPherson, April 6, 1864, OR, Ser. I, vol. 32, pt. 3, 274.

77. George S. Schmutz, ed., History of the 102d Regiment, O.V.I. (n.p.: n.p., 1907), 265.

but we have a countersign, which is "Tiger," and if you see any stranger, demand the countersign, and if he answers "Tiger" you may take him in, but if not,—well—you know what we came for.'" Leaving lookouts along the way, the main body of soldiers climbed to the top of the mountain, where they met up with the unionists. "Together they traversed the mountain, burning a few buildings, killed one man by the name of Lindsay—the home guards said he was a bushwhacker—captured another, also captured three 'critters,' and returned to the riverbank by afternoon." Having "exterminated" one "bushwhacker," the 102nd Ohio recrossed the river. The unionist rangers however, stayed behind to patrol and skirmish on their own, maintaining their independence to fight at their own behest.[78]

Other North Alabama antiguerrilla missions taken on by Federal forces in 1864–65 were similarly shaped by the knowledge and agendas of unionist partisans. For instance, the Twelfth Indiana Cavalry, stationed near Huntsville in the summer of 1864, regularly sent one or two companies out on "a little scout" to find guerrillas, often with the help of unionists. On one week-long scouting expedition, the Twelfth Indiana acted in cooperation with a local man named Harris who had worked as "Chief of Scouts for Gen. Sherman." He had been to Atlanta "3 times" that summer, but had been allowed to return to his home "with orders to clean that country out" and to "burn every house within 10 miles of there" in retaliation if "the bushwhackers fired a single shot into him." Though the Twelfth Indiana burned six houses on that particular mission, their opponents did not, evidently, stop resisting. The company returned to the same area in December and "burned every house" in the town of Vienna in retaliation for its citizens' continued harboring of "bushwhackers."[79]

Another significant aspect of Federal counterinsurgency strategy in the summer of 1864 involved cooperation between unionists and the increasing number of gunboats patrolling the Tennessee River. Working in accordance with intelligence provided by scouts, spies, and partisan fighters, their mission was to flush out guerrillas attempting to cross the river to forage, destroy the railroad, or attack Union forces. These missions involved local African Americans, as well, for Federal gunboats on

78. Ibid., 266, 267.
79. Charles A. Harper to All, September 23, 1864; and December 15, 1864, Charles Harper Diary; both in Charles A. Harper Papers, F84, IHS.

the Tennessee were manned in part by runaway slaves who enlisted at port towns like Bridgeport and Decatur all through 1864 and 1865.[80]

One gunboat commander, Captain William A. Naylor, took particularly good advantage of his contacts with civilians and home guards as he patrolled the river between Bridgeport and Decatur. On May 17, 1864, the boat made contact with "Doctor Logan (citizen)" who "reported that [Gen. Stephen D.] Lee, Forrest, and Roddey had concentrated and crossed the river above Florence." Two days later, the gunboat stopped again to have a chat with a different civilian informant: Naylor "took Mr. Rogers aboard, who reported rebel battery about two miles up the river." On May 22, Naylor left again for another expedition, this time to follow up on "reliable information that a company of rebel bushwhackers, number 150–200 men, were encamped on Town Creek." These men had a "habit" of crossing the Tennessee in small boats in order to attack the railroad. Naylor's mission was to "break up their rendezvous" and to destroy their craft hidden in the river's tributaries. To do so, he piloted his boat approximately thirty miles southwest from Bridgeport to a spot called Larkin's Landing, on the north side of the Tennessee River in southwest Jackson County. There he picked up "some citizens," men "who had formed themselves into a company of home guards for the purpose of protecting themselves." The home guard was captained by a man named J. R. Hamblin; he and his men had been working for the Union army as laborers, cutting wood for the use of Naylor's gunboat. The "reliable information" Naylor had been given about the activities of the rebel

80. Capt. William A. Naylor to Lt. Col. Wladimir Krzyzanowski, May 21, 1864, and June 1, 1864, *OR*, Ser. I, vol. 38, pt. 4, 280–1, 384–5; Maj. Gen. George H. Thomas to Brig. Gen. R. S. Granger, October 10, 1864, 10:30 P.M., *OR*, Ser. I, vol. 39, pt. 3, 198; Acting Rear Adm. S. P. Lee to Maj. Gen. George Thomas, December 27, 1864, *OR*, Ser. I, vol. 45, pt. 2, 371; see also Q.M.G. M. C. Meigs to Maj. Gen. Ulysses S. Grant, January 15, 1864, in *Official Records of the Union and Confederate Navies in the War of the Rebellion*, 30 vols. (Washington, D.C.: Government Printing Office, 1894–1922), Ser. I, vol. 25, 699 (hereinafter *ORN*); Lt. Comdr. Le Roy Fitch to Rear Adm. David D. Porter, February 7, 1864, *ORN*, Ser. I, vol. 25, 741–3; Lt. Comdr. Le Roy Fitch to Rear Adm. David D. Porter, March 18, May 11, and July 24, 1864, *ORN*, Ser. I, vol. 26, 188, 295, 488; entries for *U.S.S. General Sherman, U.S.S. General Thomas,* and *U.S.S. General Grant, ORN,* Ser. II, vol. 1, 93; and also Claim 1459, Isaac Brunston, Marshall Co., August 23, 1871, SCC. For black sailors, see Lt. Comdr. Le Roy Fitch to Rear Adm. David D. Porter, February 7, 1864, *ORN*, Ser. I, vol. 25, 742; for enlistment records, see Black Sailors Research Project of Howard University, Civil War Soldiers and Sailors Database: http://www.civilwar.nps.gov/cwss/sailorsindex.html; last accessed April 19, 2002.

"bushwhackers" likely came from Hamblin and his men in the first place.[81]

Over the next two days, Naylor transported the home guards, as well as other Union scouts and members of a company of Ohio sharpshooters (snipers), to various river landings and ferry crossings on the south bank of the Tennessee between Larkin's Landing and Gunter's Landing deep in neighboring Marshall County. At the end of the mission, the home guards had "killed 2 men and wound 2 others, [and] captured 10 or 12 horses, one of which was branded 'U.S.'" The captain of the sharpshooters, a man named Barber, also took as a prisoner "a very noted bushwhacker by the name of Whitecotton." This was likely Pete Whitecotton of Jackson County, who in addition to having "made his boasts that he ha[d] killed more Yankees than any other rebel" had, along with various kinfolk, "created terror" among unionists in southwestern Jackson County. "They were desperate men," one unionist recalled.[82]

By early June, Naylor was still working closely with the Larkin's Landing home guard, as well as Federal sharpshooters and members of the Sixty-third Illinois, to hunt down rebel fighters. Simultaneously, however, he was also doing personal favors for the home guard captain, revealing the lack of distinction some unionist partisans seemed to draw between the war for the Union and the war for their own economic security. On this occasion, Naylor and his crew picked up for safekeeping some "eleven bales of cotton" belonging to Captain Hamblin and stored at Roman's Landing, on the north side of the Tennessee River in Marshall County. Hamblin had heard that "the guerrillas had threatened to

81. Capt. William A. Naylor to Col. Wladimir Krzyzanowski, May 21 and May 24, 1864, *OR*, Ser. I, vol. 38, pt. 4, 280, 307.

82. For first quoted passage, see Capt. William A. Naylor to Col. W. Krzyzanowski, May 24, 1864, *OR*, Ser. I, vol. 38, pt. 4, 307. This was likely Capt. Greshom M. Barber, Fifth Independent Company Ohio Sharpshooters. Naylor gives only his last name and refers to his regiment as the First Ohio Sharpshooters, but there is no record of a company under that ordinal. The *Fifth* Independent Company, however, served under the Army of the Cumberland in this vicinity. Moreover, both the Capt. Barber mentioned and the Lt. Botsford mentioned in a later letter served in the Fifth. For enlistment records, see the Civil War Soldiers and Sailors System Database of the National Parks Service: http://www.civilwar .nps.gov/cwss/PersonzDetail.cfm?PerNBR = 1823526; and http://www.civilwar.nps.gov/ cwss/PersonzDetail.cfm?PerNBR = 1845296; last accessed April 22, 2002. For third and fourth quoted passages, see Claim 2384, Moses Maples, Jackson Co., December 15, 1873: Testimony of Silas P. Woodall, SCC. For Whitecotton's activities, see Col. Green B. Raum to Lt. C. L. White, May 6, 1864, *OR*, Ser. I, vol. 38, pt. 4, 51.

burn it."[83] The gunboat brought the cotton to Larkin's Landing, where the home guard was still cutting wood for the gunboat. That cotton represented gold or greenbacks in the healthy black markets of the Tennessee Valley, especially those linked to smuggling in and around Memphis. The Confederates were as likely to take advantage of such a hoard as were unionists; if they themselves could not capture and sell the cotton, they would certainly have destroyed it.[84] Naylor's willingness to expend the considerable amount of time and labor it would have taken to load eleven bales of cotton onto his gunboat indicates the closeness of his relationship with the unionist home guards, who were supplying him with a steady supply of fuel, a reliable stream of intelligence, and indefatigable willingness to destroy rebel guerrillas.

Not all unionist partisans were able to make alliances and work in concert with the Union army. When Federals were not close enough to offer help, unionist civilians took matters of self-defense and punishment into their own hands. In April 1864, a report from the Confederate provost marshal revealed the success of such efforts in Fayette County, well behind Confederate lines: "Five [soldiers] were last week found dead tied up to trees, shot through the head," he commented. The murders, he felt confident, were the "work of deserters and tories."[85] Late in the war, a group of unionists from Walker and Winston Counties, also located in Confederate territory, met together as they had done many times in the past "in solitary places in the woods . . . to council for the good of the union, and for the safety of the union people." At the meeting they decided to "break up the rebel post at Jasper," Walker County's seat, described later by Union army raiders as "the poorest excuse for a town we

83. Capt. William A. Naylor to Col. Wladimir Krzyzanowski, June 1, 1864, *OR*, Ser. I, vol. 38, pt. 4, 384. Besides being a valuable black-market commodity, such a stash of cotton had practical importance for the gunboat captain, who in a separate incident described confiscating abandoned caches of the stuff "for the purposes of protecting the boilers and magazine on the boat from the artillery fire on shore"; see Capt. William A. Naylor to Col. Wladimir Krzyzanowski, May 24, 1864, *OR*, Ser. I, vol. 38, pt. 4, 307.

84. For the various legal and illegal markets in Confederate cotton and the value of smuggling it, see Joseph H. Parks, "A Confederate Trade Center under Federal Occupation: Memphis, 1862–1865," *Journal of Southern History* 7, no. 3 (August 1941): 292–5, 299–301, 306–10; and A. Sellew Roberts, "The Federal Government and Confederate Cotton," *American Historical Review* 32, no. 2 (January 1927): 271–4.

85. Lt. Col. T. H. Baker [C.S.A.] to Maj. J. C. Denis, April 4, 1864, *OR*, Ser. I, vol. 32, pt. 3, 746.

ever did see" and situated in woods that were "horrible in the extreme" and in a "country poor beyond conjecture." This unionist band hoped that if they organized, they would be able to free the numerous loyalist prisoners held at the Confederate jail, "and to effect other purposes for the safety of ourselves."[86]

These "other purposes" arose out of several years of fighting between the Confederate military officials stationed at Jasper and area unionists. In particular, those plotting to burn down the courthouse hoped to avenge the murder of three members of the staunchly loyalist Curtis family. Thomas Pinkney Curtis, Winston's probate judge (elected by his county's unionist majority), had been "taken from his home and shot by the orders of Hokett who was then acting under the command of Colonel [Richard O.] Pickett" of the Tenth Alabama Cavalry, C.S.A. George Washington Curtis was assassinated in his front yard by "men of [John R. B.] Burtwell's [Cavalry] Regiment." And finally, Joel Jackson Curtis was arrested, taken from his home, and shot near the Confederate post at Jasper, where rebels allegedly kept "a slaughter pen for the purposes of killing all parties brought to there."[87]

In their assault on the Confederate stronghold, the Winston and Walker unionists successfully liberated unionist prisoners and torched the jail, though they failed to destroy the courthouse.[88] On the way back to their homes, the gang of arsonists made it a point to stop at the home of Dr. Andrew Kaiser. A well-known opponent of unionists, Kaiser had been one of the earliest Alabamians to report pro-Union activity to the governor in 1861.[89] Since then, he had played a significant role in the conscription and imprisonment of unionists in both Winston and Walker Counties and, it was supposed, had at least some part in the killings of the Curtis men. Someone, most likely Jim Curtis, shot Kaiser dead in

86. First two quotes, Claim 6091, James Ellis, Walker Co., December 28, 1871, SCC; third quote in B. F. McGee, *History of the Seventy-second Indiana Volunteer Infantry of the Mounted Lightning Brigade*, ed. William R. Jewell (LaFayette, Ind.: S. Vater, 1882), 531; fourth quote, Claim 10339, William V. Curtis, Winston Co., March 12, 1872, SCC.

87. Claim 10339, William V. Curtis, Winston Co., March 12, 1872, SCC. There is no enlistment record of a man by the name of Hokett in the records of the 10th Alabama Cavalry; he may well have been a civilian home guard captain who did not enlist in the army.

88. McGee, *History of the 72d Indiana Volunteer Infantry*, 531.

89. See Andrew Kaiser to Gov. J. Gill Shorter, December 3, 1861, AGP: John Gill Shorter, 1861–63.

retaliation for the murder of his kinfolk.[90] Not long afterward, a detachment of Union troops finished what the unionists had left undone, burning the Jasper courthouse as they raided through Walker County with General James H. Wilson in late March 1865.[91]

By 1864, the national and personal causes for which unionist civilians fought—whether as informants, scouts, spies, or partisan bands—had become almost inseparable from one another. That intimacy allowed them to offer vital help to Union forces—because the war was so close to home, their expertise was of immense value to occupying forces. Nevertheless, when unionists' intensely personalized agendas were backed with the power of military force, as they were in the arming and support of unionist guerrillas, the consequences could be ambiguous. On the one hand, the Union army clearly benefited from the vigor with which such partisans conducted warfare. On the other, however, unionist guerrillas rarely subordinated their own agenda to that of the Union. They wanted to remain at home to fight against the men who had persecuted them and their families—to hunt down and kill whoever had tormented them. Given this, it is not surprising that Confederate Alabamians viewed unionist partisans as the real desperadoes. One Confederate soldier bitterly denounced the "Tories" who fought in this way as cowards who "wore the blue as a cloak for their deviltry and for the protection of the Federal army. They did not have the manhood to go to the front, nor were they ever seen near a battlefield, but made war on women and old men; and, in fact, were nothing more than a band of thieves and murderers, for they did not hesitate to kill citizens as well as soldiers when it suited their purposes to do so."[92] Clearly, one side's liberation force looked awfully like a ruthless gang of bandits to the other.

90. Dodd and Dodd, *Winston: An Antebellum and Civil War History,* 106–8. Dodd and Dodd based their account of the raid and the killing of Kaiser on an oral history given by the youngest Curtis brother, Frank (Benjamin Franklin Curtis) to Probate Judge John B. Weaver of Winston in 1910. Curtis would have been in his late seventies or early eighties at the time of the telling. According to Dodd and Dodd, there is no conclusive proof that Jim Curtis killed Kaiser, but he was suspected because "he had earlier vowed to 'get' every rebel responsible for the deaths of his three brothers, Thomas Pinkney Curtis, George Washington Curtis, and Joel Jackson Curtis. All of the Curtis boys had sworn to remain loyal to the Union in response to the deathbed request of their father, Solomon Curtis."

91. McGee, *History of the 72d Indiana Volunteer Infantry,* 531.

92. J. P. Cannon, *Inside of Rebeldom: The Daily Life of a Private in the Confederate Army* (Washington, D.C.: National Tribune, 1900), 188.

Nonetheless, the desperation and fury of unionists' attempts to defend and revenge themselves goes a long way to demonstrating the stakes they felt were at play. P. P. Pike, a farmer of Walker County, illustrated this when describing his comrade James Ellis's deeds during the war. "General Grant nor any other man was never more loyal to the government of the United States than James Ellis," Pike asserted to the SCC, "and few men ran more risks and narrow escapes than he did." Ellis's efforts against the Confederacy branded him as an outlaw, and the only hope for avoiding an outlaw's fate was Union victory. "He would not have been allowed to live here, nor would [the Confederates] have allowed him the charity of a grave here, if they had succeeded in establishing a separate government."[93] With a unionist's final burial place among his ancestors at stake, not to mention his home, farm, and family, the Union cause became synonymous with defense of everything he held dear. The experience of guerrilla warfare during the last years of the war, itself rooted in several years of intimidation, abuse, and exile, made Union people believe in stringent solutions to the problem of treason against the Union. This thirst for justice and retribution, however, would result in a most bitter legacy.

93. Claim 6091, James Ellis, Walker Co., December 28, 1871: Testimony of P. P. Pike, SCC.

5

"Stripped Twice By"

THE LIMITS OF PRESIDENTIAL RECONSTRUCTION

You have no idea of the strength of principle and devotion these people exhibited toward the national government. People were hung or driven off; their houses burned down; their wives and children driven off; and still they would not deny their allegiance to the national government. I saw a beautiful woman who had walked nearly sixty miles in the sleet, and snow, with an infant on her breast, her house having been burned over her head. There have been hundreds of such cases. It would be an act of humanity to assist these people—an act of charity which would never be forgotten.

—J. J. Giers, Morgan County, before the Joint Committee on Reconstruction, 1866

These Wileys always had a grudge at us after [the war]. Old Man Wiley was the worst reb of them all. Yes it is so. They haven't got over it yet & I haven't either.

—Elizabeth Kelly, Morgan County, 1876

Alabama's unionists learned of the Confederacy's surrender while minding their posts in Federal barracks, in hidey-holes and mountain caves overlooking the Tennessee Valley, in small towns of Illinois and Indiana, and in Confederate jails. Their realization of Union victory was at once shocking and thrilling. "O!" George Watkins exclaimed upon remembering his reaction. "I felt just like a cat let out of a wallet when I heard of the final surrender. I felt released from prison. I felt revived, like a new man." Martin Middleton was told "the good news" of Lee's surrender by Federal soldiers marching through his county of Monroe.

For epigraphs, see testimony of J. J. Giers in *Report of the Joint Committee on Reconstruction, 39th Congress, 1st Sess.* (Washington, D.C.: Government Printing Office, 1866), 14; and Claim 18264, George Thrasher, Morgan Co., June 3, 1876: Testimony of Elizabeth Kelly, SCC.

"I told them I had been looking for them for a long time, and I was so damn glad to hear that Lee's company had gone up that I throwed up my hat and hollered." Federal soldier James Casteel recalled that gray-haired Solomon Lentz offered the neighborhood's returning Union soldiers "a big dinner if they would come to his house." Casteel himself happily attended and noted that Lentz "was greatly rejoiced" at the war's outcome. Elizabeth Kelly thought her old father just "seemed mighty free" when peace came.[1]

Such feelings of unmitigated joy over Union victory soon diminished, replaced with the certain knowledge that loyalists' struggle with rebels had not ended with Confederate surrender. Of the approximately thirty-five thousand Federal soldiers stationed in Alabama in May 1865, all but a tiny proportion were now free to return home. They went back to towns untouched by the devastation that marked North Alabama, and more important, free of an embittered enemy. Unionists, by contrast, found themselves in a ruined land, indelibly marked as traitors to the Confederacy, and left alone to fend for themselves amongst defeated and disillusioned rebels. Four months after Lee and Grant met at Appomattox Court House, "parties of marauders" were reported running rampant in northwestern Alabama, "burning houses [and] murdering Union men."[2] Three months later, a number of "loyal men and discharged U.S. Soldiers Resident of Jackson County" (including Union scout George W. Ridge, whose father and brother had been murdered by rebel guerrillas in 1863) were so harassed by rebels in their neighborhood that they petitioned for permission to form a loyalist militia. Without it, they argued, "union men can not live here any longer."[3] Over a year after the armi-

---

1. Claim 6858, George W. Watkins, Limestone Co., July 24, 1875; Claim 2318, Martin Middleton, Monroe Co., December 3, 1874; Claim 5202, Solomon Lentz, Limestone Co., June 13, 1876: Testimony of James H. Casteel; Claim 18264, George Thrasher, Morgan Co., June 3, 1876: Testimony of Elizabeth Kelly; all in SCC.

2. George W. Howard to Brig. Gen. R. S. Granger, July 1, 1865, OR, Ser. I, vol. 49, pt. 2, 1057.

3. J. A. Hammond et al. to Gov. Lewis E. Parsons, October 9, 1865, quoted in Clyde E. Wilson, "State Militia of Alabama during the Administration of Lewis E. Parsons, Provisional Governor, June 21st to December 18th, 1865," Alabama Historical Quarterly 14 (1952): 313–4. Ridge and his fellow petitioners were refused permission to organize a militia by Provisional Governor Lewis Parsons. Evidence suggests that Andrew Johnson or his advisers may have encouraged Parsons not to use unionists in militias; see Brooks D. Simpson, LeRoy P. Graf, and John Muldowny, Advice after Appomattox: Letters to Andrew Johnson, 1865–1866, Special vol. no. 1, Papers of Andrew Johnson, ed. LeRoy P. Graf (Knoxville: University of Tennessee Press, 1987), 111.

stice, First Alabama, U.S.A., cavalryman Joseph H. Davis and his son watched in shock as ex-rebels strode into the polling area at a local Randolph County election, gathered "about the ballot box," and began "over aweing union men, intimidating them to such an extent as to prevent their votes." When Confederate veteran Robert Richards stepped to the front of the crowd to shout curses like, "God damn the Government, hurah for secession & the Rebel army & God damn them that don't believe it," Davis and son gave vent to their own frustration. A fistfight ensued, with the Davises tearing into Richards and "his party of late rebels." In a letter to Alabama's Freedmen's Bureau, Davis made a dire prediction. "[U]nless the Union men in my part of the country can get the protection of the Government of the US," he asserted, "they are in danger of losing their lives."[4]

For unionists, the great calamity of the postwar period was that the "Government of the US" was rarely forthcoming with its support and "protection." From the start, as historian Michael Perman has argued, President Andrew Johnson reflected widespread thinking on postwar policy in his "assumption that a real reunion demanded reconciliation at the expense of reconstruction." Believing that only "time and sympathetic circumstances . . . could sow feeling of cooperation among Southerners," Johnson endorsed lenient measures to restore many former Confederates to the full rights of citizenship.[5] He thus remained quite unwilling to do what unionists wanted most: to punish in severe and lasting ways the men who had attempted to take the South out of the Union. Though this Southern-born president had vigorously opposed the Confederacy as unionists had, he nonetheless set in motion a program for reconstruction that sacrificed their most treasured ideals about political legitimacy.

Johnson was not alone in endorsing a postwar policy devoted to amnesty and conciliation. Most Republicans, too, remained ambivalent about the feasibility or legality of establishing loyalist-controlled governments in the South, especially in the Deep South where consistently loyal white men represented a tiny proportion of the population. Elevat-

4. J[oseph]. H. Davis to Gen. Wager Swayne, June 20, 1866, FB-AL, NAMS-M809, Roll 8.

5. Michael Perman, *Reunion without Compromise: The South and Reconstruction, 1865–1868* (New York: Cambridge University Press, 1973), 7, 69; also see 11–2, 68–70.

ing true-blue unionists to positions of control would mean broadly disfranchising Southern citizens, a step that many feared would upset the
peace by fostering renewed opposition in the former Confederacy. To
put such an obvious minority in charge of Southern state governments
was politically dangerous for other reasons as well. The Republican Party
had been firmly associated with violations of civil liberties during the
war, particularly Abraham Lincoln's suspension of the writ of habeas corpus to suppress antiwar dissent. After the war, Northern Democrats remained eager to exploit for political gain any Republican policies that
might be deemed equally unconstitutional or antidemocratic. The alternative of building Southern majorities was equally risky, for the only way
to do it was to enfranchise freedmen. Before 1867, most Republicans
were sure that any attempt to establish black political equality (and possible domination of Southern politics) would enrage many of their border state and Northern constituents.[6] Through calculus like this, the
political aspirations of loyal Southerners were quickly pushed aside by
the party of Lincoln.

Unionists, by contrast, gave almost overwhelming allegiance to the
Republican Party from the first. For most loyalists, the Democratic Party
remained the party of secession and copperheadism. They believed that
Republican activism offered them a chance to advance a postwar Reconstruction policy devoted to punishing traitors and to honoring and rewarding the loyal. This understanding of Reconstruction went to the
heart of their understanding of political legitimacy, and it came into direct conflict with the desire of the president and Congress to reconcile
with the South. Unionists did not seek pacification of their Confederate
enemies, but power over them. Consequently, when Federal policy during the first two years following the war allowed former rebels to take
positions of local judicial, political, and economic authority, loyalists
were stunned and bitterly disappointed. Such a program of reunification
seemed a living rebuke to unionists' sacrifice during the war. As one
group of Federal veterans complained, "It is very hard to be ruled and
governed . . . by these old Rebels, after we have served in the Union
army and under the old flag for nearly five years."[7]

6. Richard Abbott, *The Republican Party and the South, 1855–1877: The First Southern
Strategy* (Chapel Hill: University of North Carolina Press, 1986), 22, 28–9; x–xii; 43–60.

7. Many petitioners to Brig. Gen. Wager Swayne, June 8, 1866, FB-AL, NAMS-M809,
Roll 7.

The 1865 Constitutional Convention

When Andrew Johnson inaugurated his program of political reconstruction in the summer of 1865, Alabama's white unionists believed that he would, as promised, "make treason odious" and punish traitors by broadly disfranchising Confederates. In practice, however, many of Johnson's Reconstruction policies—embodied in his Proclamation of Amnesty and Pardon of May 29—differed little from the conciliatory measures most favored by Abraham Lincoln before his assassination. Moreover, like Lincoln, Johnson understood Reconstruction as an executive, rather than a legislative, matter. He thus quickly began to implement postwar policy through executive order, rather than through consultation with Congress. One of his first actions was to appoint to every Southern state provisional governors who would be acceptable to Southerners and yet palatable to the nation. Consequently, most of these governors, like Alabama's Lewis E. Parsons, had been reluctant secessionists who had "gone with the state" in 1861. They were charged with appointing moderate men like themselves as officials to maintain law and order until the state could hold elections for delegates to constitutional conventions. These conventions, in turn, were to rewrite the state constitution, officially abolish slavery, and nullify the 1861 secession ordinances. Once these conditions were satisfied, states could be readmitted to the Union.[8]

Johnson's guidelines regarding the political rights of Southern citizens likewise incorporated elements of Lincoln's early plans. Through the application of a generous amnesty oath, the vast majority of white male Southerners returned to citizenship and the franchise by promising future fidelity to the Union. However, Johnson did mandate exceptions, barring from this amnesty fourteen categories of Confederates, particularly high-level Confederate officials or military men, as well as all citizens who owned more than twenty thousand dollars in property.[9] Although considerably more stringent in its language than anything Lincoln had ever proposed, the disfranchisement failed to diminish Confed-

---

8. Sarah Woolfolk Wiggins, *The Scalawag in Alabama Politics, 1865–1881* (Tuscaloosa: University of Alabama Press, 1977), 9; Dan T. Carter, *When the War Was Over: The Failure of Self-Reconstruction in the South, 1865–1867* (Baton Rouge: Louisiana State University Press, 1985), 27–32; Eric Foner, *Reconstruction: America's Unfinished Revolution, 1864–1877* (New York: Harper & Row, 1988), 185; Abbott, *Republican Party in the South*, 47.

9. Abbott, *Republican Party in the South*, 47.

erate power significantly, because so many of the Southern elite were allowed to apply for, and received, presidential pardon.[10] By the end of 1865, fourteen thousand of the approximately fifteen thousand white Southerners who petitioned for pardon received it. In Johnson's reconstructed South, many of the leading lights of the Confederacy were very soon after the war able to stand for and vote in state and national elections.[11]

During Alabama's late summer elections for delegates to the state constitutional convention, unionists were shocked to realize that numerous leading Confederates had not only been pardoned, but had managed to get themselves elected to the convention. Of the ninety-nine delegates chosen, twenty-five were former Confederate officers, soldiers, or government officials. Two of these men had in fact signed the secession ordinance in 1861.[12] Another five had been members of the secession convention and, although they had refused to sign the ordinance, had "gone with the state" in the end.[13] Indeed, when the convention began, only ten delegates can be confirmed as having been open and consistent unionists from the date of secession throughout the war. Four of these men—Elliot P. Jones of Fayette County, Henry C. Sanford of Limestone County, Christopher C. Sheets of Winston County, and William O. Winston of DeKalb County—had been members of the secession convention in 1861, where they refused to sign the Ordinance of Secession, and had maintained their opposition throughout the war.[14]

This small cadre of unionists and their constituents had hoped that the new constitution would address the past wrongs of secession and the war. It was thus especially disconcerting for them to witness the alacrity with which former Confederates claimed the mantle—and preroga-

10. Perman, *Reunion without Compromise*, 129.

11. J. T. Dorris, "Pardon Seekers and Brokers: A Sequel of Appomattox," *Journal of Southern History* 1, no. 3 (1935): 277 n. 5, 291; Carter, *When the War Was Over*, 25; Foner, *Reconstruction*, 185.

12. Perman, *Reunion without Compromise*, 129–31; Foner, *Reconstruction*, 183, 193; Carter, *When the War Was Over*, 25; Rogers et al., *Alabama*, 231.

13. Owen, *History of Alabama and Dictionary of Alabama Biography; Journal of the Proceedings of Convention of the State of Alabama Held in the City of Montgomery, Tuesday, September 12, 1865* (1865; facsimile reprint, Washington, D.C.: Statute Law Book Co., 1934), 12–3.

14. The 1865 constitutional convention included forty-two farmers, thirty-three lawyers, nine merchants, seven ministers, six doctors, and two teachers. Fully forty-five claimed to be "old line Whigs"; over half of the delegates were over fifty years old. See McMillan, *Constitutional Development*, 92; Rogers et al., *Alabama*, 231–2.

tives—of unionism as their own. Indeed, the term "union man" was rapidly rehabilitated to mean simply that an individual "had opposed secession, regardless of subsequent service for the Confederacy."[15] Wartime unionists, of course, could never accept this. A true-blue unionist was a man who had been "steadfast" throughout—"loyal to the union cause from first to last." According to this definition, no man who had gone "with the current" could claim true unionism.[16] After the suffering they and their fellows had endured because of their loyalty, this distinction lay at the core of their identity. Usurpation of the name "unionist" transcended trivial or semantic debate—it violated honor and distorted history.

That unionists were determined to record and remedy the past sins of the state was readily apparent in the policies they proposed and supported during the constitutional convention. Take, for example, unionists' contributions to the debate over repealing the secession ordinance. Though the convention made repeal a priority because it was one of the steps necessary for Alabama's readmission to the Union, such a measure had special significance for unionists, for it offered a chance to write their ideological opposition to secession into the very foundation of the state government. They thus proposed that the new constitution declare the ordinance "*to have been and is* null and void," and thereby fully repudiate the right of secession for the future.[17] The unionist position stood in marked contrast to that embraced by the majority of delegates at the convention, who proposed simply to declare the 1861 ordinance "null and void." There would be no judgment of what came before Reconstruction, no question but that secession had been the legitimate result of the free and fair elections of the fall of 1860. Though willing to concede defeat at the hands of the Union army, most of the delegates would not, as

15. Quote in Simpson et al., *Advice after Appomattox*, 75; James Alex Baggett, *The Scalawags: Southern Dissenters in the Civil War and Reconstruction* (Baton Rouge: Louisiana State University Press, 2003), 124–6; Malcolm C. McMillan, *Constitutional Development in Alabama, 1798–1901: A Study in Politics, the Negro, and Sectionalism* (1955; reprint, Tuscaloosa: University of Alabama Press, 1992), 92; Rogers et al., *Alabama*, 231–2; Carter, *When the War Was Over*, 27.

16. Claim 2177, Green M. Haley, Marion Co., March 28, 1872: Testimony of Russell S. S. Bull; Claim 6675, Samuel H. Herron, Cherokee Co., October 12, 1877: Testimony of Andrew Herron; Claim 21355, William J. Bibb, Montgomery Co., February 24, 1873: Testimony of Thomas Joseph; all in SCC.

17. McMillan, *Constitutional Development*, 98; Rogers et al., *Alabama*, 231. (Italics are mine.)

the unionists demanded, admit wrongdoing in 1861. Consequently, when the minority amendment was put forward, it was tabled by a vote of 69 to 21. Undeterred, unionists made two further attempts to add "unauthorized" or "is and was unconstitutional" to the language of the repeal, but again, the majority easily overruled their efforts.[18]

Unionist delegate and wartime political prisoner Christopher Sheets of Winston County likewise proposed constitutional language that would codify the illegitimacy of secession. Sheets sponsored a resolution that "all amendments to the Constitution of a general character, except so much as refers to the emancipation of slaves, should be referred back to the people at the next general election for their ratification or rejection."[19] Loyalists had long cited the lack of popular referendum as evidence of secession's illegitimacy and the Confederacy's corrupt character, even though the convention had been democratically convened by elected delegates. Moreover, as one of the members of the secession convention who had advocated that step, Sheets wanted to prevent another instance of "usurpation." But, as was the case in 1861, the Winston County delegate and his fellow unionists did not have enough influence to bring the resolution to a vote. Moreover, the convention responded to Sheets's attempt by voting to repudiate altogether the principle of holding referenda to approve or disapprove the actions of a constitutional convention. The majority's sole concession was to agree that all future constitutional conventions be called by a popular vote rather than by the state legislature, as had historically been the case.[20]

Ultimately, the unionist delegates had but one success at the convention, when wartime loyalist Christopher Tompkins urged that delegates pledge the state to pay only that debt contracted before secession.[21] Across the South, unionists had successfully lobbied Andrew Johnson to add debt repudiation to his list of requirements for a state's readmission to the Union. In unionists' minds, the Confederate debt was not legally, morally, or ethically defensible. The illegality of the Confederate state

18. McMillan, *Constitutional Development*, 98; *Journal of the Proceedings of Convention, 1865*, 57–9. The Joint Committee on Reconstruction noted with dismay the failure of Southern state governments to repudiate secession; see *Report of the Joint Committee on Reconstruction*, xv.

19. *Journal of the Proceedings of Convention, 1865*, 34.

20. McMillan, *Constitutional Development*, 108.

21. Ibid., 28.

meant that any agreements undertaken by Alabama should be considered invalid. Voiding this debt implicitly asserted the illegitimacy of the Confederacy itself. Moreover, the consequences of debt repudiation promised to be widely punitive. The lion's share of the debt, of course, was held by citizens who had taken out Confederate bonds in support of the war. Tompkins's resolution would force bondholders to lose their investments, the amounts of which were staggering. In April 1865, the Confederate government owed more than $700 million in Confederate currency that, when adjusted for depreciation, totaled some $300 million in U.S. specie. Alabama citizens who lived in the strongly Confederate Black Belt and in Mobile held most of the state's $13 million in bonds. Unionists who, as a matter of principle, had not purchased Confederate or state war bonds, were insulated from the consequences of repudiation. On September 28, the convention voted 60 to 19 in support of Tompkins's resolution.[22]

Return to Rebel Rule

As they had been since 1860, die-hard unionists at the constitutional convention were outnumbered and, with the exception of debt repudiation, were ineffective in establishing their political vision through the constitution. In subsequent months, the evidence that Johnson had pardoned ever-larger numbers of former Confederates only exacerbated loyalists' feelings of impotence and heightened their forebodings about the future.[23] As loyalist William Miller complained to a friend, "I thot [the president] declared Emphatically that he will put the government in the hands of its friends make treason odious & that the leaders in the Rebellion must take back seats. [But] he then commences pardoning all of the worst & most bitter enemies of the Government."[24]

The consequences of Johnson's generous policies toward ex-Confederates were most dramatically realized during the election of November 1865, as the citizens of the newly readmitted state went back to the polls under their new constitution. In Alabama, as elsewhere in the former

22. Foner, *Reconstruction*, 194; McMillan, *Constitutional Development*, 99, 101; Carter, *When the War Was Over*, 70–3; *Journal of the Proceedings of Convention, 1865*, 77.

23. Carl Schurz to Andrew Johnson, [November, 1865], in Simpson et al., *Advice after Appomattox*, 75.

24. William Miller to Alexander Boyd, September 5, 1866, Alexander Boyd Papers, BPL.

Confederacy, Southerners elected to national, state, and local office "men who had actively participated in the rebellion."[25] So overwhelming was ex-Confederate triumph that historian Eric Foner has quipped that "service to the Confederacy emerged as a virtual prerequisite for victory" in the Deep South.[26] Lewis E. Parsons, who relinquished Alabama's provisional governorship, ran for and won a seat in the U.S. Senate; Confederate officers George C. Freeman and Cullen A. Battle and wartime state legislator C. C. Langdon were elected to the U.S. House of Representatives.[27] Even Alabama's newly elected governor, R. M. Patton, seemed an appalling choice to many unionists. As one loyalist put it, Patton "has spoken to the Rebel soldiers during the war & told them [not to give up], it would not be long before they would only have to pull out their tooth pick and the Yankeys would run."[28] Moreover, as unionist J. J. Giers testified to Congress, Patton had served as "a financial agent of the confederate government during the whole rebellion—cotton agent and tax agent."[29]

Alabama's unionists reacted to the election with outrage and disgust. As veteran surgeon of the Federal army, Hugh McVay of Limestone County reported to the Freedmen's Bureau in March 1866, "The Rebels hold almost all the offices in our state . . . the most rampant secesh are now to hear them speak the most loyal."[30] Others complained that even unpardoned citizens had managed to stand for and win elections. In June 1866, a number of "late Officers in the U.S.A. and loyal citizens of Morgan Co." protested to Federal officials that the fall elections had placed a man named George P. Charlton in the office of probate judge. His victory came despite having held "at different times two offices of trust under the so called Confederate Govt." (They included a copy of his oath of office to prove it.) Moreover, according to the veterans, Charlton had never received a pardon as required by Johnson's amnesty plan, and thus had taken his office illegally. "We hold it our duty as Union men to have

25. *Report of the Joint Committee on Reconstruction,* xvi.

26. Foner, *Reconstruction,* 196; see also Fitzgerald, "Radical Republicanism," 569–70.

27. *Report of the Joint Committee on Reconstruction,* 15; Owen, *History of Alabama and Dictionary of Alabama Biography,* 115, 614–5, 848.

28. H. W. McVay to Brig. Gen. Wager Swayne, November 27, 1866, FB-AL, NAMS-M809, Roll 8.

29. *Report of the Joint Committee on Reconstruction,* 14.

30. H. W. McVay to Brig. Gen. Wager Swayne, March 11, 1866, FB-AL, NAMS-M809, Roll 8.

the facts known that the matter may be investigated, and we protected in our rights." They tersely concluded, "As the U.S. Govet says, Union men must rule and not rebels who bid defiance to the U.S. laws."[31]

The success of ex-Confederates at the polls did not pass unnoticed by unionists' rebel neighbors. On the contrary, the victories seemed to fuel the growth of renewed antiunionist sentiment in local communities, in part because the fears former rebels had harbored about the postwar political landscape were allayed by their speedy rehabilitation. Those who, only months before seemed to be the heirs apparent of Union victory, now appeared considerably diminished. William H. Smith, a wartime unionist and First Alabama Cavalry recruiter from Randolph County, explained in testimony before the Joint Committee on Reconstruction that since the election, former Confederates "have been very bold, very intolerant, and manifest the most perfect contempt for a man who is known to be an unequivocal Union man; call him a 'galvanized Yankee,' and apply other terms and epithets to him."[32] The standing of the disloyal seemed elevated, while unionists remained degraded. As a committee of Southern unionists, one a native Alabamian who refugeed from the state during the war, chided the president, "We have neither seen treason made odious nor traitors disreputable by any act of the Executive of the Nation. We *have* seen traitors—*leading, intelligent conscious traitors*—bearing away from the national capital with exultation, in the same pocket, indemnity for the past, and endorsement and security for the future, in the form of special pardons and appointments to Federal office." Evidently, "fidelity to the Government was not the passport to Executive favor; but, on the contrary, [to] servile subserviency to the President and his 'policy.'"[33]

The consequence of this dangerous consolidation of power extended beyond the realm of formal elective politics. Indeed, wherever loyal people engaged in public life, they confronted officials who viewed "tories" with disdain. This problem was particularly evident in the operation of county courts, where unionists encountered juries and judges who harbored considerable antiunionist prejudice. In October 1866, for instance, W. J. Cooper wrote a letter to General U. S. Grant asking for help de-

---

31. Many petitioners to Brig. Gen. Swayne, June 8, 1866, FB-AL, NAMS-M809, Roll 7.

32. *Report of the Joint Committee on Reconstruction*, 11. Smith would also be the first governor of Alabama elected under Congressional Reconstruction.

33. Address of A. J. Hamilton of Texas, B. J. Saffold of Alabama, and William B. Stokes of Tennessee to [Southern unionists], July 10, 1866, Lewis E. Parsons Papers, ADAH.

fending himself and other unionists from the discrimination of leading rebels in his county. He asserted that the people of his settlement had cast 105 votes during the secession convention election in 1861, of which only three had been pro-secession. He then indignantly pointed out, "[T]hose 3 secessionists in the settlement . . . are the men that [sit] on the jury in our county court. I do not know of [a] loyal man that is on the jury in this county."[34] Unionists' opprobrium among Confederates like these seemed to have prevented a Tuscaloosa man named Roberts from being able to prosecute the ex-Confederate soldier who beat him up. According to the soldier, Roberts had made "indelicate insinuations" to the soldier's young daughter. Roberts's defender wrote to General Swayne that "Roberts swares positively that he had no such thought or intention and was only chatting with the Child . . . Roberts is an old man over 70 years of age and his Character unblemished as regards Morrality." Swayne's correspondent continued, "[U]nfortunately for him . . . he was known to have been and still is an unyielding Union Man, and for that and a closeness of dealing he is quite unpopular." Despite Roberts's appearance in the mayor's court with his "face and head awfully bruised up," the mayor found for the defendant and forced Roberts to pay the costs of the hearing. Later, the mayor admitted that there had been little proof offered and that it was doubtful that Roberts had committed any offense that warranted beating.[35]

Even in the rare cases where the tables were turned and unionists held the judicial power, their authority could be stifled by hostile citizens. One of the few loyalist judges appointed to office by Governor Parsons, William H. Smith of Randolph County found it impossible to maintain his seat on the circuit court. "I found I could not hold court without being insulted by the rebel lawyers in their speeches, in which they were upheld by the authorities," he explained to Congress when testifying before the Joint Committee on Reconstruction. One of the solicitors appointed to the circuit court by the state legislature, moreover, had "been a very violent rebel, in favor of hanging Union men." This man and the other lawyers continued to refer "to the rebellion and glory in it," which made Smith decidedly uncomfortable. "I did not feel that I ought to give my sanction to what was going on by holding position

34. W. J. Cooper to Gen. Grant, October 10, 1866, forwarded to Brig. Gen. Swayne, FB-AL, NAMS-M809, Roll 7.

35. R. Blair to Brig. Gen. Wager Swayne, April 26, 1867, FB-AL, NAMS-M809, Roll 10.

under the authorities then in power." Smith resigned his chair in protest. His departure signaled the loss of one of the few wartime unionists in positions of judicial authority in the state.[36]

The political clout of former Confederates did more than create difficulties for unionists in the courts. Rebel control of state and local politics also translated into control of economic resources, a particularly salient issue for men and women struggling with wartime destitution and the physical reconstruction of their economic livelihoods. Soldiers and refugees had returned home to find desolate farms, impoverished and weary wives and children, and the needy widows and orphans of brothers and neighbors. Between Confederate and Yankee foraging and depredations, as well as simple neglect, small farms and plantations alike had been "totally broken up."[37] In September 1865, Governor Parsons reported to Alabama's constitutional convention that at the end of the war, the state had been "furnishing meal and salt to 38,772 destitute families, the individual members of which numbered in the aggregate 139,042."[38] By late November, Governor Parsons predicted that the total white and black indigents in the state would soon number near 250,000.[39] One of the most serious problems lay with farm animals, who had been decimated to such an extent that even by 1870 the livestock population of Alabama still remained below 1860 levels.[40]

War damage was further compounded by a variety of complicating circumstances. Men arriving home during the late spring of 1865 returned too late to plant a fall crop.[41] In North Alabama, the war itself

36. *Report of the Joint Committee on Reconstruction*, 12.

37. Quote in Claim 11631, Jeremiah F. Files, Fayette Co., January 30, 1873, SCC; see also Steven Hahn, *The Roots of Southern Populism: Yeomen Farmers and the Transformation of the Georgia Upcountry, 1850–1890* (New York: Oxford University Press, 1983), 137–40; and Robert H. McKenzie, "The Economic Impact of Federal Operations in Alabama during the Civil War," *Alabama Historical Quarterly* 38, no. 1 (1976): 57.

38. *Journal of the Proceedings, 1865*, 43.

39. Phyllis LaRue LeGrand, "Destitution and Relief of the Indigent Soldiers' Families of Alabama during the Civil War" (M.A. thesis, Auburn University, 1964), 264–5; Elizabeth Bethel, "The Freedmen's Bureau in Alabama," *Journal of Southern History* 14, no. 1 (1948): 58; Brig. Gen. Clinton B. Fisk to Brig. Gen. Wager Swayne, October 10, 1865, FB-AL, NAMS-M809, Roll 6.

40. McKenzie, "Economic Impact of Federal Operations," 57; Rogers et al., *Alabama*, 228–30.

41. Gov. R. M. Patton of Alabama to the U.S. Congress, relative to the special land tax, May 16, 1866, *House Miscellaneous Documents*, No. 114, 39th Cong., 1st Sess. (Washington, D.C.: Government Printing Office, 1866), 2.

lingered through the summer—guerrillas and independent partisans put down their arms warily, and slowly at that.[42] As one Huntsville man explained, "Peace was not fully made [in the Tennessee Valley] til June, too late to plant a crop. There was no stock to plough with till July—and there was no security out of sight of a Military post till it was too late to plant a crop."[43] Even nature seemed to conspire against economic recovery. Widespread droughts, which would have made husbandry difficult in the best of times, plagued much of the South during the war and continued to do so into the early postwar period.[44] Without assistance, Alabamians feared, people would starve to death. "Our country is in a deplorable condition," citizens of Calhoun, Randolph, and Talladega Counties complained to Brigadier General Wager Swayne of the Freedmen's Bureau, "[and] destitution meets the eye at every point." Diminished stores and bad weather had brought people to desperation. "The unprecedented drouth cut the crops painfully short, few having any surplus, and many almost nothing."[45] One Tuscumbia citizen wrote bluntly in his diary in September, "Famine threatens the community & all is gloomy."[46] In DeKalb County, indigent unionists reported a range of reasons for their suffering: "in Federal army too late to make crop"; "[sustenance] destroyed by Confederates"; "Husband killed in Federal Army"; "Foraged out by Rebs"; "husband Killed by Rebs." Confederate reports mirrored these descriptions: "Rob[b]ed by Federals"; "Foraged out by Federals." Many accounts, however, testify to nothing more than the nonpartisan impact of warfare and bad times: "widow and no means"; "No horse to Plow"; or simply "Drought."[47]

Along with the destruction of farms and communities came the abolition of slavery, the institution that had undergirded antebellum Ala-

42. Carter, *When the War Was Over*, 8–12.

43. David C. Humphrey to Wager Swayne, November 25, 1865, FB-AL, NAMS-M809, Roll 5.

44. Foner, *Reconstruction*, 140; Michael W. Fitzgerald, *The Union League Movement in the Deep South: Politics and Agricultural Change during Reconstruction* (Baton Rouge: Louisiana State University Press, 1989), 18; Hahn, *Roots of Southern Populism*, 139–40; Gov. R. M. Patton of Alabama to the U.S. Congress, relative to the special land tax, May 16, 1866, *House Miscellaneous Documents*, No. 114, 39th Cong., 1st Sess., 2.

45. Many petitioners to Brig. Gen. Wager Swayne, [November?] 1865, FB-AL, NAMS-M809, Roll 6.

46. September 2, 1865, William Cooper Diary, SHC.

47. Register of Indigent Families, DeKalb Co., 1865, 344, Governors' Records, Volunteer Family Assistance Reports, SG16064, ADAH.

bama's economic and social life. While most white Southerners clearly responded to black freedom with anxiety, unionists' discussions of the postwar world in their SCC testimony or in other extant documents rarely focused with any particularity on the question of freedpeople and their future. Direct evidence of unionists' views about emancipation is rather limited prior to the advent of black franchise in 1867. Until then, white unionists' opinions about freedpeople generally pertained to questions of access to resources. For instance, in May 1866, Union veteran Henry Mitchell objected to the distribution of rations in his county of Randolph. He asked the Freedmen's Bureau "what sort of peopl" were supposed to get food aid, complaining that the Bureau agents distributed rations to "the able bodyed freed men in prefference to the poor widdow" and wondering whether "the federal solgers that served their country and was Robed by the rebels of all that they had has a rite to anything." Racial fears entered into Mitchell's assessment of this state of affairs, for he claimed to be "informed that the Agent for this County has bin offering freedwomen five dollar to whip poor white women" and demanded to know whether the Bureau approved "such conduct as that."[48] For poorer whites like Mitchell, unionists and Confederates alike, freedpeople represented an economic and social threat.[49]

Because so few Alabamians—black, white, rebel, or unionist—had the resources to survive the months between planting and harvest in 1865 or, for that matter, to provide for themselves throughout 1866–67, the U.S. Secretary of War ordered the disbursement of food relief to the destitute, and arranged for the Bureau of Refugees, Freedmen, and Abandoned Lands (Freedmen's Bureau) to manage the distribution of rations.[50] The Freedmen's Bureau had originally begun its work aiding freedpeople and refugees in the occupied South in March 1865. Although its continued existence during Reconstruction became a source of considerable conflict between President Johnson, who opposed it, and the Republican Congress, who supported it, many Alabamians understood the Bureau as an agency offering critical support to the destitute in the bleak months following the war. By January 1866, Alabama's Bureau head, Assistant Commissioner Brigadier General Wager Swayne, had

48. Henry F. Mitchell and Emely E. Pointy to Gen. Wager Swayne, May 22, 1866, FB-AL, NAMS-M809, Roll 8.

49. Kolchin, *First Freedom,* 14–5, 152–7.

50. LeGrand, "Destitution and Relief of the Indigent," 266; George R. Bentley, *A History of the Freedmen's Bureau* (Philadelphia: University of Pennsylvania, 1955), 139.

stockpiled enough supplies to issue twenty thousand rations to white and black Alabamians every day for the entire month.[51]

On the face of it, the Freedmen's Bureau ration system seemed ideal for unionists suffering from war-induced poverty: a Federal agency, not the state, had taken charge of food aid. But because of their inability to win local political offices in rebel-dominated communities, unionists were, in practice, dependant upon former Confederates, not the Bureau, to secure their rations. In January 1866, Alabama and the Freedmen's Bureau instituted an arrangement whereby local justices of the peace compiled lists of the destitute in their respective beats. The justices submitted these rolls to county commissioners and probate judges, who then made a master list from the beat returns, and afterward appointed an agent to direct the Bureau's once-monthly distribution of rations.[52] In the November elections, of course, many of the local offices responsible for overseeing the implementation of the Bureau food rationing program had been secured by former Confederates, good numbers of whom had held the same positions during the war. Consequently, many local Bureau agents had been in charge of prosecuting unionists during the war.[53]

Unionists were quick to perceive injustices in Bureau food distribution. As J. J. Giers, a wartime unionist from Morgan County, explained to the Joint Committee on Reconstruction in 1866, assistance "is distributed through the rebel-officeholders. The Judge of probate is generally a rebel, and he will not assist 'the damned tories,' as the Union people are called."[54] It was for discrimination of this sort in the summer of 1867 that a number of Calhoun County citizens petitioned Bureau official O. D. Kinsman to remove

M. Woodruff the [Bureau's] ration agent of this place Because 1st He refuses to isue Goverment rations to poor people who are friends to the Government. 2st Because He isues the Government supplies to people who are unfrinly to the Government becaus of

51. LeGrand, "Destitution and Relief of the Indigent," 267–8; Foner, *Reconstruction*, 152; Bethel, "Freedmen's Bureau in Alabama," 59.

52. Bethel, "The Freedmen's Bureau in Alabama," 59.

53. Robert A. Flimmy to Brig. Gen. Swayne, [September?] 1865, FB-AL, NAMS-M809, Roll 5; Kenneth B. White, "Wager Swayne, Racist or Realist?" *Alabama Review* (April 1978): 95–7.

54. *Report of the Joint Committee on Reconstruction*, 14.

exclusion of deserving union families. 3rd He acts unfrenly in his official capacity to poor people . . . and grants favors to those who were and still ar the enimes of the Government and that to[o] for no other re[a]son than that they are such enemies.[55]

Poverty, according to these Calhoun citizens, was not the primary reason they had been rebuffed by the ration agent; only those "poor people who are friends to the Government" were singled out for the treatment, while former Confederates were rewarded.[56]

Antiunionist recriminations like these prompted Mrs. S. M. Rogers of Colbert County to write a letter to General Swayne in the spring of 1867. In it, she explained that her husband, R. C. Rogers, "was a younited State soldier cap[t]ured by the rebes," men who had subsequently "cild" him. Widowed with small children, she had been relying on Federal army rations during the war, and since then, on Freedmen's Bureau rations to feed herself and her children. Of late, though, there had been so little corn at her local Bureau distribution point that she had not been able to draw rations at all. Upon discovering from a neighbor that a new shipment of corn had arrived at the home of a local man named Warren, Rogers "went an asked him about the corn." This man demanded further details of Rogers: "[H]e asked me if I was soldier widow, I told him that I was, he wanted to know wat a caind of a soldir, I told him that he was a feddrel soldir an he sed that the corn was onely for the rebbel soldier widdo." Stunned and confused, Rogers bitterly denounced the inequity of ex-Confederates who continued to make "a division" between the sections, especially after so many had taken advantage of the rations offered by occupying Union forces during the last part of the war. "I began to think that I [was] strip[p]ed twise by," she complained to Swayne. "[I had] lost my husban and st[oo]d the persecuison thr[ough] the war and when the feddreals prepared bred an meat the rebes was the first afte[r] hit, both man and wimman." Bitterly, she concluded that although the Federal army had "fead a many long sided reb," the same people "wo[ul]d cut the federels throt if th[ey] had the chance." After apologizing to Swayne for her letter—"hist baddly rot[e] and baddly spelt"—

55. Many Citizens of Calhoun Co. to O. D. Kinsman, June 26, 1867, FB-AL, NAMS-M809, Roll 12.
56. Ibid.

Rogers begged him to keep her communication secret, convinced that she had endangered herself by making her report.[57]

Search for Justice

Although dismayed to find themselves still on the defensive in the post-war period, some loyalists were able to harness strength in those communities where they had some numbers. One of the most effective areas of unionist organizing took place in the Union League, which during the years of Presidential Reconstruction remained a whites-only organization. North Alabama unionists had little difficulty metamorphosing their wartime networks into local Union Leagues where they could gather to share their struggles and organize for political action.[58] Founded in the North during the war as a patriotic club, the League quickly became the Republican Party's grassroots organizing arm in the postwar South. In at least a few Alabama locations, the League had first taken hold among white unionists during the war itself, and was sustained by wartime unionists until military Reconstruction ushered in black voting rights. Northern soldiers likely informed Alabamians of the existence of the group. During the war, the Northern-based Loyal Publication Society published ninety different pro-Union and pro-Lincoln pamphlets, of which they distributed some nine hundred thousand to Union Leagues,

57. Mrs. S. M. Rogers to Brig. Gen. Wager Swayne, May 9, 1867, FB-AL, NAMS-M809, Roll 12. According to Hoole, *Alabama Tories,* 115, Robert C. Rogers was a private in Company D, First Alabama Cavalry. He enlisted in April 1863, at Glendale, Mississippi, and was captured only two months later. The published roster makes no note of his death.

58. The most recent and significant study of the Union League in Alabama is Fitzgerald, *Union League Movement.* This volume, as well as Fitzgerald's "Radical Republicanism," 565–96, has been central to my understanding and analysis of unionists in Reconstruction. See also George Parsons Lathrop, *History of the Union League of Philadelphia* (Philadelphia: n.p., 1884); Walter L. Fleming, "The Formation of the Union League in Alabama," *Gulf States Historical Magazine* 2 (1903): 73–89; Susie L. Owens, "The Union League of America: Political Activities in Tennessee, the Carolinas, and Virginia, 1865–1870" (Ph.D. diss., New York University, 1943); Mario Clement Silvestro, "None But Patriots: The Union Leagues in Civil War and Reconstruction" (Ph.D. diss., University of Wisconsin, 1959) and by the same author, *Rally Round the Flag: The Union Leagues in the Civil War* (Lansing: Michigan State University Press, 1967); and Frank L. Klement, *Dark Lanterns: Secret Political Societies, Conspiracies, and Treason Trials in the Civil War* (Baton Rouge: Louisiana State University Press, 1984).

various political and service organizations, private individuals, and Union soldiers in the field. Some fifteen thousand pamphlets were sent to Union-occupied Louisiana and almost five thousand found their way to Kentucky. It is entirely possible that such pamphlets eventually circulated into Alabama via Federal occupation or by way of native soldiers who crossed the lines.[59] Certainly, men associated with the First Alabama Cavalry started a Union League very early in the war, sometime around 1863, when James Ellis, a farmer from Walker County, began organizing in and around Jasper, the county seat and Confederate military post. A. J. Sides, who headed a band of unionist partisan rangers in North Alabama, was initiated by Ellis, as were numerous other local men. Ellis even ventured "into the rebel camps" to recruit "many of the soldiers, and officers, into the Union League, that he knew entertained [unionist] sentiment."[60]

After Lee's surrender, even more Union Leagues grew out of the networks white unionists had developed over the course of the war. Leaders took to heart the national League's injunction to "enlist all loyal talent in their neighborhood," and recruited heavily among men who had been their comrades and confidants during the war.[61] The group was quite successful: one observer believed that as early as 1865–66, six thousand "Union men, white men and Federal officers" had joined the Union League in North Alabama. For unionists, one of the League's great attractions was its secrecy.[62] Over the previous four years, these men had grown quite familiar and comfortable with meeting in secret; it was a natural transition to expand their clandestine wartime networks into Union League associations. The covert nature of the organization ensured that the men within it could trust one another, just as they had as lie-outs, scouts, and spies. This, in turn, allowed the men safely to dis-

59. Frank Freidel, "The Loyal Publication Society: A Pro-Union Propaganda Agency," *Mississippi Valley Historical Review* 26, no. 3 (1939): 359–61, 363; Fitzgerald, *Union League Movement*, 18.

60. Claim 6091, James Ellis, Walker Co., December 28, 1871: Testimony of A. J. Sides; Claim 8985, Thomas Boteler, Winston Co., January 25, 1876: Testimony of James Ellis; both in SCC.

61. Fitzgerald, "Radical Republicanism," 580; Fitzgerald, *Union League Movement*, 10–1, 24–5, 73; Klement, *Dark Lanterns*, 37–9; Owen, *History of Alabama and Dictionary of Alabama Biography*, 1344; Foner, *Reconstruction*, 283.

62. Quote in *Testimony Taken by the Joint Select Committee*, 9: 894; for number of League members, see Fitzgerald, "Radical Republicanism," 571; also see Fitzgerald, *Union League Movement*, 12–4, 22; Foner, *Reconstruction*, 283.

cuss and advocate radical plans to challenge Confederates around them, and to protest Andrew Johnson's policies toward the South.

Most Leaguers were small to middling nonslaveholding farmers who had rarely held statewide or regional political office or engaged in politics as anything other than a civic duty.[63] Their lack of an antebellum political pedigree, along with their unionist pasts, led the probate judge of Blountsville to deride the League as "composed of men without reputation or brains" with whom "men of any respectability . . . will not associate on the street."[64] Though largely composed of men of little public reputation, the Union League in Alabama also attracted the interest of small slaveholders like Green Haley, who was "President" of Marion County's "organization styled the 'Union League.'" During the war, Haley had won the respect of local loyalists by publicly proclaiming his political sentiments in church, stating that he "was a union man, Socially, Publicly, and Religiously," and had "been raised as such and expected to die as such."[65] Likewise, planter Dr. William Irwin organized the first Union League in Lawrence County in 1866, designating a building on his plantation—"what is known on the place as the 'League House'"—as the regular meeting place for the group. "I was president of the League," he remembered later, "and I think I initiated about 600 men that year [1866] into the Union League."[66]

Loyalists developed strategies to hold rebels accountable for their wartime actions, attempting thereby to do for themselves what the constitutional convention could not. At the fall court in 1865, for example, Winston County citizens successfully brought charges against a Colonel

63. In 1860, William C. Ford, for instance, had owned one hundred and sixty acres but cultivated only thirty; Jesse Smith of Marshall County had an estate of $879 and cultivated about forty acres; James Cargile owned an estate worth $1,111. See Claim 5262, William C. Ford, Walker Co., August 6, 1873: Testimony of Job Richardson; Claim 15136, Jesse Smith, Marshall Co., March 28, 1874; Claim 13285, James Cargile, Jackson Co., December 7, 1872: Testimony of William A. Austin; all in SCC; 1860 U.S. Census, Alabama, Free and Slave Pop., NAMS M-653.

64. J. Moore to Gov. R. M. Patton, April 9, 1867, AGP: R. M. Patton, 1865–68.

65. Haley's total estate before the war equaled $18,500 and included eight slaves; Claim 2177, Green M. Haley, Marion Co., March 28, 1872, SCC; 1860 U.S. Census, Alabama, Free and Slave Pop., NAMS M-653.

66. Irwin owned two plantations in 1860, one of which included 1,010 acres, the other totaling 1,600 acres. He cultivated corn and cotton using the labor of fifty-one slaves; Claim 1369, William B. Irwin, Lawrence Co., April 13, 1872, SCC; 1860 U.S. Census, Alabama, Free and Slave Pop., NAMS M-653.

Cudry of General Roddey's Fourth Alabama Cavalry for having murdered unionist deserters who were hiding out in the hills. During the war, Cudry had detailed a group of his soldiers with orders "to arrest certain parties who were committing robberies upon the good citizens." He also made it clear that the squad was "not to bring [the arrested men] back" once they had been caught. The squad had located and arrested five individuals "who were lying out in the woods with arms in their hands." Then, in accordance with Cudry's orders, the captain in charge "organized a Drum Court Martial which . . . sentenced the men to be hung." Of the five, one was summarily hanged; three others were shot; only one, a young boy, was released. The accusers claimed that at one point the captain had put a pistol to his own soldiers' heads to force them to kill the Winston men. The county's grand jury indicted Cudry and over twenty of his men (deemed by their defenders to come from Winston's "best families") for these wartime killings; only some of them were successfully captured and jailed.[67]

Walker County unionists were numerous enough to prosecute a similar case in February 1866. There, the grand jury presented bills of indictment against Captain F. L. B. Goodwin, commander of the Confederate post at Jasper, who had become infamous for imprisoning and murdering Union men during the war. Brigadier General Sterling A. M. Wood of Tuscaloosa, the attorney who defended Goodwin to Alabama's governor, explained that Goodwin had been a soldier in his Confederate brigade during the war, although not at the time of the Walker County murders. Wood claimed that Goodwin had always been a "Kind, judicious, and conscientious officer," and could not accept that Goodwin "could be guilty of an act of murder." While admitting that it was "probably true that some persons were executed in Walker," he insisted that Goodwin was not to blame. Area unionists viewed Captain Goodwin in quite a different light, largely because he had commanded the post at Jasper and the "slaughter pen" they believed he ran there. One of the Curtis unionists from Winston County, for instance, was shot by men who reported to Goodwin. William C. Ford of Walker remembered that "Capt. F. Lee B. Goodwin" had threatened him with hanging "for my union sentiments" and on one occasion sent "his men to my residence after me with instruction to bring me dead or alive but I happened to be gone from home and they did not get me." And George Davis of Walker County was

---

67. H. C. Speake to Gov. R. M. Patton, September 7, 1867, AGP: R. M. Patton, 1865–68.

arrested numerous times as a conscript avoider; on the last occasion in winter 1864, he was picked up by Goodwin himself, who ordered Davis bound and taken to the jail at Jasper. There Davis remained until the Federal army liberated him in March 1865.[68]

The outcome of Goodwin's trial is unclear, for the court documents have since been destroyed or lost. It is possible that even if tried and convicted, Goodwin could have been pardoned by the governor, who by 1866 had been empowered by the state to intervene in such war crimes cases. Regardless of Goodwin's fate, the fact that Walker County's unionists could prosecute the case was remarkable. Like their Winston County counterparts, they used the courts to hold a man accountable for acting in accordance with the laws of the Confederacy and the prerogatives of the Confederate army, confirming the principle at the heart of unconditional unionism: that the Confederacy had always been a fraud, that its laws were unjust and deserved no standing in law, and that its supporters deserved to be thoroughly punished. Moreover, they did so while the force of national Reconstruction policy tended in the opposite direction.

Not surprisingly in the light of North Alabama's "hard war," violent confrontations, including vigilantism, marked many attempts by unionists to get justice. These men had nurtured outrage and fury for a long time—it had warmed them on cold nights in the bushes, formed a central part of their identities as Union men, and driven them to risk everything to escape the Confederacy to fight on the side of the Union. Furthermore, life as fugitives, guerrillas, and bushwhackers had taught hard lessons about self-defense and retribution. These men wanted revenge, pure and simple, and they believed that their suffering had justified them in seeking it out. Even ten years after the war ended, for instance, Mial Abernathy of Limestone County yearned to punish the local Confederate who had revealed Abernathy's whereabouts to the conscript cavalry. Soldiers had then come to his home, arrested him, and stolen nearly every item he owned, down to the clothes and shoes he and his family were wearing. "I know who told them I was at home," he hotly exclaimed to the Southern Claims Commission in 1875, "and Damn him, I ought to kill him for it."[69]

68. Sterling A. M. Wood to Gov. Robert M. Patton, February 13, 1866, AGP: R. M. Patton, 1865–68; Claim 10339, William B. Curtis, Winston Co., March 12, 1872; Claim 5262, William C. Ford, Walker Co., August 6, 1873; Claim 6090, George Davis, Walker Co., February 7, 1873; all in SCC. See also Marjorie Howell Cook, "Restoration and Innovation: Alabamians Adjust to Defeat, 1865–1867" (Ph.D. diss., University of Alabama, 1968), 140.

69. Claim 4806, Mial S. Abernathy, Limestone Co., July 23, 1875, SCC.

Abernathy never acted on his impulse, but others like him did, determined to settle old scores. In Fayette County, where the county court had successfully arrested a man who had imprisoned and executed unionists during the war, legal punishment would not satisfy loyalists intent on personal vengeance. Instead, a group of them rode to the jail in the middle of the night, forcibly took the keys from the jailer, and kidnapped the prisoner. "He has not been heard from," a citizen wrote to Governor Robert M. Patton, "[w]hether murdered or not, is not known."[70] A Bibb County citizen likewise wrote to Patton to report "the many deeds of horror, crime, & bloodshed, that are frequently being made in portions of Bibb & Shelby Counties, by the Tories and deserters of said & other Counties." Unionists had begun sending messages "almost daily" to the "most prominent and most influential citizens," demanding their immediate departure from the county. According to the writer, the "tories" had brought about what was doubtlessly a long-wished-for reversal of fortune:

> Several of our most worthy citizens have been shot, & murdered in cold blood; many have been compelled to leave their homes & families at the mercy of these outlaws, & seek refuge amid the thickly settled & enlightened portions of the Counties; while others have been hunted like wild beast, their stock shot down in the woods & pastures, & appropriated, & they, are forced to sacrifice property & lands, by a speedy disposal, & immediate removal.[71]

Likewise, in Shelby County during the summer of 1866, unionists James Thames, Levi Thames, and John Allen murdered a man named Martin McGraw. According to a county official, the "homicide is said to have been committed, by way of retaliation for the murder of the father of two of the prisoners, which was perpetrated during the war, under most atrocious circumstances, & in which it is charged that the deceased [participated]." Shelby's citizens had been "before and during the war . . . much divided in their political opinions"; after the war, the county was plagued by "a fierce spirit of retaliation."[72]

70. Sterling A. M. Wood to Gov. Robert M. Patton, February 13, 1866, AGP: R. M. Patton, 1865–68.

71. J. N. Suttle to Gov. Robert M. Patton, September 24, 1866, AGP: R. M. Patton, 1865–68.

72. William J. Mudd to Gov. Robert M. Patton, March 20, 1867, AGP: R. M. Patton, 1865–68.

Randolph County was similarly beset with episodes of violence and intimidation, much of it designed to settle old scores between unionists and Confederates. "Your Excellency is aware of the terrible state of affairs which has existed in the county of Randolph since the close of the late war," wrote a team of Lafayette attorneys to the governor. "You are further aware of the fact that during the war said county was filled with *so called* Union men and that after the surrender of the Southern Army the [Union] '*Leaguers*' have been banded to murder or drive out of the limits of said County every man who sympathised with the Confederate Cause." At the end of December 1865, Randolph unionists had murdered one man and beaten another because of long-standing "political animosity." A. Sidney Reaves, the son of the wounded man, described his father's assailants as "the scum of the world" who were motivated to commit this violence by an "offense, as they were pleased to say, during the war against Union men." Such vendetta campaigns by unionists were devastating for former Confederates. As one observer explained to Governor Patton, he and his neighbors felt boxed in on every side "by assaults from them who seek revenge on a people who have submitted."[73]

Violence also grew out of unionists' desires to *stay* in the woods, rather than rejoin Alabama society. For a full fourteen months after Appomattox, a band of unionist lie-outs in Blount County refused to accept the return to peace. They remained armed and resisted all attempts by county officials to collect taxes in their neighborhood—Blount's probate judge, a former Confederate sympathizer, reported that the men constituted "the major part of the population" living in the southeastern corner of the county. They appeared to work in concert with "similar organizations" in neighboring St. Clair County, through which the men were able to "give to each other mutual aid and protection." The holdouts refused to allow the tax assessor into their neighborhood, threatened both him and the sheriff with "bushwhacking" if either attempted revenue collection, and "boldly avowed that they would pay no tax to the 'rebel state,' as they call the State of Alabama."[74]

This resistance perhaps suggests that these men had become used to the life of outlaws and may even have begun to enjoy the freedoms asso-

73. Dean & McGraw, Attys., to Gov. Robert M. Patton, December 27, 1866; A. Sidney Reaves to Gov. Robert M. Patton, December 31, 1866; Sterling A. M. Wood to Gov. Robert M. Patton, February 13, 1866; all in AGP: R. M. Patton, 1865–68.

74. A. M. Gibson and J. W. Moore to Gov. R. M. Patton, August 16, 1866, forwarded to Brig. Gen. Wager Swayne, FB-AL, NAMS-M809, Roll 7.

ciated with that life. However, it is crucial to recognize that from the unionists' perspective, the county's officials were, as far as they were concerned, well-known rebels. One of the men reporting the tax resistance was justice of the peace A. M. Gibson, who had served in the Confederate army as lieutenant of Company K in "Fightin' Joe" Wheeler's Nineteenth Alabama Infantry. Gibson had also served as Blount County's representative in the state legislature during the last two years of the war and, thanks to a pardon from President Johnson, would continue to serve as a state representative for two years following the war.[75] Another official making the report, Probate Judge J. W. Moore, had held his office throughout the war and *not* by virtue of his unionism. During Reconstruction, local unionists complained of Moore's hostility toward them in matters of ration distribution and justice.[76] Moreover, the tax collector himself was a Confederate veteran named Jeremiah Ratliffe, formerly lieutenant of Company C, "Avalanche Company," of the Twenty-ninth Alabama Infantry. In fact, of the eleven Blount County officials appointed or elected in the fall of 1865, at least six—including two justices of the peace and two constables—had served in the Confederate army, three in Wheeler's Nineteenth Alabama Infantry.[77] As Wheeler's men spent some of their time fighting in North Alabama, it is no wonder that the Union men hiding in the hilly portions of Blount and St. Clair Counties looked askance at the self-proclaimed representatives of the U.S. government who said they came to collect tax in peace. Unable to accept

75. "Muster Roll of Nineteenth Alabama Infantry Regiment, 1861–1865," available from: http://www.19thalabama.org/muster.html; last accessed July 27, 1998; Alabama Secretary of State, Elections and Registration Division, Commission Registers, 1861–1865: Blount Co., 67, ADAH; Owen, *History of Alabama and Dictionary of Alabama Biography*, 160.

76. "Preamble and Resolutions Adopted by the U.S.A. Circle, Blount Co., Ala., in General Meeting on the Fourth Saturday in September, 1866," enclosure in W. C. Garrison to Col. J. B. Callis, September 3, 1866, forwarded to Brig. Gen. Swayne, FB-AL, NAMS-M809, Roll 7.

77. "Muster Roll of Company C, 'Avalanche Company,' Twenty-ninth Alabama Infantry," available from http://members.aol.com/egun/Avalanche.html; "Muster Roll of Nineteenth Alabama Infantry Regiment, 1861–1865," available from http://www.19thalabama .org/muster.html; "Muster Roll of Company F, Forty-eighth Alabama Infantry," available from http://fly.hiwaay.net/jgeorge/frame48.html; "Muster Roll of Company F 'Blount County Tiger Boys,' Twenty-ninth Alabama Infantry," available from http://members.aol .com/egun/Tiger.html; and "Muster Roll of Company B 'Blount County Hornets,' Twenty-ninth Alabama Infantry," available from http://members.aol.com/egun/Hornet.html; all accessed July 27, 1998. For election information, see Alabama Secretary of State, Elections and Registration Division, Commission Registers, 1861–1865: Blount Co., 67–8, ADAH.

the idea that such men would have been granted political appointments under a victorious Union government, the men denounced all attempts to pacify them as dirty tricks and continued to prosecute the war as bushwhackers against the now-dead Confederacy.

Just as unionists' greatest fear during the war had been that Confederate victory would mean their own expulsion from the South, their deepest hope for Union triumph had been that the South would be their own— that their fidelity to the Union would be rewarded with the political trusteeship of their state. Between 1865 and 1867, it became clear that political empowerment would not come with Union victory. The conciliatory policies of President Johnson and the Republican Congress failed to offer loyalists the tools they needed to win the peace. Stripped of the authority they believed to be theirs by right as reward for loyalty, disillusioned by reconstruction through pacification and reunification, these people felt scorned, marginalized, and outnumbered. Though many took matters into their own hands, most still feared for their future, and in some cases, their lives. As George White and ninety other petitioners from Blount County explained to Congress in 1866, "We say to you that Rebellion is [now] more strong more Resolute more Hell Bent [and] that the Rebels wold Be more savage than at any time during the war if tha had the opitunity."[78]

78. Petition to [Congress] of George White and 90 Other Loyal Citizens of Blount County, Alabama, November 21, 1866, Records of the Committee on the Judiciary, 39th Cong., HR 39A-H14.10, RG 233, NAB.

6

"The Day of Our Ruin"

RADICAL ACTIVISM AND KLAN BACKLASH

It is more than idle, it is a mockery, to contend that a people who have thrown off their allegiance, destroyed the local government which bound their States to the Union as members thereof, defied its authority, refused to execute its laws, and abrogated every provision which gave them political rights within the Union, still retain, through all, the perfect and entire right to resume, at their own will and pleasure, all their privileges within the Union, and especially, to participate in its government, and to control the conduct of its affairs. To admit such a principle for one moment would be to declare that treason is always master and loyalty a blunder.

— Report of the Joint Committee on Reconstruction, 39th Cong., 1st Sess., 1866

He was so sorely pressed by the Cluclux that he was forced to leave his home, fireside, and family and flee to the north for his own personal preservation. He was called by the KluKlux a radical and a negro equalizer.

— Thomas A. Christian, Fayette County, 1872

In June 1867, unionists joined Northerners and newly enfranchised African Americans in Montgomery, where they convened the first statewide Republican Party convention in Alabama's history. Hailing from thirty-eight counties and calling themselves "the loyal men of the State of Alabama," the delegates crafted a party platform from issues long championed by white unionists. "We believe," the platform began, "that the establishment of justice is essential to enduring peace, that patriotism should be exalted as a virtue, and that it is the duty of the State to cherish all its people." The delegates went on to affirm loyalists' long-standing

For epigraphs, see *Report of the Joint Committee on Reconstruction*, ix–x; and Claim 11632, John Hamer, Fayette Co., September 1, 1872: Testimony of Thomas A. Christian, SCC.

ideal of political legitimacy, in which fitness for office was determined by individuals' wartime loyalty to the Union. "[T]hose men who have stood firm by the cause of the Union," they asserted, "are entitled to that confidence which is the reward of patriotism and fidelity in any land."[1]

This meeting was made possible only by the stunning political developments of the previous spring. Radical Republicans in Congress had managed finally to convince the moderate majority of the party to challenge Andrew Johnson's control of Reconstruction policy. Although men like Charles Sumner and Thaddeus Stevens had long alienated their fellow party members through outspoken advocacy of black voting rights and Confederate land confiscation, developments in the South since the November 1865 elections had narrowed the gap between this minority and the dominant moderate wing of the party. Virtually all Republicans believed that loyalists had been politically intimidated and overwhelmed by former rebels. It was equally clear that former slaveholders were keeping former slaves in subjugation by virtue of black codes passed by Southern states since the end of the war. Unless Johnson's willingness to overlook these offenses was checked, the Radicals now argued persuasively, the Congress of the United States would soon be filled with unrepentant Southerners unwilling to recognize or support the changes wrought by the war.

In March 1867, Congressional Republicans of all persuasions thus began to take concrete measures to curb the power of former Confederates in Southern politics. In a series of Military Reconstruction Acts, each passed over Johnson's veto, Congress placed all the former Confederate states except Tennessee under martial law and divided the region into five military districts. Each district was to be overseen by a military governor, who would quickly register voters and hold elections for delegates to new state constitutional conventions.[2] Also proscribed from the franchise was any man who had taken an oath to the United States before 1860 and subsequently taken an oath to the Confederacy. By virtue of these limits, many former Confederate officials, including men who had gained political positions during Presidential Reconstruction, were now barred both from voting and from holding local, state, and national

1. *Elmore Standard* (Wetumpka, Ala.), June 7, 1867.

2. Gen. John Pope was appointed to take military control of the Third Military District, of which Alabama was a part.

offices.[3] Finally, Congress made the granting of suffrage rights to black men an unavoidable price for Southern states' readmission to the Union. Lawmakers mandated that in the election for delegates to the state constitutional conventions (and all subsequent electoral contests), African American men would both vote and run for office.

The political empowerment of African Americans had been long advocated by Northern Radicals, and in 1866, many white unionists had added their voices to the chorus. In September of that year, Southern loyalists gathered at an anti-Johnson conference in Philadelphia. At this meeting, representatives from Alabama and the other unreconstructed former Confederate states approved a resolution supporting the enfranchisement of blacks.[4] Pragmatism, of course, rather than magnanimity, had prompted unionists to move so far ahead of all but the most extreme members of the Northern Republican Party. African American voting rights, they believed, would solve the problem of minority rule, bolster Republican Party membership in the South, and thereby help defeat rebels in elections. Regardless of the means employed, only the creation of loyal Southern governments, they argued, would provide security to loyal people. In the words of the Union League's state council, the question was simply, "Shall we have [the freedman] for our ally or the rebel for our master?"[5] With the proscription of leading Confederates and the enfranchisement of blacks, many loyalists believed that Reconstruction was finally on the course they had advocated since the war's end.

Initially, unionists' hopes for a new political order seemed well founded, for they soon acceded to positions of greater political power, especially in North Alabama. In particular, many were called upon to fill Federal appointive offices at the county or local level, for those jobs now required the so-called ironclad oath, in which the oath-taker swore to having never supported the Confederacy. Because unionists could pass

3. Wiggins, *Scalawag in Alabama Politics*, 19–20; Foner, *Reconstruction*, 275–6. The Reconstruction Acts took much of their language regarding voter proscription from the Fourteenth Amendment, which in 1866 had been soundly rejected by all the Southern states but Tennessee. Their rejection of the amendment was one of the acts precipitating Congress's decision to take control of Reconstruction; each state had to ratify the Fourteenth Amendment to regain representation in Congress.

4. Abbott, *Republican Party and the South*, 70.

5. *Montgomery Mail*, April 17, 1867, quoted in Fitzgerald, "Radical Republicanism and the White Yeomanry," 578. Also see Foner, *Reconstruction*, 259–61; McMillan, *Constitutional Development*, 131.

this bar, they were now asked to serve as Freedmen's Bureau officials, election registrars, postmasters, and tax assessors. Unionists also began to hold other non-Federal positions because so many former office holders were now barred by virtue of having taken oaths to the Confederacy.[6] This newfound political leverage culminated in the spring of 1868, with black and white voters electing a Republican and wartime unionist, William H. Smith, to the governor's seat and giving the Republicans a majority in the state legislature.[7]

Political power, however, came at a steep price. Not long after the onset of Congressional Reconstruction, vigilante groups, particularly the Ku Klux Klan, began targeting white and black Republicans in an attempt to derail Reconstruction. Their efforts created the most repressive and violent environment loyalists had encountered since 1865. Such intimidation quickly dampened some loyalists' early enthusiasm for political organizing. As S. S. Plowman of Tuscaloosa County explained to the governor, fears of the Klan had caused many of his unionist associates to become reluctant "to own that th[ey] are members of the union league."[8] John Ramsey likewise emphasized unionists' very real fears to the SCC. "[I]t has taken almost as much nerve to be a Republican in the midst of KuKlux bands as it did during the war in the time of vigilance committees and bands of cutthroats."[9]

Though loyalists tried mightily to defend themselves and Republicanism in the face of this onslaught, they found themselves without ade-

6. For instance, Union veteran Henry Springfield acted as a voter registrar in the 1867 election; constitutional convention delegate William C. Garrison, long-time League activist and Bureau agent, became a member of the executive committee of Alabama's Republican Party in 1868; William T. Ewing took up the job of postmaster; veteran Thomas Haughey of Morgan County won a seat in the U.S. Congress as a Republican in 1868; Benjamin Saffold of Dallas County, who had refugeed during the war, became mayor of Selma; and William Skinner, a leading unionist in Franklin County, took the office of chancery court judge and held it through the rest of Reconstruction. See Richard L. Hume, "The 'Black and Tan' Constitutional Conventions of 1867–1869 in Ten Former Confederate States: A Study of Their Membership" (Ph.D. diss., Johns Hopkins University, 1972), 52–68.

7. William H. Smith had opposed secession in 1860 and fled Alabama in 1862. He remained in the North until the end of the war. When he returned, unconditional unionists favored him for the governorship, which President Johnson gave to Lewis Parsons. Under Brig. Gen. Wager Swayne's brief military governorship in 1867, Smith took charge of voter registration. See Wiggins, *Scalawag in Alabama Politics*, 38.

8. S. S. Plowman to Gov. W. H. Smith, July 12, 1868, AGP: W. H. Smith, 1867–70.

9. Claim 7252, Joseph Stricklin, Cherokee Co., May 30, 1874: Summary comments by SCC Agent John Ramsey, SCC.

quate aid. While the Klan and the Democratic Party behaved, in the words of historian Eric Foner, "as if conducting a revolution," most Republicans in the North continued to seek "stability through conciliation," despite having supported the Military Reconstruction Acts.[10] Unionists soon came to realize that though most Republicans had endorsed certain radical measures out of frustration with recalcitrant former rebels, they remained unwilling to invest the money, political clout, or military force necessary to defend those measures and the Southern Republicans charged with carrying them out.[11]

Political Organizing under Congressional Reconstruction

As a consequence of Congress implementing African American franchise, white unionists in the Republican Party quickly became involved—directly or indirectly—with interracial political organizing. Even if unionists welcomed black franchise as a buttress to Republican control of state politics, the introduction of African American voters to the body politic could not help but transform the trajectory on which loyalists had been embarked since 1861. During the secession winter and throughout the war, unionists had embedded their political choices within neighborhood and kinship; loyalty to the Union had grown out of a conservative impulse to protect the world they knew. Congressional Reconstruction, by contrast, demanded that unionists commit to defending a new and alien order, one that was not so deeply embedded in long-standing social and cultural traditions, especially those governing race relations. For while some unionists had cooperated with African Americans during the war, they had done so only when forced into the marginal social space occupied by black Southerners. Interracial cooperation was largely a matter of circumstance, not of ideology. Moreover, though wartime alliances clearly undermined slavery and the Confederacy, few unionists who participated in those alliances believed they were threatening white supremacy. By contrast, the new political order in the South required, as the price of power, that unionists recognize and support African American civil and political equality. It was a difficult challenge to which unionists responded in a range of ways.

In keeping with the resolutions of the 1866 Southern loyalist conven-

10. Foner, *Reconstruction*, 444.
11. Abbott, *Republican Party and the South*, 191–4.

tion in Philadelphia, many took black civil and voting rights in stride. Among those who were most visibly associated with African Americans' economic and political interest were unionists hired as agents for the Freedmen's Bureau. The Bureau had long had an interest in employing loyal men, for it was well aware that ex-rebels were more likely to resist enforcement of policies favorable to freedmen and white unionists alike. Nonetheless, prior to Congressional Reconstruction, only three confirmed wartime unionists—W. C. Garrison in Blount County, C. C. Sheets in Morgan County, and John Green in Franklin County—had been hired as Bureau agents in North Alabama.[12] The director of North Alabama's Bureau, Jonathan B. Callis, admitted to his superiors that he had struggled to appoint "loyal men," but had found it "next to impossible to find in the community men of fair reliability, who are admitted by all their neighbors, to be loyal." The Military Reconstruction Acts' requirement that agents take the "iron-clad" oath now mandated that nonunionists be replaced by "none but the strictly loyal," and Callis was forced to dig more deeply to find unionists to take the positions.[13] By the summer of 1867, the number of wartime unionists on the North Alabama Bureau payroll had increased markedly, with seven new loyal agents appointed to the counties of Franklin, Jackson, Jefferson, Limestone, Marion, Walker, and Winston.[14] As Bureau agents, these unionists not only helped fellow loyalists with political and economic aid, but assisted

12. "Roster of Officers, Citizens, Agents and Employees on Duty in the B.R.F. and A.L. Dist. Nor. Ala. during the Month of October 1866," FB-AL, NAMS-M809, Roll 22.

13. Jonathan B. Callis to Brig. Gen. Wager Swayne, January 15, 1867; O. D. Kinsman to Gen. Swayne, March 27, 1867; both in FB-AL, NAMS-M809, Roll 11.

14. "Special Report of Civilians Employed in the Sub-District of Alabama: July 1, 1867," FB-AL, NAMS-M809, Roll 11. These new agents—all native Alabamians—included Christopher Tompkins (Claim 6045, Franklin Co.); William A. Austin (Claim 13285, Jackson Co.); John M. Oliver (Claim 12955, Jefferson Co.); James L. Coman of Limestone (Denied Claim 1879, Report 7, 1877, NAMS-M1407, SCC Disallowed Claims; and, for his witness testimony, Allowed Claims 7088, 20403, 18475, 19483, and 20847, Limestone Co.); Frank Morton (Claim 2177, Marion Co.); James Ellis (Claim 6091, Walker Co.); and A. J. Ingle (Claims 8985 and 10339, Winston Co.); all in SCC.

Of these counties, only Limestone had a notably large 1860 slave population of 52.8 percent. Counties with 1860 slave populations between 15 and 45 percent included Jackson, Jefferson, and Franklin. Marion, Walker, and Winston Counties were of the Hill Country and had 1860 slave populations of 11.5, 6.5, and 3.4 percent, respectively. Inter-university Consortium for Political and Social Research, Study No. 3, "Historical, Demographic, Economic, and Social Data: The United States, 1790–1970" (http://fisher.lib.virginia.edu/census/).

blacks in their search for fair access to food relief, legal advocacy, labor contract assistance, and political education.[15] Consequently, loyalists in these positions found themselves on the front lines of the African American struggle for social and political justice.

Other unionists undertook the direct political organizing of African Americans through the Union League. Heretofore, the League had had no black members because only whites had the right to vote. With the advent of African American franchise, some white Leaguers were unsure of their responsibilities toward the new voters. A Shelby County League member, for instance, wrote to Governor Robert M. Patton in May 1867, asking for guidance in the matter of black membership: "As the negro Question has come up before this League it has been laid over untill the next meeting of our U. L.," in anticipation of further advice from the governor. The men questioned whether or not white Leagues should "initiate the negro" and by "what authority" such initiation could take place. They asked the governor to "explain to us" what to do.[16]

Some unionists seemed to understand immediately "what to do." Federal veteran and physician Thomas Haughey of Morgan County, and attorney and wartime refugee Robert Heflin of Randolph County, for instance, both recruited and organized black Leagues during the spring and summer of 1867.[17] In May 1867, Calhoun County's "Loyal Whitemen & Freedmen" brought together a local biracial organization that they called "the union Republican party."[18] And in August 1867, sixteen whites and nineteen blacks marched together in a Union League procession through Tuscumbia, a Tennessee River town, much to the dismay of local whites.[19] Thus, though most local Leagues remained segregated or only desegregated to the degree that leadership was white and membership was black, some clubs nonetheless initiated true interracial political cooperation in furtherance of Republican Party grassroots organizing.[20]

Not all white loyalists embraced the new civil and political freedoms

15. Bentley, History of the Freedmen's Bureau, 187–9; Foner, Reconstruction, 283–4.

16. S. M. Hare and A. H. Merrell to Gov. R. M. Patton, May 29, 1867, AGP: R. M. Patton, 1865–67.

17. Fitzgerald, Union League Movement, 16, 42; Claim 14, Robert Heflin, Randolph Co., April 18, 1871, SCC.

18. John H. Dearman to Gen. Wager Swayne, May 17, 1867, FB-AL, NAMS-M809, Roll 11.

19. Elmore Standard (Wetumpka, Ala.), August 16, 1867.

20. Fitzgerald, Union League Movement, 65; Baggett, Scalawags, 216.

accorded African Americans. In the Hill Country counties of Winston and Fayette, for instance, unionists endorsed colonization schemes to remove blacks from their counties and passed resolutions restricting immigration by blacks. Other loyalists simply abandoned the Republican Party in the wake of black franchise.[21] In May 1867, F. T. C. Sommerland of the Piedmont's Tallapoosa County, for instance, explained to the Freedmen's Bureau that he was a "Union Constitutional man . . . in favour of a Union of Hearts, a Union of Hands, A Union of People & a Union [of] Lands," but that African American franchise, among other recent political events, had caused him to fear that "a war of Races" might commence. "I have too mutch Pride in the U.S. Government," he explained, "to think that they would [cause] any more blood Shed in this unfortunate & undone Section."[22] Likewise, in November 1867, unionist Albert Collins reported that Henry H. Russell, a "good union man," had defected from the Republican cause in response to black franchise.[23]

Of the possible reasons behind such defections, the most obvious is simple racism—unionists, like their ex-Confederate neighbors and most white Northerners, harbored serious doubts about the intellectual and social fitness of African Americans for political life. Another factor, however, was the opprobrium loyalists experienced as a consequence of being associated with freedmen's rights. Indeed, regardless of the extent to which individuals were involved with black political organizing, the organizations to which unionists belonged—the Republican Party, the Freedmen's Bureau, the Union League—were all directly implicated in such activity. For men with little standing among former Confederates, these political associations only further compounded loyalists' disrepute and isolation in their communities. Alabama's most violent anti-Reconstruction newspaper editor, Ryland Randolph of the *Tuscaloosa Independent Monitor*, called all those whites who supported the Radical program in the state "moral lepers."[24] In the summer of 1867, Tuscumbia's *North Alabamian* remarked, upon viewing the interracial parade of Union Leaguers, "They were the meanest, dirtiest, hungriest, leanest, slimiest, foulest, filthiest, forlornest, most cadaverous graveyard looking set of

21. Fitzgerald, *Union League Movement*, 42–3, 23, 95; Kolchin, *First Freedom*, 18.

22. F. T. C. Sommerland to Gen. John Pope, May 31, 1867, AGP: Wager Swayne, 1867–68.

23. A. B. Collins to Gen. John Pope, November 14, 1867, FB-AL, NAMS-M809, Roll 11.

24. Quoted in Sarah Van V. Woolfolk, "The Political Cartoons of the *Tuskaloosa Independent Monitor* and *Tuskaloosa Blade*, 1867–1873," *Alabama Historical Quarterly* 27 (1965): 143.

human beings which could have been collected from the four quarters of the earth. No well trained dog would have barked at them, for they looked more harmless than whipped spaniels." The editor carefully distinguished between the native-born white Republicans—or "scalawags"—and the freedmen, however. "The negroes were by far the most decent part of the procession." The *Elmore Standard* groused that most white Alabamians would favor black voters to white Republicans any day. "[W]e can trust a Southern black man," the editor opined, "when we cannot trust a white traitor. . . . Give us the Southern negro, every time, before either a domestic or an imported Radical."[25] Just at the moment unionists began to realize some measure of political power, they found themselves accused not as traitors to the old Confederacy, a charge they embraced as a badge of honor, but as traitors to their race. Whether they agreed with the racial policies of the Republican Party or not, unionists could not escape the intense opposition those policies engendered against them.

It was amid considerable public scorn, then, that loyalists participated in the October 1–4, 1867, election. At hand were two issues: whether the state should hold a convention; and, in the event that a convention was approved, who should serve as delegates. For unionists, the results of that contest made manifest the political promise of the Military Reconstruction Acts: black and white voters overwhelmingly supported, by a margin of 90,283 to 5,583, the rewriting of Alabama's constitution. A breakdown of the votes cast indicates the invaluable role played by black voters, among whom the Union League's efforts had clearly fostered considerable voter turnout. Some 104,418 blacks registered to vote, of whom 71,730, or 68.7 percent, participated in the election; virtually all African Americans who voted approved the referendum to hold the convention and elected representatives to the same. Turnout among whites was considerably lower. Of the 61,295 whites registered, only about a third actually voted. Those who participated, however, overwhelmingly supported the convention: their 18,533 "yea" votes represented 78 percent of ballots cast by whites.[26]

The stark differences between white and black voter turnout should not be seen as a symptom of intimidation or apathy among whites. Instead, Alabama Democrats who had retained suffrage encouraged fellow

25. *North Alabamian* quoted in *Elmore Standard* (Wetumpka, Ala.), August 16, 1867; second quote, *ibid.*, August 2, 1867.

26. Rogers et al., *Alabama*, 244; Fitzgerald, *Union League Movement*, 79.

anti-convention citizens to register to vote, but then to boycott the election in order to invalidate the results. Had it worked, the plan would have taken advantage of a clause within the Reconstruction Acts stating that if the majority of registered voters failed to cast ballots in the constitutional convention contest, the election would have to be held again.[27] Although the referendum drew well over the number of voters necessary to validate the election, the paltry participation of whites allowed opponents to cast Congressional Reconstruction and the upcoming convention as illegitimate affairs run by white traitors, wily carpetbaggers, and the freedmen both had duped. As the editor of Tuscaloosa's *Independent Monitor*, Ryland Randolph, commented three days after the election, "To their credit, be it said, the great bulk of the whites avoided the polls as they would a pest house. The negroes, the yanks, and last and least, the Southern Radicals hobnobbed together on that occasion."[28] Moreover, Alabama Democrats learned an extremely important lesson from their failed boycott, one that they would apply to the next referendum held on the new constitution itself. By successfully limiting the white vote to 18,533 ballots—only 30.2 percent of the total registered—Democratic strategists had proven that it was possible to encourage a boycott among white Alabamians. In future referenda, they realized, the challenge would be to find a way to restrain not only whites, but blacks as well.

The 1867 Constitutional Convention

When the "negroes," "yanks," and "southern Radicals" arrived at the 1867 Constitutional Convention in Montgomery on November 5, they convened a meeting strikingly different from that held in 1865. One of the more significant distinctions, of course, lay with the convention's membership. Of the one hundred delegates, all but four were Republicans; of the Republicans, eighteen were African Americans.[29] Wartime

27. Foner, *Reconstruction*, 314.

28. *Tuscaloosa Independent Monitor*, October 9, 1867.

29. Rogers et al., *Alabama*, 245. Of these eighteen African American delegates, thirteen were elected from Black Belt counties, where black voters held a majority: Benjamin F. Alexander of Greene; Samuel Blandon of Lee; Simon Brunson and Benjamin Inge of Sumter; Thomas Diggs of Barbour; Peyton Finley of Montgomery; James K. Greene of Hale; Jordan Hatcher of Dallas; Washington Johnson of Russell; L. S. Latham and Benjamin F. Royal of Pike; Thomas Lee of Perry; and J. Wright McLeod of Marengo. Three delegates hailed from the Tennessee Valley (Lafayette Robinson and Columbus Jones of Madison, and James T.

unionists, many of them Union League activists, represented about 25 percent of the delegates, a far larger proportion than the 10 percent they had constituted in the 1865 Convention. At least twelve of these delegates had either fled or been driven from their homes during the war.[30] Refugees included William A. Austin of Jackson County; Arthur Bingham of Talladega County; W. T. Ewing of Etowah County; William C. Garrison of Blount County; and Benjamin Saffold of Dallas County.[31] Those who joined the Federal army upon fleeing their homes included Joseph H. Davis of Randolph County; Thomas Haughey of Morgan County, an officer from 1862 to 1865; S. F. Kennamer of Marshall County, leader of a group of Union Independent Scouts from 1863 to 1865; Henry J. Springfield of St. Clair County, head of a similar group of Union Scouts from 1864 to 1865; J. R. Walker of Shelby County, Union soldier from 1862 to 1865; and John W. Wilhite of Winston County, who, after being arrested for treason in 1861, escaped North in 1862 and enlisted in the Federal army, where he remained until 1865.[32] Other native white delegates to the 1867 convention had stayed the union course, including Thomas Adams of Clay County; James H. Autrey of Calhoun County; 1865 Constitutional Convention delegates Alfred Collins of De-

---

Rapier of Lauderdale) and John Carraway and Ovid Gregory represented Mobile County. See *Official Journal of the Constitutional Convention of the State of Alabama, Held in the City of Montgomery, Commencing on Tuesday, November 5, A.D. 1867* (Montgomery: Barrett & Brown, 1868), ii–iii; McMillan, *Constitutional Development,* 116–9 nn. 32, 33; Owen, *Dictionary of Alabama Biography,* "1867 Constitutional Convention"; Claim 11501, James T. Rapier, Montgomery, 1874, SCC; Foner, *Reconstruction,* 318.

30. McMillan, *Constitutional Development,* 114; Foner, *Reconstruction,* 317. To establish how many of the delegates had been refugees during the war, McMillan quotes the *Montgomery Daily State Sentinel,* the capital's Republican organ, of October 17, 1867. The newspaper claimed that twenty of the delegates had fled Alabama during the war. I have independently confirmed that twelve of these men crossed the lines.

31. McMillan, *Constitutional Development,* 121–2 n. 60; Owen, *Dictionary of Alabama Biography,* 13, 69, 463, 525, 556, 1165, 1372, 1412, and 1567. And see Claims 1343, 1346, and 1348, William A. Austin, Jackson Co., 1871, 1873, and 1878; Claim 5514, Charles A. Clayton (for reference to W. T. Ewing), Etowah Co., January 9, 1879; all in SCC. McMillan cites the *Montgomery Daily State Sentinel,* which remarked that Ewing, who had fled from Georgia to North Alabama to hide during the war, "was one of the 'original Moulton (Lawrence County) Leaguers who, in 1865, first organized the Radical party in Alabama.'"

32. Owen, *Dictionary of Alabama Biography,* 964; McMillan, *Constitutional Development,* 119–22 nn. 41, 60, 63; Hume, "'Black and Tan' Constitutional Conventions," 52–68; Claim 2493, Joseph H. Davis, Jr., Randolph Co., 1878, and Claim 3970, John B. Penn (for reference to John Wilhite), Morgan Co., January 29, 1879, both in SCC.

Kalb County and Early Greathouse of Tallapoosa County; George J. Dykes of Cherokee County; Gustavus Horton of Mobile County; John J. Martin of Macon County; Byron O. Masterson and Thomas M. Peters of Lawrence County; William S. Skinner of Franklin County; and Benjamin L. Whelan of Hale County. Even the president of the convention, New York–born Elisha Woolsey Peck of Tuscaloosa, had been a steadfast opponent of the Confederacy, denouncing "secession at the first, in the middle, and at the end." He had moved to Rockford, Illinois, after the war, but returned to Alabama to preside over the convention.[33]

Unionists thus faced much better prospects for shaping the state constitution in 1867 than they had in 1865. Allied with a substantial body of white Radical Republicans from the North, as well as some African American Radicals, they felt confident that they could garner a majority over more moderate native whites and freedmen.[34] And, indeed, on a number of issues—including rebel disfranchisement, repudiation of the Confederate debt, and land redistribution—unionists found common cause with many of their fellow delegates. Loyalists' motivations and plans for shaping a reconstructed Alabama, however, continued to distinguish them in important ways from the rest of the convention. As they had in 1865, unionists understood political power as a tool to punish traitors and to shape the public record about what happened during the war. As such, they approached the convention with the expectations plaintiffs might have of a court; constitutional debates represented a hearing of sorts, in which the wrongs of secession and war could be enumerated and adjudicated.[35] However deeply unionists desired this outcome, their fervor would not carry the day.

33. Quote in McMillan, *Constitutional Development*, 123; Hume, " 'Black and Tan' Constitutional Conventions," 61. And see Claim 5517, Alfred Collins, DeKalb Co., 1873; Claim 6678, George J. Dykes, Floyd Co., Ga., 1872; Claim 1, J. J. Martin, Macon Co., April 12, 1871; and Claim 129, Sarah A. Goins (for reference to William Skinner), Franklin Co., July 28, 1875; all in SCC.

34. Hume, " 'Black and Tan' Constitutional Conventions"; *Official Journal of the Constitutional Convention . . . 1867*, ii–iii; McMillan, *Constitutional Development*, 116–9 nn. 32, 33; Owen, *Dictionary of Alabama Biography*, "1867 Constitutional Convention"; Foner, *Reconstruction*, 318.

35. One of the more interesting manifestations of unionists' activism at the convention was an ordinance proposed by delegate C. P. Simmons, wartime unionist of Colbert County in the Tennessee Valley: "*Be it ordained by the people of Alabama in Convention assembled, That the county named Colbert in this State, be hereafter called the county of Brownlow.*" This motion to honor the militantly unionist William G. "Parson" Brownlow of East Tennes-

Advocacy of economic justice formed a key element of the loyalist agenda. One of the most significant issues involved the confiscation and redistribution of Confederate lands. The idea of land confiscation, while extreme, was not new. In 1864, Andrew Johnson, then acting as the military governor of Union-occupied Tennessee and in a decidedly more punitive frame of mind than he was during Reconstruction, had suggested the redistribution of confiscated Confederate lands among yeomen farmers as a way to punish and bankrupt leading rebels. Moreover, Radical Republicans like Thaddeus Stevens had long advocated the seizure of slaveholder lands to be redistributed in forty-acre plots to freedmen. Additional confiscated lands could be used to underwrite a variety of government measures, including payment of the national war debt, funding of veteran pensions, and compensation for loyal Southerners' wartime property losses.[36] After years of having these ideas pushed aside by most national leaders, Congressional Reconstruction represented Radicals' best chance to see such measures made law.

Wartime unionists and white Union Leaguers at the convention strongly supported confiscation and redistribution efforts. C. P. Simmons and Robert S. Heflin, for instance, heartily agreed with Senator Stevens's confiscation proposals; Simmons, for one, seems to have been elected as a delegate to the convention on the basis of his pro-confiscation position.[37] These men represented unionists who came out of the war poorer than they started it and who placed the blame for this squarely at the feet of the Confederacy. Postwar poverty was for them inseparable from their experience of Confederate power and abuse, for they believed rebels were not only responsible for the war and its devastation, but had caused and compounded unionists' privation. In this view, economic suffering after the war was yet another manifestation of the political and military injustices done them by the Confederate state and their rebel neighbors. Confiscation, then, promised economic relief, but just as important, it offered a way for the state to make restitution to loyalists while punishing those who had done the damage in the first place.

---

see was tabled, not surprisingly, by a vote of 76 to 12. Of the twelve who voted for it, though, eight were unionists, four of whom had served in the Union army. See *Official Journal of the Constitutional Convention . . . 1867*, 71.

36. Foner, *Reconstruction*, 183, 235.

37. Fitzgerald, *Union League Movement*, 122; Claim 14, Robert Heflin, Randolph Co., April 18, 1871: Testimony of John G. Stoke, SCC.

White unionists were not above accepting support for their cause from any and all quarters, including impoverished former rebels in North Alabama.[38] Former commander of the First Alabama Cavalry, U.S.A., and postwar Republican activist George E. Spencer pointed out to a friend that he had managed to garner interest among former Confederate soldiers who recognized in confiscation a way to recover their wartime losses.[39] For, though unionists had suffered heavily during the war, Confederate families living in areas of Federal occupation were equally "broken up" in 1865. Moreover, by 1863, conscription and privations at home had fostered considerable disaffection among North Alabamians who had originally supported the South's war effort. Like unionists, these people blamed the war—and by extension, secessionists—for their troubles. Spencer believed that, as a consequence, more than five thousand North Alabama votes could be brought to bear on any referendum for such a policy.[40] W. T. Stubblefield, a wartime unionist from Coosa County who had fled to Walker County to lie out, concurred. Asserting that "the people here are in for a confiscation of the property of the Secessionists," he argued the previous summer that the Republican Party should use the policy to enlist men who, though rebels during the war, had "merely followed their Secesh leaders, as dogs follow their masters." Relying on the support of former Confederate soldiers posed no difficulties for Stubblefield, as he believed that confiscation would ultimately benefit the right sort of people. "There is a good many abandoned lands in this section of the country," Stubblefield explained, "which ought to be put in market for the benefit of Union families so they could secure themselves good homes."[41]

Despite the broad-based support among North Alabama whites, unionists at the convention could not deliver on their radical agenda. No proposal for land confiscation or redistribution ever reached the floor for

38. For an argument emphasizing the class-based origins of unionists' radicalism at the convention, see Fitzgerald, *Union League Movement,* 20.

39. Abbott, *Republican Party and the South,* 110–2. In his advocacy, Spencer both affirmed and challenged the wisdom of national leaders. In one sense, he embraced the view of moderate Republicans that the party should appeal to a broad white base in order to avoid relying on black majorities to maintain control of Southern states. However, in choosing land confiscation as the platform by which to achieve this goal, Spencer flew in the face of the party's admonition not to upset northern voters by violating property rights in the South.

40. Fitzgerald, *Union League Movement,* 126.

41. W. T. Stubblefield to W. H. Smith, June 20, 1867, AGP: Wager Swayne, 1867–68.

debate, much less for a vote. With the exception of a few Radicals, the national Republican Party was never willing to pursue land confiscation as anything more than a threat to impress the South with the seriousness of the Reconstruction Acts. In the end, proposals to undermine the land rights of anyone, even men seen as traitors to the Union, were too revolutionary and threatening to individual property rights throughout the nation. Moreover, the national Union League, and even the black leadership of Alabama's Union League, abandoned their earlier pro-confiscation sympathies once the opposition of moderate Republicans became clear. According to historian Michael Fitzgerald, this "restraint was virtually universal among black leaders who made public statements on the matter," and marked a clear divide between African American policies and those of white unionists.[42] Without critical support at either the national or state level, then, unionists had no way to push such a measure through at the convention.

In addition to land confiscation, loyalists at the convention aggressively pursued broad-ranging rebel disfranchisement. Their hope was to permanently alter the political landscape of Alabama by denying the rights of citizenship to those they viewed as unredeemable traitors. For many, this was "the great object which ought to govern the convention." Shortly before the constitutional convention met, in fact, the Grand Council of Alabama's Union League publicly advocated that delegates should award the franchise only to wartime unionists, a resolution heartily endorsed by a number of local Leagues, particularly in North Alabama.[43] Accordingly, loyalists at the convention attempted to extend disfranchisement well beyond the provisions established by Military Reconstruction Acts (and by the as-yet-unratified Fourteenth Amendment), which nullified the voting rights of individuals who had taken an oath to the United States and subsequently aided the Confederate state.

The constitutional articles governing disfranchisement were to be debated and then proposed by the committee on the franchise, composed of two native wartime unionists, Joseph H. Davis of Randolph County and Benjamin Whelan of Hale County; Northerners Albert Griffin of Mobile County, John C. Keffer of Montgomery County, and B. W. Norris

42. Fitzgerald, *Union League Movement*, 117–25, 23–4, quote on 125; Foner, *Reconstruction*, 309–11, 235.

43. McMillan, *Constitutional Development*, quote on 128, 12; Fitzgerald, "Alabama Yeomanry during Reconstruction," 579–80.

of Elmore County; one white conservative, Joseph Speed, a former officer in the Confederate army representing Perry County; and one African
American delegate, Thomas Lee, also of Perry County.[44] Unrepresented
on the committee were convention delegates hailing from the heavily
unionist Hill Country or Tennessee Valley counties in North Alabama.

On the sixth day of the convention, the committee presented its recommendations to the convention floor. The majority report, signed by
all three Northerners and unionist Joseph Davis, recommended fairly
specific proscriptions against particular groups of rebels. A key clause
permanently disfranchised men who had "inflicted or caused to be inflicted, any cruel or unusual punishment upon any soldier, sailor, ma-
rine, employee or citizen of the United States, or who in any other way
violated the rules of civilized warfare." In proposing this rule, the Committee had squarely addressed long-standing desires among Federal veterans and civilian unionists to see guerrillas and conscript officers
permanently punished for their wartime abuses. Moreover, the majority
proposed a voter registration oath in which men, if they had "ever believed in the right of a State to secede," had to renounce that right, and
swear that they would not "in any way injure or countenance in others,
an attempt to injure any person or persons, on account of past or present
support of the Government of the United States, the policy of the Congress of the United States, or the principle of the political and civil equality of all men or of affiliation with any political party." The oath's
rhetoric went much further than eliciting a vow of future loyalty, as the
amnesty oaths of Presidential Reconstruction had done. Instead, it required a political confession, in which the citizen admitted wrongdoing
in the past, and a promise to respect the civil rights of African American
and unionist Alabamians in the future. In concluding its report, the
Committee's majority expressed its position in stark terms: "[I]t is altogether improbable that a loyal man can anywhere be found," they concurred, who is "willing to entrust with power to rule in this land, the
incarnate fiends, whose atrocious conduct during the late war, shocked
the moral susceptibilities of the civilized world." The only question remaining, they concluded, was "whether we have not been too liberal."[45]

44. *Official Journal of the Constitutional Convention . . . 1867*, 3–5. Please note that I will
refer to the members of the Democratic Party as "conservatives" to distinguish them from
the moderate and Radical factions of the Republican Party.
45. *Official Journal of the Constitutional Convention . . . 1867*, 31–2.

Many wartime unionist delegates, especially from North Alabama, believed that the recommendations were in fact "too liberal." They quickly offered a series of amendments to the article, whereby the constitution would ban even larger numbers of former rebels from voting. Moreover, each proposal embodied a judgment and exacted punishment for a particular Confederate "crime." For instance, William C. Garrison, a unionist refugee during the war, Union League organizer, and Freedmen's Bureau agent in Blount County, proposed to disfranchise "those men who were members of the State Convention of 1861, and voted or signed the ordinance of secession," or "who were members of the Confederate Congress, and voted for the conscript law." Garrison argued that the betrayals of 1861, as well as any act that resulted in the persecution of union men, should not only be remembered but also penalized. Likewise, Thomas Haughey, Union army veteran from Morgan County and Union League organizer, lobbied to disfranchise anyone who had held an officership in the Confederate army above the rank of captain, had "ever held a seat in any pretended Legislature, or held any executive, judicial, or ministerial office under any government, or pretended government, in hostility to the government of the United States," or had "killed, or otherwise abused citizens of Alabama because such citizens were known to be friends of the government of the United States." Haughey explained his proposal to the *Montgomery Daily State Sentinel* by noting "his constituents demanded the disfranchisement of nearly all who participated in the rebellion."[46]

Though unionist amendments disputed the liberality of the majority report, other delegates, white and black, pushed the debate in the opposite direction. The minority faction of the committee on the franchise—composed of one white unionist, one former Confederate, and one African American from the Black Belt—asserted in their dissenting report the principle of universal manhood suffrage and lamented that the Military Reconstruction Acts had proscribed anyone from the franchise. Instead, these delegates recommended that voters simply take oaths of future allegiance to the United States and renounce "the right of secession as a constitutional right."[47] The single black delegate on the commit-

---

46. Ibid., 53, 42; McMillan, *Constitutional Development*, 129, quote on 127. McMillan presents Haughey as a carpetbagger, which is incorrect. Haughey was a native of Scotland but had lived in Alabama since the 1840s.

47. *Official Journal of the Constitutional Convention . . . 1867*, 36.

tee, Thomas Lee of Perry County, sensed the contradiction—or perhaps the promise of self-destruction—in bestowing voting rights on freedmen while taking them away from certain whites. "I have no desire to take away any rights of the white man," he explained, "all I want is equal rights in the court house and equal rights when I go to vote. I think the time has come when charity and moderation should characterize the actions of all." Lee, like black delegates serving in constitutional conventions across the South, recognized the fragility of his situation and remained sensitive to the dangerous consequences of disfranchising hostile whites, hoping instead to depend upon black majorities at the polls to limit white political power.[48]

The majority report's measured restriction of voting rights, not to mention the strictness of wartime unionists' proposed amendments, conflicted sharply with the agenda of the national Republican Party, as well. They knew that such punitive measures would provoke resentment among former Confederates and, therefore, delay the process of Reconstruction. Others eyed their Northern constituents with unease, fearful of a backlash from voters opposed to unseating moderate white politicians in favor of a majority comprised of African Americans and white unionists, both of whom they held in doubtful esteem. Consequently, when national politicians got wind of the franchise committee's majority report, they began lobbying General John Pope, commander of the Third Military District, and General Wager Swayne, head of the Freedmen's Bureau in Alabama, to restrain the unionist delegates. Matters became so delicate at one point as to require an emissary be sent from Alabama to Washington in search of guidance "on the wording of the disfranchisement clause" in the new constitution.[49] As a consequence of opposition within the convention—fifteen conservative native whites threatened to walk out—and intervention from Washington, all the Radical amendments on the franchise were either tabled or defeated. Even the majority report's original proposal for Article VII on elections was considerably watered down by the passage of a series of conciliatory amendments.[50]

Moreover, with the exception of the clause barring those guilty of war

48. For Lee's membership on the franchise committee, see ibid.; quoted passage in McMillan, *Constitutional Development*, 129; Foner, *Reconstruction*, 324.

49. Abbott, *Republican Party and the South*, 138–9; 140–1, quote on 140.

50. McMillan, *Constitutional Development*, 131; Hume, "'Black and Tan' Constitutional Conventions," 20–1 n. 18; *Official Journal of the Constitutional Convention . . . 1867*, 95; Abbott, *Republican Party and the South*, 140–1.

crimes, all of the majority report's proposed restrictions on voting were missing from the final Constitution as well. Instead, the convention proscribed only those who had already been disfranchised by the Military Reconstruction Acts and who would continue to be barred under the Fourteenth Amendment once it was ratified. After all the debate, the constitution did little to immediately change the Alabama electorate beyond that point endorsed by Congress in its plans for Reconstruction. Those unable to vote in the June election for convention delegates remained the only significant "class" of disfranchised men in the state of Alabama, joined only by those who could be disqualified based on the war crimes clause. Furthermore, the new constitution created two enormous loopholes through which even the status quo might be undone, revealing the extent to which the Republican Party continued to tolerate, even to advocate, reconstruction through reconciliation. Anyone who "aided in the reconstruction proposed by Congress and accepted the political equality of all men before the law" would be absolved of any franchise restrictions. The convention further provided that "the General Assembly shall have power to remove the disabilities" incurred through the Reconstruction Acts or the Fourteenth Amendment. Anyone with influence in the state legislature could reverse the proscription, given sufficient majorities willing to approve the pardon. Even the majority report's voter registration oath was substantively altered to make it more palatable to Alabama conservatives. Rather than including a vow to renounce belief in the right of secession, citizens had to swear, "I will never countenance or aid in the secession of this State from the United States." Little really distinguished this oath from the old amnesty oath offered by Lincoln and Johnson.[51]

When the entire constitution was finally brought to a vote on December 5, 1867, pressures from the national Republican Party and moderates in the convention had convinced all but one unionist delegate to support the new document. The final tally was 67 for and 9 against.[52] Perhaps

---

51. Alabama Constitution of 1868, Art. VII, sect. 3 and 4.

52. *Official Journal of the Constitutional Convention . . . 1867*, 239–40. The lone unionist holdout was W. T. Ewing of Etowah Co., who had been a refugee during the war. The other dissenters were former Confederate officers J. C. Meadors of Lee Co.; Joseph H. Speed and George W. Graves of Perry Co.; and Henry C. Semple of Montgomery Co. Also voting in the negative were C. M. Cabot of Elmore Co.; J. L. Alexander of Autauga Co.; S. L. Latham of Bullock Co.; and James F. Hurst of Coosa Co. Of these, all but Hurst (who registered his vote the next day) signed the following statement: "They protest against [the constitution]

the small victories—particularly in the form of laws mandating debtor relief, declaring Alabama's war debt null and void, and protecting voters from intimidation at the polls—convinced them to accept a constitution full of compromises.[53] Perhaps loyalists balked at scuttling their alliance with the party so early into their cooperative effort at reconstruction. While unionists needed the good will of the party, the party clearly did not need their paltry numbers at the polls to win elections in Alabama. African American voters could give them that. To keep a place at the political table, unionists supported a constitution quite different from the one they had envisioned creating. The demands of partisan politics had yet again undermined their ideal of political legitimacy.

"The Day of Our Ruin"

Though unionist citizens were disappointed with the moderate features of the new constitution, their rebel neighbors viewed the document as anathema. They regarded the convention and everything it produced as illegitimate. Many Alabamians were thus determined to oppose the new constitution and the entire Federal effort to control the course of state politics. They had their first real opportunity to do so during the February 4, 1868, election to ratify the constitution itself, at which time a slate of candidates for new state officers and legislators were also offered up for consideration. Extensive attempts to "keep both whites and colored from voting" were reported by election judges across the state. In particular, opponents of the constitution used election rules to intimidate the electorate, particularly that statute which read, "Qualified voters shall have the privilege of challenging any party offering to vote." In theory, this was meant to assist loyal men in maintaining voting proscriptions against Confederates. In practice, however, vote challenging was simply an excuse whereby citizens gained entrance to polling areas and then bullied both freedpeople and white unionists. In Madison County, for example, former rebels managed to get inside the room where the election judges sat watching as people submitted their ballots, hoping to "intimidate persons as they offered their tickets." The effect was

---

because, in their opinion, a government framed upon its provisions, will entail upon the people of the State, greater evils than any which threaten them" (page 240).

53. Fitzgerald, "Alabama Yeomanry during Reconstruction," 579; Foner, *Reconstruction*, 326–7; *Official Journal of the Constitutional Convention . . . 1867*, 195–201, 243–4, 263.

electric—men who arrived to pick up pro-Constitution tickets saw what was happening, turned tail, and went home. As Republican J. H. Bone explained, "Our white unionists, with but few exceptions, were completely intimidated . . . by the leading rebels having seats with the Judges." Upon getting "to the window to offer their tickets" they spied who was inside "and failed to cast their ballott." In the Wiregrass region, A. W. Jones, a unionist delegate to the constitutional convention from Conecuh County, likewise reported "Treachery among our County candidates" who apparently destroyed pro-ratification tickets by tearing off the preprinted section that said "for the Constitution" on it. Even worse, he reported that names of "both white and black are all taken down by the rebel club." Jones fervently believed that without the continued presence of the small garrison of Federal troops stationed in the county, unionists and freedmen were "as Sheep in the night time before those who are sworn to slaughter us."[54]

Other adversaries of the constitution made no pretense of following election rules but simply patrolled local polling places, threatening and abusing Republican voters. "Union Citizens" of Wiregrass Henry County, for instance, "attempted to open the Polls" only to be made victims of "a number of outrageous acts" by three local men. In Coosa County, those who came to the polls "did so in the face of threats of violence from the Black Cavalry," a group described by one voting registrar as "a free booting organization of ex rebel soldiers and thieves who have ridden over the County from time to time since the war ended, robbing and maltreating Union men and freedmen." Whites were threatened with being expelled from the county, and blacks were told they would be thrown out of employment if they voted in the election. Those who withstood the intimidation and voted anyway were, in the opinion of one observer, "men of more than common nerve."[55]

The effective campaign of intimidation at the polls was coordinated

54. J. H. Bone to B. W. Norris, February 13, 1868; and "Circular to Judges of Election," January 31, 1868, enc., W. T. Hatchett to Gen. Supt. of Registration Col. James F. Meline, February 14, 1868; A. W. Jones to B. W. Norris, February 10, 1868; all in Box 3, General Records 1867–1868, Records of the Third Military District, NAB.

55. Supt. of Registration W. T. Hatchett, Report of the Officers for the Inspection of Election, May 9, 1868, submitted to Bvt. Brig. Gen. O. L. Shepherd, Commanding the Sub-District of Alabama; and Affidavit of A. W. McBrayer before John C. Keffer, U.S. Commissioner, February 14, 1868; both in Box 3, General Records 1867–1868, Records of the Third Military District, NAB.

with a concerted boycott of the election by antiratification citizens. As with the referendum to hold a convention, for ratification of the constitution to be valid, the document had to garner the approval of a majority of votes in an election in which at least 50 percent of the registered voters had participated.[56] Widespread registration among whites who boycotted the polls, in combination with aggressive poll intimidation, achieved the desired results. The turnout failed to meet the necessary threshold, for the election only recorded 71,817 votes, far short of a majority of the 170,000 registered electors. These effects were particularly apparent among white voters; though almost 83 percent of registered blacks cast ballots (62,194), just under 9 percent of registered whites (6,702) came to the polls. Thus, although the constitution received over seventy favorable votes to every one negative vote, the new constitution met with defeat.[57]

The news of the constitution's defeat was received with alarm and outrage by state Republicans. Many, like B. W. Norris, viewed the opposition's victory as "false in fact, wicked in morals, and most pernicious."[58] Indeed, the military governor of Alabama, General George G. Meade (General Pope's successor) determined that the election had been manipulated by constitution opponents' tactics of intimidation and boycott, and recommended that Congress call a new convention for the state. National leaders balked at this suggestion, fearful that another attempt would only produce the same result and that anti-Reconstruction voters in subsequent Southern elections would be encouraged to attempt boycotts of their own. They instead opted to rewrite the Reconstruction law altogether. In the Fourth Military Reconstruction Act, passed over President Johnson's veto on March 11, 1868, Republicans changed the guidelines for ratification of state constitutions. Now, Congress simply required that the majority of those voting approve the document. They then "grandfathered" Alabama's 1867 constitution into law under the new rules, allowing the state to rejoin the Union.[59]

56. Fitzgerald, *Union League Movement*, 83; Foner, *Reconstruction*, 333; Abbott, *Republican Party and the South*, 152.

57. Rogers et al., *Alabama*, 246–7; McMillan, *Constitutional Development*, 168.

58. B. W. Norris et al., to Maj. Gen. George G. Meade, Commanding, Third Military District, March 17, 1868, RG 393, Box 3, General Records 1867–1868, Records of the Third Military District, NAB.

59. Abbott, *Republican Party and the South*, 152–3, 155, 162; Foner, *Reconstruction*, 332–3; McMillan, *Constitutional Development*, 168–9; Rogers et al., *Alabama*, 247.

Probably nothing could have more deeply outraged former Confederates convinced of the illegitimacy of Congressional Reconstruction. Indeed, the overturn of the election, along with a visit to the state by Nathan Bedford Forrest, likely spurred a "rapid expansion" of Alabama's Ku Klux Klan in March 1868. Formed as a secret fraternal order in Tennessee in 1866, the Klan did not become an active vigilante organization until the advent of Congressional Reconstruction in 1867, and even then, most of the group's activities remained confined to Tennessee. The advent of black voting and the new state conventions in the South, however, prompted the Klan's growth into neighboring states, including Alabama, where it merged with similar groups like the Knights of the White Carnation and the Knights of the White Camellia, which had already been intimidating freedpeople in the Black Belt.[60] Anti-Reconstruction forces throughout the state quickly coalesced around the use of extralegal violence as a way to challenge and defeat all adherents, white or black, of the Republican Party and its policies. In the end, though congressional restructuring of state electoral laws may have given loyalists nominal political standing, it could do little to reshape the inequitable power relationships between unionists and their enemies.

Although most vigilantism during Congressional Reconstruction was certainly associated with the Klan, it would be a mistake to understand these groups as part of a tightly organized, centralized movement. Instead, many small groups of citizens banded together as vigilantes in sympathy with the Klan's mission to restore racial and political "order" in their neighborhoods. Victims of violence usually referred to their persecutors as "Ku Klux" less because they knew them to be part of any organization in particular than because news of "the Klan" was ubiquitous in their newspapers and communities. As unionist C. S. Cherry explained in testifying before the congressional committee investigating the Klan in 1871, the name was generic rather than specific. "The term Ku-Klux . . . is sort of understood to cover all political outrages, all these political disorders," he explained. "People are sort of called Ku-Klux whether men are in disguise or not." William Shapard concurred, noting that few loyal people were "particular about the name."[61]

60. Allen Trelease, *White Terror: The Ku Klux Klan Conspiracy and Southern Reconstruction* (Baton Rouge: Louisiana State University Press, 1971), 81–2. Though Trelease notes the date of this expansion, he links it more directly to the conflict over the constitution in February, rather than outrage over the Fourth Reconstruction Act.

61. *Testimony Taken by the Joint Select Committee to Inquire into the Condition of Affairs in the Late Insurrectionary States*, vols. 8 and 9, *Alabama* (Washington, D.C.: Government Printing Office, 1872), 8:77, 9:750.

For unionists, the name was less important than the identity of the men persecuting them. Hooded or not, Klansmen or not, their enemies were the same men whom they had been fighting for the last seven years: rebels. Take, for instance, the situation of a community of unionists in Cherokee County who had faced considerable persecution during the war. When, after the war, the Ku Klux Klan began to terrorize their neighborhood, few were surprised to find among the Klansmen the Confederates who had led efforts to intimidate and conscript unionists during the war. One of these men, R. W. Wilkes, "a violent and persecuting rebel," had organized a mob to "kill or run out of the country" the prominent unionists in his neighborhood. After the war, Wilkes became a leading advocate of "Kukluxism." One of Cherokee County's most renowned conscript officers, "a villain named Bratch Porter," likewise continued his abuse of loyalists during Reconstruction, causing neighborhood unionists to rechristen him "KuKlux Porter." Both Porter and Cherokee's loyalists understood their postwar conflict as an extension of wartime animosities. For John Smith, Bratch Porter was the embodiment of Confederate continuity—Smith referred to Porter as "a rebel and a Kuklux." This continuity of identity was perceived by Porter, too, for when he attacked Smith, swearing to have his "hearts blood," Porter also cursed the unionist as "a D——d Blue Coat."[62] The parallels between wartime and postwar violence were eagerly exploited by the most pro-Klan newspaper editor in the state, Ryland Randolph of the *Tuscaloosa Independent Monitor*. In a vitriolic assault on "the genus scallawag," Randolph alluded to unionists' wartime history of lying out and their postwar trouble with the Klan: "[He] sleeps in the woods . . . at the bare idea of a Ku-Klux raid."[63]

From the summer of 1868 through 1870, increasing numbers of disguised bands like these took to demonstrating in the public areas of Southern towns and nightriding through rural neighborhoods, intimidating, abusing, and murdering freedpeople and unionists. The goals of this violence were simple: to scare whites and blacks away from the Union League, pro-Republican political gatherings, and during elections, the polls themselves. C. P. Simmons, the unionist delegate to the 1867 constitutional convention, wrote Governor W. H. Smith in September 1868,

62. Claim 6701, Ebenezer Leath, Cherokee Co., July 2, 1875: Testimony of Joseph Baker; Claim 6701, Ebenezer Leath, Cherokee Co., July 2, 1875; Claim 6837, John Smith, Cherokee Co., May 13, 1874; all in SCC.

63. Quote in Woolfolk, "Political Cartoons," 143–4; also see Wiggins, *Scalawag in Alabama Politics*, x.

explaining that "bands of disguised men" had been spotted "in different Parts of the county," intimidating black and white Republicans into silence. "[W]e hav more trouble hear than we have ever sean." Likewise, Winston County native and long-time unionist C. C. Sheets was threatened by the Klan after he gave a "lively" pro-Republican—and anti-Klan—speech in Florence, Lauderdale County, in October 1868, just before the presidential election. That night the "Ku Klux order" arrived at his hotel, "took him out of his bed and said many harsh & improper things" to him. Sheets's experience was unusual only in that he was not hurt, for the Klan had by that time begun "riding every night" around Florence, intimidating and shooting freedpeople and "Union men."[64]

Similar incidents marked the lives of unionists across North Alabama. Henry C. Sanford—two-time unionist delegate to the 1861 secession convention and the 1865 constitutional convention—was the acknowledged Republican leader of his county. In 1868, Sanford won election "as a Radical" to Alabama's state senate and had "firmly supported the Reconstruction measures of Congress."[65] From that point forward, he was frequently insulted and threatened by his neighbors, some of whom rode by his house to shout threateningly against "tories and Radicals."[66] By 1870, matters had deteriorated so severely that Sanford was in a state of constant anxiety. In May, he reported to the governor that the "Ku Klux are raiding and going on foot in our county" whipping black men and abusing whites. One white man who lived very close to Sanford was "hanged until nearly dead." By July, he was convinced that the Republican Party was doomed in his county. "The day of our ruin is fast hastening on," he assured the governor's secretary.[67]

Vigilante attacks sometimes seemed like full-blown military maneuvers. In 1870, St. Clair County Union veteran and constitutional convention delegate Henry J. Springfield was besieged by some two hundred men "armed with Rifles, Shot guns, and revolvers" as well as members of the "county sheriff's posse." Denouncing Springfield "as a dangerous

64. Trelease, *White Terror*, 87. Quotes in C. P. Simmons to Gov. W. H. Smith, September 3, 1868; and Neander Rice to Dr. Figures, October 31, 1868, forwarded to Gov. Smith; both in AGP: W. H. Smith, 1867–70.

65. Neander Rice to Dr. Figures, October 31, 1868, forwarded to Gov. Smith, AGP: W. H. Smith, 1867–70.

66. Claim 6285, Henry C. Sanford, Cherokee Co., May 16, 1874, SCC.

67. Henry C. Sanford to Gov. W. H. Smith, May 9, 1870; H. C. Sanford to Col. D. L. Dalton, Secty. to Gov. William H. Smith, July 7, 1870; both in AGP: W. H. Smith, 1867–70.

man and a 'Scalawag'" and for his "service in the Union Army," the attackers opened fire on his house at eight in the morning, and continued firing until the morning of the next day. Springfield finally surrendered, but not before narrowly cheating death. An army officer later called in to investigate the incident examined the house and "found on the side windows of his bedroom Twelve distinct bullet holes—in the front window of same room Ten—in the side wall of same room Thirty Five, in the front Fifty, all of which passed clear through the room and partitions and cut many of his wife's dresses which were hanging on the partition." The rest of the house and its outhouses, too, were "riddled with bullet holes" to such an extent that the officer could not count them.[68]

Vigilantes aggressively attacked all advocates of the new political order, including those whose resistance took place outside the regular boundaries of politics. Among the most hard-hit of such "non-political" entities were congregations associated with the Methodist Episcopal Church. Alabamians variously referred to this denomination as the "loyal Methodist Church," the "Northern Methodist Church," or "the Republican Methodist Church," to distinguish it from the Methodist Episcopal Church, South, which in 1844 had split from the national church over the question of slavery. These nicknames also served to dissociate the church from secession and the Confederacy, and continued to be used long after Reconstruction's end. As historian William W. Sweet noted in 1915, "Every 'Northern' Methodist was a Republican, and even today in some sections of Alabama, the members of the Methodist Episcopal Church are know[n] as 'Republican' Methodists as distinguished from the Southern Methodists or 'Democrat' Methodists."[69]

An early critic of President Johnson's Reconstruction policies, the Methodist Episcopal Church had not hesitated to take up the cause of both freedpeople and Southern loyalists.[70] A church newspaper, the

---

68. M. Frank Gallagher to Lt. James Miller, July 12, 1870, AGP: W. H. Smith, 1867–70.

69. William W. Sweet, "Methodist Church Influence in Southern Politics," *Mississippi Valley Historical Review* 1, no. 4 (1915): 548. Mr. William Erwin, archivist at Duke University Special Collections, first alerted me to the byname "Republican Methodist Church," by which the Jefferson County church he attended as a child in the 1950s was commonly known.

70. Sweet, "Methodist Church Influence in Southern Politics," 548, 551–7; Fitzgerald, "Alabama Yeomanry during Reconstruction," 571; Trelease, *White Terror*, 254; Daniel W. Stowell, *Rebuilding Zion: The Religious Reconstruction of the South, 1863–1877* (New York: Oxford University Press, 1998), 134–5.

Western Christian Advocate, frequently highlighted unionists' tribulations in its editorials. One such piece, published in November 1865, drew a direct connection between Southerners' faith in the Union and their faith in God:

For the sake of the Union of these States men have renounced father, mother, wife, children, home, friends, and every thing which could seduce men into disloyalty, and, unhallowed and unknown to fame, have died in the mountain fastnesses, whither they had been hunted by dogs and men more brutal and ferocious than dogs, thanking God that they were honest men, and not rebels and traitors. Could the religion of Jesus be divine if it required any thing less than martyrdom for truth and holiness? A religion for which men would not die, could not meet the necessities of the human soul.[71]

The *Christian Advocate and Journal*, another prominent Methodist periodical, promised in February 1865 that Northern missionaries would minister to the "genuine Union men of the South whose abhorrence of the rebellion will lead them to reject the religious services of a set of men by whom they have been so fearfully misled." Indeed, according to Sweet, "[L]oyalty to the government of the United States had become practically a part of the Methodist creed, and disloyalty was discredited as much as the worst types of heresy."[72]

For its outspoken endorsement of Southern loyalty, the Methodist Episcopal Church appealed as a haven for unionists. During the war, loyalist worshippers had frequently met separately from the secessionist-dominated congregations of the M. E. Church, South. Its firm associations with the Confederacy prevented many unionists from returning to the fold after 1865. Instead, they yearned for the opportunity to build congregations associated with the regular M. E. Church. In October 1867, a mission conference of the regular M. E. Church was established in North Alabama by Bishop David W. Clark.[73] North Alabama men at-

71. *Western Christian Advocate* (Cincinnati), November 8, 1865.

72. "Church Reconstruction in Rebeldom," *Christian Advocate and Journal*, February 9, 1865, quote in Stowell, *Rebuilding Zion*, 57; Sweet, "Methodist Church Influence in Southern Politics," 522.

73. Marion Elias Lazenby, *History of Methodism in Alabama and West Florida: Being an Account of the Amazing March of Methodism through Alabama and West Florida* (N.p.: North Alabama Conference and Alabama–West Florida Conference of the Methodist Church, 1960), 362–9.

tending the organizational conference at Talladega were "from the rural districts, and have, as a general rule, suffered much, as Union men, during the war, and now, since their connection with the Old Church, have suffered almost as much from the persecutions of the ministry and membership of Churches which were rebels through the war, and remain so still." The total number of North Alabamians initiated into the new conference was 8,218. Of these, one-third were African American members who soon separated, both by their own choice and in response to white pressure for segregation, into separate congregations within the denomination.[74]

Unionist membership in the Methodist Episcopal Church represented a public statement about continuing fidelity to the Union, to Reconstruction, and to a South dominated by loyal men, not former rebels.[75] Opponents of these ideas understood perfectly well what the church and its congregants stood for. As a consequence, the church buildings, ministers, and congregants alike all became the targets of vigilante groups. In 1871, unionist Isaac Berry noted in his testimony before the Congressional Joint Committee investigating the Klan that "two or three" such churches were burned in Blount County, but by whom was never proven. Nonetheless, "[i]t was generally supposed it was these Klans that did it . . . because [the churches] were composed of loyal characters to the Government."[76] Reverend Levin Clifton of Cherokee County, who was "bitterly opposed to Ku Kluxism and [a] firm Republican," had been "much persecuted" on account of his being one of the founding members of the missionary conference and a traveling minister in its circuit.[77] Likewise, Ebenezer Leath of Cherokee County attributed his hard treatment at the hands of the Klan in part to his religious affiliations. "After the war was over . . . [I] took the liberty to join the Methodist Episcopal Church and voted for the Republican ticket and the

---

74. *Western Christian Advocate* (Cincinnati), October 30, 1867; John Lakin Brasher, "History of the Alabama Conference Methodist Episcopal Church," [typescript], John Lakin Brasher Papers, DU.

75. Sweet, "Methodist Church Influence in Southern Politics," 549; Baggett, *Scalawags*, 165–66.

76. *Testimony Taken by the Joint Select Committee*, 9:776.

77. Claim 6785, Levin A. Clifton, Cherokee Co., November 18, 1874: Testimony of John Helms, SCC; "Minutes of the Alabama Mission Conference Held in Talladega, Alabama, October 17–20, 1867," in *Annual Conferences of the Methodist Episcopal Church for the Year 1866* (New York: Carlton & Lanahan, 1868), 271.

Kuklux come after me to my house and threatened to break down my door if I did not open it."[78] Although Leath escaped unharmed, the Reverend M. B. Sullivan was not so lucky. On May 11, 1869, Sullivan was awakened to see "a band of armed men" surrounding his bed, with their "pistols . . . cocked and presented at my breast." The vigilantes forced Sullivan out of bed, ransacked his possessions, stole his pistols, and carried him outside, about two hundred yards away from the house. Telling Sullivan that he had preached his "last sermon," and swearing that no other Methodist institution should "exist South of Mason and Dixon's line but the Church South," the men began to beat Sullivan "horribly." Throughout the attack, they threatened him with even worse treatment unless he abandoned the Northern church. "If I did not join the Church South, work for my family through the week, and preach for the Church South on Sabbaths, they would kill me."[79]

Under such an onslaught against virtually all of their social and political institutions, even the most staunchly unionist Republicans became gravely concerned for their lives and shocked that such violence could occur under Republican rule. Many felt as loyalist C. P. Simmons did: abandoned and desperate. "In the name of God," he pleaded to Governor William H. Smith, "what ar[e] we to do, when will we ever get Protection in this State?" William Powell of Calhoun County demanded to have "something dun or the Union Men will have to leave their homes and farms, for their is men that has to ly out every night to keep the KK from whipping them." Without help, Union Leaguer S. S. Plowman explained, loyal men would "be crushed under foot again by the hated rebs." Dr. T. C. Brannon of Lawrence County concurred. Characterizing Klan violence as "another Bloody war," Brannon pleaded with the governor of Alabama for protection. "If this thing is suffered to go on," he predicted, "it will not be long till everybody who will say a word for Law & order & union will be intimidated one by one & the secesh will rule the country with a rod of Iron." Brannon felt confident that the Klan would kill him and demanded help "quick," adding tersely, "I shall not need it when my wife has become a widow & my children orphans." H. C. Sanford of

---

78. Claim 6701, Ebenezer Leath, Cherokee Co., July 2, 1875, SCC. As was the case during the war, Leath continued to have a reputation as a fighter. The reason he wasn't harmed, at least according to him, was that he "would kill the first man that touched the door." Apparently, his opponents took him seriously.

79. *The Nationalist* (Mobile), June 11, 1869. Also see mention of Sullivan's beating in A. S. Lakin to Gov. W. H. Smith, July 27, 1869, AGP: W. H. Smith, 1867–70.

Cherokee County spoke for these and other unionists when he wondered, "Why is it that all are blind and deaf who are at a distance from the places of disturbances?"[80]

Unionists looking for protection from Klan violence found that there was little military power to deploy on their behalf. Alabama's readmission to the Union after the ratification of the new constitution had lifted martial law, as it did elsewhere in the South. Fewer than twenty thousand troops remained in the entire South in the fall of 1868; of those, only just over six hundred were stationed in Alabama. With the exception of these troops, most of whom were assigned to two or three remaining Federal garrisons or to the Freedmen's Bureau, any national military forces had to be requisitioned from the government by civil state officers, a lengthy and complicated process. In the absence of Federal military forces, Alabama's governor could have mobilized the state militia.[81] And indeed, unionists pleaded with Governor Smith to allow them to organize branches of the state militia for their own defense. DeKalb Countians recommended that Captain T. J. Nicholson, a Federal veteran, be put in charge of a military force to suppress Klan activity in their county.[82] Likewise, J. Pinkney Whitehead and Union veteran J. F. Morton, a delegate to the 1867 constitutional convention, also nominated a number of Union men, including a First Alabama veteran, for officerships in the state militia. Morton and his fellow petitioners believed that, without a reliable militia, "Fayette County is ruined." Indicative of the dangers these men felt, Morton hastened to add this postscript: "Do not make our names Known as it would cost us our lives."[83]

Despite pleas like these, Governor Smith failed to call Alabamians to arms. He likely faced the difficulties plaguing many Southern governors.

80. C. P. Simmons to Gov. W. H. Smith, September 3, 1868; William Powell to Gov. W. H. Smith, [October 1870]; S. S. Plowman to Gov. W. H. Smith, July 12, 1868; T. C. Brannon to Gov. W. H. Smith, August 29, 1870; Henry C. Sanford to Gov. W. H. Smith, May 9, 1870; all in AGP: W. H. Smith, 1867–70. See also Claim 6285, Henry C. Sanford, Cherokee Co., May 16, 1874, SCC. In 1872, when Sanford ran again as the Republican Party's incumbent state senator for the sixth district, he was "defeated by the Democracy."

81. Trelease, White Terror, xxxiv; James E. Sefton, The United States Army and Reconstruction, 1865–1877 (Baton Rouge: Louisiana State University Press, 1967), app. B: Numbers and Locations of Troops, 260–2.

82. W. J. Haralson and G. W. Moore to Gov. W. H. Smith, August 16, 1869, AGP: W. H. Smith, 1867–70; Claim 14463-A, James Copeland, DeKalb Co., March 22, 1875, SCC.

83. J. F. Morton, J. Pinkney Whitehead, and Many Citizens to Gov. W. H. Smith, June 10, 1870, AGP: W. H. Smith, 1867–70.

In an attempt to prevent uprisings against the establishment of military rule, the Military Reconstruction Acts had prohibited the formation of militias in the former Confederacy. As a result, the entire militia system was in disarray across the South. Even if militias could be organized, impoverished Southern legislatures were unable to pay for necessary materiel. Though in July 1868, sympathetic Congressmen had proposed a bill to federally subsidize arming Southern militias in reconstructed states, the legislation was ignored by the Republican majority, which allowed Congress to recess before taking up the proposed legislation.[84]

With little, if any, assistance from the Federal military or state militias, white unionists had to turn to local authorities for help. Many such officials, however, were unwilling to act. One loyalist complained that Blount County's sheriff and justice of the peace were too intimidated to help him. "I have asked them frequently why they don't enforce the law, and they have told me they were afraid; even afraid to issue warrants."[85] Whatever the prerogatives of holding judicial or political positions, these officeholders could count on little protection against vigilante groups and the community that supported them. In DeKalb County, officers who had successfully arrested Klansmen complained that they could not keep the lawbreakers in jail for very long before fellow riders broke into the jail and liberated their comrades. Cursing the Klan for its seeming immunity to authority, they exclaimed, "It rides with high handed impunity over all who do not bow to its miserable behests."[86]

For many unionists, there seemed to be only one real solution: taking matters into their own hands, just as they had during the war. As William Powell of Calhoun County explained to the governor, "If I can find out whar the K K will pass, I will get my Radical croud and I will find . . . if Powder and led will do any exicution . . . I am willing to do any thing to Stop the K. K." W. T. Beard of Marshall County likewise killed "one of the ring-leaders of a K. K. Klan" who had contrived one of the most "hellish murderous plots" against him. Although Beard had reported the plan to local officials, they had refused to issue warrants for the arrest of the men implicated. Frustrated to the point of recklessness, Beard acted where the law would not and killed the Klansman himself:

84. Trelease, White Terror, xxxiv; Abbott, Republican Party and the South, 189.
85. Testimony Taken by the Joint Select Committee, 9:775.
86. W. J. Haralson and G. W. Moore to Gov. W. H. Smith, August 16, 1869, AGP: W. H. Smith, 1867–70.

"I had been abused as long as it was human to bear."[87] Similarly, Union veteran Henry Smith of DeKalb County resorted to using violence of his own. After having been continually harassed by the Klan for his unionism and steadfast association with the Republican Party, Smith killed at least two Klansmen in the spring of 1869.[88]

In Blount and Morgan Counties, Union men determined to put down the Klan were able to garner enough support among neighbors, unionists and former rebels alike, to actually end the reign of terror in their counties. As veteran Isaac Berry explained to the congressional committee investigating the Klan in 1870, "Loyal men—men for the Government— what we term Union men" formed in these counties "an organization of what we call the anti-Ku-Klux." The objective of the organization was "to protect all good, loyal peaceable citizens" from the Klan. Berry himself became the acknowledged leader of this group, largely because he had "a good deal of influence . . . with the Union boys who belonged to the Federal Army, and all who held that way."[89] In all, the group attracted nearly one hundred followers.

Berry's activism did not go unnoticed. The "threat was hung out" against him, and neighbors who supported the Klan began visiting Berry's house with ominous warnings. "They would brag about it, and all these things," he explained, "that I had the day long enough; that I had been in the Federal service and come out conqueror . . . and that I had been organizing the Union League . . . and I would have to get farther," that is, leave the area. In the wake of these threats of exile, and in response to the whipping of one of Berry's neighbors, he and about forty anti–Ku Kluxers rode out to confront the Klansmen and their families. "One night we met at the brink of the mountain . . . and went to these Ku-Klux fellows, young fellows, and called them out, and if they were not at home, we called their parents out, and told them that they were

---

87. William Powell to Gov. W. H. Smith [October 1870]; and W. T. Beard to Gov. W. H. Smith, July 23, 1869; both in AGP: W. H. Smith, 1867–70.

88. *The Nationalist* (Mobile), June 11, 1869; for Henry Smith's wartime record, see Claim 4194, John Barnes, DeKalb Co., May 26, 1875: Testimony of Henry H. Smith, SCC. Although a refugee who claimed to have served the Union Army, Smith was denied his claim before the Southern Claims Commission. See Claim 6237, Henry H. Smith, DeKalb Co., Office No. 80, Report 6, 1876, NAMS-M1407, SCC Disallowed Claims.

89. *Testimony Taken by the Joint Select Committee*, 9:778. Trelease describes a similar organization also developed in Fayette County. Composed largely of wartime unionists, the group called themselves the "Mossy Backs," a common term used for those who spent the war lying out "'til the moss grew on their backs'"; Trelease, *White Terror*, 267–9.

Ku-Klux and their sons were Ku-Klux." Berry explained that he wanted the men "to quit it"—if they persisted and "rode upon loyal people, or anybody who was good citizens," Berry and his friends promised to return. "We didn't intend to suffer it." By the end of their trek, the anti–Ku Kluxers had traveled twenty-five miles, going from farm to farm spreading the word. According to Berry, the stratagem worked. His neighborhood saw no more disguised terrorists.[90]

It was not until May 1870 that Republicans in Congress, worried about their prospects in upcoming midterm elections, acted to rein in the violence of the Klan. They did so in response to public outrage, but not that emanating from Southern unionists; instead, it took growing protest from Northerners, appalled by Klan violence, to galvanize Congress to intervene. In the first of two Enforcement Acts, Republicans made conspiracy to prevent blacks or whites from exercising their right to vote a federal crime. Though the law required that such activities be tried in federal courts, and mandated that U.S. troops monitor the polls at areas particularly troubled by Klan violence, it did not authorize the increase in military presence necessary to prevent intimidation before the forthcoming election. Consequently, violence and intimidation across Alabama went virtually unabated, and the Republicans lost heavily, returning the governorship and much of the state legislature to the Democrats. Similar outcomes elsewhere in the Deep South states finally roused congressional Republicans into aggressive efforts to clamp down on the violence, passing the second Enforcement Act on February 28, 1871, as well as a new Ku Klux Act on April 20, 1871. The latter, in particular, addressed the long-standing problems of effective law enforcement by giving the president the power to suspend the writ of habeas corpus and to declare martial law in areas of intense violence. Both laws markedly increased the numbers of Klansmen arrested and tried in federal court.[91]

These efforts, while certainly appreciated by beleaguered unionists, came far too late to save the Republican cause in Alabama. As early as 1868, the majority of the Union League's white members had fled the organization because of Klan intimidation; by 1869, the League had officially disbanded in Alabama. The inability or unwillingness of the Republican Party and the U.S. government to defend unionists caused many to

90. *Testimony Taken by the Joint Select Committee*, 9:778–9.
91. Abbott, *Republican Party and the South*, 210–3; Rogers et al., *Alabama*, 251.

228

deeply question the integrity of the political order they had so long advocated. As one witness before the Klan Trials of 1872 noted, some former Federal soldiers even abandoned the Republican Party in favor of the opposition, becoming "the most ultra and bitter democrats" because they felt the "sting of disappointment and ingratitude" on the part of the government and did not believe that they had been treated any better than "the balance of the community."[92]

Racism played a role in the party's demise as well. As unconditional unionist Archibald Steele of Madison County explained to the Congress, the sympathies of some loyalists were turned not simply because they felt abandoned by the party, but because they supported the Klan's terrorization of blacks. In his early sixties when the war commenced, Steele had been a successful planter; he owned twenty-three slaves and over five hundred acres of farmland, of which he cultivated two hundred throughout the war.[93] After the war, Steele's laborers had been visited by "bands of men in disguise" on five or six different occasions. At first, these visits seemed designed solely to intimidate, for the men just rode around in costume and "declared themselves to be friends to the white men and black men both and did not interfere with anything or anybody." By August 1871, however, the pattern had shifted; the freedmen on Steele's plantation began to suffer physical abuse. Steele admitted having been taken aback by these incidents, because, as he put it, he had never had "a cross word" with any of his laborers and did not want them harmed. His surprise also arose, however, from learning that the disguised men were *unionists* from his neighborhood. "It is strange the way this all has occurred," he explained. "We are all Union. These bad fellows up there and me, we got through the war like brothers; we are Union men."[94]

Other white unionists backed away when they realized that repudiation of the Republican Party—and by extension, the party's active assertion of black political rights—was often enough to protect white unionists from harm at the hands of the Klan. For instance, although Isaac Berry testified to the SCC that "a great many outrages" were perpetrated against "loyal characters" in northern Alabama after the war,

92. Fitzgerald, *Union League Movement*, 83–6; Abbott, *Republican Party and the South*, 205; *Testimony Taken by the Joint Select Committee*, 9:884.

93. Claim 2652, Archibald J. Steele, Madison Co., August 1, 1872, SCC.

94. *Testimony Taken by the Joint Select Committee*, 9:944–7, 952–3.

when asked by Congress whether veterans or other white unionists were vulnerable as a consequence of their wartime allegiance, Berry equivocated. While asserting that abuse of unionists or Union veterans was part of the Klan's motivation—a fact the organization wanted to keep "hid as much as possible"—Berry also noted that Klansmen only attacked those unionists who maintained active association with the Republican regime in Alabama. "Well, it is this way sorter," he explained. "I see that they don't like a man who served in the Federal Army unless he joins them and is one of their sort; then they like him pretty well." Unless a unionist, and especially a Union veteran, became "one of their sort," the "disguised Klan" looked upon such men "as low-down characters" and called them "Tories."[95] Upon repudiating his support of the Republican Party, however, a man's chances of being attacked diminished significantly.

Subjected to unrelenting violence, Republican "rule" in Alabama quickly degenerated into a disastrous mess. Although the party managed to regain the governorship in 1872, it did so only with the help of a belated infusion of Federal troops sent to guard polling places from intimidation or attack. Gubernatorial success, moreover, was overshadowed by legislative chaos, for two legislatures—one Democratic, one Republican—claimed victory in the election. From November 1872 to March 1873, the state wobbled between these two bodies until the state's attorney general established a compromise under which the Republicans gained the majority in a bipartisan legislature. Though Alabama unionists and freedmen voted heavily for Grant in the presidential election of 1872, the Republican Party was unable to parlay their remaining support into sustained domination of state politics. Capitalizing on a combination of national Republican apathy and state-level factionalism, native white distrust of radical economic policies, black suspicion of white party leaders, and continuing vigilante intimidation of voters, Alabama's "Democracy" overthrew Republican control in 1874, making it the second state (after Georgia) to be "redeemed" from Radical rule. The only Alabama county to maintain a Republican majority in the 1874 election was strongly unionist Winston County. Since 1861, Winston had been the one county in Alabama where loyalists had always been able to muster majorities at the beat level. Heavily white to begin with, Winston's un-

95. Claim 12986, John N. Nesmith, Blount Co., October 31, 1873: Testimony of Isaac Berry, SCC; *Testimony Taken by the Joint Select Committee*, 9:769, 772, 689.

ionists were numerous enough after the war not to need an alliance with freedmen, or Northern whites, to maintain electoral strength in their county.[96]

The inability of Alabama's wartime unionists to put forward similar majorities elsewhere does not necessarily indicate that all white unionists in Alabama abandoned their dissident ways, or even the Republican Party. As historian Eric Foner has shown, loyalists throughout the South continued to run as Republican candidates well into the twentieth century and were the only white Southerners to do so. In Alabama's Morgan County, unionist C. C. Sheets stood for governor as a Republican in 1876; a decade later, Arthur Bingham, prominent Union Leaguer and radical, did the same; and W. T. Ewing, also a wartime unionist and 1867 convention delegate, followed suit in 1888. The adherence of some white unionists to the Republican Party does not change our picture of Alabama politics after 1870. In none of these above cases did a Republican come close to winning the governorship; moreover, in 1886 and 1888, the Republicans won no legislative seats at all.[97] However, these pockets of lasting party loyalty do indicate the continued power of wartime identity for unionists and their descendants. In the futility of supporting the Republican Party, individuals honored a loyalist tradition of stubborn nonconformity and remained people of consequence where they had always had their greatest influence: within their small circles of kin and friends.

---

96. Rogers et al., *Alabama*, 250–3; Foner, *Reconstruction*, 442, 553. For those who volunteered information about their continued support for the Republican Party into the 1870s, see Claim 10347, Alexander McDonald, Fayette Co., March 8, 1872; Claim 7531, Young R. Amerson, Fayette Co., March 16, 1872; Claim 11640, Green P. Stovall, Fayette Co., February 9, 1872; Claim 6514, Samuel Studdard, Fayette Co., February 23, 1872; Claim 1755, Frederick H. Anderson, Franklin Co., September 8, 1871; Claim 13285, James Cargile, Jackson Co., December 7, 1872; Claim 19480, John V. Gross, Jackson Co., September 1, 1873; Testimony of David M. Cowley; Claim 5406, Thomas T. Allington, Lauderdale Co., September 14, 1871; Claim 9819, William Simons, Lauderdale Co., April 2, 1873; Claim 12483, Murphy Bruce, Limestone Co., February 21, 1873; Claim 5846, Leonard Weir, Limestone Co., July 14, 1873; Claim 5604, James S. Armstrong, Winston Co., March 2, 1872; Claim 15136, Jesse Smith, Marshall Co., March 28, 1874; all in SCC.

97. Foner, *Reconstruction*, 442, 553; Allen Johnston Going, *Bourbon Democracy in Alabama, 1874–1890* (1951; reprint, Tuscaloosa: University of Alabama Press, 1992), 50–4.

Epilogue

I think I have told all I remember now and hope I have forgotten nothing.
—William Ridge, Jackson County, 1875

It seems most fitting to conclude this study as it began—by noting the continuing hold Civil War loyalties have over individual identity in Alabama. For the modern-day heirs of unionists, war stories tether the present to a past they did not create, but somehow defines them nonetheless. In this, unionist descendants share some fundamental similarities with the men and women they honor. Loyalists at the time of Alabama's secession understood their obligations in corporate and historical terms, too. The political culture of loyalty was for them a family and community affair. It was rooted in the desire to protect the place and the people they valued most. In this they were duty-bound, for to do otherwise would violate the imperatives of both personal and familial honor. This belief was not an abnegation of unionists' Southern selves—indeed, it was an affirmation of their understanding of the South's history and their hopes for its future. In the end, unionists' experiences illustrate in a profound way how an idea as personal, and sometimes as idiosyncratic, as "loyalty" can bind people so tightly to the abstract and impersonal notion of "nation." And that tie, ultimately, is what compels people to fight wars.

This connection is still honored today, in large and small ways, by the descendants of Alabama's unionists. In Winston County, citizens hold annual recreations of the 1861 meeting at Looney's Tavern, where loyalists gathered from surrounding hill counties to resist secession by establishing the "Free State of Winston." The event takes place in an outdoor amphitheater near Double Springs. Situated in a stand of pines, the site also boasts a miniature golf course carved out of the red clay, as well as a nice array of refreshment stands. The most striking element of the place, however, is its enormous American flag, which presents a striking sight from the rural Alabama highway. Every summer, with "Old Glory" flying

For epigraph, see Claim 20467, William Ridge Estate, Jackson Co., November 10, 1875: Testimony of George W. Ridge, SCC.

above them, the progeny of Alabama unionists ritually recognize and honor their ancestors. Similar commemorative efforts have been launched by the descendants of First Alabama Cavalry soldiers. These men and women maintain a website dedicated to historical accounts of the cavalry, rosters and genealogy of the soldiers, essays and stories, and news of regimental re-enactment events. In a state recognized for its Confederate, and neo-Confederate, history, these Alabamians have carved out different arenas for remembering their Civil War.[1]

Over the years of this study, I have been exceedingly fortunate to communicate with many of the people engaged in this work of commemoration. They have shared with me bits and pieces of family history and local lore, photographs and documents, all of which confirmed for me that generations of unionists had dutifully told and retold the stories of their war. Jim Gilbert, whose ancestors hailed from Winston County, explained that when he was "a very young child," his mother would pick up his "Grandmother Roxanna Barton Gilbert" and drive her to a local cemetery so that she could decorate the graves of her parents. "She would talk about them," Jim remembered, "and her Father's love for the 'Union.'" Her father, Jonathan Barton, known to his descendants as Grandfather Jonathan, died in 1910; he was a veteran of the First Alabama Cavalry. His gravestone at Sardis No. 1 Cemetery near the town of Lynn, Alabama, bears a United States military insignia, along with his unit and company name.[2]

Most compelling are tales about relations between Confederate and unionist neighbors both during and after the war. Larry Whitehead of Pinson, Alabama, tells the story of his great-great-grandfather and First Alabama cavalryman Drury (Drew) Cox Whitehead, who after the war returned home to live next door to a man named Tucker, whose sons had all joined the Confederate army. The two "hated each other" until Whitehead died in 1914; nonetheless, three Whitehead sons married three Tucker daughters. Larry Whitehead believes that the children overcame the bad blood of the fathers through the conciliatory influence of the local Church of Christ, which relied heavily on "family ties to cement

1. Many descendants of unionists with whom I have spoken immediately pointed me to the Looney's Tavern meeting, its recreation, and the books written about it. Some simply retold the story to me themselves. As of August 2003, the First Alabama website is: http://swannco.net/1stAlaCav. The moderator of the site is Glenda Todd.

2. Personal email correspondence of Jim Gilbert with the author, June 24, 1997. Gilbert also noted that Winston County families "were [a] very close [k]nit group."

the church" and, unlike the regular Methodist Episcopal Church, welcomed former unionists and former Confederates alike.[3]

Other stories testify to the bitterness that outlived the war. In correspondence begun about unionists in Jackson County, Thomas E. Jacks of Arizona shared with me a story long-told on the Confederate side of his family. In a graveyard in a lovely valley near New Market, Alabama, a unionist named Shedrick Golden is buried under a remarkable obelisk, on which the following is inscribed:

> In Memory of
> Shedrick
> Golden
> was Born
> July 4th 1808
> In the Year
> of our Lord
>
> ———
>
> on the 13th of
> Januay 1865
> he was taken
> off and murdred
> for mantaining
> the Union and
> Constation of
> the United States

This particular strain of family lore has it that Golden was murdered by Confederate citizens who believed he had been spying on them on behalf of the occupying Union forces. Thomas Jacks's grandmother heard the story of Golden's demise from her own grandmother, a Confederate woman named Sallie Bailes Bragg, who lived next door to Shedrick Golden's father. Sallie Bragg explained to her children and grandchildren that when Shedrick was murdered—*exactly by whom* always seems to be missing from the story—the occupying Union forces got wind of the killing

---

3. Telephone interview with Larry Whitehead, June 29, 1997, in possession of the author. Most living descendants of Civil War soldiers are separated by an additional generation from their ancestors, but Larry Whitehead's great-grandfather was one of the younger sons of a man who had twenty-four children by two wives (seven from the first, and seventeen from the second). At the time of our interview, Larry's parents, age ninety, were still living.

and "out of spite" buried the unionist in the Bragg family cemetery under a special, and no-doubt expensive, obelisk. Bragg anger over this act festered for generations. As Jacks remembered, "My grandmother and family viewed Golden with the utmost contempt. When Bragg Cemetery was cleaned, the trash was always heaped on Golden's grave. My grandmother always made a point to tell everyone that 'we do not have a drop of Golden blood in us.' "[4]

Unionism has never been the principal story of the Deep South's Civil War's narrative; considering the relative paucity of unionists in the region, it should not be. But family stories like these demonstrate that the events of the home front, perhaps as much as those on the battlefield, defined local understanding about the war and its meaning. Moreover, they show that while the Union may have abandoned the loyalists who aided the Federal cause, loyalist families never forgot their own contributions or patriotism. However incomplete, these traditions do the important task of commemorating loyalists, regardless of whether the "larger narrative" takes them into account. In recreating the incident at Looney's Tavern, in etching "U.S.A." on a headstone, or in naming a child "Grant" or "Sherman," loyalty has always been remembered. And in that tenacious memory, perhaps, lies the heart of Union people's "Southernness." Like their Confederate neighbors, unionists and their children nurtured a Lost Cause, too.

4. Personal correspondence of Thomas Jacks with the author, May 16, 1998. This story is confirmed and augmented by James A. Barnes, James R. Carnahan, and Thomas H. B. McCain, *The Eighty-Sixth Regiment Indiana Volunteer Infantry: A Narrative of Its Services in the Civil War of 1861–1865* (Crawfordsville, Ind.: Journal Company, 1895), 521–3; see also Lilla Bullington Brackeen, *All in Our Family: A Family Book of the Bullington, Halbert, Legg, Golden, Vickrey, Brackeen, Eastep, and Other Related Families* (Decatur, Ala.: Decatur Printing, 1976), 103.

Appendix 1

A NOTE ON THE SOURCES

Because the papers of the Southern Claims Commission represent a sizable proportion of the evidence used by this study, some attention to the history of the agency and the ways SCC files were created is appropriate. The commission was established by the Federal government in 1871 to hear the claims of loyal Southerners, black and white, who had lost real and personal property to the Union army through foraging during the Civil War. According to the commission's primary historian, Frank Klingberg, by the time it closed its doors in 1880, the SCC had heard over twenty-two thousand cases and considered the testimony of more than two hundred thousand witnesses. Seven thousand of the applicants, or about one-third, appear to have received some compensation; approximately eight hundred claims were awarded to Alabamians. (The number of allowed claims is somewhat uncertain because a good many cases that were initially disallowed by the SCC were later appealed to the Congressional Court of Claims under the Bowman Act of 1881, after the discontinuation of the SCC. Neither the files of the Allowed Claims nor the records of the Court of Claims, however, include a list of the appealed cases.) Klingberg has established that awards typically equaled about 50 percent of the amount originally claimed. This rate of compensation was lower among the 405 allowed claims from Alabama utilized in this study (a total which represents about half of all allowed claims from the state). On average, Alabama's allowed claimants requested $1,343 and received $519.[1]

1. Frank Wysor Klingberg, The Southern Claims Commission, University of California Publications in History, vol. 50 (Berkeley: University of California Press, 1955), vii; Klingberg, "The Southern Claims Commission: A Postwar Agency in Operation," Mississippi Valley Historical Review 32, no. 2 (1954): 211. For the most up-to-date list of Alabama's allowed claims, see Michael E. Pilgrim and Paul Crissman, Introduction to Southern Claims Commission Approved Claims, 1871–1880: Alabama, NAMS-M2062, RG 217. Pilgrim and Crissman

As historian Gary B. Mills explained in his expansive index of all the claims (allowed, disallowed, and barred), *Southern Loyalists in the Civil War*, the commissioners' determinations about what they would pay for fell into four main categories. Anything taken or destroyed as a matter of "military necessity" was almost always disallowed; items the Federal army officially "contracted for" were almost always allowed. Mills further notes that the commission took "mixed action" on two other categories of property claimed. Claims for any lost property for which payment was promised through "verbal agreements between civilians and U.S. officers" were usually met with considerable disputation. Claims for property destroyed or stolen by "unauthorized soldiers" was likewise heavily disputed—this was a frequent issue for unionists living in guerrilla warfare zones and those living in areas heavily foraged by official troops who often went beyond their orders to pillage and loot. Claims like these were only granted after aggressive scrutiny of the circumstance and the character of the claimant.[2]

The process of adjudicating the claims began when special commissioners, traveling on circuits between county seats or sizable towns throughout the South, posted announcements of the SCC's program in local newspapers, encouraging claimants to file claims, and at a later date, to appear before the commissioner to testify.[3] In part to deter frivolous claims, the SCC instituted a number of fees and costs associated with filing a claim. Initial preparation prior to an appearance before the special commissioner, for instance, cost most claimants approximately one hundred dollars. Upon submission, claimants were charged ten cents per folio if the amount claimed totaled less than a thousand dollars. For claims over a thousand dollars (but less than ten thousand dollars),

---

introduce the 1999 microfilm publication of all the allowed claims from Alabama, comprising thirty-six rolls of microfilm. These records were not available on film when I did the research for this study, but were available only at the National Archives in Washington, D.C. (Most SCC papers from other southern states are still accessible only in manuscript form.) This microfilming project was a joint effort by NARA and The Family and Regional History Program at Wallace State Community College in Hanceville, Alabama.

2. Gary B. Mills, *Southern Loyalists in the Civil War: The Southern Claims Commission. A Composite Directory of Case Files Created by the U.S. Commissioner of Claims, 1871–1880, includ-ing those appealed to the War Claims Committee of the U.S. House of Representatives and the U.S. Court of Claims* (Baltimore: Genealogical Publishing, 1994), x, Table 1: Classes of Claims and Their General Treatment.

3. See for example, the "Notice to Claimants," in the *Lauderdale* [Florence, Ala.] *Times,* September 12, 1871.

the special commissioner charged three dollars for each day that he appeared in a particular locale. This fee was pro-rated among all claimants whose cases were heard on a specific day. Attorneys who represented a successful claim generally collected 50 percent of the award.

At the deposition, the special commissioner conducted and transcribed (or had a clerk transcribe) local interviews based on a standard questionnaire (see appendix 2), and submitted this testimony and appropriate supporting materials to the SCC office in Washington, often attaching his own recommendation for or against an award. Men and women who requested over ten thousand dollars from the government had to travel to Washington to be deposed by the three head commissioners, A. O. Aldis, Orange Ferriss, and William Howell.[4] As the head commissioners explained to Congress, detailed and careful examination of claimants and their milieu during the war was critical to the SCC's ability to pinpoint the deserving while thwarting pretenders. Because the objective of claimants was monetary gain, the SCC was duly cautious. Then, as now, these documents bore the weight of self-interest.

The Southern Claims Commission made little room for half-hearted or late-coming unionism. As historian Frank Klingberg has noted, the SCC was renowned for "being 'very severe upon the question of loyalty.'"[5] Indeed, commissioners assumed from the outset that all claimants were disloyal—"Voluntary residence in an insurrectionary State during the war is *prima facie* evidence of disloyalty"—and demanded that "satisfactory evidence" be brought forth to prove otherwise.[6] To most fully document unionism, the agency wanted to know the "condition of affairs" in a particular locale, as well as the prevailing "state of public opinion." Concerned to adequately account for intimidation and violence meted out against unionists, the SCC inquired into the "kinds and degrees of duress and insecurity" under which loyalists lived. These factors, the commission realized, would determine the extent to which individuals could demonstrate "loyalty by word or act."[7]

Lending assistance to Union army prisoners of war, avoiding conscription by hiding in the woods, joining a resistance group, refusing to accept Confederate money, provoking violent harassment from home

4. Klingberg, "Southern Claims Commission in Operation," 73, 79 n. 21, 87–9, 211.
5. Ibid., 211.
6. Quote in Klingberg, *Southern Claims Commission*, 89.
7. Fifth General Report of the Commissioners of Claims, *House Miscellaneous Documents*, 46th Cong., 2d Sess., vol. 2, no. 30, 2.

guard units or arrest by Confederate authorities represented sufficient evidence of active resistance to the secessionist government. In this regard, the SCC was sensitive to the pressures felt by unionists in different areas of Confederate authority; they distinguished between the circumstances of unionists in Montgomery and those living in Federally occupied Tennessee, for instance. Regardless of a unionist's locale, though, any transgression or perceived inconsistency could easily prevent a claim from passing. Providing a gun to a son in the Confederate army, serving in the home guard or local vigilance committee, holding Confederate office, voluntarily aiding the Confederate military, knitting socks for Confederate soldiers, or exhibiting any "cooperationist" behavior in an effort to appease local secessionists and avoid violent retribution—all of these could undermine a claim.[8]

Because the commissioners were fully aware that Federal funds might represent easy money to Southerners suffering through postwar privation, they constantly fought against fraud by investigating and reinvestigating claims. At its inception, the commission established a corps of special agents whose members moved from place to place reexamining claims of a suspicious or difficult nature. Arriving unannounced, these agents watched and collected information without revealing their identity or business to local inhabitants. Like the SCC itself, they assumed that claimants lied more often than not. As John D. Edwards, a special agent from Little Rock, explained while traveling in northern Mississippi in August of 1875, "[I will] spend the week out in the country driving from house to house of claimants, and witnesses; this is better than summonsing them in town, because I can catch them unprepared, and they are more likely to tell the truth about their claims from the sheer inability to manufacture a lie on short notice." Special commissioners urged known unionists to inform on neighbors who tried to cheat. They posted public lists that revealed the names and addresses of petitioners, along with the amount of claimed property. Klingberg notes that this practice could be very dangerous for unionists, who were already targeted by the Ku Klux Klan for their Republican Party affiliation. The commissioners maintained this strategy, however, because it was better than nothing. Even with these precautions in place, though, the SCC was clearly unable to avoid awarding fraudulent claims. To engineer such a deception, however, required widespread conspiracy among the citizens, and per-

8. Ibid., 92, 98–100.

haps the special commissioner himself, to cover up compromising evidence. Ultimately, by setting very high standards of proof for loyalty, the agency likely excluded more honest unionists than it compensated defrauders.[9]

Another evidentiary challenge posed by the claims is the expanse of time—six to fifteen years—that stretched between claimants' wartime experiences and their testimony before the SCC. We must, therefore, always be cautious about the reliability of unionists' memories and consider the ways that time, and the great political difficulties of the postwar era, affected unionists' special pleading before the commission. As I argue in this study, unionists carefully catalogued their own wartime experiences and those of their kin and neighbors—they needed desperately to know who among them was loyal, how loyal particular individuals were, and whether they could be trusted in matters of life and death. During the war, the recounting of trials and tribulations became the vehicle for this evaluation; after the war, these stories became badges of honor. Unionists cultivated their memories and viewed them as the taproot of personal identity. SCC agents simply provided a Federal and generally sympathetic audience for remembrances that unionists had been nurturing since 1860.

Another significant factor to keep in mind is that the claims do not represent a statistical sample of unionists; therefore, statistical evidence gleaned from them can be seen as reliably descriptive of a certain group of unionists, but not as a way to isolate causal or correlative factors behind unionism. The most significant reason not to use SCC records in this way is simply that not all unconditional unionists made claims. In the first place, the only way to make a claim was to have lost property to the Union army. The army did not visit every unionist's neighborhood; consequently, significant numbers of unionists fell outside the SCC's purview. Because Alabama's allowed claims are most numerous in the state's northern counties—geographic regions well documented through other sources to have been unionist areas—this problem is mitigated somewhat for this particular study. However, this is largely a matter of coincidence and may well not apply to situations elsewhere in the South.

9. Klingberg, "Southern Claims Commission in Operation," 202; Special Commissioner Enos Richmond to Honorable Commissioners of Claims, June 3, 1876, and John D. Edwards, Reports of August 7, 1875 and September 7, 1865, Holly Springs, Mississippi, both in Records of the Commissioners of Claims, 1871–1881, NAM Publ. No. 87, RG 56, Reel 11, EU; Klingberg, *Southern Claims Commission*, 74 n. 4.

Other factors limited unionists' participation in the claims process. I have come to believe, for example, that many Union veterans did not apply to the SCC, perhaps because they had been paid for their service during the war, or perhaps because they knew they could rely on government pensions. Other unconditional unionists doubtless moved west (along with many other Southerners) or north before the commission began its work and were thereby outside the familial and friendship networks that could help them file claims. Others likely died and had no executors to carry a claim on their behalf. Some probably could not afford the cost of filing; others may well have been able to afford the monetary outlay but were loath to pay the social cost of publicly asserting their wartime unionism in the heat of Reconstruction controversy. And finally, it is surely the case that the claims of numerous loyalists were disallowed for reasons that might seem unfair or arbitrary, such as following procedures incorrectly or claiming property not covered under the SCC's mandate.

New Counties and Their Predecessors, 1865–1874

Baine County, December 7, 1866, from Cherokee, DeKalb, Marshall, Blount, St. Clair, and Calhoun Counties; abolished December 1, 1868, and reestablished as Etowah County;

Baker County, December 30, 1868 (renamed Chilton County, December 17, 1874), from Autauga, Bibb, Perry, and Shelby Counties;

Bullock County, December 8, 1866, from Barbour, Pike, Montgomery, and Macon Counties;

Clay County, December 7, 1866, from Randolph and Talladega Counties;

Cleburne County, December 6, 1866, from Calhoun, Randolph, and Talladega Counties;

Colbert County, February 6, 1867, from Franklin County;

Crenshaw County, November 30, 1866, from Butler, Coffee, Covington, Pike, and Lowndes Counties;

Cullman County, January 24, 1877, from Blount, Morgan, and Winston Counties;

Elmore County, February 15, 1866, from Autauga, Coosa, Montgomery, and Tallapoosa Counties;

Escambia County, December 10, 1868, from Baldwin and Conecuh Counties;

Etowah County, December 1, 1868, reestablishment of abolished Baine County (see above);

Hale County, January 30, 1867, from Tuscaloosa, Greene, Perry, and Marengo Counties;

Geneva County, December 2, 1868, from Coffee, Dale, and Henry Counties;
Jones County, February 4, 1867, from Marion and Fayette Counties; abolished
  November 13, 1867; reestablished as Sanford County (see below);
Lee County, December 5, 1866, from Chambers, Tallapoosa, Macon, and Russell
  Counties;
Sanford County, 1868, reestablishment of abolished Jones County (see above);
  name changed again February 8, 1877, to Lamar County.

Appendix 2

QUESTIONS USED IN INTERROGATION BY THE
SOUTHERN CLAIMS COMMISSION

The following version of the SCC's standard interrogatories was final-ized around 1874. Prior to that point, at least two other incarnations of the questionnaire had been employed; subsequent revisions seem only to make the questions more specific and detailed.

Source: Allowed Case Files, SCC.

1. What is your name, your age, your residence, and how long has it been such, and your occupation?

2. If you are not the claimant, in what manner, if any, are you related to the claimant or interested in the success of the claim?

The following questions will be put to every claimant, except claimants who were slaves at the beginning of the war:

[*NOTE—If the original claimant be dead, these questions are to be an-swered by each of the heirs or legatees who were not less than sixteen years of age when the war closed.*]

3. Where were you born? If not born in the United States, when and where were you naturalized? Produce your naturalization papers, if you can.

4. Where were you residing and what was your business for six months before the outbreak of the rebellion, and where did you reside and what was your business from the beginning to the end of the war? And if you changed your residence or business, state how many times, and why such changes were made.

5. On which side were your sympathies during the war, and were they on the same side from beginning to end?

6. Did you ever do anything or say anything against the Union cause; and if so, what did you do and say, and why?

7. Were you at all times during the war willing and ready to do what-ever you could in aid of the Union cause?

8. Did you ever do anything for the Union cause or its advocates or defenders? If so state what you did, giving times, places, names of persons aided, and particulars. Were the persons aided your relations?

9. Had you any near relatives in the Union Army or Navy; if so, in what company and regiment, or on what vessel, when and where did each one enter service, and when and how did he leave service? If he was a son, produce his discharge-paper, in order that its contents may be noted in this deposition, or state why it cannot be produced.

10. Were you in the service or employment of the United States Government at any time during the war; if so, in what service, when, where, or how long, under what officers, and when and how did you leave such service or employment?

11. Did you ever voluntarily contribute money, property, or services to the Union cause; and if so, when, where and to whom and what did you contribute?

12. Which side did you take while the insurgent States were seceding from the Union in 1860 and 1861, and what did you do to show on which side you stood?

13. Did you adhere to the Union cause after the States had passed into rebellion, or did you go with your State?

14. What were your feelings concerning the battle of Bull Run or Manassas, the capture of New Orleans, the fall of Vicksburgh, and the final surrender of the confederate forces?

15. What favors, privileges, or protections were ever granted you in recognition of your loyalty during the war, when and by whom granted?

16. Have you ever taken the so-called "iron-clad oath" since the war, and when and on what occasions?

17. Who were the leading and best-known Unionists of your vicinity during the war? Are any of them called to testify to your loyalty; and if not, why not?

18. Were you ever threatened with damage or injury to your person, family, or property on account of your Union sentiments, or were you actually molested or injured on account of your Union sentiments? If so, when, where, by whom, and in what particular way were you injured or threatened with injury?

19. Were you ever arrested by any confederate officer, soldier, sailor, or other person professing to act for the confederate government, or for any State in rebellion? If so, when, where, by whom, for what cause; how long were you kept under arrest; how did you obtain your release;

did you take any oath or give any bond to effect your release; and if so, what was the nature of the oath or bond?

20. Was any of your property taken by confederate officers or soldiers, or any rebel authority? If so, what property, when, where, by whom; were you ever paid therefor [sic], and did you ever present an account therefor to the confederate government, or any rebel officers?

21. Was any of your property ever confiscated by rebel authority, on the ground that you were an enemy to the rebel cause? If so, give all the particulars, and state if the property was subsequently released or compensation made therefor.

22. Did you ever do anything for the confederate cause, or render any aid or comfort to the rebellion? If so, give the times, places, persons, and other particulars connected with the transaction.

23. What force, compulsion, or influence was used to make you do anything against the Union cause? If any, give all the particulars demanded in the last question.

24. Were you in any service, business, or employment, for the confederacy, or for any rebel authority? If so, give the same particulars as before required.

25. Were you in the civil, military, or naval service of the confederacy, or any rebel State, in any capacity whatsoever? If so, state fully in respect to each occasion and service.

26. Did you ever take any oath to the so-called Confederate States while in any rebel service or employment?

27. Did you ever have charge of any stores, or other property, for the Confederacy, or did you ever sell or furnish any supplies to the so-called Confederate States, or any State in rebellion; or did you have any share or interest in contracts, or manufactures in aid of rebellion?

28. Were you engaged in blockade-running, or running through the lines, or interested in the risks or profits of such ventures?

29. Were you in any way interested in any vessel navigating the waters of the confederacy, or entering or leaving any confederate port? If so, what vessel, when and where employed, in what business, and had any rebel authority any direct or indirect interest in vessel or cargo?

30. Did you ever subscribe to any loan of the so-called Confederate States, or of any rebel State; or own confederate bonds or securities, or the bonds or securities of any rebel State issued between 1861 and 1865? Did you sell, or agree to sell, cotton or produce to the confederate government; or to any rebel State, or to any rebel officer or agent, and if so,

did you receive or agree to receive confederate or State bonds or securities in payment; and if so, to what amount, and for what kind and amount of property?

31. Did you contribute to the raising, equipment, or support of troops, or the building of gunboats in aid of the rebellion; or to military hospitals or invalids, or to relief-funds or subscriptions for the families or persons serving against the United States?

32. Did you ever give information to any person in aid of military or naval operations against the United States?

33. Were you at any time a member of any society or organization for equipping volunteers or conscripts, or for aiding the rebellion in any other manner?

34. Did you ever take an oath of allegiance to the so-called Confederate States? If so, state how often, when, where, for what purpose, and the nature of the oath or affirmation.

35. Did you ever receive a pass from rebel authority? If so, state when, where, for what purpose, on what conditions, and how the pass was used.

36. Had you any near relatives in the confederate army, or in any military or naval service hostile to the United States? If so, give names, ages on entering service, present residence, if living, what influence you exerted, if any, against their entering the service, and in what way you contributed to their outfit and support.

37. Have you been under the disabilities imposed by the fourteenth amendment to the Constitution? Have your disabilities been removed by Congress?

38. Have you been specially pardoned by the President for participation in the rebellion?

39. Did you take any amnesty oath during the war, or after its close? If so, when, where, and why did you take it?

40. Were you ever a prisoner of the United States authorities, or on parole, or under bonds to do nothing against the Union cause? If so, state all the particulars.

41. Were you ever arrested by the authorities of the United States during the war? If so, when, where, by whom, on what grounds, and when and how did you obtain your release?

42. Were any fines or assessments levied upon you by the authorities of the United States because of your supposed sympathy for the rebellion? If so, state all the facts.

43. Was any of your property taken into possession or sold by the United States under the laws relating to confiscation, or to captured and abandoned property?

The following questions will be put to all male claimants or beneficiaries who were not less than sixteen years of age when the war closed:

44. After the presidential election of 1860, if of age, did you vote for any candidate or on any questions, during the war, and how did you vote? Did you vote for or against candidates favoring secession? Did you vote for or against the ratification of the ordinance of secession, or for or against separation in your state?

45. Did you belong to any vigilance committee, or committee of safety, home-guard, or any other form of organization or combination designed to suppress Union sentiment in your vicinity?

46. Were you in the confederate army, State militia, or any military or naval organization hostile to the United States? If so, state when, where, in what organizations, how and why you entered, how long you remained each time, and when and how you left. If you claim that you were conscripted, when and where was it, how did you receive notice, and from whom, and what was the precise manner in which the conscription was enforced against you? If you were never in the rebel army or other hostile organization, explain how you escaped service. If you furnished a substitute, when and why did you furnish one, and what is his name, and his present address, if living?

47. Were you in any way connected with or employed in the confederate quartermaster, commissary, ordnance, engineer, or medical department, or any other department, or employed on any railroad transporting troops or supplies for the confederacy or otherwise engaged in transportation of men and supplies for the confederacy? If so, state how employed, when, where, for how long, under whose direction, and why such employment was not giving "aid and comfort" to the rebellion.

48. Did you at any time have charge of trains, teams, wagons, vessels, boats, or military supplies or property of any kind for the confederate government? If so, give all the particulars of time, place, and nature of service or supplies.

49. Were you employed in saltpeter-works, in tanning or milling for the confederate government, or making clothing, boots, shoes, saddles, harness, arms, ammunition, accouterments, or any other kind of munitions of war for the confederacy? If so, give all the particulars of time, place, and nature of service or supplies.

50. Were you ever engaged in holding in custody, directly or indirectly, any persons taken by the rebel government as prisoners of war, or any person imprisoned or confined by the confederate government, or the authorities of any rebel State, for political causes? If so, when, where, under what circumstances, in what capacity were you engaged, and what was the name and rank of your principal?

51. Were you ever in the Union Army or Navy, or in any service connected therewith? If so, when, where, in what capacity, under whose command or authority, for what period of time, and when and how did you leave service? Produce your discharge-papers so that their contents may be noted herein.

The following questions will be put to every person testifying to the loyalty of claimants or beneficiaries:

52. In whose favor are you here to testify?

53. How long have you known that person altogether, and what part of that time have you intimately known him?

54. Did you live near him during the war, and how far away?

55. Did you meet him often, and about how often, during the war?

56. Did you converse with the claimant about the war, its causes, its purposes, its progress, and its results? If so, try to remember the more important occasions on which you so conversed, beginning with the first occasion, and state with respect to each when it was, where it was, who were present, what caused the conversation, and what the claimant said, in substance, if you cannot remember his words.

57. Do you know of anything done by the claimant that showed him to be loyal to the Union cause during the war? If you do, state what he did, when, where, and what was the particular cause or occasion of his doing it. Give the same information about each thing he did that showed him to be loyal.

58. Do you know of anything said or done by the claimant that was against the Union cause? If so, please state, with respect to each thing said or done, what it was, when it was, and what particular compulsion or influence caused him to say or do it.

59. If you have heard of anything said or done by the claimant, either for the Union cause or against it, state from whom you heard it, when you heard it, and what you heard.

60. What was the public reputation of the claimant for loyalty or disloyalty to the United States during the war? If you profess to know his

public reputation, explain fully how you know it, whom you heard speak of it, and give the names of other persons who were neighbors during the war that could testify to his public reputation.

61. Who were the known and prominent Union people of the neighborhood during the war, and do you know that such persons could testify to the claimant's loyalty?

62. Were you, yourself, an adherent of the Union cause during the war? If so, did the claimant know you to be such, and how did he know it?

63. Do you know of any threats, molestations, or injury inflicted upon the claimant or his family, or his property, on account of his adherence to the Union cause? If so, give all the particulars.

64. Do you know of any act done or language used by the claimant that would have prevented him from establishing his loyalty to the confederacy? If so, what act or what language?

65. Can you state any other facts within your knowledge in proof of the claimant's loyalty during the war? If so, state all the facts and give all the particulars.

The following questions concerning the ownership of property charged in claims will be put to all claimants, or the representatives of deceased claimants.

66. Who was the owner of the property charged in this claim when it was taken, and how did such person become owner?

67. If any of the property was taken from a farm or plantation, where was such farm or plantation situated, what was its size, how much was cultivated, how much was woodland, and how much was waste land?

68. Has the person who owned the property when taken since filed a petition in bankruptcy, or been declared a bankrupt?

The following will be put to female claimants:

69. Are you married or single? If married, when were you married? Was your husband loyal to the cause and Government of the United States throughout the war? Where does he now reside, and why is he not joined with you in the petition? How many children have you? Give their names and ages. Were any of them in the confederate service during the war? If you claim that the property named in your petition is your sole and separate property, state how you came to own it separately

from your husband; how your title was derived; when your ownership of it began. Did it ever belong to your husband? If the property for which you ask pay is wood, timber, rails, or the products of a farm, how did you get title to the farm? If by deed, can you file copies of the deeds? If single, have you been married? If a widow, when did your husband die? Was he in the confederate army? Was he in the civil service of the confederacy? Was he loyal to the United States Government throughout the war? Did he leave any children? How many? Are any now living? Give their names and ages. Are they not interested in this claim? If they are not joined in this petition, why not? State fully how your title to the property specified in the petition was obtained. Did you ever belong to any sewing-society organized to make clothing for Confederate soldiers or their families, or did you assist in making any such clothing, or making flags or other military equipments, or preparing or furnishing delicacies or supplies for confederate hospitals or soldiers?

The following questions will be put to colored claimants:

70. Were you a slave or free at the beginning of the war? If ever a slave, when did you become free? What business did you follow after obtaining your freedom? Did you own this property before or after you became free? When did you get it? How did you become owner, and from whom did you obtain it? Where did you get the means to pay for it? What was the name and residence of your master, and is he still living? Is he a witness for you; and if not, why not? Are you in his employ now, or do you live on his land or on land bought from him? Are you in his debt? What other person besides yourself has any interest in this claim?

The following questions will be put to all colored witnesses in behalf of white claimants:

71. Were you formerly the slave of the claimant? Are you now in his service or employment? Do you live on his land? Are you in his debt? Are you in any way to share in this claim, if allowed?

The following questions will be put to claimants and witnesses who testify to the taking of property, omitting in the case of each claimant or witness any questions that are clearly unnecessary:

72. Were you present when any of the property charged in this claim was taken? Did you see it actually taken? If so, specify what you saw taken.

73. Was any of the property taken in the night-time, or was any taken secretly, so that you did not know of it at the time?

74. Was any complaint made to any officer of the taking of any of the property? If so, give the name, rank, and regiment of the officer, and state who made the complaint to him; what he said and did in consequence; and what was the result of the complaint.

75. Were any vouchers or receipts asked for or given? If given, where are the vouchers or receipts? If lost, state fully how lost. If asked and not given, by whom were they asked; who was asked to give them, and why were they refused or not given? State very fully in regard to the failure to ask or obtain receipts.

76. Has any payment ever been made for any property charged in this claim? Has any payment been made for any property taken at the same time as the property charged in this claim? Has any payment been made for any property taken from the same claimant during the war; and if so, when, by whom, for what property and to what amount? Had this property, or any part of it, been included in any claim heretofore presented to Congress, or any court, department, or office of the United States, or to any board of survey, military commission, State commission or officer, or any other authority? If so, when and to what tribunal was the claim presented, was it larger or smaller than this claim, and how is the difference explained, and what was the decision, if any, of the tribunal to which it was presented?

77. Was the property charged in this claim taken by troops encamped in the vicinity, or were they on the march; or were they on a raid or expedition; or had there been any recent battle or skirmish?

78. You will please listen attentively while the list of items, but not the quantities, is read to you, and as each kind of property is called off, say whether you saw any such property taken.

79. Begin now with the first item of property you have just said you saw taken, and give the following information about it: First. Describe its exact condition—as, for instance, if corn, whether green or ripe, standing or harvested, in shuck or husked, or shelled; if lumber, whether new or old, in building or piled; if grain, whether growing or cut, &c. Second. State where it was. Third. What was the quantity? Explain fully how you know the quantity; and if estimated, describe your method of making the estimate. Fourth. Describe the quality, to your best judgment. Fifth. State as nearly as you can the market-value of such property at the time in United States money. Sixth. Say when the property was taken. Seventh.

Give the name of the detachment, regiment, brigade, division, corps, or army taking the precise property, and the names of any officers belonging to the command. Eighth. Describe the precise manner in which the property was taken into possession by the troops, and the manner in which it was removed. Ninth. State as closely as you can how many men, animals, wagons, or other means of transport, were engaged in the removal; how long they were occupied, and to what place they removed the property. Tenth. State if any officers were present; how you knew them to be officers; what they said or did in relation to the property; and give the names of any, if you can. Eleventh. Give any reasons you may have for believing that the taking of the property was authorized by the proper officers, or that it was for the necessary use of the Army.

80. Now take the next item of property you saw taken, and give the same information, and so proceed to the end of the list of items.

Appendix 3

DEMOGRAPHIC TABLES

The following tables have all been compiled from data recorded in Alabama's free and slave population schedules of the 1860 U.S. Census, Alabama (NAMS M-653), the Inter-University Consortium for Political and Social Research Study No. 3, "Historical, Demographic, Economic, and Social Data: The United States, 1790–1970" (http://fisher.lib.virginia .edu/census/; last accessed August 21, 2001), and the allowed case files of the Southern Claims Commission (RG 217).

TABLE A.1: *Slave Population and Improved Acreage, Alabama, 1860 (By Subregion and County)*

Subregion and County	% of Population Enslaved	Improved Acreage as % of Total Land
Tennessee Valley	42.7	38.5
Franklin	45.6	32.3
Jackson	18.6	31.4
Lauderdale	38.7	32.7
Lawrence	48.6	41.5
Limestone	52.8	44.9
Madison	55.1	52.7
Morgan	32.7	34.2
Hill Country	12.0	20.3
Blount	6.1	21.2
Cherokee	16.4	32.9
DeKalb	7.9	36.1
Fayette	13.3	14.7
Marion	11.5	10.7
Marshall	15.9	31.2
St. Clair	16.1	20.3

(Table A.1 continued)

Subregion and County	% of Population Enslaved	Improved Acreage as % of Total Land
Walker	6.5	13.7
Winston	3.4	14.5
Central Piedmont	*33.4*	*31.0*
Bibb	32.3	24.5
Calhoun	20.2	33.7
Chambers	51.0	52.3
Coosa	27.0	28.0
Jefferson	22.6	25.8
Pickens	54.6	34.6
Randolph	9.5	23.1
Shelby	28.7	27.2
Talladega	37.7	31.1
Tallapoosa	28.0	33.7
Tuscaloosa	43.7	24.4
Black Belt	*61.4*	*44.3*
Autauga	57.4	30.0
Barbour	49.3	39.2
Butler	37.6	24.6
Dallas	76.6	47.7
Greene	76.5	32.3
Lowndes	69.8	46.7
Macon	67.8	50.4
Marengo	78.3	42.3
Monroe	55.6	28.0
Montgomery	66.0	46.6
Perry	65.7	46.1
Pike	36.0	32.0
Russell	58.8	51.8
Sumter	75.3	47.5
Wilcox	72.3	34.6
Wiregrass	*24.5*	*24.0*
Coffee	14.7	21.0
Conecuh	43.2	29.8

(Table A.1 continued)

Subregion and County	% of Population Enslaved	Improved Acreage as % of Total Land
Covington	12.7	17.0
Dale	14.8	21.9
Henry	29.7	27.7
Piney Woods	50.7	20.4
Choctaw	51.1	26.3
Clarke	49.4	18.2
Washington	53.4	13.6
Coastal Plain	31.0	9.2
Baldwin	49.3	12.2
Mobile	27.7	7.4

Source: Inter-University Consortium for Political and Social Research, Study No. 3, "Historical, Demographic, Economic, and Social Data: The United States, 1790–1970" (http://fisher.lib.virginia.edu/census/; last accessed August 21, 2001).

TABLE A.2: *Distribution of Wealth among Allowed SCC Claimants, White Males and Females, Alabama, 1860*

Decile	Total Value of Wealth	% Share of Wealth	Mean Wealth
Top decile	$1,388,567	70.90	$52,597
Second	263,074	13.43	9,965
Third	112,516	5.75	4,262
Fourth	66,270	3.38	2,510
Fifth	44,870	2.29	1,700
Sixth	32,475	1.66	1,230
Seventh	22,695	1.16	860
Eighth	16,805	.86	637
Ninth	10,015	.51	379
Tenth	1,170	.06	44
Totals	$1,958,457	100.00	$7,418

Sources: SCC; 1860 U.S. Census, Alabama, Free Pop., NAMS M-653.

Note: The total for this table is 264; it includes only those white claimants whose real and personal property was recorded in the 1860 census; men eighteen and younger still living in their parents' households were excluded. However, sons over eighteen living in their father's or mother's household were included, whether or not they independently owned property.

TABLE A.3: *Percentage of Slaveholders among Adult White Population, Alabama, 1860 (Hill Country Subregion)*

County	Number of Slaveholders	Adult White Population	% Adult White Population
Blount	125	4,017	3.1
Cherokee	498	6,376	7.8
DeKalb	165	3,901	4.2
Fayette	330	4,530	7.3
Marion	204	3,861	5.3
Marshall	224	4,019	5.6
St. Clair	257	3,734	6.9
Walker	102	2,853	3.6
Winston	14	1,403	1.0
Total for Subregion	1,919	34,694	5.5
Total for State	33,730	226,269	14.9

Sources: 1860 U.S. Census, Alabama, Free and Slave Pop., NAMS M-653; Inter-University Consortium for Political and Social Research Study No. 3, "Historical, Demographic, Economic, and Social Data: The United States, 1790–1970."

Note: The adult white population was calculated based on the prearranged age categories in the aggregate census returns, which do not break at eighteen or twenty-one, but instead at twenty. Thus, the figure for adult white population includes all whites twenty years of age and older.

TABLE A.4: *Percentage of Slaveholders among Adult White Population, Alabama, 1860 (Tennessee Valley Subregion)*

County	Number of Slaveholders	Adult White Population	% Adult White Population
Franklin	519	4,289	12.1
Jackson	482	6,272	7.7
Lauderdale	522	4,605	11.3
Lawrence	391	3,144	12.4
Limestone	661	3,196	20.7
Madison	1,117	5,448	20.5
Morgan	391	3,273	11.9
Total for Subregion	4,083	30,227	13.5
Total for State	33,730	226,269	14.9

(Table A.4 continued)

Sources: 1860 U.S. Census, Alabama, Free and Slave Pop., NAMS M-653; Inter-University Consortium for Political and Social Research Study No. 3, "Historical, Demographic, Economic, and Social Data: The United States, 1790–1970."

Note: The adult white population was calculated based on the prearranged age categories in the aggregate census returns, which do not break at eighteen or twenty-one, but instead at twenty. Thus, the figure for adult white population includes all whites twenty years of age and older.

TABLE A.5: *Occupations of Allowed SCC Claimants, White Males, Alabama, 1860*

Occupation	Number	% of Total
Farmer	204	68.0
Artisan	22	7.0
Artisan-Farmer	19	6.0
Tenant Farmer	7	2.0
Professional	5	2.0
Merchant	5	2.0
Preacher-Farmer	5	2.0
Day Laborer	5	2.0
Planter	4	1.0
Merchant-Farmer	4	1.0
Miller	4	1.0
Family Farm Laborer	3	1.0
Saw Mill Operator/Owner	3	1.0
Oysterman/Fisherman	3	1.0
Schoolteacher	2	1.0
Other	6	2.0
Totals	301	100.0

Sources: SCC; 1860 U.S. Census, Alabama, Free Pop., NAMS M-653.

Note: Artisanal trades represented here included blacksmithing, carpentry, wagon making, other mechanic trades, tanning, shoemaking, printing, and tailoring. The category "other" includes an overseer, an auctioneer, a steamboat engineer, a railroad yardmaster, a grocer, and a manufacturer. In the Tennessee Valley, there were thirteen artisans, while the Hill Country only included five; artisan-farmers were more evenly distributed, with ten Valley claimants and seven Hill Country claimants naming both farming and a trade as their occupation.

TABLE A.6: *Occupations of Allowed SCC Claimants, White Females, Alabama, 1860*

Occupation	Number	% of Total
Housekeeper for family farm	25	43.85
Farmer	18	31.58
Housekeeper for tenant farm	3	5.26
Tenant farmer	2	3.51
Planter	1	1.75
Housekeeper for plantation	1	1.75
Housekeeper for professional household	1	1.75
Housekeeper for artisan household	1	1.75
Seamstress	1	1.75
Schoolteacher	1	1.75
Trader	1	1.75
Spinster (no other occupation given)	1	1.75
Widow (no other occupation given)	1	1.75
Totals	57	100.00

Sources: SCC; 1860 U.S. Census, Alabama, Free Pop., NAMS M-653.

Note: Most of the women who filed SCC claims on their own, or who became the administratrices of claims after the death of husband claimants, usually ascribed to themselves the job of keeping house for a farming or artisanal family. One-third of unionist women, however, were independent yeomen farmers in 1860, having been widowed, divorced, or never married before the war.

TABLE A.7: *Nativity of Allowed SCC Claimants, White, Alabama, 1860 (By Region and State)*

Region and State	Total Number Born in Each Region and State	As % of Total
Deep South	165	53.6
Alabama	69	22.4
Georgia	44	14.3
Mississippi	2	0.6
South Carolina	50	16.2
Upper South	124	40.3
Kentucky	7	2.3
Maryland	2	0.6
North Carolina	48	15.6

(Ttable A.7 continued)

Region and State	Total Number Born in Each Region and State	As % of Total
Tennessee	55	17.9
Virginia	12	3.9
North	16	5.2
Connecticut	1	.3
Delaware	1	.3
Indiana	1	.3
Massachusetts	3	.98
New Jersey	2	.6
New York	2	.6
Pennsylvania	3	.98
Rhode Island	1	.3
Vermont	2	.6
Abroad	3	.98
Ireland	2	.6
Scotland	1	.3

Sources: SCC; 1860 U.S. Census, Alabama, Free Pop., NAMS M-653.

Note: Total is 308 and includes all white allowed claimants whose birthplace was recorded in the 1860 census or at the time of SCC interview.

TABLE A.8: *Age of Allowed SCC Claimants, White, Alabama, 1860 (By Age Cohort and Average)*

Age in 1860	Men	Women
18–29	21	11
30–39	62	11
40–49	52	5
50–59	59	10
60+	27	0
Average Age	44.7	37.4

Sources: SCC Papers; 1860 U.S. Census, Alabama, Free Pop., NAMS M-653.

Note: Total is 258; universe includes only white claimants whose age in 1860 could be confirmed through manuscript census records.

TABLE A.9: *Occupations of Allowed SCC Claimants, Enslaved and Free African Americans, Alabama, 1860*

Occupation	Status			Totals
	Enslaved	Enslaved, Hiring Own Time	Free	
General Laborer	23			23
Blacksmith	2	1	3	6
Carpenter		2		2
Livery Stable Worker		1	2	3
Shoemaker	1		1	2
Carriage Driver	1			1
Brick Mason	1			1
Basket Maker	1			1
Cotton Gin Maker/Repairman			1	1
Tanner		1		1
Housemaid (female)	1			1
Cook (f)		1		1
Seamstress (f)			1	1
Washerwoman (f)	1			1
Totals	31	6	8	45

Sources: SCC Papers; 1860 U.S. Census, Alabama, Free and Slave Pop., NAMS M-653.

Bibliography

PRIMARY SOURCES

Archival and Manuscript Sources

Alabama Department of Archives and History, Montgomery
Civil War and Reconstruction Files
Governor Albert B. Moore Papers, 1857–61
Governor J. Gill Shorter Papers, 1861–63
Governor Thomas Watts Papers, 1863–65
Governor Lewis E. Parsons Papers, 1865
Governor Robert M. Patton Papers, 1865–67
Governor Wager T. Swayne Papers, 1867–68
Governor William H. Smith Papers, 1868–70
Governors' Unprocessed Administrative Records (Shorter, 1861–63)
Lewis E. Parsons Papers, 1817–95
Secretary of State, Elections and Registration Division, Commission Registers,
    1861–1865
Volunteer Family Assistance Reports

Birmingham Public Library, Birmingham, Alabama
Alexander Boyd Papers

*The Gilder Lehrman Collection on deposit at the Morgan Library,
New York City*
Eb Allison Papers, GLC 3523.24
Edward Amsden Papers, GLC 2156
Joseph Jones Letters, GLC 2739
"To the People of Alabama . . ." [opposing secession without plebiscite], GLC
    5987.13

*National Archives and Records Administration, National Archives Building,
Washington, D.C.*
Compiled Service Records of Volunteer Union Soldiers Who Served in Organizations from the State of Alabama, NAMS-M276

Records of the Assistant Commissioner of the Freedmen's Bureau for the State of Alabama, Bureau of Refugees, Freedmen, and Abandoned Lands, 1865–1870, RG105, NAMS-M809

Records of the Commissioners of Claims (Southern Claims Commission), 1871–1881, RG 56, NAMS-M87

Records of the Committee on the Judiciary, 39th Congress, Records of the United States House of Representatives, RG 233

Records of the United States Army Continental Commands, 1821–1920, 1817–1940. Records of the Third Military District and the Department of Alabama, RG 393

Settled Case Files for Claims Approved by the Southern Claims Commission, 1871–1880. Records of the Land, Files, and Miscellaneous Division, Records of the Accounting Officers of the Department of the Treasury, RG 217

Southern Claims Commission Disallowed Claims, 1871–1880, RG 233, NAMS-M1407

United States Census Office, *Eighth Census of the United States, 1860.* Alabama Free and Slave Populations, Manuscript Returns. NAMS-M653

Indiana Historical Society, Indianapolis
John M. Barnard Letters
George W. Baum Civil War Diaries
Helen Floyd Carlin Papers
Robert H. Crowder Papers
Stephen Emmert Letters
Charles A. Harper Papers
Edward F. Reid Papers
William A. Swayze Civil War Letters and Papers

Southern Historical Collection, University of North Carolina, Chapel Hill
William Cooper Diaries
D. H. Duryea Letters
Edward Asbury O'Neal Papers

State Historical Society of Iowa, Des Moines
Grenville Mellen Dodge Papers

William R. Perkins Library, Duke University, Durham, N.C.
John Lakin Brasher Papers
Benson-Thompson Family Papers
Mary Jane Cook Chadick Diary
Robert Anderson McClellan Papers

Eugene Marshall Papers
Henry Watson Papers

Newspapers

Elmore Standard (Wetumpka, Ala.)
Lauderdale Times (Florence, Ala.)
Montgomery Weekly Advertiser
The Nationalist (Mobile)
Tuscaloosa Independent and Monitor
Western Christian Advocate (Cincinnati)

Published Primary Sources

Annual Conferences of the Methodist Episcopal Church for the Year 1866. New York: Carlton & Lanahan, 1868.

Barnes, James A., James R. Carnahan, and Thomas H. B. McCain. *The Eighty-Sixth Regiment Indiana Volunteer Infantry: A Narrative of Its Services in the Civil War of 1861–1865*. Crawfordsville, Ind.: Journal Company, 1895.

Cannon, J. P. *Inside of Rebeldom: The Daily Life of a Private in the Confederate Army*. Washington, D.C.: National Tribune, 1900.

Curry, W. L. *Four Years in the Saddle: History of the First Regiment Ohio Volunteer Cavalry: War of the Rebellion—1861–1865*. Columbus, Ohio: Chaplin, 1898.

Fifth General Report of the Commissioners of Claims, House Miscellaneous Documents, 46th Cong., 2d Sess., no. 30. Washington D.C.: Government Printing Office, 1879.

Franklin, John Hope, ed. *The Diary of James T. Ayers, Civil War Recruiter*. Occasional Publications of the Illinois State Historical Society. Springfield: Illinois State Historical Society, 1947.

Harris, Sherry, ed. *1862 Alabama Salt List*. Granada Hills, Calif.: Harris Press, 1993.

Hartpence, William R. *History of the Fifty-First Indiana Veteran Volunteer Infantry: A Narrative of Its Organization, Marches, Battles, and Other Experiences in Camp and Prison, from 1861 to 1866, with Revised Roster*. Cincinnati: Robert Clarke, 1894.

History of the Ninety-Second Illinois Volunteers. Freeport, Ill.: Journal Steam Publishing, 1875.

Holbrook, William C. *A Narrative of the Services of the Officers and Enlisted Men of the 7th Regiment of Vermont Volunteers (Veterans) from 1862 to 1866*. New York: American Bank Note, 1883.

House Miscellaneous Documents, 39th Cong., 1st Sess. Washington, D.C.: Government Printing Office, 1866.

Hubert, Charles. *History of the Fiftieth Illinois Volunteer Infantry in the War of the Rebellion*. Kansas: Western Veteran, 1894.

Jones, Jenkin Lloyd. *An Artilleryman's Diary.* N.p.: Wisconsin History Commission, 1914.

Journal of the Proceedings of Convention of the State of Alabama Held in the City of Montgomery, Tuesday, September 12, 1865. 1865. Facsimile reprint, Washington, D.C.: Statute Law Book Co., 1934.

Kimbell, Charles. *History of Battery "A," First Illinois Light Artillery Volunteers.* Chicago: Pushing, 1899.

Lovejoy, Daniel. *Adventures of a Varied Career.* Chicago: N.p., 1894.

McGee, B. F. *History of the 72d Indiana Volunteer Infantry of the Mounted Lightning Brigade,* edited by William R. Jewell. Lafayette, Ind.: S. Vater, 1882.

Mahaffey, Joseph H., ed. "Carl Schurz Letter from Alabama, August 15–6, 1865." *Alabama Review* 3 (April 1950): 134–45.

Morrison, Marion. *A History of the Ninth Regiment Illinois Volunteer Infantry.* Monmartin, Ill.: John S. Clark, 1907.

Official Journal of the Constitutional Convention of the State of Alabama Held in the City of Montgomery Commencing on Tuesday, November 5th A.D. 1867. Montgomery, Ala.: Barrett & Brown, 1868.

Pike, James. *The Scout and Ranger: Being the Personal Adventures of Corporal Pike of the Fourth Ohio Cavalry . . . Fully Illustrating the Secret Service.* Cincinnati: J. R. Hawley, 1865.

Potter, Johnny L. T. N., comp. *First Tennessee and Alabama Independent Vidette Cavalry Roster, 1863–1864: Companies "A," "B," "C," "D," "E," "F," "G," "H."* Chattanooga: Mountain Press, 1995.

Proceedings of the Conventions at Charleston and Baltimore. Published by Order of the National Democratic Convention, Maryland Institute, Baltimore and under the Supervision of the National Democratic Executive Committee. Washington, D.C.: N.p., 1860.

Report of the Joint Committee on Reconstruction, 39th Cong., 1st Sess. Washington, D.C.: Government Printing Office, 1866.

Richardson, Wade H. *How I Reached the Union Lines.* Milwaukee: Meyer-Rotier Print Co., 1905.

Schmutz, George S., ed. *History of the 102d Regiment, O.V.I.* N.p., 1907.

Seventy-third Indiana Regimental Association, *History of the Seventy-Third Indiana Volunteers in the War of 1861–65.* Washington D.C.: Carnahan Press, 1909.

Simpson, Brooks D., LeRoy P. Graf, and John Muldowny. *Advice after Appomattox: Letters to Andrew Johnson, 1865–1866.* Special volume no. 1, *Papers of Andrew Johnson,* edited by LeRoy P. Graf. Knoxville: University of Tennessee Press, 1987.

Smith, William R. *The History and Debates of the Convention of the People of Alabama, January 1861.* Atlanta: Rice, 1861.

Testimony Taken by the Joint Select Committee to Inquire into the Condition of Af-

fairs in the Late Insurrectionary States. Vols. 9–11, *Alabama*. Washington, D.C.: Government Printing Office, 1872.

Tharin, Robert Seymour. *Arbitrary Arrests in the South; Or, Scenes from the Experience of an Alabama Unionist, by R. S. Tharin, A.M., a Native of Charleston, S. C.; For Thirty Years a Resident of the Cotton States, and Commonly Known in the West as "The Alabama Refugee."* New York: John Bradburn, 1863.

United States Census Office. *Statistics of the United States in 1860: Compiled from the Original Returns and Being the Final Exhibit of the Eighth Census, under the Direction of the Secretary of the Interior*. 4 vols. 1866. Reprint, New York: Normal Ross Publishers, 1990.

United States Naval War Records Office. *Official Records of the Union and Confederate Navies in the War of the Rebellion*. 30 vols. Washington, D.C.: Government Printing Office, 1894–1922.

United States War Department. *The War of the Rebellion: A Compilation of the Official Records of the Union and Confederate Armies*. Washington, D.C.: Government Printing Office, 1880–1901.

Wulsin, Lucien, ed. *The Story of the Fourth Regiment Ohio Veteran Volunteer Cavalry*. Cincinnati: N.p., 1912.

Wyeth, John Allen. *With Sabre and Scalpel: The Autobiography of a Soldier and Surgeon*. New York: Harper & Brothers, 1914.

Electronic Primary Sources

Black Sailors Research Project of Howard University, National Park Service: http://www.civilwar.nps.gov/cwss/sailorsindex.html

Civil War Soldiers and Sailors Database, National Park Service: http://www.civilwar.nps.gov/cwss

Inter-University Consortium for Political and Social Research Study No. 3, "Historical, Demographic, Economic, and Social Data: The United States, 1790–1970": http://fisher.lib.virginia.edu/census/

Muster Roll of Company B, "Blount County Hornets," Twenty-ninth Alabama Infantry: http://members.aol.com/egun/Hornet.html

Muster Roll of Company C, "Avalanche Company," Twenty-ninth Alabama Infantry: http://members.aol.com/egun/Avalanche.html

Muster Roll of Company F, "Blount County Tiger Boys," Twenty-ninth Alabama Infantry: http://members.aol.com/egun/Tiger.html

Muster Roll of Company F, Forty-eighth Alabama Infantry: http://fly.hiwaay.net/~jgeorge/frame48.html

Muster Roll of Nineteenth Alabama Infantry Regiment, 1861–1865: http://www.19thalabama.org/muster.html

Roster of the Sixty-fourth Illinois Infantry, Illinois State Archives: http://www.sos.state.il.us

SECONDARY SOURCES

Books

Abbott, Richard H. *The Republican Party and the South, 1855–1877: The First Southern Strategy.* Chapel Hill: University of North Carolina Press, 1986.

Abernethy, Thomas Perkins. *The Formative Period in Alabama, 1815–1828.* 1965. Reprint, Tuscaloosa: University of Alabama Press, 1990.

Alexander, Roberta S. *North Carolina Faces the Freedmen: Race Relations during Presidential Reconstruction, 1865–1867.* Durham, N. C.: Duke University Press, 1985.

Amlund, Curtis Arthur. *Federalism in the Southern Confederacy.* Washington, D.C.: Public Affairs Press, 1966.

Anderson, Bern. *By Sea and by River: The Naval History of the Civil War.* New York: Knopf, 1962.

Ash, Stephen V. *Middle Tennessee Society Transformed, 1860–1870: War and Peace in the Upper South.* Baton Rouge: Louisiana State University Press, 1988.

———. *When the Yankees Came: Conflict and Chaos in the Occupied South, 1861–1865.* Chapel Hill: University of North Carolina Press, 1995.

Ayers, Edward. *Vengeance and Justice: Crime and Punishment in the Nineteenth-Century American South.* New York: Oxford University Press, 1984.

Baggett, James Alex. *The Scalawags: Southern Dissenters in the Civil War and Reconstruction.* Baton Rouge: Louisiana State University Press, 2003.

Bailey, Anne, and Daniel E. Sutherland, eds. *Civil War Arkansas: Beyond Battles and Leaders.* Fayetteville: University of Arkansas Press, 2000.

Bailey, Richard. *Neither Carpetbaggers nor Scalawags: Black Officeholders during the Reconstruction of Alabama, 1867–1878.* Montgomery: By the author, 1995.

Barney, William L. *The Secessionist Impulse: Alabama and Mississippi in 1860.* Princeton, N. J.: Princeton University Press, 1974.

Beaver, Patricia Duane. *Rural Community in the Appalachian South.* Lexington: University Press of Kentucky, 1978.

Bentley, George R. *A History of the Freedmen's Bureau.* Philadelphia: University of Pennsylvania Press, 1955.

Berlin, Ira, Barbara Fields, Thavolia Glymph, Joseph P. Reidy, and Leslie S. Rowland, eds., *Freedom: A Documentary History of Emancipation, 1861–1867.* Cambridge, U.K.: Cambridge University Press, 1992.

Berlin, Ira, Barbara J. Fields, Steven F. Miller, Joseph P. Reidy, and Leslie S. Rowland, eds. *Slaves No More: Three Essays on Emancipation and the Civil War.* Cambridge, U.K.: Cambridge University Press, 1992.

———. *Free at Last: A Documentary History of Slavery, Freedom, and the Civil War.* New York: New Press, 1992.

Berlin, Ira, and Philip D. Morgan, eds. *The Slaves' Economy: Independent Production by Slaves in the Americas.* London: Frank Cass, 1991.

Berlin, Ira, Joseph P. Reidy, and Leslie S. Rowland, eds. *Freedom: A Documentary History of Emancipation, 1861–1867, Selected from the Holdings of the National Archives of the United States.* Series 2, *The Black Military Experience.* New York: Cambridge University Press, 1982.

————. *Freedom's Soldiers: The Black Military Experience in the Civil War.* New York: Cambridge University Press, 1998.

Blair, William. *Virginia's Private War: Feeding Body and Soul in the Confederacy, 1861–1865.* New York: Oxford University Press, 1998.

Blassingame, John W. *The Slave Community: Plantation Life in the Antebellum South.* Rev. ed., New York: Oxford University Press, 1979.

Bond, Horace Mann. *Negro Education in Alabama: A Study in Cotton and Steel.* Washington, D.C.: Associated Publishers, 1939.

Boritt, Gabor S., ed. *Why the Confederacy Lost.* New York: Oxford University Press, 1992.

Brackeen, Lilla Bullington. *All in Our Family: A Family Book of the Bullington, Halbert, Legg, Golden, Vickrey, Brackeen, Eastep, and Other Related Families.* Decatur, Ala.: Decatur Printing, 1976.

Brown, Lynda W., Donald B. Dodd, Lloyd H. Cornett, Jr., and Alma D. Steading, comps. *Alabama History: An Annotated Bibliography.* Bibliographies of the States of the United States, no. 7. Westport, Conn.: Greenwood Press, 1998.

Brownlee, Richard S. *Gray Ghosts of the Confederacy: Guerrilla Warfare in the West, 1861–1865.* Baton Rouge: Louisiana State University Press, 1958.

Bruce, Dickson D., Jr. *Violence and Culture in the Antebellum South.* Austin: University of Texas Press, 1979.

Buker, George E. *Blockaders, Refugees, and Contrabands: Civil War on Florida's Gulf Coast, 1861–1865.* Tuscaloosa: University of Alabama Press, 1993.

Burton, Orville Vernon. *In My Father's House Are Many Mansions: Family and Community in Edgefield, South Carolina.* The Fred W. Morrison Series in Southern Studies. Chapel Hill: University of North Carolina Press, 1985.

Bynum, Victoria E. *The Free State of Jones: Mississippi's Longest Civil War.* Chapel Hill: University of North Carolina Press, 2001.

Carmichael, Flossie, and Ronald Lee. *In and around Bridgeport.* Collegedale, Tenn.: College Press, 1969.

Carter, Dan T. *When the War Was Over: The Failure of Self-Reconstruction in the South, 1865–1867.* Baton Rouge: Louisiana State University Press, 1985.

Cashin, Joan E. *A Family Venture: Men and Women on the Southern Frontier.* New York: Oxford University Press, 1991.

Cimbala, Paul A. *Under the Guardianship of the Nation: The Freedmen's Bureau and the Reconstruction of Georgia, 1865–1870.* Athens: University of Georgia Press, 1997.

Coleman, Charles H. *The Election of 1868: The Democratic Effort to Regain Control.*

Studies in History, Economics, and Public Law, no. 392. New York: Columbia University Press, 1933.

Cooper, William J., Jr. *Liberty and Slavery: Southern Politics to 1860.* New York: Alfred A. Knopf, 1983.

Cornish, Dudley T. *The Sable Arm: Negro Troops in the Union Army, 1861–1865.* 1953. Reprint, New York: W. W. Norton, 1966.

Craven, Avery O. *The Growth of Southern Nationalism, 1848–1861.* Baton Rouge: Louisiana State University Press, 1953.

Crawford, Martin. *Ashe County's Civil War: Community and Society in the Appalachian South.* Charlottesville: University Press of Virginia, 2001.

Crenshaw, Ollinger. *The Slave States in the Presidential Election of 1860.* Johns Hopkins University Studies in Historical and Political Science, ser. 58, no. 3. Baltimore: Johns Hopkins University Press, 1945.

Crofts, Daniel W. *Old Southampton: Politics and Society in a Virginia County, 1834–1869.* Charlottesville: University of Virginia Press, 1992.

———. *Reluctant Confederates: Upper South Unionists in the Secession Crisis.* Chapel Hill: University of North Carolina Press, 1989.

Current, Richard Nelson. *Lincoln's Loyalists: Union Soldiers from the Confederacy.* New York: Oxford University Press, 1992.

Davidson, Donald. *The Tennessee,* 2 vols. New York: Rhinehart, 1946.

Davis, Charles S. *The Cotton Kingdom in Alabama.* Montgomery: Alabama State Department of Archives and History, 1939.

Degler, Carl. *The Other South: Southern Dissenters in the Nineteenth Century.* New York: Harper & Row, 1974.

Denman, Clarence Phillips. *The Secession Movement in Alabama.* Montgomery: Alabama State Department of Archives and History, 1933.

Dodd, Donald B. *Historical Atlas of Alabama.* Tuscaloosa: University of Alabama Press, 1974.

Dodd, Donald B., and Wynelle S. Dodd. *Winston: An Antebellum and Civil War History of a Hill County of North Alabama.* Vol. 4, *Annals of Northwest Alabama,* compiled by Carl Elliott. Jasper, Ala.: Oxmoor Press, 1972.

Dorman, Lewy. *Party Politics in Alabama from 1850 through 1860.* 1935. Reprint, Tuscaloosa: University of Alabama Press, 1995.

Doyle, Don Harrison. *The Social Order of a Frontier Community: Jacksonville, Illinois, 1825–1870.* Urbana: University of Illinois Press, 1978.

Duncan, Russell. *Freedom's Shore: Tunis Campbell and the Georgia Freedmen.* Athens: University of Georgia Press, 1986.

Dunnavant, Robert, Jr. *Decatur, Alabama: Yankee Foothold in Dixie, 1861–1865.* Athens, Ala.: Pea Ridge Press, 1995.

Dupre, Daniel S. *Transforming the Cotton Frontier: Madison County, Alabama, 1800–1840.* Baton Rouge: Louisiana State University Press, 1997.

Durrill, Wayne K. *War of Another Kind: A Southern Community in the Great Rebellion.* New York: Oxford University Press, 1990.

Dyer, Frederick H. *A Compendium of the War of the Rebellion.* 3 vols. 1908. Reprint, New York: Thomas Yoseloff, 1959.

Dyer, Thomas. *Secret Yankees: The Union Circle in Confederate Atlanta.* Baltimore: Johns Hopkins University Press, 1999.

Edwards, Laura. *Scarlett Doesn't Live Here Anymore: Southern Women in the Civil War Era.* Urbana: University of Illinois Press, 2000.

Engle, Stephen D. *Struggle for the Heartland: The Campaigns from Fort Henry to Corinth.* Lincoln: University of Nebraska Press, 2001.

Escott, Paul D. *After Secession: Jefferson Davis and the Failure of Confederate Nationalism.* Baton Rouge: Louisiana State University Press, 1978.

Faust, Drew Gilpin. *The Creation of Confederate Nationalism: Ideology and Identity in the Civil War South.* Baton Rouge: Louisiana State University Press, 1988.

————. *Mothers of Invention: Women of the Slaveholding South in the American Civil War.* Chapel Hill: University of North Carolina Press, 1996.

Fellman, Michael. *Inside War: The Guerrilla Conflict in Missouri during the Civil War.* New York: Oxford University Press, 1989.

Fields, Barbara. *Slavery and Freedom on the Middle Ground: Maryland during the Nineteenth Century.* New Haven: Yale University Press, 1985.

Finley, Randy. *From Slavery to Uncertain Freedom: The Freedmen's Bureau in Arkansas, 1865–1869.* Fayetteville: University of Arkansas Press, 1996.

Fisher, John E. *They Rode with Forrest and Wheeler: A Chronicle of Five Tennessee Brothers' Service in the Confederate Western Cavalry.* Jefferson, N.C.: McFarland, 1995.

Fisher, Noel C. *War at Every Door: Partisan Politics and Guerrilla Violence in East Tennessee, 1860–1869.* Chapel Hill: University of North Carolina Press, 1997.

Fite, Emerson D. *The Presidential Campaign of 1860.* New York: Macmillan, 1911.

Fitzgerald, Michael W. *The Union League Movement in the Deep South: Politics and Agricultural Change during Reconstruction.* Baton Rouge: Louisiana State University Press, 1989.

Fleming, Walter Lynwood. *Civil War and Reconstruction in Alabama.* 1905. Reprint, New York: Columbia University Press, 1949.

Flynn, Charles L., Jr. *White Land, Black Labor: Caste and Class in Late Nineteenth-Century Georgia.* Baton Rouge: Louisiana State University Press, 1983.

Foner, Eric. *Reconstruction: America's Unfinished Revolution, 1864–1877.* New York: Harper & Row, 1988.

Forster, Stig, and Jörg Nagler, eds. *On the Road to Total War: The American Civil War and the German Wars of Unification, 1861–1871.* Cambridge, U.K.: Cambridge University Press, 1997.

Foscue, Virginia O. *Place Names in Alabama.* Tuscaloosa: University of Alabama Press, 1989.

Fox-Genovese, Elizabeth. *Within the Plantation Household: Black and White Women of the Old South.* Chapel Hill: University of North Carolina Press, 1988.

Freehling, William W. *The South vs. the South: How Anti-Confederate Southerners Shaped the Course of the Civil War.* New York: Oxford University Press, 2001.

Friedman, Jean. *The Enclosed Garden: Women and Community in the Evangelical South, 1830–1900.* Chapel Hill: University of North Carolina Press, 1985.

Gallagher, Gary. *The Confederate War: How Popular Will, Nationalism, and Military Strategy Could Not Stave Off Defeat.* Cambridge, Mass.: Harvard University Press, 1997.

Genovese, Eugene D. *Roll, Jordan, Roll: The World the Slaves Made.* New York: Random House, 1972.

Gerteis, Louis S. *From Contraband to Freedman: Federal Policy toward Southern Blacks, 1861–1865.* Contributions in American History, no. 29. Westport, Conn.: Greenwood Press, 1973.

Glatthaar, Joseph T. *Forged in Battle: The Civil War Alliance of Black Soldiers and White Officers.* New York: Free Press, 1990.

Going, Allen Johnston. *Bourbon Democracy in Alabama, 1874–1890.* 1951. Reprint, Tuscaloosa: University of Alabama Press, 1992.

Goodrich, Thomas. *Black Flag: Guerrilla Warfare on the Western Border, 1861–1865.* Bloomington: Indiana University Press, 1995.

Gray, Louis Cecil. *History of Agriculture in the Southern United States to 1860.* Carnegie Institution of Washington Publication, no. 430, vol. 1. Washington, D.C.: Carnegie Institution of Washington, 1933.

Grimsley, Mark. *The Hard Hand of War: Union Military Policy toward Southern Civilians, 1861–1865.* Cambridge, U.K.: Cambridge University Press, 1995.

Grimsley, Mark, and Brooks D. Simpson, eds. *The Collapse of the Confederacy.* Lincoln: University of Nebraska Press, 2001.

Grodzins, Morton. *The Loyal and the Disloyal: Social Boundaries of Patriotism and Treason.* Cleveland: World, 1966.

Gutman, Herbert G. *The Black Family in Slavery and Freedom, 1750–1925.* New York: Pantheon, 1976.

Hahn, Steven. *The Roots of Southern Populism: Yeomen Farmers and the Transformation of the Georgia Upcountry, 1850–1890.* New York: Oxford University Press, 1983.

Hargrove, Hondon B. *Black Union Soldiers in the Civil War.* Jefferson, N. C.: McFarland, 1988.

Heidler, David S. *Pulling the Temple Down: The Fire-Eaters and the Destruction of the Union.* Mechanicsburg, Pa.: Stackpole Books, 1994.

Hollandsworth, James G., Jr. *The Louisiana Native Guards: The Black Military Experience during the Civil War.* Baton Rouge: Louisiana State University Press, 1995.

Hoole, William Stanley. *Alabama Tories: The First Alabama Cavalry, U.S.A., 1862–1865.* Confederate Centennial Studies, no. 16. Tuscaloosa: Confederate Publishing, 1960.

Hoole, William Stanley, and Elizabeth Hoole McArthur. *The Yankee Invasion of West Alabama, March to April, 1865, Including the Battle of Trion (Vance), the Battle of Tuscaloosa, the Burning of the University, and the Battle of Romulus.* University, Ala.: Confederate Publishing, 1985.

Howard, Victor B. *Black Liberation in Kentucky: Emancipation and Freedom, 1862–1884.* Lexington: University Press of Kentucky, 1983.

Hudson, Larry E., Jr., ed. *Working toward Freedom: Slave Society and Domestic Economy in the American South.* Rochester, N.Y.: University of Rochester Press, 1994.

Hurst, Jack. *Nathan Bedford Forrest: A Biography.* New York: Vintage Books, 1993.

Hyman, Michael R. *The Anti-Redeemers: Hill-Country Political Dissenters in the Lower South from Redemption to Populism.* Baton Rouge: Louisiana State University Press, 1990.

Inscoe, John C., ed. *Appalachians and Race: The Mountain South from Slavery to Segregation.* Lexington: University Press of Kentucky, 2001.

———. *Mountain Masters, Slavery, and the Sectional Crisis in Western North Carolina.* Knoxville: University of Tennessee Press, 1989.

Inscoe, John C., and Robert C. Kenzer, eds. *Enemies of the Country: New Perspectives on Unionists in the Civil War South.* Athens: University of Georgia Press, 2001.

Inscoe, John C., and Gordon B. McKinney. *The Heart of Confederate Appalachia: Western North Carolina in the Civil War.* Chapel Hill: University of North Carolina Press, 2000.

Jaynes, Gerald D. *Branches without Roots: Genesis of the Black Working Class in the American South, 1862–1882.* New York: Pantheon, 1986.

Johnson, Eric A., and Eric Monkkonen. *The Civilization of Crime: Violence in Town and Country since the Middle Ages.* Urbana: University of Illinois Press, 1996.

Johnson, Michael. *Toward a Patriarchal Republic: The Secession of Georgia.* Baton Rouge: Louisiana State University Press, 1977.

Jones, Jacqueline. *Soldiers of Light and Love: Northern Teachers and Georgia Blacks, 1865–1873.* Chapel Hill: University of North Carolina Press, 1980.

Jones, James Pickett. *Yankee Blitzkrieg: Wilson's Raid through Alabama and Georgia.* Athens: University of Georgia Press, 1976.

Jordan, Ervin L., Jr. *Black Confederates and Afro-Yankees in Civil War Virginia.* Charlottesville: University Press of Virginia, 1995.

Jordan, Thomas, and J. P. Pryor. *The Campaigns of Lieut. Gen. N. B. Forrest, and of Forrest's Cavalry, with Portraits, Maps, and Illustrations.* 1867. Reprint, Dayton, Ohio: Morningside Bookshop, 1977.

Jordan, Winthrop. *Tumult and Silence at Second Creek: An Inquiry into a Civil War Slave Conspiracy.* Rev. ed., Baton Rouge: Louisiana State University Press, 1995.

Kennamer, John Robert. *History of Jackson County.* Winchester, Tenn.: Southern Printing, 1935.

Kenzer, Robert C. *Kinship and Neighborhood in a Southern Community: Orange County, North Carolina, 1849–1881.* Knoxville: University of Tennessee Press, 1987.

Klement, Frank L. *Copperheads in the Middle West.* Chicago: University of Chicago Press, 1960.

———. *Dark Lanterns: Secret Political Societies, Conspiracies, and Treason Trials in the Civil War.* Baton Rouge: Louisiana State University Press, 1984.

Klingberg, Frank W. *The Southern Claims Commission.* University of California Publications in History, vol. 50. Berkeley: University of California Press, 1955.

Kolchin, Peter. *First Freedom: The Responses of Alabama's Blacks to Emancipation and Reconstruction.* Contributions in American History, no. 20. Westport, Conn.: Greenwood Press, 1972.

Lathrop, George Parsons. *History of the Union League of Philadelphia.* Philadelphia, Pa.: N.p., 1884.

Lazenby, Marion Elias. *History of Methodism in Alabama and West Florida: Being an Account of the Amazing March of Methodism through Alabama and West Florida.* N.p.: North Alabama Conference and Alabama–West Florida Conference of the Methodist Church, 1960.

Letford, William, and Allen W. Jones. *Location and Classification and Dates of Military Events in Alabama, 1861–1865.* University, Ala.: Alabama Civil War Commission, 1961.

Linderman, Gerald F. *Embattled Courage: The Experience of Combat in the American Civil War.* New York: Free Press, 1987.

Litwack, Leon F. *Been in the Storm So Long: The Aftermath of Slavery.* New York: Alfred A. Knopf, 1979.

Lonn, Ella. *Desertion during the Civil War.* New York: American Historical Association, 1928.

———. *Salt as a Factor in the Confederacy.* New York: Walter Neale, 1933.

Loveland, Anne C. *Southern Evangelicals and the Social Order, 1800–1860.* Baton Rouge: Louisiana State University Press, 1980.

Lowry, Thomas P. *The Story the Soldiers Wouldn't Tell: Sex in the Civil War.* Mechanicsburg, Pa.: Stackpole Books, 1994.

McCurry, Stephanie. *Masters of Small Worlds: Yeoman Households, Gender Relations, and the Political Culture of the Antebellum South Carolina Low Country.* New York: Oxford University Press, 1995.

McGregory, Jerrilyn. *Wiregrass Country.* Folklife in the South Series. Jackson: University Press of Mississippi, 1997.

McKenzie, Robert T. *One South or Many? Plantation Belt and Upcountry in Civil War Era Tennessee.* Cambridge, U.K.: Cambridge University Press, 1994.

McMillan, Malcolm C. *The Alabama Confederate Reader.* Tuscaloosa: University of Alabama Press, 1963.

————. *Constitutional Development in Alabama, 1798–1901: A Study in Politics, the Negro, and Sectionalism.* 1955. Reprint, Tuscaloosa: University of Alabama Press, 1992.

————. *The Disintegration of a Confederate State: Three Governors and Alabama's Wartime Home Front, 1861–1865.* Macon, Ga.: Mercer University Press, 1986.

McPherson, James M. *The Negro's Civil War: How American Negroes Felt and Acted during the War for the Union.* New York: Pantheon, 1965.

Malone, Ann Patton. *Sweet Chariot: Slave Family and Household Structure in Nineteenth-Century Louisiana.* Chapel Hill: University of North Carolina Press, 1992.

Martin, Bessie. *Desertion of Alabama Troops from the Confederate Army: A Study in Sectionalism.* New York: Columbia University Press, 1932.

Merrill, James M. *The Rebel Shore: The Story of Union Sea Power in the Civil War.* Boston: Little, Brown, 1957.

Mills, Gary B. *Southern Loyalists in the Civil War: The Southern Claims Commission. A Composite Directory of Case Files Created by the U.S. Commissioner of Claims, 1871–1880, Including Those Appealed to the War Claims Committee of the U.S. House of Representatives and the U.S. Court of Claims.* Baltimore: Genealogical Publishing, 1994.

Mitchell, Memory F. *Legal Aspects of Conscription and Exemption in North Carolina.* Chapel Hill: University of North Carolina Press, 1965.

Mohr, Clarence L. *On the Threshold of Freedom: Masters and Slaves in Civil War Georgia.* Athens: University of Georgia Press, 1986.

Moore, Albert Burton. *Conscription and Conflict in the Confederacy.* New York: Macmillan, 1924.

Moore, Winfred B., Jr., ed. *Developing Dixie: Modernization in a Traditional Society.* Westport, Conn.: Greenwood Press, 1988.

Neely, Mark E., Jr. *The Fate of Liberty: Abraham Lincoln and Civil Liberties.* New York: Oxford University Press, 1991.

————. *Southern Rights: Political Prisoners and the Myth of Confederate Constitutionalism.* Charlottesville: University Press of Virginia, 1999.

Nieman, Donald G., ed. *The Day of the Jubilee: The Civil War of Black Southerners.* Volume 1, *African American Life in the Post Emancipation South, 1861–1900.* New York: Garland, 1994.

Noe, Kenneth W., and Shannon H. Wilson, eds. *The Civil War in Appalachia: Collected Essays.* Knoxville: University of Tennessee Press, 1997.

O'Brien, Michael. *Mountain Partisans: Guerrilla Warfare in the Southern Appalachians, 1861–1865.* Westport, Conn.: Praeger, 1999.

Otto, John S. *Southern Agriculture during the Civil War Era, 1860–1880*. Westport, Conn.: Greenwood Press, 1994.

Oubre, Claude F. *Forty Acres and a Mule: The Freedmen's Bureau and Black Land-ownership*. Baton Rouge: Louisiana State University Press, 1978.

Owen, Thomas McAdory, and Marie Bankhead Owen. *History of Alabama and Dictionary of Alabama Biography*. 4 vols. Chicago: S. J. Clarke, 1921.

Owsley, Frank L. *Plain Folk of the Old South*. Baton Rouge: Louisiana State University Press, 1949.

———. *States Rights in the Confederacy*. Chicago: University of Chicago Press, 1925.

Paludan, Phillip Shaw. *Victims: A True Story of the Civil War*. Knoxville: University of Tennessee Press, 1981.

Perman, Michael. *Reunion without Compromise: The South and Reconstruction: 1865–1868*. New York: Cambridge University Press, 1973.

———. *The Road to Redemption: Southern Politics, 1869–1879*. Chapel Hill: University of North Carolina Press, 1984.

Potter, David. *The South and the Sectional Conflict*. Baton Rouge: Louisiana State University Press, 1968.

Pruitt, Wade. *Bugger Saga: The Civil War Story of Guerrilla and Bushwhacker Warfare in Lauderdale County, Alabama*. Columbia, Tenn.: P-Vine Press, 1977.

Quarles, Benjamin. *The Negro in the Civil War*. Boston: Little, Brown, 1953.

Rable, George C. *The Confederate Republic: A Revolution against Politics*. Chapel Hill: University of North Carolina Press, 1994.

Radley, Kenneth. *Rebel Watchdog: The Confederate States Army Provost Guard*. Baton Rouge: Louisiana State University Press, 1989.

Ramsdell, Charles W. *Behind the Lines in the Southern Confederacy*. Walter Lynwood Fleming Lectures in Southern History. Baton Rouge: Louisiana State University Press, 1944.

Randall, James. *Constitutional Problems under Lincoln*. New York: D. Appleton, 1926.

Rappaport, Anatole. *The Origins of Violence: Approaches to the Study of Conflict*. New York: Paragon House, 1989.

Rawick, George P., ed. *The American Slave: A Composite Autobiography*. Ser. 1, vol. 4, *Texas Narratives*, pt 1. 1941. Reprint, Westport, Conn.: Greenwood Press, 1972.

———. *The American Slave: A Composite Autobiography*. Ser. 1, vol. 6, *Alabama and Indiana Narratives*. 1941. Reprint, Westport, Conn.: Greenwood Press, 1972.

Roark, James L. *Masters without Slaves: Southern Planters in the Civil War and Reconstruction*. New York: W. W. Norton, 1977.

Robinson, William M., Jr., *Justice in Grey: A History of the Judicial System of the Confederate States of America*. Cambridge, Mass.: Harvard University Press, 1941.

Rogers, William Warren, Jr. *Black Belt Scalawag: Charles Hays and the Southern Republicans in the Era of Reconstruction*. Athens: University of Georgia Press, 1993.

———. *Confederate Home Front: Montgomery during the Civil War*. Tuscaloosa: University of Alabama Press, 1999.

Rogers, William Warren, Jr., Robert David Ward, Leah Rawls Atkins, and Wayne Flynt, eds. *Alabama: The History of a Deep South State*. Tuscaloosa: University of Alabama Press, 1994.

Royce, Josiah. *The Philosophy of Loyalty*. 1908. Reprint, New York: Hafner, 1971.

Saville, Julie. *The Work of Reconstruction: From Slave to Wage Laborer in South Carolina, 1860–1870*. Cambridge, U.K.: Cambridge University Press, 1994.

Schweninger, Loren. *Black Property Owners in the South, 1790–1915*. Urbana: University of Illinois Press, 1990.

Scott, Joan Wallach. *Gender and the Politics of History*. Rev. ed., New York: Columbia University Press, 1999.

Sefton, James E. *The United States Army and Reconstruction, 1865–1877*. Baton Rouge: Louisiana State University Press, 1967.

Sellers, James Benson. *Slavery in Alabama*. 1950. Reprint, Tuscaloosa: University of Alabama Press, 1994.

Sifakis, Stewart. *Compendium of the Confederate Armies: Alabama*. New York: Facts on File, 1992.

Silvestro, Mario Clement. *Rally Round the Flag: The Union Leagues in the Civil War*. Lansing: Michigan State University Press, 1967.

Starr, Stephen Z. *The War in the West, 1861–1865*. Vol. 3, *The Union Cavalry in the Civil War*. Baton Rouge: Louisiana State University Press, 1985.

Stewart, Mrs. Frank Ross. *Cherokee County History, 1836–1956*, vol.2. Centre, Ala.: Birmingham Printing, 1959.

Stowell, Daniel W. *Rebuilding Zion: The Religious Reconstruction of the South, 1863–1877*. New York: Oxford University Press, 1998.

Sumner, Christine. *Jackson County, Alabama, Records*. 3 vols. Scottsboro, Ala.: By the author, 1971–1976.

Sutherland, Daniel E., ed. *Guerrillas, Unionists, and Violence on the Confederate Home Front*. Fayetteville: University of Arkansas Press, 1999.

Sutherland, Daniel, and Anne J. Bailey, eds. *Civil War Arkansas: Beyond Battles and Leaders*. Fayetteville: University of Arkansas Press, 2000.

Sydnor, Charles S. *The Development of Southern Sectionalism, 1819–1848*. Baton Rouge: Louisiana State University Press, 1948.

Tatum, Georgia Lee. *Disloyalty in the Confederacy*. 1934. Reprint, Lincoln: University of Nebraska Press, 2000.

Taylor, Joe Gray. *Louisiana Reconstructed, 1863–1877*. Baton Rouge: Louisiana State University Press, 1974.

Thomas, Emory. *The Confederacy as a Revolutionary Experience*. 1971. Reprint, Columbia: University of South Carolina Press, 1991.

Thompson, Wesley S. *"The Free State of Winston": A History of Winston County, Alabama.* Winfield, Ala.: Pareil Press, 1968.

Thornton, J. Mills, III. *Politics and Power in a Slave Society: Alabama, 1800–1860.* Baton Rouge: Louisiana State University Press, 1978.

Trelease, Allen. *White Terror: The Ku Klux Klan Conspiracy and Southern Reconstruction.* Baton Rouge: Louisiana State University Press, 1971.

Turner, George Edgar. *Victory Rode the Rails: The Strategic Place of the Railroads in the Civil War.* New York: Bobbs-Merrill, 1953.

Walker, Clarence E. *A Rock in a Weary Land: The African Methodist Episcopal Church during the Civil War and Reconstruction.* Baton Rouge: Louisiana State University Press, 1982.

Wallenstein, Peter R. *From Slave South to New South: Public Policy in Nineteenth-Century Georgia.* Chapel Hill: University of North Carolina Press, 1987.

Webb, Samuel L. *Two-Party Politics in the One-Party South: Alabama's Hill Country, 1874–1920.* Tuscaloosa: University of Alabama Press, 1997.

Westwood, Howard C. *Black Troops, White Commanders, and Freedmen during the Civil War.* Carbondale: Southern Illinois University Press, 1992.

Wiggins, Sarah Woolfolk. *The Scalawag in Alabama Politics, 1865–1881.* Tuscaloosa: University of Alabama Press, 1977.

Williams, David. *Rich Man's War: Class, Caste, and Confederate Defeat in the Lower Chattahoochee Valley.* Athens: University of Georgia Press, 1998.

Wooster, Ralph A. *The Secession Conventions of the South.* Princeton, N.J.: Princeton University Press, 1962.

Wright, Marcus J. *Tennessee in the War.* Williamsbridge, N.Y.: A. Lee, 1908.

Wyatt-Brown, Bertram. *The Shaping of Southern Culture: Honor, Grace, and War, 1760s–1890s.* Chapel Hill: University of North Carolina Press, 2001.

———. *Southern Honor: Ethics and Behavior in the Old South.* New York: Oxford University Press, 1982.

Articles and Essays

Agee, Rucker. "Forrest–Streight Campaign of 1863: Preliminary Report." Address delivered before the 100th Meeting of the Civil War Roundtable. Milwaukee: N.p., 1958.

Alexander, Thomas B. "Ku Kluxism in Tennessee, 1865–1869." *Tennessee Historical Quarterly* 8 (1949): 195–219.

———. "Neither Peace Nor War: Conditions in Tennessee in 1865." *East Tennessee Historical Society Publications* 21 (1949): 33–51.

———. "Persistent Whiggery in Alabama and the Lower South, 1860–1867." *Alabama Review* 12 (January 1959): 35–52.

Ash, Stephen V. "Poor Whites in the Occupied South, 1861–1865." *Journal of Southern History* 57, no. 1 (1991): 37–62.

Baggett, James Alex. "Origins of Early Texas Republican Party Leadership," *Journal of Southern History* 40, no. 3 (1974): 441–54.

Bailey, Hugh C. "Disaffection in the Alabama Hill Country, 1861." *Civil War History* 4 (1958): 183–93.

———. "Disloyalty in Early Confederate Alabama." *Journal of Southern History* 23 (November 1957): 522–8.

Bearss, Edwin C. "A Federal Raid up the Tennessee River." *Alabama Review* 17 (October 1964): 261–70.

Bethel, Elizabeth. "The Freedmen's Bureau in Alabama." *Journal of Southern History* 14, no. 1 (1948): 49–92.

Blassingame, John W. "The Recruitment of Colored Troops in Kentucky, Maryland, and Missouri, 1863–1865." *Historian* 29 (August 1967): 533–45.

Bond, Horace Mann. "Social and Economic Forces in Alabama Reconstruction." *Journal of Negro History* 23 (July 1938): 290–348.

Bowen, Don R. "Guerrilla War in Western Missouri, 1862–1865: Historical Extensions of the Relative Deprivation Hypothesis." *Comparative Studies in Society and History* 19 (1977): 30–51.

Brantley, William H. "Alabama Secedes," *Alabama Review* 7 no. 3 (1954): 165–85.

Brooks, R. P. "Conscription in the Confederate States of America, 1862–1865." *Military Historian and Economist* 1 (October 1916): 419–42.

Bryan, Charles F. " 'Tories' amidst Rebels: Confederate Occupation of East Tennessee, 1861–63." *East Tennessee Historical Society Publications* 60 (1988): 3–22.

Burns, Zed H. "Abel D. Streight Encounters Nathan Bedford Forrest." *Journal of Mississippi History* 30 (1968): 245–69.

Campbell, Randolph B. "Grass Roots Reconstruction: The Personnel of County Government in Texas, 1865–1876." *Journal of Southern History* 58, no. 1 (1992): 99–116.

Coclanis, Peter. "The American Civil War in Economic Perspective: Basic Questions and Some Answers." *Southern Cultures* 2 (winter 1996): 163–75.

Cody, Cheryll Ann. "Naming, Kinship, and Estate Dispersal: Notes on Slave Life on a South Carolina Plantation, 1786 to 1833." *William and Mary Quarterly*, 3d ser., 35 (January 1982): 192–211.

Davis, Thomas J. "Alabama's Reconstruction Representatives in the U.S. Congress, 1868–1878: A Profile." *Alabama Historical Quarterly* 44 (spring/summer 1982): 32–49.

Dodd, Donald B. "The Free State of Winston." *Alabama Heritage* 28 (spring 1993): 8–19.

Dorris, J. T. "Pardon Seekers and Brokers: A Sequel of Appomattox," *Journal of Southern History* 1, no. 3 (1935): 276–92.

Doster, James F. "Land Titles and Public Land Sales in Early Alabama." *Alabama Review* (April 1963): 108–24.

Dyer, J. P. "Some Aspects of Cavalry Operations in the Army of Tennessee." *Journal of Southern History* 8, no. 2 (1942): 210–25.

Eaton, Clement. "Mob Violence in the Old South." *Mississippi Valley Historical Review* 29 (December 1942): 351–70.

Farish, Hunter Dickinson. "An Overlooked Personality in Southern Life." *North Carolina Historical Review* 12 (October 1935): 341–53.

Fitzgerald, Michael W. "Radical Republicanism and the White Yeomanry during Alabama Reconstruction, 1865–1868." *Journal of Southern History* 54, no. 4 (1988): 565–96.

———. "Railroad Subsidies and Black Aspirations: The Politics of Economic Development in Reconstruction Mobile, 1865–1879." *Civil War History* 39 (September 1993): 240–56.

———. "Republican Factionalism and Black Empowerment: The Spencer-Warner Controversy and Alabama Reconstruction, 1868–1880." *Journal of Southern History* 64 (August 1998): 473–94.

———. "'To Give Our Votes to the Party': Black Political Agitation and Agricultural Change in Alabama, 1865–1870." *Journal of American History* 76 (September 1989): 489–505.

———. "Wager Swayne, the Freedmen's Bureau, and the Politics of Reconstruction in Alabama." *Alabama Review* 48 (July 1995): 188–232.

Fleming, Walter L. "The Formation of the Union League in Alabama." *Gulf States Historical Magazine* 2 (1903): 73–89.

———. "The Peace Movement in Alabama during the Civil War." *South Atlantic Quarterly* 2 (1903): 114–24 and 246–60.

Freidel, Frank. "The Loyal Publication Society: A Pro-Union Propaganda Agency." *Mississippi Valley Historical Review* 26, no. 3 (1939): 359–76.

Gates, Paul Wallace. "Federal Land Policy in the South, 1866–1888." *Journal of Southern History* 6, no. 3 (1940): 303–30.

Granade, Ray. "Violence: An Instrument of Policy in Reconstruction Alabama." *Alabama Historical Quarterly* (fall/winter 1968): 181–202.

Grant, C. E. "Partisan Warfare Model, 1861–1865." *Military Review* 38 (1958): 42–56.

Greenberg, Kenneth S. "The Nose, the Lie, and the Duel in the Antebellum South." *American Historical Review* 95, no. 1 (1990): 57–74.

Hamilton, J. G. DeRoulhac. "The State Constitutions and the Confederate Constitution." *Journal of Southern History* 4 (November 1938): 425–48.

Harris, William C. "The Southern Unionist Critique of the Civil War." *Civil War History* 3 (1969): 20–61.

Heier, Jan Richard. "The Effect of the Civil War on Taxation in Alabama." *Essays in Economic and Business History* 8 (1990): 187–203.

Henretta, James A. "Families and Farms: *Mentalité* in Pre-Industrial America." *William and Mary Quarterly*, 3d ser., 35, no. 1 (1978): 3–32.

Hesseltine, William B., and Larry Gara. "Confederate Leaders in Post-war Alabama." *Alabama Review* (January 1951): 5–21.

Higginbotham, Don. "The Early American Way of War: Reconnaissance and Appraisal." *William and Mary Quarterly*, 3d ser., 44, no. 2 (1987): 230–73.

Hollman, Kenneth W., and Joe H. Murrey, Jr. "Alabama's State Debt History, 1865–1921." *Southern Studies* 24 (fall 1985): 306–32.

Honey, Michael K. "The War within the Confederacy: White Unionists of North Carolina." *Prologue* 18 (summer 1986): 75–93.

Horton, Paul S. "Submitting to the 'Shadow of Slavery': The Secession Crisis and Civil War in Alabama's Lawrence County." *Civil War History* 44, no. 2 (1998): 111–36.

Johnson, Kenneth R. "Confederate Defenses and Union Gunboats on the Tennessee River: A Federal Raid into Northwest Alabama." *Alabama Historical Quarterly* 30 (summer 1968): 39–60.

Kerber, Linda. "Separate Spheres, Female Worlds, Women's Place: The Rhetoric of Women's History." *Journal of American History* 75, no. 1 (June 1988): 9–39.

Klingberg, Frank Wysor. "The Southern Claims Commission: A Postwar Agency in Operation." *Mississippi Valley Historical Review* 32, no. 2 (September 1954): 195–214.

Kolchin, Peter. "Reevaluating the Antebellum Slave Community: A Comparative Perspective." *Journal of American History* 70 (December 1983): 579–601.

———. "Scalawags, Carpetbaggers, and Reconstruction: A Quantitative Look at Southern Congressional Politics, 1868–1872." *Journal of Southern History* 45, no. 1 (1979): 63–76.

Krebs, Sylvia. "Funeral Meats and Second Marriages: Alabama Churches in the Presidential Reconstruction Period." *Alabama Historical Quarterly* 37 (fall 1975): 206–16.

Kyriakoudes, Louis M. "The Rise of Merchants and Market Towns in Reconstruction-Era Alabama." *Alabama Review* 49 (April 1996): 83–107.

Larson, Sarah. "Records of the Southern Claims Commission." *Prologue* 12 (winter 1980): 207–18.

Long, Durwood. "Unanimity and Disloyalty in Secessionist Alabama." *Civil War History* 11 (September 1965): 257–73.

Longacre, Edward G. "Black Troops in the Army of the James, 1863–65." *Military Affairs* 45, no. 1 (1981): 1–8.

McGee, David H. "'Home and Friends': Kinship, Community, and Elite Women in Caldwell County, North Carolina, during the Civil War." *North Carolina Historical Review* 74 (October 1997): 363–88.

McKaughan, Joshua. "'Few Were the Hearts . . . That Did Not Swell with Devotion': Community and Confederate Service in Rowan County, North Carolina, 1861–1862." *The North Carolina Historical Review* 73 (April 1996): 156–61.

McKenzie, Robert H. "The Economic Impact of Federal Operations in Alabama during the Civil War." *Alabama Historical Quarterly* 38, no. 1 (1976): 51–68.

Malone, Ann Patton. "Slave Kinship: A Case Study of the South Carolina Good Hope Plantation, 1835–1856." *Journal of Family History* 6 (1981): 294–308.

Mann, Ralph. "Family Group, Family Migration, and the Civil War in the Sandy Basin of Virginia." *Appalachian Journal* 19 (summer 1992): 374–92.

———. "Mountains, Land, and Kin Networks: Burkes Garden, Virginia, in the 1840s and 1850s." *Journal of Southern History* 58, no. 3 (1992): 411–34.

Mathis, Robert Neil. "Freedom of the Press in the Confederacy: A Reality." *Historian* 37 (August 1975): 633–48.

Mitchell, Reid. "The Creation of Confederate Loyalties." In *New Perspectives on Race and Slavery in America: Essays in Honor of Kenneth M. Stampp*, edited by Robert H. Abzug and Stephen E. Maizlish, 93–108. Lexington: University Press of Kentucky, 1986.

Mohr, Clarence L. "Before Sherman: Georgia Blacks and the Union War Effort, 1861–1864." *Journal of Southern History* 45, no. 3 (1979): 331–52.

Moneyhon, Carl H. "The Failure of Southern Republicanism, 1867–1876." In *The Facts of Reconstruction: Essays in Honor of John Hope Franklin*, edited by Eric Anderson and Alfred A. Moss, Jr., 99–119. Baton Rouge: Louisiana State University Press, 1991.

Morgan, Philip D. "The Ownership of Property by Slaves in the Mid-Nineteenth Century Low Country." *Journal of Southern History* 49 (August 1983): 399–420.

Morris, Chris. "An Event in Community Organization: The Mississippi Slave Insurrection Scare of 1835." *Journal of Social History* 22 (1988): 93–112.

Myers, John B. "The Freedmen and the Law in Post-Bellum Alabama, 1865–1867." *Alabama Review* (January 1970): 56–69.

Noe, Kenneth W. "Who Were the Bushwhackers? Age, Class, Kin, and Western Virginia's Confederate Guerrillas, 1861–1862." *Civil War History* 49, no. 1 (2003): 5–26.

O'Brien, Gail W. "The Systematic Study of Power in the Nineteenth Century South." In *Class Conflict, and Consensus: Antebellum Southern Community Studies*, edited by Orville Vernon Burton and Robert C. McMath, Jr., 263–90. Westport, Conn.: Greenwood Press, 1982.

Owsley, Frank L. "Defeatism in the Confederacy." *North Carolina Historical Review* 3 (1926): 446–56.

———. "Local Defense and the Overthrow of the Confederacy." *Mississippi Valley Historical Review* 11 (1925): 490–525.

———. "The Pattern of Migration and Settlement on the Southern Frontier." *Journal of Southern History* 11 (February/November 1945): 147–76.

Parks, Joseph H. "A Confederate Trade Center under Federal Occupation: Memphis, 1862–1865." *Journal of Southern History* 7 (August 1941): 289–314.

Penningroth, Dylan. "Slavery, Freedom, and Social Claims to Property among African Americans in Liberty County, Georgia, 1850–1880." *Journal of American History* 84, no. 2 (September 1997): 405–35.

Pitt-Rivers, Julian. "Honour and Social Status." In *Honour and Shame: The Values of Mediterranean Society*, edited by J. G. Peristiany, 19–77. Chicago: University of Chicago Press, 1966.

Purcell, Douglas Clare. "Military Conscription in Alabama during the Civil War." *Alabama Review* 34, no. 2 (1981): 94–106.

Robbins, John B. "The Confederacy and the Writ of *Habeas Corpus*." *Georgia Historical Quarterly* 55 (summer 1971): 83–101.

Roberts, A. Sellew. "The Federal Government and Confederate Cotton." *American Historical Review* 32, no. 2 (January 1927): 262–75.

Robinson, William M., Jr. "Legal System of the Confederate States." *Journal of Southern History* 2, no. 2 (1936): 453–67.

Rodabaugh, Karl. "The Prelude to Populism in Alabama." *Alabama Historical Quarterly* (summer 1981): 111–52.

Russ, William A., Jr. "Registration and Disfranchisement under Radical Reconstruction." *Mississippi Valley Historical Review* 21, no. 2 (1934): 163–80.

Rutman, Darrett B. "The Social Web: A Prospectus for the Study of the Early American Community." In *Insights and Parallels: Problems and Issues of American Social History*, edited by William L. O'Neill, 57–188. Minneapolis: Burgess, 1973.

Schweninger, Loren. "Alabama Blacks and the Congressional Reconstruction Acts of 1867." *Alabama Review* (July 1978): 182–98.

———. "Black Citizenship and the Republican Party in Reconstruction Alabama." *Alabama Review* 29 (April 1967): 83–103.

Sloan, John Z. "The Ku Klux Klan and the Alabama Election of 1872." *Alabama Review* (April 1965): 113–23.

Smallwood, James. "Disaffection in Confederate Texas: The Great Hanging at Gainesville." *Civil War History* 22 (1976): 349–60.

Steckel, Richard K. "Slave Marriage and the Family." *Journal of Family History* 5 (winter 1980): 406–21.

Sutherland, Daniel E. "Guerrilla Warfare in the Confederacy." *Journal of Southern History* 68, no. 2 (May 2002): 259–92.

Sweet, William W. "Methodist Church Influence in Southern Politics." *Mississippi Valley Historical Review* 1, no. 4 (1915): 546–60.

Sydnor, Charles S. "The Southerner and the Laws." *Journal of Southern History* 6 (February 1940): 3–23.

Thornton, J. Mills, III. "Fiscal Policy and the Failure of Radical Reconstruction in the Lower South." In *Region, Race, and Reconstruction: Essays in Honor of C. Vann Woodward*, edited by J. Morgan Kousser and James M. McPherson. New York: Oxford University Press, 1982.

Trelease, Allen W. "Who Were the Scalawags?" *Journal of Southern History* 29, no. 4 (1963): 445–68.

Watson, Elbert L. "The Story of the Nickajack." *Alabama Review* 20 (January 1967): 17–26.

White, Kenneth B. "Black Lives, Red Tape: The Alabama Freedmen's Bureau." *Alabama Historical Quarterly* (winter 1981): 241–58.

———. "Wager Swayne: Racist or Realist?" *Alabama Review* (April 1978): 92–109.

Wiggins, Sarah Woolfolk. "Alabama: Democratic Bulldozing and Republican Party Folly." In *Reconstruction and Redemption in the South,* edited by Otto H. Olson, 48–77. Baton Rouge: Louisiana State University Press, 1980.

———. "Ostracism of White Republicans in Alabama During Reconstruction." *Alabama Review* 27, no. 1 (1974): 52–64.

———. "Unionist Efforts to Control Alabama Reconstruction." *Alabama Historical Quarterly* (spring 1968): 51–64.

Williams, Clanton W., ed. "Notes and Documents: Presidential Election Returns and Related Data for Ante-Bellum Alabama." *Alabama Review* 2 (January 1949): 63–73.

Williams, Frank B., Jr. "The Poll Tax as a Suffrage Requirement in the South, 1870–1901." *Journal of Southern History* 18, no. 4 (1952): 469–96.

Wilson, Clyde E. "State Militia of Alabama during the Administration of Lewis E. Parsons, Provisional Governor, June 21st to December 18th 1865." *American Historical Quarterly* 14 (1952): 313–23.

Woolfolk, Sarah Van V. "Amnesty and Pardon and Republicanism in Alabama." *Alabama Historical Quarterly* 26 (1964): 240–8.

———. "Carpetbaggers in Alabama: Tradition versus Truth." *Alabama Review* 15 (April 1962): 133–44.

———. "Five Men Called Scalawags." *Alabama Review* 17 (January 1964): 45–55.

———. "George E. Spencer: A Carpetbagger in Alabama." *Alabama Review* 19, no. 1 (January 1966): 41–52.

———. "The Political Cartoons of the *Tuskaloosa Independent Monitor* and *Tuskaloosa Blade,* 1867–1873." *Alabama Historical Quarterly* 27 (fall/winter 1965): 140–65.

Wyatt-Brown, Bertram. "Community, Class, and Snopesian Crime: Local Justice in the Old South." In *Class, Conflict, and Consensus: Antebellum Southern Community Studies,* edited by Orville Vernon Burton and Robert C. McMath, Jr., 173–206. Westport, Conn.: Greenwood Press, 1982.

Dissertations and Theses

Barr, Michael D. "An Assessment of Guerrilla Activity in Northern and Western Virginia, 1861–1865." M.A. thesis, Southwest Texas State University, 1986.

Breen, Whilden P. "The Alabama and Chattanooga Railroad Bond Affair during the Lindsay Administration in Alabama, 1871–1872." M.A. thesis, University of Alabama, 1966.

Brownlee, Richard. "Guerrilla Warfare in Missouri, 1861–1865." Ph.D. diss., University of Missouri, 1955.

Cash, William M. "Alabama Republicans during Reconstruction: Personal Characteristics, Motivations, and Political Activity of Party Activists, 1867–1880." Ph.D. diss., University of Alabama, 1973.

Cook, Marjorie Howell. "Restoration and Innovation: Alabamians Adjust to Defeat, 1865–1867." Ph.D. diss., University of Alabama, 1968.

Daniel, John S., Jr. "Special Warfare in Middle Tennessee and Surrounding Areas, 1861–1862." M.A. thesis, University of Tennessee, 1971.

Dodd, Donald Bradford. "Unionism in Confederate Alabama." Ph.D. diss., University of Georgia, 1969.

———. "Unionism in Northwest Alabama through 1865." M.A. thesis, Auburn University, 1966.

Evans, William David. "Rousseau's Raid, July 10–July 22, 1864." Ph.D. diss., University of Georgia, 1982.

Gilmour, Robert. "The Other Emancipation: Studies in the Society and Economy of Alabama Whites during Reconstruction." Ph.D. diss., John Hopkins University, 1972.

Hume, Richard L. "The 'Black and Tan' Constitutional Conventions of 1867–1869 in Ten Former Confederate States: A Study of Their Membership." Ph.D. diss., Johns Hopkins University, 1972.

Jones, Freeman E. "Mosby's Rangers and Partisan Rangers." M.A. thesis, United States Army Command and General Staff College, 1993.

King, Jerry McDowell. "Shadow Warriors of the Confederacy." M.A. thesis, University of South Florida, 1990.

LeGrand, Phyllis LaRue. "Destitution and Relief of the Indigent Soldiers' Families of Alabama during the Civil War." M.A. thesis, Auburn University, 1964.

Martin, James Brent. "'Have Them Shot at Once': Guerrilla Warfare in Kentucky, 1863–1865." M.A. thesis, University of Texas, 1986.

———. "The Third War: Irregular Warfare on the Western Border, 1861–1865." Ph.D. diss., University of Texas, 1997.

Melton, Maurice K. "Major Military Industries of the Confederate Government." Ph.D. diss., Emory University, 1978.

Owens, Susie L. "The Union League of America: Political Activities in Tennessee, the Carolinas, and Virginia, 1865–1870." Ph.D. diss., New York University, 1943.

Roush, Gerald Lee. "Aftermath of Reconstruction: Race, Violence, and Politics in Alabama, 1874–1884." M.A. thesis, Auburn University, 1973.

Sarris, Jonathan D. "'Hellish Deeds in a Christian Land': Southern Mountain Communities at War." Ph.D. diss., University of Georgia, 1998.

Silvestro, Mario Clement. "None But Patriots: The Union Leagues in Civil War and Reconstruction." Ph.D. diss., University of Wisconsin, 1959.

Smith, Thomas Alton. "Mobilization of the Army in Alabama, 1859–1865." M.A. thesis, Alabama Polytechnic Institute, 1953.

Stelluto, Donald Louis, Jr. "In the Absence of a National Supreme Court: Conscription and Exemption in the State Supreme Courts of the Confederacy." M.A. thesis, California State University at Fullerton, 1993.

Index

Abolitionism: unionists and, 22–4, 203; equated with treason, 26–7

African Americans: collaboration of with white unionists, 51–5, 80–1, 99, 109, 149–51; as Union soldiers, 52–3, 89, 102, 113, 114–7; and federal foraging, 129–32; offer aid and comfort to Union soldiers, 141, 143; enlist in Union navy, 163–4; and voting rights during Reconstruction, 173, 197–8; unionists advocate suffrage for, 198; and Reconstruction political organizing, 200–4; opposed to Confederate disfranchisement, 212–3; terrorized by Ku Klux Klan, 218, 219–30; and Methodist Episcopal Church, 223. *See also* Refugees (African American); Slaves; Women (African American)

Alabama: counties and subregions of, 10, 242–3; state policy regarding unionists, 56–63, 108; strategic importance of, 90–4; Union army occupation of, 93–4; postwar economy of, 182–4. *See also* North Alabama; South Alabama; Union occupation of Alabama

Alabama: First Regiment Cavalry (Union), 103, 104–5, 107, 109, 129, 161–2, 188

Arson, 82–3, 167

Bell, John: support for among Alabama unionists in 1860, 23–4, 27, 28

Bourlier, E. (Union spy), 157

Bowman Act of 1881, 237. *See also* Southern Claims Commission

Bragg, Braxton: and conscription enforcement, 68; mentioned, 93

Breckinridge, John C., 24, 28

Buell, Don Carlos: maneuvers of in North Alabama, 93

Bureau of Refugees, Freedmen, and Abandoned Lands. *See* Freedmen's Bureau

Bushwhackers, 138 n. 13. *See also* Guerrillas; Partisan fighters

Butler, Benjamin: "contraband" policy of, 112

Callis, Jonathan B., 201

Confederacy: and political prisoners, 59; role in conscription enforcement, 67–8

Confederate frontier: defined, 96

Conscript cavalry, 57, 68–9, 70–1, 79, 82–4, 159, 190

Conscription: Act to Provide for the Public Defense (April 1862), 57, 66; enforcement of, 57, 66–9, 81–4; unionist resistance to, 57–8, 70–84; bounties and, 67; exemptions to, 70–4. *See also* Lying out

Constitutional convention of Alabama, 1865: former Confederate members of, 175–6; unionist members of, 175; unionist agenda for, 176–8

Constitutional convention of Alabama, 1867: membership of, 205–7; unionists' agenda for, 207; and land confiscation, 208–10; and Confederate disfranchisement, 210–4; and war crimes, 212, 213; and referendum on Constitution, 215

Constitutional Union Party, 24

Cooperationism: defined, 30

Debt (Confederate): voided during Reconstruction, 177–8, 207, 215

Democratic Party: 1860 split of, 24; unionists and, 173; regains control of Alabama government, 230

Desertion, 77–8. *See also* Lying out

Index of Loyal Alabamians

Note: The following includes only those white unionists and pro-Union African Americans who receive mention in the text.